Gold Rush Societies and Migrant Networks in the Tasman World

Studies in British and Irish Migration

Series Editors: T. M. Devine, University of Edinburgh, and
Angela McCarthy, University of Otago

Showcasing the histories of migration into and out of Britain and Ireland from the seventeenth century to contemporary times and their impact at home and abroad

From the 1600s to the current day, millions of British and Irish migrants have sought new lives around the world. Britain and Ireland have also received returning migrants and other newcomers of diverse ethnicities. This series will examine the causes, consequences, representations and legacies of these movements on the homelands, the migrants and the destinations in which they settled. The series incorporates not just the inward and outward movement of people, but of ideas, products and objects. It specifically encourages transnational and comparative cross-disciplinary approaches across groups, space and time.

Titles available in the series:

New Scots: Scotland's Immigrant Communities since 1945
Edited by T. M. Devine and Angela McCarthy

Death in the Diaspora: British and Irish Gravestones
Edited by Nicholas J. Evans and Angela McCarthy

Gold Rush Societies and Migrant Networks in the Tasman World
Daniel Davy

edinburghuniversitypress.com/series/bims

Gold Rush Societies and Migrant Networks in the Tasman World

Daniel Davy

EDINBURGH
University Press

Edinburgh University Press is one of the leading university presses in the UK. We publish academic books and journals in our selected subject areas across the humanities and social sciences, combining cutting-edge scholarship with high editorial and production values to produce academic works of lasting importance. For more information visit our website: edinburghuniversitypress.com

© Daniel Davy, 2021, 2023

Edinburgh University Press Ltd
The Tun – Holyrood Road
12 (2f) Jackson's Entry
Edinburgh EH8 8PJ

First published in hardback by Edinburgh University Press 2021

Typeset in 10.5/13pt Sabon by
Servis Filmsetting Ltd, Stockport, Cheshire

A CIP record for this book is available from the British Library

ISBN 978 1 4744 7734 5 (hardback)
ISBN 978 1 4744 7735 2 (paperback)
ISBN 978 1 4744 7736 9 (webready PDF)
ISBN 978 1 4744 7737 6 (epub)

The right of Daniel Davy to be identified as author of this work has been asserted in accordance with the Copyright, Designs and Patents Act 1988 and the Copyright and Related Rights Regulations 2003 (SI No. 2498).

Contents

List of Figures	vi
Acknowledgements	vii
Series Editors' Introduction	xi
List of Abbreviations	xiii
Glossary	xiv
Editorial Notes	xv
Map 1: The Tasman World	xvi
Map 2: The Otago Goldfields	xvii

	Introduction	1
1	'To Return Home with ... Satisfaction and Pleasure': Home and Family Networks	23
2	'A Great Many People I Know from Victoria': The Victorian Dimension of the Otago Gold Rushes	64
3	Work and Environments	96
4	Leisure Sites and Cultures	141
5	'We Return Home in Glory': Chinese Networks and Gold Seeking in Otago	174
6	'Monuments of Industry'? The Otago Gold Rushes in Public and Private Memory	207
	Conclusion	240
	Bibliography	251
	Index	276

Figures

1.1	*Otago Witness*, 14 February 1880	47
2.1	Individuals boarding vessels in Melbourne harbour, bound for Otago	68
3.1	Rattray Street, Dunedin, 1862	103
3.2	Bell Hill excavations, 1863	105
3.3	View looking over Maclaggan Street, Dunedin	105
3.4	Gabriel's Gully, 1861	108
3.5	Gabriel's Gully, 1862	109
3.6	Shotover River	114
6.1	Former gold seekers assembled outside the Lawrence Presbyterian Church	207
6.2	Gabriel's Gully Semi-Centennial Jubilee Procession, 1911	212
6.3	Gabriel's Gully Jubilee pamphlet	214
6.4	*Otago Daily Times*, 2 March 1911	218

Acknowledgements

As an American doctoral student at the University of Otago who had never travelled to Australasia, the topic and the locality of this book were as unfamiliar to me as they were to prospectors who preceded me a century and a half ago. It was through my own encounters with place in Dunedin and central Otago that the project first began to be reshaped from an abstracted study of identity into a story of communities and relationships in Dunedin, central Otago and elsewhere. Travelling from a sprawling Washington, DC suburb, living and researching in Dunedin – which is a small town by American standards – brought the role of locality to the foreground. As I transcribed diaries, letters and autobiographies and pored over thousands of pages of newspapers, writers highlighted time and again the importance of local and transnational relationships. Perhaps in some ways similar to the Victorian prospector, the friendships I made and the support I received both locally and overseas were instrumental to the work of writing this book. *Gold Rush Societies*, therefore, would have been impossible without a wide network of friends and family in New Zealand, Australia, the United Kingdom and the United States.

I am deeply grateful for my doctoral supervisor, Angela McCarthy, who took an unruly dissertation proposal and helped to fashion it into a focused study on transnational networks and local communities during the gold rushes. She read multiple drafts of each chapter and always challenged me to rethink my perspectives, broaden my secondary reading and interrogate my primary sources in new ways. Angela struck the perfect balance between offering guidance and letting this project be my own. This book would not have been possible without her direction, encouragement and support. The degree to which the book succeeds is due to her guidance. Any limitations or failings of the book are my own.

I am also indebted to the Department of History and Art History at the University of Otago. This book truly grew out of its rich academic community. *Gold Rush Societies'* exploration of multiple entangled bodies of scholarship is the result of multiple Department members' generosity in reading drafts, recommending secondary literature and discussing methodology. Tom Brooking sharpened my understanding of the Otago rushes and environmental history. Tony Ballantyne encouraged me to think concretely about the role of space and place in colonial history. John Stenhouse developed my grasp of New Zealand history, while Brian Moloughney deepened my understanding of Chinese migration. Erik Olssen always offered support and encouragement. Vanessa Ward and Mark Seymour read multiple drafts and constantly encouraged me to write as a reader. Barbara Brookes, as Department Chair, fostered a sense of community within the Department and provided funding for multiple research trips throughout central Otago, which were vital to the conceptual framework of the book. A network of fellow postgraduate students, particularly Kenton Storey and Scott Campbell, provided a sense of community and challenged me to improve as an historian.

I am also grateful to several historians who have provided critical insights and feedback at various stages of the book's development. Conversations with Terry Hearn, Keir Reeves, Lloyd Carpenter, David Goodman, Antoinette Burton, Rory Sweetman, Lyndon Fraser, Rainer Buschmann, Colin Barr, Kirsten McKenzie and Marjory Harper have influenced this book in various ways. My curiosity in the Tasman World was nurtured during postgraduate studies at the University of Edinburgh under the supervision of Tom Devine and Enda Delaney. Though Tom and Enda were not involved in this project, their guidance is nevertheless imprinted on this book.

I was also supported by archivists at the Central Stories Museum (Otago), the Lakes District Museum (Otago), the Lawrence Museum (Otago), the Mitchell Library, the State Library of Victoria, the Alexander Turnbull Library, the Library of Congress, the Scottish National Library, the Presbyterian Church Research Centre Archive (Otago), the Hokitika Museum, the Dunedin Public Library and the Hocken Collections. I owe a special debt to the staff of the Toitū Otago Settlers Museum, particularly Seán Brosnahan and Jill Haley, who is now at the Canterbury Museum. In the midst of renovations at the Museum, Jill granted access to several valuable uncatalogued manuscripts and unwearyingly accommodated my endless string of requests. Sarah Foyle and Jen Daly at Edinburgh University Press also provided support and endless patience throughout the publication process during the time of the coronavirus.

At Ave Maria University, I am grateful to Roger Nutt for his encouragement and understanding of the difficulties of writing, teaching and serving in administration. Michael Dauphinais has similarly provided assistance throughout my time at AMU. My colleagues, particularly Paul Baxa, Michael Breidenbach, Mary Blanchard, Gabriel Martinez and James Patterson, have benefited me through their support and friendship. The AMU library staff provided exceptional support in obtaining several books not easily accessible in the United States via interlibrary loans. My students, particularly those in British Empire, Historiography and the American West – who I forced to give feedback on chapter drafts – have taught me the joys of combining research and teaching.

I owe the greatest debt to Julie Davy, who agreed to leave her world behind three months after our wedding day and travel to New Zealand so I could pursue what I love. Whether it was driving on the edge of a cliff in the Lakes District or getting lost outside of Middlemarch, Julie was there at every step of this book's development. She never wavered in her support as I juggled the book alongside teaching and administrative responsibilities at AMU. Finally, I want to thank Joseph, Simeon, Max, Therese and Edy, whose Nerf battles and baby dolls always continue to keep me grounded.

Series Editors' Introduction

Gold rushes were a colourful and significant feature of the society and economy of the new lands settled and colonised by Europeans and others in the nineteenth century. Major rushes occurred in Australia, Brazil, Canada, New Zealand, South Africa and the United States. They have attracted a significant historiography because not only did they trigger permanent and temporary migration but they also influenced the trade, economy, colonisation, investment practices and environment of their host countries as well as those of the world beyond.

Daniel Davy's book is a pioneering study of gold rushes which adopts a new methodology and contains much of interest for specialists in the history of New Zealand, Australia and the interconnected Tasman World in the mid-Victorian era, as well as of diaspora, mining labour, ethnicities, masculinities and the environment.

By situating his study of New Zealand's Otago gold rushes within a broader Tasman World framework, Davy emphasises the Victorian dimension of the Otago rushes, examining the reciprocal movement not just of people, but of commodities and ideas. Deploying the techniques of comparative and transnational history, he brings out fresh perspectives on the miners' socio-economic and environmental impact as well as the lives and identities of the mining populations. Davy also shines intriguing light on a fascinating aspect of diaspora history at the time, the 'coming and going' of the miners between separate geographical areas and how those movements influenced their life experiences.

Yet, though Davy has internationalised and contextualised the story of these two gold rushes, he never forgets the importance of the local. The book therefore evolves as neither a local nor a transnational history but one which blends the two in a single study and offers fresh perspectives on each in the process. It is a work, therefore, that denationalises the gold rushes by highlighting a range of connections to Australia, the British Isles and North America.

The volume is constructed on a rich foundation of wide reading and careful research in a range of original materials. Chief among them are the impressive collections of migrant letters which have been explored, as well as the systematic investigation of newspaper files in both Australia and New Zealand. Davy also draws upon diaries, autobiographies, published accounts and death certificates. Evocative contemporary photographs further enrich his account.

It is through such material that we learn in intimate and graphic detail of the miners' journeys, their occasional successes and frequent failures, and their mining cultures and societies. Whether through the haunting account of a miner's last breath in a blizzard, tracing the mobility of miners between international shores and within local environs, or charting the harmony and conflict between individuals and cultures on the goldfields, Daniel Davy is ever alert to the human stories as well as broader structural factors in this evocative account of Tasman World gold rush societies.

Tom Devine and Angela McCarthy

Abbreviations

AJHR *Appendices to the Journals of the House of Representatives* (New Zealand)
ATL   Alexander Turnbull Library, Wellington
CNZ   *The Cyclopedia of New Zealand*
HC   Hocken Collections, University of Otago, Dunedin
LDM   Lakes District Museum, Arrowtown
OSM   Toitū Otago Settlers Museum, Dunedin
SLV   State Library of Victoria

Glossary

cradle: A box on rockers with a perforated iron tray on top, into which gold-bearing gravel is shovelled. Water is poured continuously into the top of the tray, the force of which when combined with the rocking motion applied by the operator, allows gold and heavier materials to fall through the false bottom and behind riffles inside the cradle, as lighter materials are carried away by the flow of water.

gold pan: A dish a gold seeker uses to sift gold-bearing dirt. The prospector covers the soil with water and swirls the contents of the pan. This separates lighter material from the gold, which sinks to the bottom of the dish.

quartz mining: Quartz reefs containing veins of gold are quarried from hillsides. Stamping batteries are erected to pulverise the quartz, thereby separating out the gold, which is then sifted by pan or cradle.

sluicing: Various methods of sluicing rely on a heavy and constant flow of water to break up earth and separate gold from other materials. Usually this relies on a sluice box, which is a rectangular box open at the top and on both ends. The bottom of the sluice box contains a canvas or tussock mat and several riffles along the width. As in a cradle, water that passes through the sluice box carries away soil and lighter minerals, while gold collects behind the riffles and in the fabric of the mat. Water often is transported to the sluice box via a water race.

water race: An artificial waterway cut out of a hillside. It is intended to convey water to 'dry' claims, where it is used to separate gold from other materials.

Editorial Notes

Authentic oddities: manig [*manage*]
Clarifications: privile*d*ge
Illegible words: [*word illegible*]
Illegible words with suggestions: [?all]
Words deleted or omitted: [*omitted:* he]

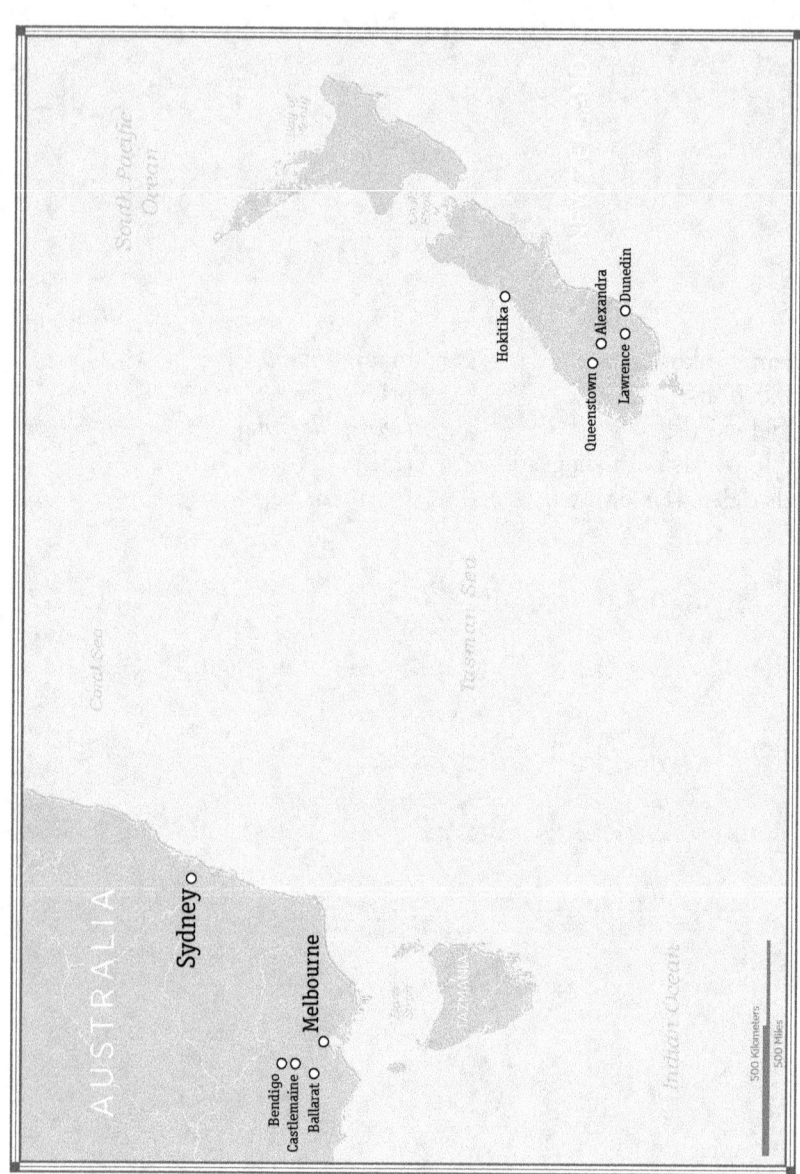

Map 1 The Tasman World.

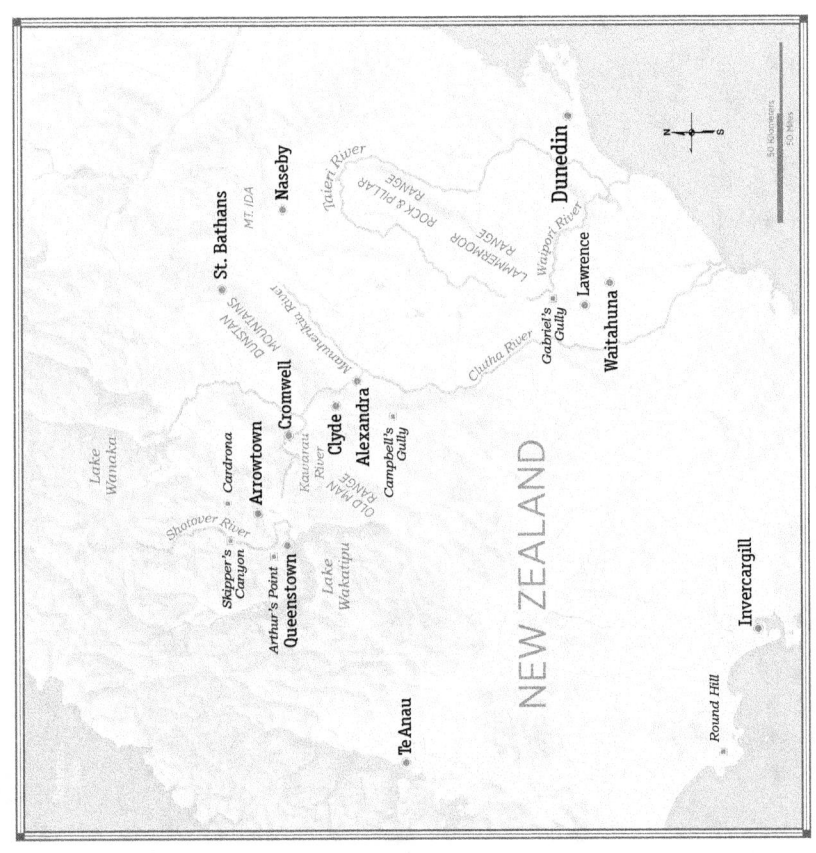

Map 2 The Otago Goldfields.

Introduction

In November 1863 four gold seekers, Robert Mattheson, William Gwillen, George Hyde and John Love, left their flooded claim along the Kawarau River on the Dunstan goldfield in Otago, New Zealand, for Campbell's Gully, a small goldfield to the southwest, hidden at the foot of the Old Man Range. After a brief and unsuccessful bout of prospecting in Campbell's and the surrounding area, the party retraced their steps back to the Dunstan. Within a few hours of leaving the gully, the group was caught in a blizzard of snow and sleet, which limited visibility to a few metres. After another two hours of walking, Hyde was overcome with cold and crumbled into a snowdrift. Love and Gwillen turned back to help their partner, but they lost sight of Mattheson, who continued to walk ahead of the party's packhorse. When Hyde was unable to stand, Love and Gwillen picked him up and carried their mate through the blizzard with snow up to their armpits. Unable to carry Hyde any farther, Love and Gwillen laid him down beside a rock and constructed a snow embankment to shelter him from the wind. The two miners then wandered on to find more permanent shelter, promising Hyde they would return for him. After searching for twenty minutes, Love and Gwillen found a rock behind which to take cover, hoping the storm would subside. During the night, Love became paralysed from cold and Gwillen, too weak to hold him up, could only listen to his mate's whispered pleadings with God, which lasted only a few minutes before he died. When morning came and the storm dissipated, Gwillen discovered a stone hut some thirty metres from where he and Love took shelter the night before. Hyde was also dead by the time he was discovered that morning.

When George Hyde died, he had among his few possessions a letter from a long-time mining partner at Lambing Flat, New South Wales, with whom he shared all of his earnings. John Love's body was later found with a handful of letters from his wife and a few portraits of their child in Glasgow. Local miners and townspeople collected a monetary donation that was sent to Love's wife along with a notice that her husband, whom she had kissed goodbye a year ago, froze to death half a world away. A funeral procession of prospectors and townspeople conveyed the bodies to the town's cemetery across the river. The local correspondent for the *Otago Daily Times* described the burial of the two diggers:

> In one grave, side by side, the two dead mates were placed. They had worked together, lived together, and died together; and in one small spot of ground, in close contiguity to several others who had met their end through like circumstances on the same mountain, found their last worldly halting place.[1]

This narrative illustrates several key themes about the societies and cultures of the Tasman World's gold rushes explored in this book. Firstly, the rushes cannot be understood without first placing them in the natural landscapes and natural environments that made the events extremely unstable and unpredictable. Few gold seekers ever faced such dire circumstances as those discussed above, but every prospector fought against floods and droughts, landslips and blizzards, enduring weather patterns that were far more volatile than those many experienced before arriving in Otago. These weather patterns had a profound impact on both the course of the rushes and the meanings individuals ascribed to gold seeking. The story also illuminates local relationships on the diggings. Strong bonds, like that between Gwillen and the other prospectors, often crystallised through the daily social experiences of swirling wash dirt in a pan or gin in a glass with mates. Moreover, gold rush societies were profoundly local and often possessed enough social cohesion to secure collections for gold rush widows and mass funeral processions for deceased diggers. Finally, this incident reveals the difficulty of framing the Otago rushes solely as events within New Zealand history. Some prospectors remained connected to loved ones in Britain, Ireland or China or mates and relatives across the Tasman Sea throughout their time in Otago. All these elements stress the need to position the Tasman World gold rushes at the junction of local societies and environments and the networks and identities that extended to Australia, Britain, Ireland and China.

PLACE, NATION AND THE OTAGO GOLD RUSHES

The gold rushes in Australia and the United States are embedded within the national histories of the countries in which they occurred. In the United States, historians have long understood the American rushes as part of a western frontier that defined national identity.[2] While less research has been undertaken on the gold rushes in Australia than the United States, the Australian gold seekers, writes Ian McCalman, have stood 'between the convicts and the Anzacs as landmarks on the road towards a national self-image built on "mateship" and a sceptical distrust of authority'.[3] In contrast to these American and Australian historiographies, New Zealand's South Island gold rushes never really found a home in a national history centred on Māori–Pakeha relations in the North Island. The rushes were too rapid, too transitory and too far removed from the larger Māori iwi in the North Island to fit within this national narrative. For this reason, the general histories of New Zealand often treat the gold rushes of the 1860s as a mere footnote to the New Zealand Wars in the North Island. Michael King, in his 2003 *Penguin History of New Zealand*, only remarks briefly that the gold rushes brought more immigrants and more capital to New Zealand.[4] Forty-four years earlier, in *A History of New Zealand*, Keith Sinclair simply offers a paragraph on the gold rushes, justifying this cursory treatment with the brief claim that the rushes 'have not lived on in the New Zealand imagination outside of the gold provinces ... [although] what they did do was to add to the variety of New Zealand life'.[5] While James Belich provides a slightly more detailed account of the rushes in the first of his two-volume history of New Zealand published in the 1990s, the events form a relatively minor episode between what he terms 'crusader' colonisation and the 'progress industry' in nineteenth-century New Zealand.[6] In her 2005 general history of New Zealand, Philippa Mein-Smith similarly surveys the New Zealand rushes briefly in a chapter otherwise devoted to the Māori–Pakeha conflicts in the North Island and the creation of New Zealand as a 'neo-Britain' through immigration and public education.[7]

Some of the best work on the gold rushes has been undertaken by historians moving away from the 'two nations' approach to understanding colonial society independent of interactions with Māori. Such studies tend to focus on the South Island, bringing the gold rushes into clearer focus. In his study of nineteenth-century New Zealand society, entitled *A Man's Country? The Making of the Pakeha Male*, Jock Phillips seeks to explain the historical origins of male culture in New Zealand. He begins his book by stating his interest in studying the 'ideas, stereotypes and images' of colonial masculinity that have been carried down to the present day rather than simply colonial male behaviour, but he quickly conflates reality with myth.[8] Phillips argues that the scarcity of women, the strenuousness of work, the sparseness of settlement and the fluid nature of social bonds combined to make colonial society masculine, open and egalitarian: male colonists scorned elitism, preferred bachelorhood to marriage and stressed male bonding and physical prowess over more 'refined' skills.[9] He contends that these environmental conditions amplified 'a regional variant of Victorian British attitudes', which in turn created an image of nineteenth-century New Zealand as a distinctive 'man's country'.[10] Phillips identifies the gold rushes – especially mobility, leisure cultures and the cooperative nature of gold seeking – as one of the primary foundations of this masculine culture and therefore profoundly important to national identity. The image of the gold rushes that emerges from Phillips' account is a largely cohesive, cooperative society of heavy-drinking and hard-working bachelors, whose friendships may not have been passionate and enduring but were strong and potent nonetheless.[11]

As Phillips acknowledges in his prologue, *A Man's Country* is an attempt to explain the origins of late twentieth-century gender stereotypes. He writes, 'It is my hope that by uncovering some of the values of the traditional male stereotype in New Zealand, the wounds inflicted upon men and women in the past may be opened to the air and the healing begin.'[12] Writing for a New Zealand audience, Phillips describes the gold rushes as part of a chequered 'our past' that the nation, collectively, needs to move beyond. A similar theme can be traced in Stevan Eldred-Grigg's volume entitled *Diggers, Hatters and Whores*. While Phillips seeks to explain the origins of masculine culture for contemporary New Zealanders, Eldred-Grigg sets out to use the gold rushes to strip New Zealand's colonial past of its Victorianism and prudery. Under Eldred-Grigg's pen, the rushes emerge as a scene of anarchy and adventure, dripping with 'blood, crime, death, [and] shameful acts' by gold seekers decked out in gold earrings and bracelets.[13]

Miles Fairburn, in his influential book on New Zealand colonial society, *The Ideal Society and Its Enemies*, offers another explanation of colonial New Zealand, and like Phillips and Eldred-Grigg, draws heavily from the rushes for his conclusions. Fairburn is concerned with what made New Zealand different from every other society. According to Fairburn, colonial New Zealand, and especially the goldfields, were 'gravely deficient' in social bonding, possessing the highest level of atomisation in the nineteenth century.[14] This resulted from mass transience, anonymity, sparse settlement and extreme individualism, creating an environment on the diggings and elsewhere where robbery, violence and loneliness were the dominant characteristics. According to Fairburn, modern New Zealand is shaped by the increased rate of immigration and urbanisation from the 1870s, rather than the gold rushes a decade earlier, as Phillips stresses.[15]

Because of the contentiousness of Fairburn's argument, *The Ideal Society* received much more attention than *A Man's Country*. Fairburn's work has spurred a flurry of articles, theses and monographs, most of which criticise his atomisation theory. Most of these studies have argued that local communities or ethnic networks bonded colonists, and in the case of ethnic networks, connected individuals to loved ones in Britain and Ireland or across the British Empire.[16] Fairburn dismisses this evidence as unrepresentative of broader New Zealand trends, stressing the importance of using statistics to discern typicalities across the colony.[17] Yet although the gold rushes form a core pillar of the atomisation thesis, Fairburn does not utilise statistical data to make claims about the rushes. He therefore is forced to rely on a handful of reminiscences published decades later, anecdotal evidence and rates of violence in Wellington, which tell us little about social bonding on the goldfields.[18] While Fairburn is able to use personal accounts to show that atomisation did exist on the goldfields, he is less successful in showing that it was the defining feature of goldfield life. Like that of Phillips, Fairburn's claims towards a master variable are unable to support themselves when there was none.

This book is not intended as a simple refutation of Fairburn's or Phillips' theses, though it can be seen as contributing to that discussion.[19] Historians too often have argued about which particular locality most accurately represented New Zealand. While there are several problems with the ways in which Phillips and Fairburn reach their conclusions, both scholars force historians to think critically about New Zealand in new ways. Rather than simply providing a new case study to critique a master variable, the analysis here follows pleas by Peter Gibbons and Tony Ballantyne to push beyond concerns with determining which locality was the most 'New Zealand' by interrogating whether the nation is the appropriate geographic scale to understand places within the New Zealand archipelago.[20] This is not to say that the gold rushes were unimportant to the development of New Zealand. Its provincial capital, Dunedin, was the largest city in New Zealand after the gold rushes, and Otago gold financed the agricultural boom in the North Island during the 1870s.²¹ Rather, this book argues that preoccupations with the national significance of the rushes tend to apply the least useful context for understanding gold rush cultures and societies in colonial Otago during the early 1860s. Whether scholars understand the rushes as the 'single biggest events in the history of colonial New Zealand', as Stevan Eldred-Grigg asserts, or (more often) as unimportant affairs because they never transcended locality into the 'New Zealand imagination outside of the gold provinces', as Sinclair contends, the Otago rushes have been both remembered and forgotten because of their supposed role in national development.²² This book pushes against these nationalising frameworks that understand the Otago rushes only as either a New Zealand story or a New Zealand footnote. The rushes are not valuable because they were 'big' – in fact, the Otago rushes were quite small when compared to rushes in Australia and North America²³ – but because the events can tell us about the ways that societies and cultures operated beneath and beyond national space. Historians must instead, as Antoinette Burton reminds us, think 'with and through the nation', rather than accept it as the primary unit of analysis.²⁴ However, local history also needs to recognise the placement of a locality within wider networks and geographies – a neglect in an otherwise exceptional body of local histories of gold rush Otago.

Such an interrogation of scale and scope reveals that the Otago gold rushes, although occurring in the archipelago known as New Zealand, are not best termed New Zealand events. Few participants would have considered themselves New Zealanders. Most migrated from Victoria, Australia. Some only resided in New Zealand for a month or less, while others migrated seasonally between Otago and Victoria before eventually leaving New Zealand shores permanently. Among those who stayed, '"New Zealand" was of relatively less importance as a frame of reference' than a particular locality, where individuals shared the rhythms of life with family members and neighbours.²⁵ This stress on locality is the greatest strength of the above-mentioned local studies of the Otago rushes; it is also why historians have consistently neglected them.²⁶ To return to Sinclair's claim, the gold rushes are valuable precisely because they were local, as well as transnational.

TRANSNATIONAL PERSPECTIVES

This book presents what David Thelen calls an 'internationalised' history that recognises that 'people, ideas and institutions' in gold rush Otago did not have 'clear national identities' but 'began or ended somewhere else'.²⁷ The term 'transnational' is used throughout this book to investigate 'movements, flows and circulation [of people, cultures, knowledge and money], not simply as a theme or motif but as an analytic set of methods which defines the endeavour itself'.²⁸ While most studies of the gold rushes in Australasia and North America mention that prospectors came from other countries or colonies, these comments are usually side notes to studies that are firmly bound within national history. However, transnational links during the gold rushes 'were too far reaching to allow us to tinker around the edges of any general accepted sketch'.²⁹ *Gold Rush Societies*, therefore, stresses the need to look across to Victoria, Britain, Ireland and China to understand these societies' impacts on and pervasiveness in colonial Otago during the gold rushes. However, the broadening of scale does not obliterate a micro-perspective. As James Ng and H. D. Min-his Chan show, while Chinese prospectors in Otago were part of a global diaspora, their sense of 'home' was rooted in a distant small village composed of members of the same family lineage.³⁰ Studies of Irish diasporic networks by David Emmons, Angela McCarthy and David Fitzpatrick have similarly discussed the role of kinship networks in facilitating and directing overseas migration, as well as the pervasiveness of the concept of 'home' as a small group of relatives and neighbours at a distinct locality that migrants left.³¹ This all links up with calls by Enda Delaney, Charles Tilly and Donna Gabaccia to understand overseas migration as a multitude of flows emanating from local communities and kinship networks and connecting to multiple overseas localities.³²

These diasporic networks and identities overlapped with the Tasman World. Few historians have investigated links between Australia and New Zealand during the gold rushes. There is no recent study that stresses the trans-Tasman connections in a similar way to Philip Ross May's analysis of the West Coast gold rushes, when he observed that the West Coast was a Victorian frontier and its chief port, Hokitika, was 'an Australian port'.³³ Across the Tasman Sea, connections to the Otago goldfields are even more absent in the histories of the Victorian rushes. The two major histories of the Victorian rushes only state that many prospectors left for 'New Zealand' in the early 1860s and make no mention of return migrations.³⁴ By neglecting the 'perennial interchange' between Otago and Victoria, these histories treat gold seekers as 'Australian' while in Victoria and 'New Zealanders' while in Otago.³⁵ This book contends that framing the Australasian rushes within the national histories of Australia and New Zealand leaves gold seekers, who migrated back and forth across the Tasman Sea, as '"nowhere men" occupying a historiographical nowhere land'.[36] It also neglects the ways in which the rushes transformed Otago into a periphery of Melbourne. The book instead investigates the migration paths of prospectors that, as Bruno Ramirez demonstrates in his study of Anglo-Canadians in the United States, was often as important as origins for understanding personal identities and networks.[37] By embedding the Otago rushes in the Tasman World, the investigation also responds to the plea by Carl Bridge and Kent Fedorowich to analyse the multiple regional metropoles in the British Empire, rather than only discern connections between the United Kingdom and colonial sites.[38]

This neglect of the trans-Tasman is perhaps surprising, given the growing interest in the Tasman World among historians in the last twenty years. Most of this scholarship is written by historians of New Zealand, rather than Australia, and it emerges from criticisms of the central thesis in James Belich's *Reforging Paradise*. Belich argues that New Zealand in the nineteenth century was 'part of "Australia", to the extent that any such thing existed' but became culturally independent in 1901 when it did not confederate with the Australian colonies and instead 'recolonised' itself through imitation of Britain.[39] Several historians, most notably Philippa Mein Smith, challenge Belich's conclusions by stressing the cultural, political, social and intellectual connections between Australia and New Zealand after Federation. In the debate over the endurance of the Tasman World into the twentieth century, nineteenth-century connections are merely assumed with little comment, which gives us only a fractured idea of what exactly it was that continued.[40] Sixty years after A. H. McLintock first drew attention to this neglect, the Victorian gold seekers in Otago are still hidden under 'the iniquity of Oblivion'.[41] Acknowledging these gaps, *Gold Rush Societies* emphasises the Victorian dimension of the Otago rushes through analysing both the relevance of prospectors' Victorian experience and the constant traffic of people, supplies and knowledge that made the gold rushes trans-Tasman events.

LOCAL AND ENVIRONMENTAL PERSPECTIVES

Historical geographers working in the wake of the 'spatial turn' have understood place through the networks and flows that connect it to the outside world.[42] 'Places', as David Lambert and Alan Lester argue, 'are not so much bounded entities, but rather specific juxtapositions or constellations of multiple trajectories.'[43] In their 'ever-changing coming together', they produce combinations that are unique, giving an unrepeatable character to each place.⁴⁴ Localities on the goldfields were defined by the constant coming and going of people, supplies, knowledge and gold. This shuffling was magnified in a gold rush society that often prized the most immediate and spectacular piece of knowledge, making the rushes extremely changeable events.⁴⁵ A goldfield or a township could be transformed overnight from a bustling honeycomb of industry into a heap of abandoned machinery and supplies with the arrival of news of a recently discovered field elsewhere in the province. This point connects to Doreen Massey's assertion that places were 'ever changing . . . constantly disconnected by new arrivals, constantly waiting to be determined . . . by construction of new relations'.⁴⁶ The control of knowledge became central when the rushes at any moment were characterised more by how the newspapers described them than by how much gold lay in the earth. As Chapter Two of the book argues, when knowledge of the rushes flowed across the Tasman Sea, the Victorian and Otago press often fought for readers in an itinerant trans-Tasman population.

Place also implies a particular location, a 'somewhere', which contains a particular blend of environmental characteristics, such as topography, weather patterns and geology. Fairburn and Phillips both have strong environmental currents running through their studies, prioritising environmental factors over British and Irish origins. However, neither scholar engages critically with the environment. Fairburn's analysis of the environment does not move beyond merely stating that there were few people in colonial New Zealand and they were spread out.⁴⁷ Phillips contends that digging for gold or felling trees was hard work and therefore bonded people together.⁴⁸ This book argues that environment during the gold rushes meant far more to gold seekers, who very quickly discovered that nature possessed enough force and power to dictate the course of the rushes. There was perhaps no single event in the nineteenth century more grounded in natural environments than the gold rushes. Individuals, day in and day out, fought with the earth for wealth that had laid dormant for centuries. They waded through water, trudged through snowdrifts and shovelled masses of mud and rock in near endless repetition. Moreover, when success usually depended on an abundance and easy conveyance of water over an arid landscape, natural factors continued to influence the rushes as streams froze overnight or snow melted in the mountains. Otago's changeable weather patterns compounded uncertainty and made the rushes very fluid and unstable events. In a society where spending habits depended on how much gold prospectors dug up, human and natural environments were always interconnected.⁴⁹

Portable and immobile entities collided daily on street corners and claims across Otago. Diggers migrating from Victoria quickly found that the Otago environment was more volatile than they expected as they fought against nature for gold, which then was laid down for brandy from London, flour from Adelaide, tea from India, or used to post a letter to a family member living in Melbourne or Manchester. Comings and goings in Otago during the rushes also had a profoundly tangible impact on places. As Kathryn Morse observes, 'What we choose to value in the earth shapes what we do with the earth, what we take from it to sustain ourselves.'[50] In Dunedin, on the goldfields and everywhere in between, the pursuit of gold transformed natural and human landscapes. The road along Lake Waihola on the way to the Tuapeka goldfield became a muddy quagmire when thousands of diggers and hundreds of wagons filed ceaselessly along the shoreline, while the road to the Dunstan was lined with animal carcasses and broken wagons. Dunedin was filled with excrement, squalor and cesspools as diggers flooded into the city in pursuit of golden riches. On the diggings, hordes of rats and tons of excrement were often more the materials of goldfield life than the gold that drew people there. As Terry Hearn shows, the impacts of prospectors' arrival and presence remained, even if they did not.[51]

This point also underscores a further theme. These mobile characteristics did not always flow freely, for there were multiple points of local friction that impeded the easy transplantation of cultures and societies. Some scholars who depend on transnational analysis risk overstating their case in this regard.[52] While transnationalism offers a fresh vision of the past beyond fixed national boundaries, using flows and networks as the sole methodology of historical research runs the risk of divorcing societies and cultures from local factors that inhibited the development of transnational identities. This, in turn, implicitly makes place irrelevant. This is one difficulty with the literature on the Tasman World: it stresses the unity and uniformity of a trans-Tasman identity in place of a national identity.[53] Just as a national scaffold is difficult to apply to the Otago rushes, an analysis that only uses a trans-Tasman framework creates problems. Connections to Victoria were clearly evident in Dunedin and on the goldfields during the rushes, as argued in Chapter Two. However, as Chapters Four and Five show, gold rush societies and cultures often were grounded more in local environments and topographies that were vastly different from Victoria and forced prospectors to adopt new forms of gold extraction in the province.[54] Here again the analysis stresses the importance of using the transnational and the local to counteract each other.

Prospectors who swirled gold and constructed water races in gullies and flats across Otago also possessed a 'sense of place', to use John Agnew's term, which was a 'symbolic identification with a place as distinctive and constitutive of a personal identity and a set of personal interests'.[55] From the moment gold seekers arrived in central Otago, they infused the landscape with the 'expectations, fears, rumours, desires and meanings' that could all be linked to the quest for gold hidden under rock, dirt and water.[56] In pursuit of golden dreams, prospectors created quagmires, clogging waterways, uprooting trees and eroding soil.[57] As diggers arrived with mates from Victoria or created new relationships with other miners, publicans or barmaids, their sense of place also came to be the local community that crystallised around the everyday routines of work and leisure. Here it is important to stress the importance of social structures and networks to understand cultural formation. This book presents culture as a 'concrete and bounded world of beliefs and practices'.[58] Following E. P. Thompson, this study also highlights the 'social and cultural contradictions [and] the fractures and oppositions within the whole' that push against a 'cosy invocation of consensus'.[59] Finally, it draws on the work of James Carey to analyse the role of everyday communication in local cultural formation. Such daily, local interactions are often forgotten in historical writing and yet are so constitutive of identity.[60]

MIGRATION AND ETHNICITY

Gold seekers' sense of place, which entangled transplanted kinship networks with a relatively egalitarian gold-mining community, inhibited the expression of a strong ethnic identity among miners from the British Isles. This aligns with Lyndon Fraser's argument of Irish migrants in New Zealand's West Coast rushes that absence of political elites and the 'relative economic homogeneity of its inhabitants [prevented] the maturation of intensified ethnic consciousness'.[61] As Rogers Brubaker maintains, ethnicity is not simply a pre-existing category but an ongoing process of self-identification through interactions with other groups and with a dominant host society.[62] It usually develops as either ethnic solidarity in resistance to a dominant host society or other groups, or through 'situation selection', whereby individuals choose pragmatically to adopt an ethnic identity for social, political or economic benefit.[63] Most studies of British and Irish migration use ethnicity as the primary or sometimes the only unit of analysis. This impressive body of literature can tell us a lot about a migrant's self-identification, memory and sense of belonging; however, as Nancy Green and Enda Delaney remind us, an exclusive focus on it can sometimes run the risk of missing other cultural frames that were more meaningful to migrants than ethnicity.[64]

In Gold-rush Otago, gold seekers did not find a dominant host society conducive to ethnic identity, nor did many consider ethnic identity a useful means of association. If anything, the volume and speed of the rush that overwhelmed the province solidified the ethnicity of earlier Scottish settlers who fashioned themselves the 'Old Identity' and the Victorian influx as the 'New Iniquity'.[65] The paths miners took to Otago were also more important than the country of origin. Prospectors and those that followed them to Otago drew heavily on their experiences in Victoria, where economic realities and fluid social dynamics were not conducive to the development of ethnicity. As Chapter Three argues, gold seekers in Otago instead drew on Victoria experiences by employing Chartist language as a form of solidarity and agency against the Provincial Government. Many of the Chartist-leaning gold seekers in Otago were likely among the flow of Chartist migrants to south-eastern Australia in the 1840s and 1850s – a reminder that ethnicity was just one of multiple identities that migrants brought with them.[66] Chartism provided a stronger associational language than ethnicity in Otago because it was more familiar and better reflected the labour and environmental concerns of gold seeking for miners who were preoccupied with immediate and local concerns. Rather than accept the ethnic group as the primary point of analysis, *Gold Rush Societies* therefore follows Kathleen Neils Conzen's plea to acknowledge 'the full range of immigrant expressive behaviour, not just the overtly ethnic ... if we are to understand the kinds of lives they were constructing, and the frustrations and satisfactions they encountered'.[67]

While social and economic conditions in 1860s Otago were not conducive to British and Irish ethnicities on the goldfields, ethnicity remained an important frame of reference for Chinese gold miners who arrived in the province from the 1870s through the 1910s. This was due to the changes within the host society, as well as internal dynamics within the Chinese community in Otago. As the province shifted out of prospecting towards more industrial and capital-intensive forms of gold extraction, a nascent working-class movement developed that drew on transnational concepts of 'whiteness' in North America and Australasia. Within this context, miners sought to expel Chinese migrants they interpreted as a capitalist ploy to drive down wages. While these political, economic and cultural factors in the host society helped to coalesce Chinese migrants into an ethnic group, members of the Chinese community also actively articulated multiple variations of Chinese ethnicity through religion, mutual aid and the purchase of commodities.

OVERVIEW OF THIS BOOK

This book is organised into three sections along chronological and spatial themes. In doing so, it moves beyond an approach that understands the Otago gold rushes as New Zealand events to show how they existed at the junction of local communities and environments and networks extending to Victoria, China and the United Kingdom. Chapters One and Two look at connections between the Otago goldfields, Britain, Ireland and Victoria. Chapter One discusses the British and Irish origins of gold seekers, their paths to Australasia and gold seekers' personal connections to communities and families in Britain and Ireland. The chapter argues that the Otago goldfields population was heavily influenced by migration streams to the Australian colonies which later converged on the Victorian goldfields, stressing the role of kinship and community networks in facilitating and direction migration. The chapter further shows how these kinship bonds were transplanted in Otago, as well as the degree to which some individuals retained connections to loved ones in Britain or Ireland through the exchange of correspondence. By analysing migrant correspondence, the chapter frames gold seeker identities within communities at home and the degree to which these relationships were maintained after overseas migration.

Chapter Two places the Otago gold rushes within the Tasman World by considering the links between Otago and Victoria during the gold rushes. It discusses the impacts of the contraction and industrialisation of the Victorian goldfields on facilitating migration to Otago. It further analyses the two-way traffic of people, information and commerce that wedded the Otago and Victorian goldfields into a single economic and social trans-Tasman community. Gold seekers also transplanted social networks in Otago, where they dug and drank alongside Victorian mates. Meanwhile, the Otago and Victorian press competed for itinerant gold seekers. Despite the attempts of the Otago newspapers, few had any attachment to Otago and their experiences in Otago were a temporary sojourn rather than permanent settlement.

Chapters Three and Four move beneath the nation to understand the importance of place in the Otago rushes, informed through the weekly and seasonal routines of work and leisure. Chapter Three looks at work on the Otago goldfields, emphasising particularly the daily practices and randomness of gold deposits in Otago. This chapter rubs against approaches that stress the vivid characteristics of the gold rushes to highlight the importance of the ordinary and mundane on an individual's habits, beliefs and language.[68] Moreover, it shows the impacts of the environment on the frequent transformations of the Otago rushes. Chapter Four elucidates the leisure worlds of the Otago gold rushes. While it recognises that gold seekers placed leisure in binary opposition to work, Chapter Four also stresses the commercialised production of entertainment spaces. It calls attention to the cultural work of leisure. While leisure practices often drew upon metropolitan cultural forms, they also offered individuals a prism into the society they were forming on the goldfields.

Chapters Five and Six are broadly framed between the waning of the Otago rushes in 1865 and the semi-centennial jubilee celebration of the gold rushes in 1911. Chapter Five draws on the diary of Alexander Don, a Presbyterian missionary to the Chinese in Otago. It charts the migration of Chinese prospectors and the means by which they attempted to maintain connections to home and kin. It also maps Chinese societies onto the diggings where individuals lived and worked with migrants from the same family or village. The second half of the chapter maps the responses of European colonists to Chinese gold seeking in Otago after the European gold rushes, and the ways in which debates about Chinese migration to Otago drew on similar debates occurring in California and Australia.

The intention of the chapter is not to quarantine Chinese participants in the rushes as entirely distinct from their European counterparts. Historians of the gold rushes often overlook significant similarities between Chinese, Irish and British migrants. Chinese prospectors in Otago were as discerning as British and Irish miners, established similar transnational and local networks and, although often described as sojourners, were less itinerant than other European gold seekers. The Chinese gold rush is described in a separate chapter because it was a different stream and occurred over a different period than the European rushes. Whereas the European gold rushes occurred in Otago between 1861 and 1865, most Chinese migrants arrived in the province during the 1870s. The Chinese sources therefore relate to a different period than their European counterparts, giving rise to a different set of contexts. By the time Chinese miners began arriving, most European prospectors had left the province and those that remained shifted into waged labour on the goldfields or in Dunedin, where they became crucial to the nascent New Zealand nationalism developing in the colony. Chinese experiences and identities were therefore affected by differing economic circumstances and the changing nature of colonial society.

Chapter Six continues this discussion of the development of New Zealand nationalism to examine how memories of the Otago gold rushes intersected closely with contemporary social debates about New Zealand. It also discusses how the rushes were remembered and forgotten among those who left New Zealand.

NOTES

1. *Otago Daily Times*, 23 December 1863, 5.
2. See, for example, Susan Lee Johnson, *Roaring Camp: The Social World of the California Gold Rush* (New York: W. W. Norton and Company, 2000); Brian Roberts, *American Alchemy: The California Gold Rush and Middle-Class Culture* (Chapel Hill: University of North Carolina Press, 2000); Kevin Starr, *Americans and the California Dream, 1850–1915* (New York: Oxford University Press, 1973); Malcolm J. Rohrbough, *Days of Gold: The California Gold Rush and the American Nation* (Berkeley: University of California Press, 1998); Paula Mitchell Marks, *Precious Dust: The American Gold Rush Era, 1848–1900* (New York: William Morrow and Co., 1994); H. W. Brands, *The Age of Gold: The California Gold Rush and the New American Dream* (New York: Doubleday, 2002). One exception is Jay Monaghan, *Chile, Peru, and the California Gold Rush of 1849* (Los Angeles: University of California Press, 1973).
3. Iain McCalman, Alexander Cook and Andrew Reeves, 'Introduction', in Iain McCalman, Alexander Cook and Andrew Reeves (eds), *Gold: Forgotten Histories and Lost Objects of Australia* (Cambridge: Cambridge University Press, 2001), 2. Also see David Goodman, *Gold Seeking: Victoria and California in the 1850s* (Stanford: Stanford University Press, 1994), 1–45. More recently, however, the gold rushes have been marginalised in Australian historiography, with greater emphasis being placed on convict transportation, urbanisation, gender history and the 'History Wars' surrounding aboriginal–settler conflicts. See Ann Curthoys, 'We've Just Started Making National Histories, and You Want Us to Stop Already?', in Antoinette Burton (ed.), *After the Imperial Turn: Thinking with and through the Nation* (Durham, NC: Duke University Press, 2003), 70–89. A few key works on the Australian rushes are Iain McCalman, Alexander Cook and Andrew Reeves (eds), *Gold: Forgotten Histories and Lost Objects of Australia* (Cambridge: Cambridge University Press, 2001); Geoffrey Serle, *The Golden Age: A History of the Colony of Victoria, 1851–1861* (Melbourne: Melbourne University Press, 1963); Geoffrey Blainey, *The Rush That Never Ended: A History of Australian Mining*, 4th edn (Melbourne: Melbourne University Press, 1993); Kerry Cardell

and Cliff Cumming (eds), *A World Turned Upside Down: Cultural Change on Australia's Goldfields 1851–2001* (Canberra: Australian National University Press, 2001).
4. Michael King, *The Penguin History of New Zealand* (Rosedale: Penguin Books, 2003), 241–5.
5. Keith Sinclair, *A History of New Zealand*, 4th edn (Auckland: Penguin Books, 1988), 106–7.
6. James Belich, *Making Peoples: A History of the New Zealanders from Polynesian Settlement to the End of the Nineteenth Century* (Auckland: Penguin, 1996), 345–9.
7. Philippa Mein Smith, *A Concise History of New Zealand* (Cambridge: Cambridge University Press, 2005), 81–5.
8. Jock Phillips, *A Man's Country?: The Image of the Pakeha Male, a History*, 2nd edn (Auckland: Penguin Books, 1996), viii.
9. Ibid., especially 5–38.
10. Ibid., 4. In a later criticism of Miles Fairburn's conclusions that are discussed below, Phillips argued that historians need to recognise the 'home' cultures migrants brought with them to New Zealand. However, *A Man's Country* similarly stresses the role of environment over cultural 'baggage', which figures only marginally in his book. See ibid., 4–6, 11, 23. Also see Jock Phillips, 'Of Verandahs and Fish and Chips and Footie on Saturday Afternoon: Reflections on 100 Years of New Zealand Historiography', *New Zealand Journal of History* 24, no. 2 (1990): 132–3.
11. Phillips, *A Man's Country*, 28–35.
12. Ibid., ix.
13. Stevan Eldred-Grigg, *Diggers, Hatters and Whores: The Story of the New Zealand Gold Rushes* (Auckland: Random House, 2008), 25, 270–1. For an excellent critique of *Diggers, Hatters and Whores*, see Tom Brooking, 'Gold in Otago: Digging for a New Perspective', in Richard Stedman (ed.), *A Golden Opportunity: Proceedings of the New Zealand Society of Genealogists Annual Conference* (Dunedin: New Zealand Society of Genealogists, 2011), 17–22.
14. Miles Fairburn, *The Ideal Society and Its Enemies: The Foundation of Modern New Zealand Society, 1850–1900* (Auckland: Auckland University Press, 1989), 11.
15. As Erik Olssen notes, Fairburn pushes against a 'Reevesian paradigm' that described an egalitarian and united society. See Erik Olssen, 'Where to from Here? Reflections on the Twentieth-Century Historiography of Nineteenth-Century New Zealand', *New Zealand Journal of History* 26, no. 1 (1992): 71.
16. Angela McCarthy, *Irish Migrants in New Zealand, 1840–1937: 'The Desired Haven'* (Woodbridge: Boydell Press, 2005); Tanja Bueltmann, *Scottish Ethnicity and the Making of New Zealand Society, 1850–1930* (Edinburgh: Edinburgh University Press, 2011), especially 4–7; Caroline

Daley, *Girls and Women, Men and Boys: Gender in Taradale, 1886–1930* (Auckland: Auckland University Press, 1999), Chapter 2; Scott Campbell, 'Community Formation in a Colonial Port Town: Port Chalmers, 1860–1875' (MA thesis, University of Otago, 2012), 7–14. The best and most balanced critique of *The Ideal Society* is Erik Olssen, 'Where to from Here? Reflections on the Twentieth-Century Historiography of Nineteenth-Century New Zealand', *New Zealand Journal of History* 26, no. 1 (1992): especially 71–2.

17. Miles Fairburn, 'A Discourse on Critical Method', *New Zealand Journal of History* 25 (1991): 161.
18. Fairburn, *The Ideal Society*, 222, 230–2.
19. For criticisms of Fairburn's atomisation thesis, see the articles in *New Zealand Journal of History* 25, no. 2 (1991).
20. Peter Gibbons, 'The Far Side of the Search for Identity: Reconsidering New Zealand History', *New Zealand Journal of History* 37, no. 1 (2003): 38–49; Tony Ballantyne, 'Thinking Local: Knowledge, Sociability and Community in Gore's Intellectual Life, 1875–1914', *New Zealand Journal of History* 44, no. 2 (2010): 138–56. For two excellent studies applying a similar approach, see Scott Campbell, 'Community Formation in a Colonial Port Town: Port Chalmers, 1860–1875' (MA thesis, University of Otago, 2012); and Rollo Arnold, *New Zealand's Burning: The Settlers' World in the Mid-1880s* (Wellington: Victoria University of Wellington Press, 1994).
21. Belich, *Making Peoples*, 369–70.
22. Eldred-Grigg, *Diggers, Hatters and Whores*, 494. Alan Mayne makes a similar critique of the Australian gold rush historiography, when he argues that Australian scholars usually stress technological and national development 'and disdain the local and the 'ordinary' except for those elements that can be slotted easily into the stories of "grand" events that historians want to tell … They traffic in fables, clichés and stereotypes: depicting a "matesy" egalitarian democracy that triumphed over tyranny.' Mayne underlines the importance of the local and particular as a means of increasing popular interest in the Australian gold rushes. See Alan Mayne, 'Family and Community on the Central Victorian Goldfields', in Charles Fahey and Alan Mayne (eds), *Gold Tailings: Forgotten Histories of Family and Community on the Central Victorian Goldfields* (North Melbourne: Australian Scholarly Publishing, 2010), 234–43.
23. The Otago gold rushes contributed only about 4 per cent of the world's output in gold during the early 1860s, when compared to 25 per cent from California and Victoria. See Brooking, 'A Golden Opportunity', 17.
24. Antoinette Burton, 'Introduction: On the Inadequacy and the Indispensability of the Nation', in Antoinette Burton (ed.), *After the Imperial Turn: Thinking with and through the Nation* (Durham, NC: Duke University Press, 2003), 1–23. See also Ian Tyrrell, 'Making Nations/Making States:

American Historians in the Context of Empire', *The Journal of American History* 86, no. 3 (1999): 1015–44; Tyrrell, 'American Exceptionalism in an Age of International History'; David Thelen, 'The Nation and Beyond: Transnational Perspectives on United States History', *The Journal of American History* 86, no. 3 (1999): 965–75; Richard White, 'The Nationalization of Nature', *The Journal of American History* 86, no. 3 (1999): 976–86.
25. Arnold, *New Zealand's Burning*, 118.
26. On the value of local and provincial histories and their neglect among New Zealand historians, see Olssen, 'Where to from Here?'.
27. David Thelen, 'Of Audiences, Borderlands, and Comparisons: Toward the Internationalization of American History', *The Journal of American History* 79, no. 2 (1992): 436.
28. C. A. Bayly et al., 'AHR Conversation: On Transnational History', *The American Historical Review* 111, no. 5 (2006): 1444. This quotation is taken from Isabel Hofmeyr during the panel discussion.
29. Ian Tyrrell, *Transnational Nation: United States History in Global Perspective Since 1789* (New York: Palgrave Macmillan, 2007), 2.
30. James Ng, *Windows on a Chinese Past*, vol. 1 (Dunedin: Otago Heritage Books, 1993), 27–9; H. D. Min-hsi Chan, 'Qiaoxiang and the Diversity of Chinese Settlement in Australia and New Zealand', in Tan Chee-Beng (ed.), *Chinese Transnational Networks* (Abingdon and New York: Routledge, 2007), 153–71. For similar findings among the Chinese in Australia and North America, see Adam McKeown, *Chinese Migrant Networks and Cultural Change: Peru, Chicago, Hawaii, 1900–1936* (Chicago and London: University of Chicago Press, 2001); Liping Zhu, *A Chinaman's Chance: The Chinese on the Rocky Mountain Mining Frontier* (Niwot: University Press of Colorado, 1997); Michael Williams, 'Destination Qiaoxiang: Pearl River Delta Villages and Pacific Ports, 1849–1949' (PhD thesis, University of Hong Kong, 2002).
31. David M. Emmons, *The Butte Irish: Class and Ethnicity in an American Mining Town, 1875–1925* (Campaign: University of Illinois Press, 1989), 13, 15; David Fitzpatrick, *Irish Emigration, 1801–1921* (Dundalk: Economic and Social History Society of Ireland, 1984), 30; Fitzpatrick, *Oceans of Consolation*, 622–6; McCarthy, *Irish Migrants in New Zealand, 1840–1937: 'The Desired Haven'*, 2–3, 173–4, 209. Also see Hearn, 'Irish on the Otago Goldfields, 1861–1871', in Lyndon Fraser (ed.), *A Distant Shore: Irish Migration and New Zealand Settlement* (Dunedin: University of Otago Press, 2000), 75–85; Lyndon Fraser, *Castles of Gold: A History of New Zealand's West Coast Irish* (Dunedin: Otago University Press, 2007); Tom Brooking, 'Weaving the Tartan and the Flax: Networks, Identities, and Scottish Migration to Nineteenth-Century Otago, New Zealand', in *A Global Clan: Scottish and Migrant Networks Since the Eighteenth Century* (London: Tauris Academic Studies, 2006), 183–202;

and Bueltmann, *Scottish Ethnicity*, Chapter 2. Anne Kelly Knowles makes a similar argument of Welsh migrant networks: Anne Kelly Knowles, *Calvinists Incorporated: Welsh Immigrants on Ohio's Industrial Frontier* (Chicago: University of Chicago Press, 1997), 120–6.
32. Enda Delaney, 'Our Island Story? Towards a Transnational History of Late Modern Ireland', *Irish Historical Studies* 37, no. 148 (2011): 102–5; Charles Tilly, 'Transplanted Networks', in Virginia Yans-McLaughlin (ed.), *Immigration Reconsidered: History, Sociology, and Politics* (Oxford: Oxford University Press, 1990), 11–12; Gabaccia, 'Is Everywhere Nowhere?', 1124–5. Also see John Bodnar, *The Transplanted: A History of Immigrants in Urban America* (Bloomington: Indiana University Press, 1985), 57–71.
33. Philip Ross May, *The West Coast Gold Rushes*, 2nd edn (Christchurch: Pegasus Press, 1967), 125. More recently, Lyndon Fraser also observes these connections between the West Coast and Victoria; however, he notes that his is not a study of the gold rushes so much as an analysis of the 'role of *ethnicity* in the adaptation of migrants to new environments'. Fraser, *Castles of Gold*, 18. He, therefore, does not analyse these connections to Victoria to the same extent as May.
34. See Serle, *The Golden Age*, 217, 228, 247; Blainey, *The Rush That Never Ended*, 81. In a more recent article, Blainey incorporates the New Zealand goldfields into the 'Australasian' gold rushes. See Geoffrey Blainey, 'The Momentous Gold Rushes', *Australian Economic History Review* 50, no. 2 (2010): 214. Among the handful of edited collections published over the last decade, only one article appears tracing the movement of Irish migrants from Victoria to the West Coast. Cook and Reeves, *Gold: Forgotten Histories and Lost Objects of Australia*; Cardell and Cumming, *A World Turned Upside Down*; Alan Mayne and Charles Fahey (eds), *Gold Tailings: The Hidden History of Victoria's Central Goldfield Region* (Canberra: Australian Scholarly Publishing, 2010), 119, 238. The only essay in an edited collection that discusses in detail migrations between Victoria and New Zealand is Lyndon Fraser, 'The Working Lives of Irish Men on the Antipodean Goldfields', in Keir Reeves and David Nichols (eds), *Deeper Leads: New Approaches to Victorian Goldfields History* (Ballarat: Ballarat Heritage Services, 2007), 21–38.
35. Rollo Arnold, 'Some Australasian Aspects of New Zealand Life', *New Zealand Journal of History* 4, no. 1 (1970): 54.
36. Donna R. Gabaccia, 'Is Everywhere Nowhere? Nomads, Nations and the Immigrant Paradigm of United States History', *The Journal of American History* 86, no. 3 (1999): 1115.
37. Bruno Ramirez, *Crossing the 49th Parallel: Migration from Canada to the United States, 1900–1930* (Ithaca: Cornell University Press, 2001), 186–8.
38. Carl Bridge and Kent Fedorowich, 'Mapping the British World', *Journal of Imperial and Commonwealth History* 31, no. 2 (2003): 2.

39. James Belich, *Reforging Paradise: A History of the New Zealanders from the 1880s to the Year 2000* (Auckland: Penguin Press, 2001), 46.
40. See, for example, Philippa Mein Smith, Peter Hempenstall and Shaun Goldfinch, *Remaking the Tasman World* (Christchurch: Canterbury University Press, 2008); Peter Hempenstall, 'Overcoming Separate Histories: Historians as "Idea Traders" in a trans-Tasman World', *History Australia* 4, no. 1 (2007): 04.01–04.16; Donald Denoon, 'Re-membering Australasia: A Repressed Memory', *Australian Historical Studies* 34, no. 122 (2003): 290–304; Philippa Mein Smith, 'The Tasman World', in Giselle Byrnes (ed.), *The New Oxford History of New Zealand* (Melbourne: Oxford University Press, 2009), 297–319.
41. A. H. McLintock, *The History of Otago* (Dunedin: Otago Centennial Historical Publications, 1949), 481.
42. For an overview of the spatial turn in history and geography, see Charles W. J. Withers, 'Place and the "Spatial Turn" in Geography and in History', *Journal of the History of Ideas* 70, no. 4 (October 2009): 637–58.
43. David Lambert and Alan Lester, 'Introduction: Imperial Spaces, Imperial Subjects', in David Lambert and Alan Lester (eds), *Colonial Lives Across the British Empire: Imperial Careering in the Long Nineteenth Century* (Cambridge: Cambridge University Press, 2006), 13.
44. Alan Lester, 'Imperial Circuits and Networks: Geographies of the British Empire', *History Compass* 4, no. 1 (2006): 135.
45. Tony Ballantyne, 'On Place, Space and Mobility', *New Zealand Journal of History* 45, no. 1 (2011): 62.
46. Doreen Massey, *For Space* (London: Sage Publications, 2005), 107.
47. Fairburn attempts to dodge this criticism by stating that his book was not a study of New Zealand society but of social bonding. However, it is difficult to have a study about *social* bonding not be about *society*. See Fairburn, 'A Discourse', 163.
48. Phillips, *A Man's Country*, 26–38.
49. I am influenced here by Kathryn Morse, *The Nature of Gold: An Environmental History of the Klondike Gold Rush* (Seattle: University of Washington Press, 2003), 89–114; White, 'The Nationalization of Nature', 976–80; Richard White, 'Discovering Nature in North America', *The Journal of American History* 79, no. 3 (1992): 874–6; Elliott West, *The Contested Plains: Indians, Goldseekers, and the Rush to Colorado* (Lawrence: University of Kansas Press, 1998), xvii–xxiii; Ian Tyrrell, 'Peripheral Visions: Californian–Australian Environmental Contacts, c. 1850s–1910', *Journal of World History* 8, no. 2 (1997): 278.
50. Morse, *The Nature of Gold: An Environmental History of the Klondike Gold Rush*, 7.
51. Terry Hearn, 'Mining the Quarry', in Eric Pawson and Tom Brooking (eds), *Environmental Histories of New Zealand* (New York: Oxford University Press, 2002), 84–99.

52. A few studies on the gold rushes that deemphasise place by stressing cultural and population flows are Goodman, *Gold Seeking*; Roberts, *American Alchemy*; Eldred-Grigg, *Diggers, Hatters and Whores*; Denoon, Mein Smith, and Wyndham, *A History*, 140–58.
53. Mein Smith, Hempenstall and Goldfinch, *Remaking the Tasman World*. This stress on cultural flows is prevalent in the historiography of the American rushes. See Starr, *Americans and the California Dream*; Rohrbough, *Days of Gold*: Roberts, *American Alchemy*.
54. My discussion of local 'frictions' is influenced by discussions with Tony Ballantyne and C. A. Bayly's comments in C. A. Bayly, 'AHR Conversation', 1441–64.
55. John A. Agnew, *Place and Politics in Modern Italy* (Chicago and London: University of Chicago Press, 2002), 16.
56. White, 'Discovering Nature', 874.
57. Tyrrell, 'Peripheral Visions', 279.
58. William H. Sewell, Jr, 'The Concept(s) of Culture', in Victoria E. Bonnell and Lynn Hunt (eds), *Beyond the Cultural Turn: New Directions in the Study of Society and Culture* (Berkeley: University of California Press, 1999), 39–40.
59. Edward P. Thompson, *Customs in Common: Studies in Traditional Popular Culture* (London: Merlin Press, 2009), 6.
60. James W. Carey, *Communication as Culture: Essays on Media and Society* (Boston: Unwin Hyman, 1989), 23–4.
61. Rogers Brubaker, 'Ethnicity without Groups', *European Journal of Sociology* 43, no. 2 (2002): 166.
62. Ibid.
63. Donald Handelman, 'The Organization of Ethnicity', *Ethnic Groups* 1 (1977): 188.
64. Nancy Green, 'The Comparative Method of Poststructural Structuralism: New Perspectives for Migration Studies', *Journal of American Ethnic History* 13, no. 4 (1994): 3–22; Enda Delaney, 'Our Island Story?': 98–102.
65. As Kim Sullivan shows, the sudden multi-ethnic influx of gold seekers in 1861 led to the creation of the first Caledonian Games in Otago, as 'Otago's unique Scottish hegemony came under threat'. Kim Sullivan, 'Scots by Association: Scottish Diasporic Identities and Ethnic Associationalism in the Nineteenth–Early Twentieth Centuries and the Present Day', PhD thesis (University of Otago, 2011), 64–5.
66. David Goodman, 'Gold Fields/Golden Fields: The Language of Agrarianism and the Victorian Gold Rush', *Australian Historical Studies* 23, no. 90 (1988): 32–3; Serle, *The Golden Age*, 110–13, 183–4. This argument is also influenced by Enda Delaney, 'Our Island Story?'.
67. Kathleen Neils Conzen, 'Mainstreams and Side Channels: The Localization of Immigrant Cultures', *Journal of American Ethnic History* 11, no. 1 (1991): 12.

68. See, for example, Eldred-Grigg, *Diggers, Hatters and Whores*; John Milton Hutchins, *Diggers, Constables and Bushrangers: The New Zealand Gold Rushes as a Frontier Experience, 1852–1878* (Lakewood: Avrooman-Apfelwald Press, 2010).

1

'To Return Home with . . . Satisfaction and Pleasure': Home and Family Networks

In 1856 John Lees left his home in Oldham, Lancashire, for the Australasian goldfields. This, however, was not his first departure from home. In 1847 Lees travelled to London, Hull, Birmingham and York when the contraction of Oldham's cotton and engineering industries, in which his family was involved, induced him to seek employment elsewhere in England. By 1852 Lees was living in London, from where he migrated to Victoria for the first time with two brothers also from Oldham, Daniel and John Evans. The three went out to join Lees' brother, James, who had rushed to the diggings in the colony the previous year. The Lees and Evans brothers were one of the few gold-seeking parties that actually succeeded on the Victorian diggings. A year after their arrival, the four diggers discovered a 1,319 ounce nugget worth £3,532, and they returned home in wealth shortly after. By 1856 John Lees returned to Oldham where he married, had a son and purchased a row of houses in the town along a street, which he named Nugget Street, with his own house, the largest, named Ballarat House. Yet, with money still in the bank, John once again travelled out to the Victorian goldfields with James and the Evans brothers, this time with the intention of returning to his wife and child within two years. However, he remained away from home for seven years, rushing to Otago early in 1862.

During this second tour of the goldfields John wrote twenty-nine letters home to his wife, faithfully sending one every three months on receipt of his wife's letter in the English mail. Most letters ran over a thousand words and were laborious to compose, especially when he often was surrounded by a din of diggers playing cards, or singing and dancing, which he commented all combined to 'excite a muddle of a man's ideas'.[1] In his letters, he peppered his wife with requests for news about neighbours and friends, and promised her he would soon return home. By 1862 Lees' prospect of a speedy return had long vanished, and he felt obliged to justify to his wife his delay and reiterate his intention to return home. As mindful of Oldham gossip as much as his wife's loneliness, he validated his prospecting in Otago:

> Through all the hardships, disappointments and long weary years of hope deferred there still remains one lingering smouldering spark of pride left (call it false pride if you will) that ... rebelles [*rebels*] against returning empty handed. I think, therefore, that my not having the means to return should be sufficient apology for doing so, to the stupidly sceptical of those who might be inclined to misconstrue my conduct. I cling to this trip [to Otago] as a sort of a last resort, a kind of forlorn hope after the manner of drawing and clutching at a strand to save himself. I earnestly hope that by [?*all*] means I may be enabled to return home with some degree of pleasure and satisfaction.[2]

When many of his letters home contained instructions for the fortune he collected during his last trip to Victoria and plans to invest or lend the savings on interest, poverty never inhibited Lees from rejoining his wife and child.[3] Rather, honour and reputation in Oldham delayed his return; the digger who returned in 1853 to Oldham with the largest nugget discovered up to that point in Victoria was ashamed to return seven years later poorer than when he left home. When his wife's reply to this letter was 'written in such a desponding state of mind', Lees reassured her in his next letter that he would 'swallow as best I may, this great and bitter pill, to return to my home, my Wife and my Child, at the very earliest opportunity'.[4] Shortly before leaving to return home, he lamented to his wife that 'it grieves me ... that I am bringing you nothing but an honest heart, ... an almost worn out carcass, crowned by a crop of grey hair'.[5] John Lees, who had built his castles of gold, returned home seven years later, wearied, despondent and shamed.

John Lees' story illustrates several themes that will be discussed in this chapter. Nineteenth-century gold seekers are often understood by historians as a 'restless, feverish' population, set apart from the condition of other migrants.[6] However, most were like Lees, whose mobility arose out of local conditions within Britain and Ireland and was structured by family networks. This chapter follows Nancy Green's call to de-emphasise national origins and adopt a micro-perspective to migration that properly pays attention to individual decisions, framed by social structures rooted in particular localities or family group.[7] This approach reveals a kaleidoscope of migration networks and correspondences that linked prospectors back to hamlets and towns. In their letters home and in their movements across Otago, they were more migrants from places like Glendevon and Bangor, Tiree and Drumahoe than the broader nations of England and Wales, Scotland and Ireland.

Lees' correspondence also questions some historians' conclusions that letters were important to migrants simply as a way to 'live vicariously in a community [when such] relationships were forbidden to them by the new dissocialised environment'.[8] Such dichotomy between home and local communities is not easily reconciled with the experiences of gold seekers like Lees, who faithfully wrote home to his wife in Oldham as he dug in Victoria and Otago alongside his brother and neighbours from the same town. Moreover, Lees' frequent, copious and affectionate correspondence with his wife was more indicative of the strength of their relationship than the weakness of local relationships in Otago. In fact, his preoccupations with local gossip in a village half a world away paradoxically delayed his journey home at the same time that his devotion to his family ultimately induced his return seven years later.

LEAVING THE UNITED KINGDOM

The migration of over 30,000 European gold seekers to 7,000 square kilometres of dusty hills and gullies in central Otago 'can only be understood with reference to the society of origin, in particular with reference to local occupational and social experiences' before overseas migration.[9] Overwhelmingly, these migrants came from Britain and Ireland or were Australasian-born but of British or Irish descent. Most prospectors arrived from Victoria, where only 9 per cent of the population was foreign-born. Because most of these non-British or Irish residents were Chinese, who did not arrive in Otago until after the European rushes, the percentage of British and Irish gold seekers in Otago was likely larger.[10] Because the Otago rushes relied almost exclusively on these arrivals from Victoria, they were events that remained largely within the British and Irish diasporas.

Across Britain and Ireland, the Industrial Revolution transformed local economic communities in the first half of the nineteenth century. Individuals responded to these changes in a variety of ways that usually stressed the centrality of the family. Whether across counties or across oceans, migration was often a family decision and migrants repeatedly relied upon kinship networks for knowledge about potential destinations, finance and assistance upon arrival.[11] These personal networks often overlapped with governmental structures. For example, most Irish gold seekers in Otago had previously relied on nomination schemes, in which a friend or family member in Victoria could select friends or relatives from home and pay a portion of their government-subsidised fare to the colony.[12]

This focus on economic changes and local responses stresses the importance of understanding mobility through a micro-perspective. For Otago's gold seekers the decision to migrate to Australasia was fundamentally a localised event, stimulated by local conditions and directed by translocal[13] family and neighbourhood networks at distinct places within the United Kingdom and the Australasian colonies. Moreover, overseas migration sometimes grew out of practices of local and regional mobility within and between Britain and Ireland. Some individuals who later dug for gold in Otago travelled across county or national borders within the United Kingdom years before they travelled out to Australasia.[14]

However, the decision to leave home cannot be reduced solely to economic and social structures. Overseas migration during the nineteenth century occurred during the period of modernity, in which roads, railways, steamships, mail systems and newspapers made a variety of places familiar to individuals who viewed occupations and livelihoods elsewhere as superior to their current situation.[15] It was certainly true, as Charles Tilly contends, that some structures and networks pulled some individuals in one direction while other systems pulled other individuals in different directions.[16] However, historians must also analyse 'individual and group choices' that operate within social and economic structures.[17] Some migrants were impulsive and heedless, deciding to emigrate for adventure and excitement rather than economic advantage. T. E. Crowhurst turned down an offer for a farm in England in order to travel abroad, stating that 'if I could only be the proud possessor of a horse, a dog and a gun I would have everything that could make life worth living'.[18] The sight of Greenland whalers visiting his home village in Fife encouraged James Strachan to seek adventure by enlisting aboard the *Strathmore*, a merchant vessel sailing from Glasgow. After sailing to China, Strachan jumped ship in Port Chalmers in 1858 and was employed as a labourer in Otago when he joined the Tuapeka rush.[19] Although adventurers have been overstated in the literature about the gold rushes, there were certainly many individuals to whom the word 'rush' is most aptly applied.[20] Charles Ferguson rushed from his home in Illinois to the California diggings in 1849. In 1853 he joined the rush to the Victorian diggings, where he remained for ten years before rushing to the Dunstan.[21] Arthur Scoullar quit his job as a cabinet maker near Glasgow when he heard about the Victoria rushes.[22] Thomas Monk recalled that the sight of an acquaintance returning from Victoria with 2,000 sovereigns was 'more than I could stand' and shortly after he rushed to the Victorian goldfields.[23] William Smith also set out 'in search of a fortune' when news of the Victorian rush reached Scotland in 1862.[24]

This section discusses the migration of individuals from Britain and Ireland who would later join the Otago gold rushes. It draws on a sample of 1,364 Otago gold seekers whose regional and occupation details were extracted from New Zealand death registers by Jock Phillips and Terry Hearn.[25] This source is not without problems. It records only those who died in New Zealand after 1873, ignoring those who died during the rushes and the majority of gold seekers who left New Zealand after the rushes. It is unlikely that there would have been a direct correlation between one's family occupation and one's willingness to remain in New Zealand. A more significant limitation of the source is that the information contained in death certificates may be incorrect because it was given by local acquaintances without any means of objectively verifying its accuracy. Despite these limitations, New Zealand death certificates present the best window into the origins of gold seekers of any nineteenth-century gold rush population.

England

In England, the Industrial Revolution transformed the structures of everyday life for individuals across the nation; however, its influence was not universal but trickled down in a multitude of ways into local communities and family groups. Moreover, these transformations were inseparable from the impact of global trade on reorganising economic space in the first half of the nineteenth century. Approximately 36 per cent of English gold seekers to Otago, according to Phillip and Hearn's data, came from the southwest of England. While cotton from the southeastern American states and wool from the southeastern Australian colonies drove the growth of textile manufacturing in Yorkshire and Lancashire, it also crumbled the pastoral industry in the southwest counties of Devon, Somerset and Dorset. Moreover, these regions were highly reliant on European and imperial markets, and a series of wars with France and the ending of the East India Company's monopoly on Chinese trade combined to further depress this region. Meanwhile, the extension of the railway to Exeter in 1844 and Plymouth in 1849 flooded the local market in the southwest with cheaper staples than those produced nearby, pushing farmers and tradesmen out of the region.[26]

In 1859 John Fox emigrated with his family from their family farm in Devonshire to Victoria, where he began gold mining until he travelled to Otago in 1862 at the beginning of the Dunstan rush.[27] James Marshall was born in Ilfracombe, Devonshire, where he worked as a carter until the collapse of the wool industry. He then relocated to London, where he worked as a journeyman. In 1852 he migrated to Australia and began prospecting in Victoria, rushing to Otago in 1861 and 1863.[28] As the example of Marshall illustrates, mobility sometimes began within Britain years before an individual left British shores.

Alongside the contraction of the regional pastoral industry, Cornwall and Devonshire also faced the collapse of the area's mining industry. Local copper deposits began to dry up in the 1850s at the same time that copper from newly opened mines in New Guinea and Australia flooded the global market.[29] These two contexts combined to facilitate extensive emigration to mining regions in Brazil, the United States and South Australia. Most of the Cornish population on the Otago diggings first emigrated in the 1850s to the South Australian mines.[30] One of these was William Phillips, who came from a typical Cornish emigrant family. His father emigrated from Cornwall to South Australia in 1849 and travelled to the Victorian diggings during the 1850s. William followed his father out nine years later at the age of thirteen, and the two worked together at Bendigo and Castlemaine before William rushed to Gabriel's Gully in Otago. From there, William joined the Wakamarina and West Coast rushes, eventually settling at Picton.[31] Another Cornish miner was John Lawn, who emigrated from Cornwall with his two brothers in the late 1850s. Shortly after arriving, the brothers began mining in Victoria, where they remained for four years before joining the rush to Gabriel's Gully. Over the next several years, the Lawns criss-crossed the Tasman multiple times, gold seeking in Victoria and on the West Coast, copper mining in South Australia, and finally settling at Reefton on New Zealand's West Coast.[32]

Some 9 per cent of Otago gold seekers recorded by Phillips and Hearn were from the southeast and east of England, where the quickening of transportation diminished regional wages as it had done in the southwest. These regions traditionally had some of the highest agricultural wages in England, because the industry could always rely on a high demand for produce in nearby London. However, when the railway began flooding London with crops grown elsewhere in Britain, prices in the region plummeted and many landlords converted their grain farms into orchards and hop farms in order to profit from a newly established national market.[33] These industries only required a seasonal workforce and created landless and itinerant labourers who could not rely on employment all year round. Against this backdrop many individuals began looking for work abroad, when all England provided was the choice of urban employment or unsteady rural labour with little hope of land ownership.[34]

Wales

Welsh gold seekers made up 2 per cent of Otago's prospectors from Britain and Ireland.[35] The Welsh population on the diggings was split roughly evenly between North Wales and South Wales. This regional profile was also reflected in the migration from Wales to Victoria during the 1850s, indicating that most travelled to Otago through the Victorian diggings.[36] The North and South Welsh came from two very different societies and followed different paths to the diggings. In North Wales, the enclosure of agricultural land and the contraction of the wool industry induced many sons of tenant farmers and agricultural labourers to migrate to England in search of work. English cities were often the preferred destination of Welsh migrants over the coal and iron mines and factories in South Wales.[37] Few of these North Welsh migrants, then, had any hard rock-mining experience before they emigrated, and many probably were living in England when they sailed for Australasia.

In contrast, South Wales was dominated by coal mining and iron manufacturing. Like elsewhere in Britain, the quickening of transportation caused by the railway transformed this region's economies and induced mobility. The expansion of the railway to Wales in 1839 allowed coal to be more cheaply transported elsewhere in Britain, stimulating the regional coal economy's growth at the same time it crippled the local iron-manufacturing trade.[38] Meanwhile, as coal flowed out of South Wales, subsequent waves of Welsh, Scottish and Irish migrants, responding to other economic pressures, arrived in the region. In 1851 there were 20,000 Irish and 120,000 English and Scottish living in Wales, the overwhelming majority of whom were living in South Wales.[39] That year, the English-born alone made up one-tenth of the country's total population, and their percentage only increased throughout the rest of the nineteenth century.[40] While some Welsh labourers previously employed in iron manufacturing shifted into coal mining, the industry was unable to absorb this population alongside the labourers arriving from England, Ireland, Scotland and North Wales. Moreover, the railway also strengthened the connection between individuals living in South Wales and communities of Welsh migrants living in Liverpool and

London, inducing many to migrate. In 1851 there were 48,000 Welsh-born migrants living in Lancashire and Cheshire and another 18,000 living in London alone.[41] Moreover, as information about Canada and the United States was read in Welsh-language newspapers and in private correspondence with family members already living overseas, 60,000 Welsh travelled to the United States between 1850 and 1870. Most of these migrants had no background in agriculture and chose to settle in areas with a heavy industry of coal mines.[42] Wide coverage in the Welsh-language press of the Cariboo diggings in British Columbia also induced a rush from South Wales.[43] Otago never enjoyed similar coverage anywhere in Britain and, therefore, relied upon streams to the Victorian diggings. The migration flow from Victoria to Otago will be taken up in Chapter Three.

By 1861 over 6,000 Welsh had migrated to Victoria. Most migrants were single men or married men who left their wives and families in Britain. Indeed, the Welsh population on the diggings contained a higher proportion of men, 63 per cent by 1871, than any other ethnic group from the United Kingdom. Like other ethnic groups, many of the Welsh possessed some vague desire to 'get rich' and return home.[44] The Otago diggings drew many of the migrants in much the same way as other Victorian diggings exerted their pull, and the roughly equal representation of the North and South Wales movement was extended to Otago. One of these Welsh migrants was David Jones, who left the village of Caernarfon in North Wales and sailed for Victoria in 1857. After prospecting at Ballarat for five years he rushed to Otago in 1862, returning across the Tasman the following year.[45] As Jones' case illustrates, these flows could sometimes become self-perpetuating. His letters home to his family were packed with information about prices and wages, which were intended to be mined by kin intending to emigrate. In response to a letter from his parents stating that his brother, Thomas, wanted to join him overseas, he wrote from Otago that he would nominate Thomas as an assisted migrant and deposited £7 in Victoria to cover his passage.[46]

Scotland

Thirty-one per cent of Otago gold seekers in Phillips' and Hearn's data set were born in Scotland. The Scottish Lowlands and Borders sent approximately 13 per cent of Otago's gold seekers. Land use in the Scottish Lowlands was transformed by the Industrial Revolution. The influx of migrants from the Scottish Highlands and Ireland into Lowland Scotland combined with a natural population increase to bring drastic changes in the region. Beginning in the 1780s, landholdings in the region were consolidated, tenancies were made redundant and subdivision was outlawed. These enlarged farms also increasingly relied on seasonal or annual labourers.[47] By the 1840s, most Lowland inhabitants were the non-inheriting sons of tenant farmers, labourers or farm servants, who migrated to urban areas looking for work.[48] Glasgow became the predominant destination because of a recent shipbuilding and manufacturing boom.[49]

For many Lowland prospectors, this rural to urban migration often preceded emigration to Australasia.[50] One of these migrants was James Allison, who left his home in Wigtownshire for Glasgow, where he worked in the shipbuilding industry until he sailed to Adelaide in 1859. Over the next two years he travelled to Bendigo and Gippsland before rushing to the Tuapeka in 1861.[51] Another was John Muir, who was born in southern Lanarkshire and worked as a tailor in Glasgow and London for five years. He journeyed to Melbourne during the 1850s and migrated across the Tasman in 1864, digging in Otago and on the West Coast.[52] There were also many Lowlanders who arrived directly from Scotland before the rushes as part of the Otago Company's colonisation scheme.[53] William Martin was trained as a carpenter in Glasgow before he migrated to Otago sometime before 1861; he then left a job as a labourer in Oamaru to join the Tuapeka rush.[54] Kinship networks in the province guaranteed the continual influx of migrants from Scotland before the rushes. Archibald Henderson sailed from the Clyde to join his brother in Dunedin early in 1861. He began gold seeking two years later and prospected in Otago and on the West Coast until 1869.[55]

The Scottish Highlands and Islands accounted for 14 per cent of all diggers on the Otago goldfields. Like other regions of Britain, the Highlands and Islands were connected to the wider British economy through the Industrial Revolution; however, the greater dependence on volatile markets in Europe and Britain magnified the effects of these transformations felt in Scotland. As Highland landlords adapted to fluctuations in distant markets, they often shifted production to kelping, fishing and livestock. Moreover, the French Wars of the late eighteenth and early nineteenth centuries stimulated demand for these commodities, driving population growth in the Highlands. This magnified the financial collapse of the region after the wars. A severe potato blight in 1846 further intensified the fragility of this region and threw many crofting families into destitution.[56]

Migrants from the Highlands and Islands were more reliant than other British emigrants on government and bounty assistance to finance emigration. Most of the Highland and Island gold seekers in Otago who travelled to Australia emigrated between 1837 and 1858 as part of government recruitment schemes in South Australia and New South Wales. The first large-scale migration from the Highlands and Islands to Australia occurred between 1837 and 1841, when some 4,000 Highlanders travelled to New South Wales as part of a colonial bounty system.[57] The second group came out to Australia between 1852 and 1858 through the actions of the Highland and Islands Emigration Society (HIES). The organisers of this recruitment were motivated by complaints from colonial employers about desertion to the goldfields and British humanitarian concerns about the economic deterioration of the Highlands. Under this scheme, Society agents bypassed landlords and directly recruited 5,000 shepherds and labourers who were unable to finance their own emigration. Preference was given to family groups, because recruiters believed these family connections, as well as the Highlander's clan-based society, would make him more resistant to rushing to the diggings.[58] This assumption largely proved incorrect, with Highlanders over-represented on both the Victorian and Otago goldfields.[59] The HIES sent out more than 5,000 migrants, most of whom left from Skye, Inverness and the northern and western coasts of Sutherland and Ross. Lachlan McDonald probably relied upon this government assistance. He sailed from his home on the Isle of Tiree to Victoria, where he was working as a labourer in 1858. In 1862 he travelled to Otago and prospected for gold along the Waipori River.[60]

The Otago diggings also drew heavily from Caithness and the offshore islands of Orkney and Shetland in the Far North of Scotland, despite their under-representation among both assisted migrants to Australia and the Victorian goldfields population.[61] Although the region contained only 4 per cent of Scotland's population, it accounted for 14 per cent of Scottish miners and 6 per cent of all miners – the same percentage as the English Midlands and Yorkshire combined. Jock Phillips and Terry Hearn postulate that many of these diggers were sailors who deserted their ships in Port Chalmers or Bluff when they heard news of the Otago rushes.[62] While this speculation is difficult to substantiate, the collapse of the fishing industry and several poor harvests in the region probably induced many to abandon their father's occupation and travel out to sea.[63]

Ireland

While Britain experienced high rates of internal mobility, Ireland had much larger rates of emigration than internal migration, both before and after the Famine.[64] Irish migrants to Australasia sometimes travelled to Britain first, where they saved enough of their wages to purchase a ticket to Melbourne or Sydney.[65] Whether directly from Ireland or stepwise through Britain, most Irish migrants relied on government assistance to obtain passage to Australasia, often travelling to the Australian colonies before rushing to Otago. Between 1853 and 1859, when most of Otago's gold seekers arrived in Australia, more than 70 per cent of Irish migrants to New South Wales, South Australia and Victoria had travelled out under government assistance.[66] The most common form of government assistance was the nomination scheme, in which a relative or friend in Australia would recommend a prospective migrant, and the colonial government would subsidise the transportation costs, provided a portion of the fare was deposited in the colony and the individual met the age and occupation requirements.[67] At Forrest Creek, Victoria, a year before he travelled to Otago, Hamilton McCance helped facilitate the migration of kin from County Down, forwarding £25 from his brother-in-law, William Boyce, to bring out Boyce's sister and nephew to Victoria.[68]

The reliance on government assistance among Irish migrants to Australia created a relatively selective profile of Irish prospectors in Otago, when government recruiters could canvass certain regions of the country and earlier migrants relied on the nomination scheme to bring out friends and siblings.[69] Thirty-two per cent of Otago prospectors were born in Ireland. More than 70 per cent of these Irish gold seekers, or 26 per cent of all gold seekers, came from Munster or Ulster. Most Munster migrants came from Clare, Tipperary, Kerry and Limerick, while those from Ulster came predominantly from Antrim, Londonderry, Cavan and Down. Three-quarters came from families engaged in agriculture, and many were likely semi-skilled agricultural labourers, or the children of labourers, whose employment was made redundant by the shift in Ireland to livestock production from the 1830s.[70] Moreover, especially among Munster emigrants, the recent experiences of the Famine often left individuals with 'little psychological resistance to emigration', which became part of the 'life-cycle' of the Irish living in post-Famine Ireland.[71]

As this brief overview shows, emigration from Britain and Ireland to Otago often operated through Victoria. For British migrants, travel overseas, let alone 'gold-rushing', was usually not the beginning of itinerancy; many travelled across county borders before they left British shores. In contrast, the Irish were more likely to migrate overseas than travel within Ireland, but some still shifted to Britain before travelling to Australasia. These practices of mobility were later manifested in frequent movements during gold seeking on both sides of the Tasman Sea. Most gold seekers were not mobile because of the pursuit of freedom or the licence that the gold rushes embodied, nor were many prospectors somehow of a different temperament from the millions who filled the gangways for ships bound for Boston or New York, or who travelled instead to London or Glasgow. Their movements on and between the goldfields were often in response to local economic conditions and structured by local social and familial networks, rather than a unique trait or desire they shared, as has been argued by some historians of the gold rushes.[72] Moreover, itinerancy did not end with gold seeking. Mobility often extended long after gold seeking, when 'the possibility of future migration only [ended] at death'.[73]

For both British and Irish gold seekers the decision to emigrate and the choice of where to go was largely determined by kinship and community networks, even when passage was funded by governmental sources. Individuals relied on friends and relatives for information about potential destinations, nominations to colonial governments and financing of the passage costs. As will be shown below, these family and community networks were often transplanted into central Otago during the gold rushes, when individuals prospected for gold alongside neighbours or siblings while composing letters for loved ones in the United Kingdom. However, for individuals who possessed varying degrees of willingness and ability to correspond, and faced the everyday realities of gold seeking, connections to home sometimes disappeared.

COLONIAL NETWORKS

The social networks which directed migration to Australasia were often mapped onto colonial Otago, as individuals dug alongside brothers, cousins or former neighbours. Some scholars of the gold rushes argue that the lure of gold and the multi-ethnic nature of goldfield life broke down kinship and neighbourhood bonds on the diggings. In his study of Irish gold seekers on the Victorian diggings, Chris McConville argues that Irish prospectors relied on government recruiters rather than kin to finance and organise overseas migration and worked and lived among the non-Irish on the diggings, which disintegrated any attachment individuals had to kin when they arrived in Victoria.[74] Discussing Welsh organisation on the Victorian diggings, Kerry Cardell similarly remarks that 'stronger than family life or friendship networks... were the exigencies of seeking for gold'.[75] Patrick O'Farrell puts forth a similar argument when he states that Irish migrants in Australia brought with them a kinship mentality that quickly disintegrated after arrival.[76] This depiction of the Victorian goldfields lacking kinship ties finds a corollary in Miles Fairburn's depiction of New Zealand. Fairburn argues that few individuals migrated together and those that did tended to lose touch after arrival in the colony.[77] He does not take networks seriously, instead arguing that there was little kinship or neighbourhood bonding in the colony 'because rarely did a village come out together to New Zealand'.[78] As Angela McCarthy remarks, there is an untested assumption in Fairburn's conclusion that mobility necessarily weakened family connections in New Zealand.[79] Moreover, Fairburn's neglect of correspondence and diaries overlooks the sources most likely to record such networks. Through an analysis of Irish–New Zealand correspondence, McCarthy finds that 'family and neighbourhood connexions not only initiated, but also sustained and facilitated Irish migration to and settlement in New Zealand'.[80] The evidence from the Otago goldfields confirms McCarthy's conclusion by arguing that frequent movements between Victoria and Otago and mobility within Otago were in fact structured by such kinship and neighbourhood networks. From the moment some individuals left the emigrant ship, they found themselves amid the same kinship networks they left. This can be best explained through a discussion of William Walker, who left his family's home in London for Christchurch in 1860. In a letter William sent home shortly after arrival he told his mother that

> [Upon arrival], we made our way to the Post Office where I found one letter from you and another from Mary Anne. (Has John's miscarried or did he not write?) ... From the P. O. we went to J. Hall's house. (I suppose you know he has gone home) and there we saw Mrs. Hamilton ... We stopped there about an hour – that is Goodrich and myself, he having a letter to Hall from Fitzgerald. As we were going away to Hamilton's office ... we met Tucker who had found out the Boarding house where his cousin stopped when in town. [The next day we ...] went to Mr. T. Hall but [*omitted:* he] was not at home, having gone up country to Mr. G. Hall. His wife was very kind and immediately claimed acquaintance with me as she said I was her second cousin.[81]

Emigration for William did not constitute a clear break from his acquaintances, so much as transplanting home networks onto colonial Canterbury. The social world in which William travelled in Canterbury immediately after arrival was filled with familiar faces and relatives. Moreover, communication with his mother and siblings continued seamlessly after arrival. These networks also facilitated the emigration of William's brother, John George, two years later and the two worked together and corresponded regularly with their mother until 1863 when they returned to London.[82] Throughout their time in Otago, the Walker brothers' immediate concern was 'building lives of their own within rather narrow boundaries'.[83]

Lyndon Fraser, in his history of the West Coast Irish, remarks that prospectors often worked alongside relatives and neighbours from home.[84] William and John George Walker dug together throughout their time in Otago.[85] In 1863 Anne Lindsay wrote to her sister in Britain that her son had rushed to the diggings with friends and relatives from home.[86] In 1863 Thomas Andrew rushed from Dunedin to the Molyneux with two of his brothers from Fifeshire.[87]

Diggers arriving on the diggings also sometimes found the fields full with acquaintances from home. Hamilton McIlrath told his father at Balloo, County Down, in a letter that 'We saw almost all the boys from Killinchy. We wrought close to David Osborne and Natheniel Heron's three sons on the Digings. William Gebby, he was there too.'[88] A bewildered Scottish digger, Robert McCrae, at first pretended, unsuccessfully, to be an Irishman, before he recognised Alexander McKay as a former neighbour at home.[89]

This is not to say that all diggers considered kinship networks important, or even relevant enough to maintain. While there were some who continued to work alongside friends and relatives from home, there were also many who lost connections.[90] Sometimes, this was a conscious abandonment of family networks, especially when the scale and speed of the rushes made it easy to become anonymous. Most probably did so gradually as they drifted between diggings and between jobs. The independence and freedom of movement that characterised gold seeking also sometimes made party formation extremely fluid. Andrew Roy lost touch with James White after the latter joined the Picton rush.[91] John Henry Watmuff frequently complained in his diary that his brother, Ned, failed to correspond with the family throughout his time in Otago and Victoria.[92] In 1866 Watmuff heard through another gold seeker that his brother had died on the West Coast from fever and dysentery.[93] As gold deposits diminished and prospectors left the diggings, siblings and friends also sometimes separated. In 1875 Archibald Henderson remarked that he had not seen his brother in New Zealand for nine years after settling into farming in Taranaki, though they corresponded regularly.[94]

TRANSNATIONAL TIES TO HOME

Just as we need a local perspective to understand British and Irish migration to the Otago goldfields, we also need a local perspective to understand the nature of migrant connections to 'home'. David Fitzpatrick remarks in his magisterial study of Irish–Australian correspondence that few migrant correspondents characterised a nation or country as home; rather, home usually was constituted by a concrete locality and a small network of friends and relatives.[95] The following discussion relies on 188 letters in seventeen collections sent by gold seekers in Otago to relatives and friends in Britain or Ireland to show the ways in which some diggers remained connected to communities and individuals after emigration.[96] This is not intended to be a representative sample of gold seekers in Otago. Absent are individuals who chose not to write. Moreover, this is a very small sample of the approximately 290,000 letters that were sent from Otago to the United Kingdom between 1861 and 1864.[97] Nevertheless, these letters are able to tell us some information about how, for at least some diggers, their social identities, and for that matter their daily routines of swirling gold in a pan or rocking it in a cradle, were infused with connections to friends and family members at home. As illustrated by the case of John Lees at the beginning of this chapter, there were some diggers who were consumed with what digging for gold, and often their inability to find it, meant to former neighbours at the other end of the globe. Few diggers were probably as affected by home gossip as Lees, yet many considered these relationships meaningful enough to hastily put an end to the workday and scribble down a few notes to a sibling or parent to be passed on to another digger on his way to the post office.[98]

Unlike historians of migration, few historians of the gold rushes take these relationships seriously. In the United States, gold rush correspondence is either drawn for juicy quotes about life on the diggings or is stripped of its relational contexts and understood as a means through which wealthy diggers moulded a national middle-class culture.[99] In Australia, historians of the rushes have paid more attention to the formation of local ethnic identities on the goldfields rather than the ways in which identities were maintained transnationally through correspondence.[100] New Zealand historians, often viewing the rushes along a continuum from colonisation to nationhood, have been largely unconcerned with how identities extended beyond national borders.[101] However, just as mobility did not begin or end with overseas migration, these connections to kin did not necessarily evaporate the moment an individual left the United Kingdom.

Nearly every correspondent bemoaned the delivery times and the unreliability of the postal system. After William Wilson left the Otago diggings, he complained to his brother in Fife that he never received any letters his brother sent.[102] In 1862 William Ruskin wrote with a tinge of despondency to his brother John, in Midlothian, saying that 'every letter i have got yet has been miscarried some way'.[103] In 1864, while carting goods to the Arrow River diggings, Andrew Roy simply expressed frustration to his brother James, in London, at how letters could so frequently be lost or delayed.[104] Lachlan McDonald justified the lateness of his writing by explaining to his brother John, in Tiree, that he had not written until then because he only just then received two letters that were posted five months previously.[105] Compounding this difficulty was the speed with which the rushes pushed beyond existing communication networks. After working on claims all week long, travelling back to goldfield townships was an exhausting task for many. Diggers sometimes had to walk fifteen miles to the post office, only to stand for three hours waiting for letters from home.[106] At Waitahuna, one very overworked postman handed out letters for ten hours straight. When this proved to be excessively slow, one group of frustrated diggers threatened to tear down the post office.[107] This distance from the post office and delays receiving letters was the excuse William Crawford gave his parents for not writing while he was at the diggings.[108]

Mobility on and off the goldfields compounded difficulties associated with the delivery of letters. Thomas Armstrong moved between three different jobs in Victoria before he began working on a vessel trading between Victoria and New Zealand. A few months later he rushed to Otago but left after six months 'in disgust'. He again went to sea, trading along the New Zealand and eastern Australian coastlines, before joining the crew of another ship trading between Sydney and Hong Kong. Armstrong did not receive a letter from home until he finally settled down in Melbourne in 1869.[109] William Chapman lost touch with his brother in England when he travelled to 'nearly all the Diggings in Australia' then rushed to Otago, before travelling to Canterbury where he worked as a carter and later operated a schooner out of Port Cooper.[110] In the midst of constant mobility, some individuals explained in detail where to direct letters. When Andrew Roy arrived in Bluff in 1863, he took up a job driving cattle to Invercargill and Dunedin. He relocated in January 1864 to Maori Point in the Lakes District, where he began carting goods to the diggings. In June he moved to Fox's Flat, along the Arrow River, and by August he was sheep shearing on Mount Torlesse in Canterbury. In September he moved back to Fox's Flat, where he bought shares in a mining company and began erecting a water race, but by January 1865 he had returned to Canterbury where he was employed as a shepherd along the Waimakariri River. By the beginning of July he travelled to Hokitika, where he remained until he drowned in August 1866. While Armstrong and Chapman did not maintain correspondence with family throughout their frequent movements, Roy wrote at least seventeen letters to family members during his three-year residence in Southland, Otago and on the West Coast, and he often provided detailed instructions of his intended future movements and where to send letters. Roy commented to his family that his 'wandering about so much' made his receiving and sending letters difficult and irregular.[111]

Maintaining relationships through correspondence was also hindered by the difficulties in composing and reading letters. Absent in the historical record are individuals who were illiterate, and there is no mention of any Otago gold rush correspondence being dictated to a friend or mate for composition. Even among those who did compose letters, the act of letter writing was a 'strenuous undertaking' for many who struggled to convey their thoughts and personal details through the written word.[112] In 1864 the Welsh prospector, William Jones, switched frequently between Welsh and English phonetic pronunciations in a letter he wrote to his sister in Bangor, Wales:

> I have left the diggins again and mea [*may*] be for good. I am taieard [*tired*] and wareid [*wearied*] of them . . . the diggins is very poore hare in genral and a great el [*deal*] of hrdsip.[113]

Upon the receipt of a letter detailing the death of his father in 1862, William Wilson responded in a brief letter to his brother:

> I writ a few lines to let you no [*know*] that i received your lettar [*letter*]. I was very sorry to hear the news of my father daying [*dying*] so suddenly but I hope you will manig [*manage*] every thing right.[114]

Wilson's later correspondence with family indicates a close relationship with his father, which implies that the abruptness of his response was probably more the result of his difficulty conveying emotion than apathy at his father's death. Lachlan McDonald, a prospector from the Isle of Tiree, also composed letters with stunted syntax, phonetic spellings and a number of words scribbled out. The sixteen surviving letters that he sent to his brother, Donald McDonald, indicate that letter writing was a laborious task that consumed both time and mental energy. In 1866, writing to his brother from a hospital bed after he was kicked by a horse, Lachlan expressed mid-sentence his frustration that he lacked the tools to effectively articulate himself: 'Now Brother i Wish my Schoolen[*schooling*] wood alow me to tall[*tell*] you of all i come trou [*through*] her [*here*] and What i have seen.'[115] McDonald was likely less literate than most of his fellow Scots on the Otago diggings, many of whom were from the Lowland counties.[116] However, even Andrew Roy, the eldest son of a wealthy Lowland farming and brewing family, wrote in 1865 to his parents in Glendevon that he spent several days composing one letter.[117]

Despite the irregularity of correspondence and frustrations with letter composition, many gold seekers took time to compose letters for home by campfire or candlelight after a long arduous day of shovelling dirt and panning gravel. Between 1861 and 1865 some 100,000 letters were sent annually from Otago to Britain and Ireland, approximately three letters per adult resident in the province. This number was nearly five times the quantity of letters shipped to the United Kingdom in 1860, the final full year before the gold rushes, indicating that most of these letters probably were sent from the goldfields.[118] This large number of letters sent to Britain and Ireland is further remarkable given the cost of postage. In 1865 mailing a letter between Otago and the United Kingdom cost one shilling, which was the equivalent of a day's wages in the colony.[119] Even when the diggings dried up or weather changes brought destitution, there were many prospectors in the province whose connections to loved ones were important enough to lay down what little wealth they had obtained from gold seeking or waged work to post a letter.[120] The shilling required to post a letter to Otago was even more prohibitive for some correspondents in Britain and Ireland. For example, the average daily wage for a labourer in London that year was seven and a half pence.[121] When the maintenance of relationships depended on the expense of postage, letters were 'carefully constructed, earnest in tone and packed with messages, advice and information'.[122]

Goldfield correspondents devoted even more ink to complaints about the absence of letters from home than about the barrenness of the goldfields or the harshness of the climate. This constant plea for more frequent correspondence shows that the most important purpose of letters was that they constituted a link back to a community of friends and family members at home. When diggers described in their letters a network of friends and relations from the homeland, this was not simply a desperate grasp for any social interaction but indicative of the strength of these connections. As Angela McCarthy remarks, 'the anxiousness with which news was awaited and the joy at receiving it highlights the importance of correspondence for separated kinfolk'.[123] Without any other means of obtaining news from loved ones, the letter was 'often pictured as a lifeline, and its absence as a harbinger of death'.[124] Daniel Calwell told his brother in a letter from the Kawarau River in 1863 that

'I was glad to here [*hear*] that you wh*e*re all in good helth, on [*one*] of the grate blesings in life.'[125] In 1862 William Nixon Chapman began a letter to his brother by 'hoping [this letter] will find you in good state of health. It is a long time since we have seen each other and I dare say that we shall never see each other again.'[126] David Jones told his family in Wales that 'I am often possessed with fear when having a letter in case it convey bad news, but when I see that all is well, my heart is as if it is created again by reading your letters, [and] my breast warms up with regard towards you.'[127]

Letter writers were also reminded by home correspondents of the emotional relief their letters provided, and how the failure to write could be construed among loved ones. As John McIlrath, writing from Balloo, Ireland, told his sons James and Hamilton:

> You may conc*e*ive with what emotion your letter was read. You have travelled over various regions and Seas, many perilous adventures and difficulties you must have had since you left home. Little thought we at Christmas that Hamilton was on sea again, and you at the New Zealand digging.[128]

John Walker's letter to his mother, which he wrote in 1863 inside a tent on a rainy night on the Dunstan, probably elicited a strong emotional response from his mother in England:

> You will see that the ink has run just here. It is on account of the rain. It is pouring and I am afraid it will last as it comes from the south west. A little comes through the tent. I am sitting cosily covered up with the waterproof sheet.[129]

Holding the letter in her hands, with ink smeared from rain that was pouring down on her son as he sat huddled in a tent, probably served to even further solidify the maternal love this woman felt for her sons.[130]

As goldfield letters offered parents and siblings a glimpse into the wanderings of their sons and brothers in the antipodes, letters from home offered prospectors a view back into the community they left. Every goldfield correspondent bombarded relatives with pleas for more news from home. Lachlan McDonald asked his brother about marriages and deaths among kin and neighbours.[131] Archibald Henderson showered his niece with questions about family members.[132] From Maori Point, Andrew Roy enquired about a recent party his parents had thrown at their farm in Perthshire.[133] As individuals were forming community around the rhythms of work and leisure in the hidden gullies of central Otago, many also pored over letters that transplanted them back into the local communities of friends and relatives that they left behind.

As diggers travelled between Victoria and Otago, home correspondents reiterated expectations that they would eventually travel home. John McIlrath told his two sons in Otago that he looked forward to a time when the 'rolling Seas shall no more divide us and when You shall again breath the air of your Native Home'.[134] Gold seekers often responded to these spoken and unspoken expectations of return. When John Lees received a letter from his wife which was written 'in such a desponding state of mind' because of his absence, he told her that he intended to soon return.[135] In response to a letter pleading for his return, David Jones reassured his parents that 'I am also grievous to see you too, and I hope the time is near that i shall see your smiling faces again.'[136] John Brown used these pleas for reunification to encourage the emigration of family members: 'I hope I will se you in new Zealand. I often think my self loansom away from you all.'[137] William Ruskin assured his mother and father that if they permitted William's brother to join him in Otago, '[they] would never want for him'.[138]

While most migrants had some vague intention to return home, few prospectors ever made the journey.[139] There were some diggers like Lees who saw in gold seeking an opportunity to return home wealthy – the diggings provided immense and immediate riches unrivalled in any other colonial endeavour. Since the Victorian rushes, the most common name diggers ascribed to a lucrative claim was a 'homeward bounder'. Moreover, newspaper editors, always mindful of retaining their gold rush populations, only seemed to confirm this image of the rushes with frequent reports of diggers who returned home with wealth from the profits of a lucrative claim. In 1862 the *Otago Daily Times* published an account of a party of diggers who returned to Britain on the profits of a rich claim.[140] In 1863 the paper published reports of a group of Welsh prospectors who were returning home after obtaining nine hundred ounces of gold. The following year the *Times* reported that another party of six Scottish prospectors were returning home after digging £18,000 of gold in six months.[141] Many prospectors took to the diggings in order to obtain riches, yet such wealth often proved elusive and dreams of returning prosperous quickly evaporated on the diggings. John Lees lamented to his wife in Lancashire that 'I often find myself building castles in the air respecting [his son's] future [before] these airel structures ... come trembling down so mercilessly ... extinguishing the last lingering of hope.'[142] Archibald Henderson told his niece that he saw 'bright rays [of gold] around me but alas only a constant dark gloomy cloud again [?*covered*] me'.[143]

Amid the instability and uncertainty of the rushes, some prospectors still provided for elderly parents and struggling siblings in Britain or Ireland. By the time of the gold rushes, remittances had evolved into an important part of the domestic economy for families across the United Kingdom, and prospectors often regarded providing such assistance as a source of pride.[144] As David Fitzpatrick remarks, migrants who sent home money to aged relatives or distressed kinsmen 'were not inspired by fear of sanctions but by adherence to a code of obligations and entitlements'.[145] In 1862 William Nixon Chapman sent his parents £12 he earned from prospecting.[146] David Jones sent £10 in a letter to his parents.[147] Diggers also sent home gold inside letters for family members. William Dewar and John George Walker each sent home a 'pinch of gold dust' to siblings in Britain.[148] More often gold seekers offered apologies for not sending money and promises to send it soon. Andrew Roy apologised in seven letters, spanning a year, before he sent £10 to his parents.[149] John Brown promised that 'if I am forchanot [fortunate] on the digings this time [and am not able to] se you next sumher ... I will send you some monney'.[150]

Pleading poverty in an occupation that was understood by many as simply picking wealth off the ground was an excuse met with scepticism among correspondents in Britain or Ireland. This is especially relevant given that home correspondents likely read, or were at least aware of, other narratives of the gold rushes circulating in the British press. As David Goodman demonstrates, 'the Australian (and Californian) gold rushes were major literary events in Britain'.[151] Since the first years of the California gold rushes, a plethora of published guidebooks and travel narratives circulated in Britain and Ireland about gold seeking in North America and Australasia. Virtually all of these accounts sensationalised gold seeking and exaggerated the riches of the diggings. Moreover, newspapers across the United Kingdom frequently published letters from diggers who found immense wealth on the goldfields.[152]

This scepticism, combined with distance and irregular communication, sometimes frayed relationships between gold seekers and their home correspondents. These factors and the differing expectations of filial duty slowly disintegrated the relationship between the Scottish prospector Lachlan McDonald and his brother, Donald, who had migrated from the Isle of Tiree to Lancashire, England.[153] Sometime before 1858 Lachlan McDonald migrated to Victoria. By 1862 he had travelled to Otago and was one of the first gold seekers at Waipori, and he remained in Otago until at least 1868. Between 1858 and 1862 he sent at least seventeen letters to his brother in Lancashire. Many of Lachlan's letters were filled with requests for more letters containing more news about relatives and friends. In an 1858 letter from Geelong, he wrote that

> It should always give me the greatest pleasure to hear of your good health and also to hear often from you. I expected a letter from you in the last mail but did not get one. I hope i shall not be disappointed in the next.[154]

Again in 1866, he wrote from Tokomairiro, 'Now Brother, I am to spek [*speak*] sharp to you for not writing me or my last laters [*letters*].'[155] If Lachlan complained that Donald did not fulfil his duty to write, he also defended himself against criticisms for not returning or sending money home.

This tension began to escalate in 1863 when Lachlan received a letter from his brother describing his family's destitution caused by the collapse of the cotton industry in Lancashire. Despite his brother's requests, Lachlan refused to send money, stating that he previously made £110 in prospecting but lost it all in a mining speculation, and so was now unable to send any money.[156] Moreover, Lachlan repeatedly refused his brother's requests for him to return home and instead encouraged his brother to migrate to Otago or America.[157] Donald chose to remain in Lancashire and face starvation rather than travel overseas, which he probably saw as severing his connection to Tiree. The following year, when Lachlan received a letter detailing the further destitution of Donald's family, Lachlan only offered a brief note of condolence: 'I am varey sorey about the sicness cosnannang [*concerning*] your famely and the rest of the [*word illegible*] childrin.'[158] The situation reached its climax three months later when Lachlan received a terse letter from his brother, stating that their youngest sister, Catriona, had recently died from starvation. Lachlan chastised his brother for the cold, unfeeling note about the death of his beloved sister, 'as if she was a dog'. Lachlan then stated that while Donald had often reprimanded him for being careless with his relatives, Donald committed the greater sin by not even mentioning that Catriona was sick. Moreover, Lachlan castigated his brother for not returning her body to Tiree for burial among her ancestors, but to be left on 'alien soil'.[159]

The McDonald correspondence shows the difficulty with binding the social history of the Otago gold rushes within New Zealand. In his laboriously composed letters, Lachlan was consumed with news about relatives in Britain and Ireland as he dug for gold in colonial Otago. Moreover, the news of his sister's death troubled him in a way nothing in Otago could have, and he begged his brother to tell him 'if she talked about me when you last saw her'. While acknowledging the need to locate identities across borders, the McDonald correspondence also highlights the fact that relationships were often destabilised by both the separation caused by emigration and the nature of local gold deposits in central Otago, which influenced remittances and, therefore, relationships with loved ones at home. Lachlan may have emigrated to pursue wealth and independence, yet he continually found his efforts frustrated by speculation that proved ruinous and gold seeking that appeared to be fruitless. As he told his brother, the barrenness of his claim inhibited him from providing relief to his kin. Moreover, despite failure in Australasia, he refused to return home when his pre-migration experiences and his brother's letters revealed only destitution and dependency.[160] Yet, his brother was unwilling to make such a clean break from their homeland and migrate to Otago. Furthermore, Donald saw a rejection of kith and kin in Lachlan's unwillingness to return or provide assistance while in the golden lands of Australasia. This tension was magnified by the irregularity of correspondence, when each brother only had a snapshot of each other's life every four to six months. Alongside transnational networks, attention also needs to be paid to the points of stress or friction caused by separation, with all its potential for misunderstanding and disbelief, which made such connections to home extremely weak and tenuous.

McDonald's correspondence also reveals the ambiguous nature of personal identities on the goldfields. Letters between relatives were not simply to facilitate chain migration or organise family resources. The preoccupation among goldfield correspondents with news from home and the stress placed by relatives on return migration reveal that letters were chiefly important for maintaining personal connections to separated relatives. As David Gerber argues, personal identity 'is dependent on continuity' and inseparable from 'personal relationships with our most significant others'.[161] Correspondence, then, captures the point in time when identities were ambiguous, when individuals separated themselves from friends and relatives as they pursued wealth, yet still connected themselves back to the communities they left.[162] For many who rushed to Otago, gold seeking was a part of this process – a means to accumulate enough wealth to one day settle down into business or agriculture. Gold rush correspondents provided their readers with a picture of the diggings filled with acquaintances and community, a place very similar to home, yet to prospectors the goldfields were never home.

Goldfield correspondents rarely used the word 'home' to describe their colonial environments or dwellings. John George and William Walker provided copious details about their tent and a 'jolly comfortable little place now with sod walls and calico roof' but the brothers used the word 'home' only in reference to England. As William told his mother in 1860, 'You seem to think that I shall find a home in N. Zealand, but I do not while i have you and others in England who I so long to see.'[163] Andrew Roy used the word thirty-seven times in his surviving thirteen letters to family members in Glendevon and London. For Roy, 'home' was most often used as a point of contrast with local societies and landscapes in Otago or to describe the family farm and a small group of neighbours and relatives. When he referred to home in Otago, he usually described a place of residence connected to acquaintances from Britain: 'Uncle and Aunt and Cousins [in Invercargill] were very kind, and altogether I was quite at home.'[164] For other diggers home was an emotional connection to loved ones in Britain or Ireland. Because of the absence of his parents and siblings in Otago, David Jones told his parents that 'I haven't a home this side of the globe.'[165] In a letter written to his sister after he left the diggings, William Jones pondered how gold seeking had so long delayed his return to family in Bangor, Wales:

> The digers is liven in hops [*hope*]. Year a[f]ter year passis a way with out [?*succeeding*]. I am getin perfectly satisfaid of diggin; however, when I bring to maind [*mind*] the time I spent on [the goldfields] I cant bleave [*believe*] my self [*word illegible*] that maney years is gon over me in this pleas [*place*] and when I think of you at home tist seims somewhat a hapy drame [*dream*] of satisfaction to the hart thats cravg [*craving*] still for your precans [*presence*].[166]

To John Lees, home was simply a life lived alongside his wife and child: 'I am heartily sick and tired of my captivity,' Lees wrote to his wife, 'weary of this pilgrimage and long to be with you and at home again. I am often with you in my dreams, but I invariably awake before I have had speech with you ... and find myself in a colico [*calico*] tent camped on the very outer edge of civilisation sixteen thousand miles away from [you].'[167] In response to a letter from his son, Fred, which 'took [him] a little time to make all the crooked letters out', he promised Fred to build a stable for his pony and 'bring you a great many things when I come home if you are as good as mama wishes you to be'.[168]

Few diggers had the intention of remaining in Otago as the rushes began to wane, and fewer still intended to prospect for gold until life's end. For most who had first left British or Irish shores in response to the impacts of the Industrial Revolution, gold seeking was a means towards economic independence and many intended to eventually return home to Britain or Ireland. However, the difficulty of finding gold on fields that always seemed more barren and more expensive to live on than first

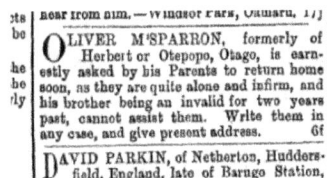

Figure 1.1 *Otago Witness*, 14 February 1880.

expected constantly delayed their return home. Some, like John Lees, eventually returned home. The newspapers and personal accounts of gold seekers indicate that most individuals did not. As the diggings dried up, the army of prospectors was transformed into a crowd of merchants and farmers, which dispersed and settled down into communities across Australasia. In this context, these individuals' social affiliations began to shift from a small group of friends and relatives in Britain or Ireland to a new group of friends and neighbours with whom they shared the rhythms of life, effectively transitioning from translocal communities with kin in the United Kingdom to local communities and neighbourhoods in New Zealand or Australia.

This gradual fraying of relationships between gold seekers and their correspondents at home was characteristic of many of the series of letters discussed here. In 1880 tension flared between Oliver McSparron and his father, Archibald, when Archibald published a missing person's notice for Oliver in the *Otago Witness* after several failed demands for his son to return home (see Figure 1.1). The notice offended Oliver, 'to be advertised for like some lost spalpeen', and the relationship further deteriorated two years later when Oliver demanded repayment of a loan from his father from over twenty years previously.[169]

The correspondence of Otago gold seekers discussed here points to this gradual shifting of social identity. Not everyone had control over this process. Sometimes the correspondence ended at the other end when home correspondents stopped writing to relatives or friends they had not seen in decades. Shortly after he arrived in Otago, Archibald Henderson lost touch with his relatives in Scotland who did not respond to several letters he wrote other than a brief note, received fourteen months after it was postmarked, that stated his mother died.[170] While most individuals did experience an 'ache of separation', these communications do not reveal the traumatic cleavage from the 'Old World' that has been described by some historians, but rather a gradual shifting of affiliation from families and local communities in Britain or Ireland to local communities and neighbourhoods in New Zealand or Australia.[171]

For the majority of prospectors, gold seeking was part of the quest for economic independence. The scarcity of gold which delayed their return home eventually served to transform their meaning of 'home' from the place and community they left into the communities they began forming after they left the diggings. The requests from parents and siblings to return to Britain or Ireland increasingly exerted less pull on individuals who were slowly become detached from these networks. Moreover, these pleas were also becoming less frequent.

The case of Archibald Henderson discussed above illustrates a further point about identities. For some gold seekers whose correspondence with home grew increasingly scarce as they made lives for themselves in the colonies, these connections to home never completely vanished. However, when communication was re-established, individuals found their families drastically different. After ten years of silence, William Nixon Chapman began a letter to his brother by stating that 'I understand that Father is dead some years, but I cannot give you any information to his death.'[172] William Ruskin reflected in a letter to his brother after a long silence:

> Ever since Mother died i never had the same love for home, although father was always kind and good father to us all. Hopping he is still in the land of the living that i might do something for him now that i should have done before. And our dear Allison also departed this life before she cam [*came*] to the age of womanhood hopping all the rest are still alive.[173]

William Smith also slowly lost connection to friends and family in Ayrshire as he settled into life in New Zealand. In 1884 he decided to visit Scotland. He later recalled in his reminiscences that

> I was glad to find my Mother and Father and the rest of the family in good health, but everything seemed strange. The young people I had left twenty-five years ago had all grown up, and i felt as though i were being introduced to strangers ... I could not reconcile myself to the idea of living in the Old Country again, and they on the other hand had no desire to leave it. I gave my Father a hand in harvesting again and, as the summer was drawing to a close, I said 'Good-Bye' to them all once more and started off for London on my return journey to New Zealand.[174]

Smith had returned to Britain only to find that it was no longer home. Slowly, through joining the Otago, West Coast and Thames rushes, his family in Ayrshire had grown more distant and his life more rooted in his colonial experiences and colonial networks.

It is perhaps unsurprising that long absences from kith and kin sometimes frayed gold seekers' connections to home. Miles Fairburn and

Patrick O'Farrell argue that overseas migration and settlement cleaved individuals from their social identities rooted in a network of friends and relatives left behind in the Old World. Both scholars argue that colonial letters indicate a desire among 'settlers to live vicariously in a community [when such] relationships ... were forbidden to them by the new dissocialised environment in Australia or New Zealand'.[175] However, this study confirms the findings of David Fitzpatrick and Angela McCarthy that most correspondence portrays a voluntary migrant who had adapted to new surroundings, rather than an atomised individual struggling to establish a personal identity in a bondless society.[176] Moreover, as discussed above, Otago gold seekers' letters reveal that migration did not constitute a dramatic break from these home networks when many letters were filled with references to friends and relatives with whom writers reconnected on and off the goldfields. What makes this especially revealing is that many of these prospectors had first emigrated several years before they began prospecting in Otago. This indicates, at least for the correspondents discussed in this chapter, that migration was not a traumatic event that immediately stripped individuals of their social identities. Rather, these transnational relationships remained intact despite the ongoing physical separation from loved ones, difficulties with composing letters and frequent frustrations with posting and collecting letters from goldfield post offices that sometimes could not even be depended on to exist if a new rush drew diggers elsewhere.

The seventeen collections of letters discussed here cannot be assumed as a representative sample of all gold seekers in Otago. The content of the vast majority of gold seeker letters which have been destroyed or lost is beyond historical inquiry. However, louder than the particular content of these letters is the volume of letters that were sent from Otago to Britain and Ireland during the gold rushes. Gold seekers and colonists in Otago sent an average of three letters annually to the United Kingdom, which indicates that a substantial number of prospectors chose to retain connections with relatives and neighbours in Britain or Ireland. What is left unrecorded are the contents of letters that were never written. Letters always only capture a snapshot in time – a certain collection of emotions and thoughts rooted in a particular moment that compelled an individual to write home. These moments of composition can be combined into a narrative of the ongoing maintenance (or transformation) of identity. What they rarely describe are the endings of these narratives when letters fall silent. Absent are periods when relatives and neighbours from Britain or Ireland were of diminished importance or relevance to individuals in Australasia who had already begun to establish homes and carve out new lives with a new set of local residents. As David Fitzpatrick observes, 'emigrants . . . fell silent as their cultural transition was completed. Letters enable us to overhear their words, and the words they read, in that phase of migration when home's hemisphere remained ambiguous.'[177]

CONCLUSION

This chapter has attempted to dislodge the history of the Otago gold rushes from a New Zealand-centred perspective that often naturalises gold seeking as a restless and rowdy rush after riches. It has done this in two ways. Firstly, the chapter argued that in order to understand itinerancy during the rushes, we need to understand practices of mobility in Britain and Ireland. Most individuals first left home years before they ever rushed to Victoria or Otago. These migrations arose in response to local economic transformations in the United Kingdom and were frequently structured by family decisions and kinship networks. These networks were often mapped onto Otago, as individuals dug for gold alongside relatives and neighbours from home.

Secondly, the chapter has revealed that an appreciation of the connections with loved ones in the United Kingdom is crucial to forming an understanding of what prospecting in Otago meant to those who engaged in it. As prospectors waded through rivers and dragged equipment over mountains, many pored over letters about a small group of loved ones at 'home'. This, however, was not a testament to the weakness of colonial relationships so much as the enduring importance of loved ones, despite extended absences. In correspondence, prospectors constantly associated 'home' with the communities they left. However, these connections were constantly under stress when remittances and return migration partially depended on how much gold was dug from the ground. When few ever returned home, most diggers gradually lost touch with friends and family at home. Translocal connections to 'home' became replaced by the community of friends and neighbours with whom individuals interacted after they left the goldfields.

The following chapter continues this networked approach to show the two-way traffic of gold seekers and those that followed them between Victoria and Otago during the Otago rushes. The chapter tracks the ways in which Victorian connections were mapped onto colonial Otago and extended back across the Tasman Sea, joining the Victorian and Otago goldfields into a single, trans-Tasman community. By moving beyond the nation, both Chapter One and Chapter Two highlight the need to understand these transnational connections beneath the nation, highlighting the local economic and social contexts in the United Kingdom or Victoria that stimulated and structured migration to Otago and the personal connections that extended identities and cultures across borders.

NOTES

1. John Lees (Melbourne) to his wife (Oldham, Lancashire, England), 21 January 1862, SLV, MS-10083.
2. John Lees (Melbourne) to his wife (Oldham), 21 January 1862.
3. For examples, see John Lees (Johnson's Gully, Navarre, Victoria) to his wife (Oldham), 16 September 1860; John Lees (Paddy's Point) to his wife (Oldham), 10 May 1862; John Lees (Donkey Hill, Victoria) to his wife (Oldham), September 1862.
4. John Lees (Paddy's Point) to his wife (Oldham), 10 May 1862.
5. John Lees (Melbourne) to his wife (Oldham), 25 April 1863.
6. Quotation taken from Stevan Eldred-Grigg, *Diggers, Hatters and Whores: The Story of the New Zealand Gold Rushes* (Auckland: Random House, 2008), 217. Some scholars who naturalise gold seeking as a restless search for riches are John Milton Hutchins, *Diggers, Constables and Bushrangers: The New Zealand Gold Rushes as a Frontier Experience, 1852–1878* (Lakewood: Avrooman-Apfelwald Press, 2010); Philip Ross May, *The West Coast Gold Rushes*, 2nd edn (Christchurch: Pegasus Press, 1967); Geoffrey Blainey, *The Rush That Never Ended: A History of Australian Mining*, 4th edn (Melbourne: Melbourne University Press, 1993); Geoffrey Serle, *The Golden Age: A History of the Colony of Victoria, 1851–1861* (Melbourne: Melbourne University Press, 1963); H. W. Brands, *The Age of Gold: The California Gold Rush and the New American Dream* (New York: Doubleday, 2002); Malcolm J. Rohrbough, *Days of Gold: The California Gold Rush and the American Nation* (Berkeley: University of California Press, 1998); Paula Mitchell Marks, *Precious Dust: The American Gold Rush Era, 1848–1900* (New York: William Morrow and Co., 1994).
7. Nancy L. Green, 'The Comparative Method and Poststructural Structuralism: New Perspectives for Migration Studies', *Journal of American Ethnic History* 13, no. 4 (1994): 6–7, 16–17. Also see Donna R. Gabaccia, 'Is Everywhere Nowhere? Nomads, Nations and the Immigrant Paradigm of United States History', *The Journal of American History* 86, no. 3 (1999): especially 1123–8; Charles Tilly, 'Transplanted Networks', in Virginia Yans-McLaughlin (ed.), *Immigration Reconsidered: History, Sociology, and Politics* (Oxford: Oxford University Press, 1990), 79–95.

8. Quotation taken from Miles Fairburn, *The Ideal Society and Its Enemies: The Foundation of Modern New Zealand Society, 1850–1900* (Auckland: Auckland University Press, 1989), 201. Also see Patrick O'Farrell, *Letters from Irish Australia: 1825–1925* (Sydney: New South Wales University Press, 1984), 4; Frances Porter and Charlotte Macdonald (eds), *My Hand Will Write What My Heart Dictates: The Unsettled Lives of Women in Nineteenth-Century New Zealand as Revealed to Sisters, Family and Friends* (Auckland: Auckland University Press, 1996).
9. Dirk Hoerder, 'Introduction. From Dreams to Possibilities: The Secularization of Hope and the Quest for Independence', in Dirk Hoerder and Horst Rössler (eds), *Distant Magnets: Expectations and Realities in the Immigrant Experience, 1840–1930* (New York and London: Holmes and Meier, 1993), 2.
10. Merle, *The Golden Age*, 371.
11. McCarthy, *Irish Migrants*, 79–80; Lyndon Fraser, *Castles of Gold: A History of New Zealand's West Coast Irish* (Dunedin: Otago University Press, 2007), 16–17; Eric Richards, *Britannia's Children: Emigration from England, Scotland, Wales and Ireland Since 1600* (Hambledon and London: Continuum International Publishing Group, 2004), 13.
12. David Fitzpatrick, *Irish Emigration, 1801–1921* (Dundalk: Economic and Social History Society of Ireland, 1984), 24.
13. 'Translocal' and 'translocality', as used in this thesis, 'means being identified with more than one location': Tim Oakes and Louisa Schein, *Translocal China: Linkages, Identities and the Reimagining of Space* (London and New York: Routledge, 2005), xiii. Also see Elliott R. Barkan, 'America in the Hand, Homeland in the Heart: Transnational and Translocal Immigrant Experiences in the American West', *The Western Historical Quarterly* 35, no. 3 (1 October 2004): 331–54, doi:10.2307/25443011; Antoinette Burton, 'Not Even Remotely Global? Method and Scale in World History', *History Workshop Journal* 64, no. 1 (2007): 323–8.
14. Biographical notes, John Lees Letters; James Randall Gascoigne, 'The Adventures of a Norfolk Boy for a Half Century from 1847 Onwards. His Early Life as a Sailor, Life on a Copper Mine in 1850, His Goldfields Experience in New South Wales in 1851, in California from 1852 to 1858, in British Columbia from 1858 to 1860, in Victoria in 1861, on the Otago Goldfields from 1861 to 1881', autobiography, OSM, DC-0483; MacLeod Orbell, autobiography, OSM, C-84.
15. Frank Thistlethwaite, 'Migration from Europe Overseas in the 19th and 20th Centuries', in Rudolph J. Vecoli and Suzanne M. Sinke (eds), *A Century of European Migration, 1830–1930* (Urbana: University of Illinois Press, 1991), 38.
16. Tilly, 'Transplanted Networks', 87.
17. Green, 'The Comparative Method', 17.

18. T. E. Crowhurst, *Life and Adventures in New Zealand, Including 'The Invisible Hand', 'The Power Within' and 'Why I Became a Spiritualist'* (Auckland: Whitcombe and Tombs, 1920), 2.
19. James Strachan, reminiscences, HC, MS-563.
20. See, for example, Eldred-Grigg, *Diggers, Hatters and Whores*; Hutchins, *Diggers, Constables and Bushrangers*.
21. Charles D. Ferguson, *The Experiences of a Forty-Niner During Thirty-Four Years' Residence in California and Australia* (Cleveland: Williams Publishing Company, 1888).
22. Arthur Scoullar, 'Arthur Scoullar of Scoullar and Chisholm', no date, OSM, DC-3028.
23. Edith Mary Story, 'Stories of the Gold Diggings', no date, ATL, fMS-Papers-7868.
24. William Smith, 'Reminiscences of a Long and Active Life by an Old Colonist', Reminiscences, 1837, OSM.
25. Jock Phillips and Terry Hearn, 'The Provincial and Gold-rush Years, 1853–70', *New Zealand History Online*, 4 February 2010, http://www.nzhistory.net.nz/files/documents/peopling3.pdf. Tables and graphs of the regional and occupational origins of Otago gold seekers are compiled in appendix 1. Also see Terry Hearn, 'Irish on the Otago Goldfields, 1861–1871', in Lyndon Fraser (ed.), *A Distant Shore: Irish Migration and New Zealand Settlement* (Dunedin: Otago University Press, 2000), 75–85; Terry Hearn, 'Scots Miners in the Goldfields, 1861–1870', in Tom Brooking and Jennie Coleman (eds), *The Heather and the Fern: Scottish Migration and New Zealand Settlement* (Dunedin: Otago University Press, 2003), 67–86. Because I have not obtained the raw data compiled by Phillips and Hearn, this section draws upon letters, autobiographies and entries in the *Cyclopedia of New Zealand* as supplemental examples. These accounts have not been used to expand upon Phillips and Hearn's data set because of the risk of counting individuals twice.
26. Shorter, Ravenhill and Gregory, *Southwest England*, 158–67.
27. *The Cyclopedia of Victoria*, vol. 2 (Melbourne: F. W. Niven and Co., 1904), 194.
28. *The Cyclopedia of New Zealand: Otago and Southland Provincial Districts* (Christchurch: Horace J. Weeks, 1903), 311.
29. Philip Payton, 'Cornish Emigration in Response to Changes in the International Copper Market in the 1860s', *Cornish Studies* 2, no. 3 (1995): 60–82; P. J. Payton, *The Cornish Miner in Australia: Cousin Jack Down Under* (Trewolsta: Trewirgie, 1984); Jock Phillips and Terry Hearn, *Settlers: New Zealand Immigrants from England, Ireland and Scotland, 1800–1945* (Auckland: Auckland University Press, 2008), 96–7. The collapse of the mining industry in southwest England would continue to shed population throughout the second half of the nineteenth century. The region experienced a net loss in population between 1851 and 1911.

Richard Lawton, 'Population', in *Atlas of the Industrializing Britain, 1780–1914* (London: Methuen and Co., 1986), map 2.8, 13.
30. Philip Payton, *The Cornish Overseas* (Fowey: Alexander Associates, 1999), 228, 231–6, 297.
31. *The Cyclopedia of New Zealand: Nelson, Marlborough and Westland Provincial Districts*, 371.
32. R. G. Lawn, 'Lawn, John 1840–1905', *DNZB*, accessed 21 March 2011, http://www.dnzb.govt.nz/. Cited in Phillips and Hearn, *Settlers*, 97.
33. E. J. T. Collins, *The Agrarian History of England and Wales 2 Volume Set* (Cambridge: Cambridge University Press, 2000), 367–72.
34. For these same reasons, the Captain Swing Riots in the 1830s and the Revolt of the Field in the 1870s spread throughout this region. See Rollo Arnold, *The Farthest Promised Land: English Villagers, New Zealand Immigrants of the Nineteenth Century* (Wellington: Victoria University of Wellington Press, 1981).
35. Phillips and Hearn, 'The Provincial and Gold-rush Years, 1853–70', 89–90.
36. Aled Jones and Bill Jones, 'The Welsh World and the British Empire, c. 1851–1939: An Exploration', *Journal of Imperial and Commonwealth History* 31, no. 2 (2003): 62.
37. Dudley Baines, *Migration in a Mature Economy: Emigration and Internal Migration in England and Wales, 1861–1900* (Cambridge: Cambridge University Press, 1985), 276–8. Interestingly, the North Welsh were twice as likely to travel to England as to the coal and iron mines of South Wales, which were overwhelmingly populated by the Irish, English and Scottish rather than the Welsh. In 1851 there were 20,000 Irish and 120,000 English and Scottish living in South Wales.
38. John Davies, *A History of Wales* (London: Allen Lane, 1994), 383–4.
39. Alun Howkins, 'In the Sweat of Thy Face: The Labourer and Work', in G. E. Mingay (ed.), *The Vanishing Countryman* (London: Routledge, 1989), 44–7; Paul O'Leary, *Immigration and Integration: The Irish in Wales, 1798–1922* (Cardiff: University of Wales Press, 2000), 314. Howkins does not break down the Scottish and English populations separately.
40. Davies, *A History of Wales*, 385–6.
41. Ibid., 382.
42. Ibid., 411.
43. Gethin Matthews, 'Gold Fever: The Stampede from South Wales to British Columbia in 1862', *North American Journal of Welsh Studies* 5, no. 2 (2005): 54–83.
44. Jones and Jones, 'The Welsh World', 62.
45. Jones Family Letters, ATL, MS-Papers-6249, biographical notes.
46. David Jones (Otago) to his parents and siblings (Wales), 10 August 1862, ibid.

47. T. M. Devine, *The Scottish Nation, 1700–2000* (London: Viking, 1999), 134–51.
48. T. M. Devine, 'Introduction: The Paradox of Scottish Emigration', in T. M. Devine (ed.), *Scottish Emigration and Scottish Society: Proceedings of the Scottish Historical Studies* (Edinburgh: John Donald, 1992), 6.
49. Devine, *The Scottish Nation*, 255–9.
50. Rosalind McClean, 'Scottish Emigrants to New Zealand, 1840–1880: Motives, Means and Background' (PhD thesis, University of Edinburgh, 1990), 113–14. Malcolm Prentis postulates that Scottish migrants to Victoria during this period came from industrial backgrounds, but he ignores previous mobility and occupational origins. See Malcolm Prentis, *The Scots in Australia* (Sydney: University of New South Wales, 2008), 10–37.
51. CNZ: Otago, 956–7.
52. *The Cyclopedia of New Zealand: Auckland Provincial District* (Christchurch: The Cyclopedia Company, 1902), 884.
53. Rosalind McClean found that 60 per cent of the Otago settlers who came out with the New Zealand Company between 1839 and 1851 emigrated from the western Lowlands, while only 12 per cent came from the eastern Lowlands. McClean, 'Scottish Emigrants to New Zealand, 1840–1880: Motives, Means and Background', 120.191–193.
54. William Martin, reminiscences, 1, HC, MS-0203.
55. Archibald Henderson (Patea, Taranaki) to his niece (?Scotland), 2 December 1869, Archibald Henderson Letters, OSM, DC-2399.
56. T. M. Devine, *Clearance and Improvement: Land, Power and People in Scotland, 1700–1900* (Edinburgh: John Donald, 2006), 9–18.
57. See David S. Macmillan, *Scotland and Australia: Emigration, Commerce and Investment* (London: Oxford University Press, 1967).
58. Eric Richards, 'Highland and Gaelic Immigrants', *The Australian People: An Encyclopedia of the Nation, Its People and Their Origins* (Cambridge: Cambridge University Press, 2001); Eric Richards, 'St Kilda and Australia: Emigrants at Peril, 1852–3', *Scottish Historical Review* 71 (1992): 129–55; Robin Haines, *Emigration and the Labouring Poor: Australian Recruitment in Britain and Ireland: 1831–1860* (New York: St Martin's Press, 1997), Chapter 6; David S. Macmillan, 'Sir Charles Trevelyan and the Highland and Island Emigration Society', *Journal of the Royal Australian Historical Society* 44 (1963): 161–88.
59. Donna Hellier, '"The Humblies": Scottish Highland Migration into Nineteenth Century Victoria', in Patricia Grimshaw, Chris McConville and Ellen McEwen (eds), *Families in Colonial Australia* (Sydney: Unwin Hyman, 1985), 9–18.
60. Lachlan McDonald (Geelong) to his brother, Donald McDonald (?Tiree), 9 May 1858; Lachlan McDonald (Waipori) to Donald McDonald (?Tiree), Lachlan McDonald Letters, OSM, DC-2810.

61. Although the region only contained 4 per cent of Scotland's population, they accounted for 14 per cent of Scottish diggers and 6 per cent of the entire goldfield population born in the United Kingdom.
62. Phillips and Hearn, *Settlers*, 111.
63. Phillips and Hearn also note that a series of letters appearing in the *Shetland Advertiser* in 1862 also encouraged emigration to Otago. The authors, however, do not cite this collection and the letters are not contained in the full 1862 run of the newspaper located in the National Library of Scotland. Phillips and Hearn, 'The Provincial and Gold-rush Years, 1853–70', 93.
64. Patrick Fitzgerald and Brian Lambkin, *Migration in Irish History, 1607–2007* (Houndmills: Palgrave Macmillan, 2008), 42–3, 168, 197.
65. Fitzpatrick, *Irish Emigration*, 24.
66. Richard E. Reid, *Farewell My Children: Irish Assisted Emigration to Australia, 1848–1870* (Spit Junction: Anchor Books, 2011), 2.
67. Fitzpatrick, *Irish Emigration 1801–1921*, 24; Patrick James O'Farrell, *The Irish in Australia: 1788 to the Present* (Sydney: University of New South Wales Press, 2000), 69.
68. Hamilton McCance (Forest Creek, Victoria) to William Orr (Grey Abbey, County Down, Ireland), 23 June 1861, in David Fitzpatrick, *Oceans of Consolation: Personal Accounts of the Irish Migration to Australia* (Ithaca and London: Cornell University Press, 1995), 221.
69. Donald Harman Akenson, *The Irish Diaspora: A Primer* (Toronto: P. D. Meany, 1993), 97; McCarthy, *Irish Migrants*, 79–80.
70. R. F. Foster, *Modern Ireland, 1600–1972* (London: Penguin Books, 1989), 333–4.
71. Fitzpatrick, *Irish Emigration 1801–1921*, 26.
72. Eldred-Grigg, *Diggers, Hatters and Whores*, 217–22; William Parker Morrell, *The Gold Rushes* (London: Macmillian Company, 1941), 411–12; Douglas Fetherling, *The Gold Crusades: A Social History of Gold Rushes, 1849–1929* (Toronto: University of Toronto Press, 1997), 3–10.
73. Fitzpatrick, *Oceans of Consolation*, 534.
74. Chris McConville, 'The Victorian Irish: Emigrants and Families, 1851–91', in Patricia Grimshaw, Chris McConville, and Ellen McEwen (eds), *Families in Colonial Australia* (Sydney: Allen and Unwin, 1985), 1–8.
75. Kerry Cardell et al., 'Welsh Identity on the Victorian Goldfields in the Nineteenth Century', in Kerry Cardell and Cliff Cumming (ed.), *A World Turned Upside Down: Cultural Change on Australia's Goldfields, 1851–2001* (Canberra: Australian National University Press, 2001), 37. Also see other articles in *A World Turned Upside Down*, which discuss the breakdown of kinship bonds among other ethnic groups.
76. O'Farrell, *The Irish in Australia*, 3–8.
77. Fairburn, *The Ideal Society*, 163–7.

78. Ibid., 165.
79. McCarthy, *Irish Migrants*, 168–9.
80. Ibid., 168. Similar conclusions about the strength of kinship and neighbourhood bonds are made in Fraser, *Castles of Gold*, 41–5.
81. William Walker (Canterbury) to his mother, Anne Walker (London), ?June 1860, William and John George Walker Letters. Mary Anne was William's sister and John was his brother.
82. For other examples of gold seekers who relied upon home networks for migration, see Archibald Henderson Letters; Peter Warren diary; William Dewar (Waihola) to his mother (unknown), 11 December 1864, John and William Dewar Letters; John Lees Letters; Archibald McKinlay (Bendigo) to his parents (Rothesay, Argyll, Scotland), 20 March 1854, Herbert and Company Store papers, private collection.
83. Lyndon Fraser, *To Tara via Holyhead: Irish Catholic Immigrants in Nineteenth-Century Christchurch* (Auckland: Auckland, 1997), 52.
84. Cf. Fraser, *Castles of Gold*, 44–5.
85. William and John George Walker papers.
86. Anne Lindsay (Blackburn) to her sister (Britain), 12 January 1863, Anne Lindsay Letters.
87. Thomas Andrew (Molyneux) to his brother and sister (?Crossgate, Fifeshire), 1 February 1863, Thomas Andrew Letters.
88. Hamilton McIlrath (Rangiora, Canterbury) to his parents and siblings (Balloo, Ireland), 12 August 1862. Many thanks to Angela McCarthy for providing a transcript of these letters, which appear in Angela McCarthy, '"Seas May Divide": Irish Migration to New Zealand as Portrayed in Personal Correspondences, 1840–1937', vol. 2 (PhD thesis, Trinity College, Dublin, 2000), 201–60.
89. Alexander McKay to his brother, Robert McKay (Carsphairn, Dumfries), 10 April 1864, Alexander McKay Letters.
90. Cf. Fitzpatrick, *Irish Emigration 1801–1921*, 35–6.
91. Andrew Roy (Christchurch) to his parents (Glendevon), 11 January 1865, Andrew Roy Letters.
92. John Henry Watmuff, diary, 22 November 1863 [4/30]; 2 February 1864 [4/62]; 19 April 1864 [4/90]; 12 June 1864 [94/104]; 30 July 1864 [4/113].
93. Ibid., 15 April 1866 [6/16].
94. Archibald Henderson (Manutahi, Taranaki) to his brother and sister, 11 February 1875, Archibald Henderson Letters, OSM, DC-2399.
95. Fitzpatrick, *Oceans of Consolation*, 624.
96. William Jones Letter, ATL, MS-Papers-10303; Thomas Armstrong Letter, SLV, MS 12164; James McVicar Letters, HC, no call number; Francis and Susan Mapleson Letters, SLV, MS 10869; Lachlan McDonald Letters, OSM, DC2810; The McIlrath Correspondence, transcribed by Angela McCarthy, in McCarthy, 'Seas May Divide', 201–11; The McSparron

Correspondence, transcribed by idem., in ibid., 50–7; John Lees Letters, SLV, MS 10083; William Crawford Letters, HC, Misc-MS-0095; William Nixon Chapman Letter, private collection; Andrew Roy Letters, OSM-DC-0683, John and William Dewar Letters, HC, MS-2373/001; John Brown Letters, ATL, MS-Papers 8869-2; Lachlan McDonald Letters, OSM, DC-2810; William and John George Walker correspondence, OSM, C-128; Arch Henderson Letters, OSM, DC-2399; Jones Family Letters, translated by Mairwen Cook, ATL, MS-Papers-6249.

97. 'Annual Report of the Postmaster General of New Zealand', *Appendices to the Journals of the House of Representatives* (AJHR), 1861–1865, D-1.
98. Cf. Archibald Henderson (Dunedin) to his brother and sister (Scotland), 4 November 1860, Archibald Henderson Letters; David Jones (Otago) to his family (Wales), 12 May 1862; Andrew Roy (Maori Point, Shotover) to his parents (Perthshire), 10 January 1864, Andrew Roy Letters.
99. Brian Roberts, *American Alchemy: The California Gold Rush and Middle-Class Culture* (Chapel Hill: University of North Carolina Press, 2000); Kevin Starr and Richard J. Orsi (eds), *Rooted in Barbarous Soil: People, Culture, and Community in Gold Rush California* (Berkeley: University of California Press, 2000); Malcolm J. Rohrbough, *Days of Gold: The California Gold Rush and the American Nation* (Berkeley: University of California Press, 1998); Marks, *Precious Dust*; Susan Lee Johnson, *Roaring Camp: The Social World of the California Gold Rush* (New York: W. W. Norton and Company, 2000).
100. Bill Jones, 'Welsh Identities in Colonial Ballarat', *Journal of Australian Studies* 25, no. 68 (2001): 34–43; Philip Payton, 'Cousin Jacks and Ancient Britons: Cornish Immigrants and Ethnic Identity', *Journal of Australian Studies* 25, no. 68 (2001): 54–64; Hugh Dan MacLennan, 'Gu Fearann an Òir: To the Land of Gold', *Journal of Australian Studies* 25, no. 68 (2001): 44–53; and several of the articles in Kerry Cardell and Cliff Cumming (eds), *A World Turned Upside Down: Cultural Change on Australia's Goldfields 1851–2001* (Canberra: Australian National University Press, 2001).
101. See, for example, Jock Phillips, *A Man's Country?: The Image of the Pakeha Male, a History*, 2nd edn (Auckland: Penguin Books, 1996); Fairburn, *The Ideal Society*; James Belich, *Making Peoples*; Eldred-Grigg, *Diggers, Hatters and Whores*. One notable exception is Lyndon Fraser, *Castles of Gold: A History of New Zealand's West Coast Irish* (Dunedin: Otago University Press, 2007).
102. William Wilson (Hokitika) to George Wilson (Fife, Scotland), 29 November 1868, William Wilson Letters, OSM, DC-0454.
103. William Ruskin (Oamaru) to John Ruskin (Pathhead, Scotland), 25 November 1862, OSM, DC-0676.
104. Andrew Roy (Arrowtown) to James Roy (London), 5 August 1864, OSM, DC-0683.

105. Lachlan McDonald (Tokomairiro) to his brother, Donald McDonald (?Tiree, Scotland), 2 May 1867, OSM, DC-2810.
106. *Colonist*, 15 December 1862, 16 January 1864; *Otago Daily Times*, 12 December 1861.
107. *Otago Daily Times*, 23 December 1861.
108. William Crawford (Dunedin) to his parents (unknown), 15 May 1862.
109. Thomas Armstrong (Melbourne) to Eliza (unknown), 27 August 1869, Thomas Armstrong Letters, SLV, MS-12164.
110. William Nixon Chapman (Lyttleton) to his brother (unknown), December 1862, private collection.
111. Andrew Roy (Mount Torlesse, Canterbury) to James Roy (London), no date (instructions to open after 9 September 1864). See, for example, Andrew Roy (Southland) to his parents and siblings (Glendevon, Perthshire), 12 August 1863; Andrew Roy (Maori Point, Shotover) to his parents and siblings (Glendevon, Perthshire), 10 January 1864.
112. Fitzpatrick, *Oceans of Consolation*, 473.
113. William Jones (Port Chalmers) to his sister, Mrs Richards (Bangor, Wales), 17 April 1864, ATL, MS-Papers-10303.
114. William Wilson (Lyttleton) to his brother, George Wilson (Fife), 1 June 1862.
115. Lachlan McDonald (Dunedin) to his brother, Donald McDonald (?Tiree), 14 August 1866, OSM DC-2810.
116. Rosalind McClean estimates that the ratio of Scottish migration to New Zealand roughly resembled population trends in Scotland: 10 per cent of both the population of Scotland and Scottish migrants to New Zealand were from the Highlands and Islands, with the rest coming from the Lowlands. See 'Scottish emigration to New Zealand, 1840–1880: Motives, means and background', PhD thesis (University of Edinburgh, 1990).
117. Andrew Roy (Hokitika, West Canterbury), to his father, James Roy, and his mother, Catherine Roy (Frandy Farm, Glendevon, Scotland), 19 December 1865, OSM DC-0683.
118. 'Annual Report of the Postmaster General of New Zealand', *Appendices to the Journals of the House of Representatives* (AJHR), 1861–1865, D-1.
119. Gerald J. Elliott, *New Zealand Routes and Rates* (Howick: The Postal History Society of New Zealand, 1986), vol. 1, plate 1-11; James Belich, *Making Peoples: A History of the New Zealanders from Polynesian Settlement to the End of the Nineteenth Century*, (Auckland: Penguin Books, 1996), 346.
120. Lachlan McDonald (Otago) to Donald McDonald (Scotland), 22 April 1863, Lachlan McDonald Letters; William Jones (Port Chalmers) to his sister (Wales), 17 April 1864, William Jones Letters.
121. Dale H. Porter, *The Thames Embankment: Environment, Technology, and Society in Victorian London* (Akron: University of Akron Press, 1998), 176.

122. David Fitzpatrick, 'Irish Emigration and the Art of Letter-Writing', in Bruce S. Elliott, David A. Gerber and Suzanne M. Sinke, *Letters Across Borders: The Epistolary Practices of International Migrants* (New York: Palgrave Macmillan, 2006), 97.
123. McCarthy, *Irish Migrants*, 89.
124. Fitzpatrick, *Oceans of Consolation*, 479.
125. Daniel Calwell (Cromwell) to his brother, Davis Calwell (unknown), 17 March 1862, Davis Calwell Letters, SLV, MS 11492.
126. William Nixon Chapman (Lyttleton, Canterbury) to his brother (England), December 1862, private possession. Also see David Jones (Otago) to his family (Wales), 8 April 1862; Andrew Roy (Charleston, Southland) to his brother, James Roy (London), 4 June 1864; Thomas Andrew (Dunstan) to his brother and sister (Fifeshire, Scotland?), 1 February 1863, Thomas Andrew Letters, ATL, MS Papers 4802; William Crawford (Dunedin) to his parents (unknown), William Crawford Letter, HC, Misc-MS-0095.
127. David Jones (Otago) to his family (Wales) 8 April 1862, Jones Family Letters.
128. John McIlrath (Baloo) to his sons, James McIlrath and Hamilton McIlrath (New Zealand), 23 March 1862, in McCarthy, 'Seas May Divide', 206. There is no mention of which goldfield James was on, but most likely he was on the Dunstan goldfields which began in the autumn of 1862 and peaked around the time his father John was writing. Alternatively, he could have been on the Tuapeka goldfields, which were still active after the Waipori rush in September 1861.
129. George Walker, 8.
130. William Walker, 2.
131. Lachlan McDonald (Waipori) to Donald McDonald (Scotland), 2 May 1862, Lachlan McDonald Letters.
132. Archibald Henderson (Patea) to his niece (unknown), 2 December 1869.
133. Andrew Roy (Maori Point) to his parents (Glendevon, Perthshire), 8 April 1864, Andrew Roy Letters.
134. John McIlrath (Baloo) to his sons, James McIlrath and Hamilton McIlrath (Otago), 23 March 1862, in McCarthy, 'Seas May Divide', 206.
135. John Lees (Waitahuna) to his wife (Oldham), 10 May 1862.
136. David Jones (Otago) to parents and siblings (Wales), 8 April 1862, Jones Family Letters.
137. John Brown (Wanganui) to his parents (unknown), 21 September 1862, John Brown Letters.
138. William Ruskin (Waikouaiti) to his parents (?England), 8 June 1861, William Ruskin Letters.
139. Cf. McCarthy, *Irish Migrants*, 193–7.
140. *Otago Daily Times*, 3 February 1862.
141. *Otago Daily Times*, 2 February 1864.

142. John Lees (Navarre, Victoria) to his wife, Catherine Lees (Oldham), 16 September 1862, John Lees Letters.
143. Archibald Henderson (Patea) to his niece (unknown), 2 December 1869, Archibald Henderson Letters.
144. Gary B. Magee and Andrew W. Thompson, 'The Global and the Local: Explaining Migrant Remittance Flows in the English-speaking World, 1880–1914', *Journal of Economic History* 66, no. 1 (2006): 177–202; Akenson, *The Irish Diaspora*, 77.
145. Fitzpatrick, *Oceans of Consolation*, 503.
146. William Nixon Chapman (Dunedin) to his parents (England), 15 May 1862.
147. David Jones (Otago) to his relatives (Wales), 8 April 1862, Jones Family Letters.
148. William Dewar (Waihola) to his brother, 15 May 1864, John and William Dewar Letters; John George Walker (Dunstan) to 'Fred' (unknown), 4 January 1863, John George and William Walker Letters.
149. Andrew Roy (Arrow River) to his parents (Glendevon), 5 August 1864, Andrew Roy Letters.
150. John Brown (Pelorus Valley, Auckland) to his parents (unknown), 21 September 1862, John Brown Letters.
151. David Goodman, 'Making an Edgier History of Gold', in Iain McCalman, Alexander Cook, and Andrew Reeves (eds), *Gold: Forgotten Histories and Lost Objects of Australia* (Cambridge: Cambridge University Press, 2001), 27–8.
152. David Goodman, *Gold Seeking: Victoria and California in the 1850s* (Stanford: Stanford University Press, 1994), Chapter 1. David Goodman forms this conclusion about colonial Victorian society, but he relies largely upon published guidebooks and travel narratives which were published in Britain and marketed to British readers. Also see R. A. Stafford, 'Preventing the "Curse of California": Advice for English Emigrants to the Australian Goldfields', *Historical Records of Australian Science* 7, no. 3 (1987): 215–30; Serle, *The Golden Age*, 37–59. For a discussion of English travel narratives of the American West, see Robert G. Athearn, *Westward the Briton* (New York: Charles Scribner's Sons, 1953).
153. It is unclear if Lachlan was from the Scottish Isle of Tiree, where his brother then lived, or was from Ireland and corresponded with his brother, who had migrated to Tyree, Lancashire. Determining the origin of Lachlan and Donald's place of residence is difficult because Lachlan used both 'Tiree' and 'Tyree' in his letters. Moreover, the destitution described in the correspondence could have characterised either region at this time: a famine destroyed most of the crops on Tiree in 1864, while there was simultaneously widespread destitution in Lancashire because of the collapse of the region's cotton industry. My best guess is that the brothers were from Tiree, because Lachlan refers to relatives throughout

the Highlands. However, when Lachlan almost certainly relied upon the HIES to obtain passage to Victoria I have been unable to locate him in the passenger records of the Society's vessels. Most likely, Lachlan emigrated with his family to mainland Britain, possibly Lancashire, before emigrating to Victoria. Either way, Donald was living on mainland Britain during the correspondences, given Lachlan's complaint that their sister died on 'alien soil'.

154. Lachlan McDonald (Geelong) to Donald McDonald (Scotland), 9 May 1858.
155. Lachlan McDonald (Tokomaririro) to Donald McDonald (Scotland), 3 October 1866.
156. Lachlan McDonald (Tuapeka) to Donald McDonald (Scotland), 30 August 1863.
157. Lachlan McDonald (Geelong) to Donald McDonald (Scotland), 9 May 1858; 30 August 1863.
158. Lachlan McDonald (Tuapeka) to Donald McDonald (Scotland), 11 April 1864.
159. Lachlan McDonald (Tuapeka) to Donald McDonald (Scotland), 13 July 1865.
160. Cf. McCarthy, *Irish Migrants*, 144.
161. David A. Gerber, 'What is it We Seek to Find in First-Person Documents? Documenting Society and Cultural Practices in Irish Immigrant Writings', *Reviews in American History* 32 (2004): 313.
162. Fitzpatrick, *Oceans of Consolation*, 627.
163. William Walker (Dunedin) to his mother, Anne Walker (London), 1860; William Walker (Molyneux) to his mother, Anne Walker (London), 10 May 1863; 4 May 1863; John George Walker (Dunstan) to his mother, 25 December 1862; 4 January 1863. William and John George Walker papers.
164. Andrew Roy (Maori Point) to his brother, Johnny Roy (London), 10 January 1864, Andrew Roy Letters. In another instance, the meaning was ambiguous when he referred to his place of residence and family in Perthshire both as home: 'I came home that time when I got my leg broken to send some money home.' Andrew Roy (Hokitika) to his parents (Glendevon), 7 August 1866, Andrew Roy Letters.
165. David Jones (Otago) to his parents (Wales), 10 August 1862.
166. William Jones (Port Chalmers) to his sister, Mrs Richards, 17 April 1864, William Jones Letters.
167. John Lees (Johnson's Gully, Victoria) to his wife (Oldham), 16 September 1860, John Lees Letters.
168. John Lees (unknown) to his son, Fred Lees (Oldham), undated (between 18 April 1861 and 21 July 1861), John Lees Letters.
169. D. H. Akenson, 'Reading the Texts of Rural Immigrants: Letters from the Irish in Australia, New Zealand, and North America', *Canadian Papers*

     of Rural History 7 (1990): 401. A spalpeen is a term commonly used to refer to an Irish seasonal labourer.
170. Archibald Henderson (Patea) to his niece (?Scotland), 2 December 1869.
171. Cf. Porter and McDonald, *My Hand Will Write What My Heart Dictates*; Oscar Handlin, *The Uprooted: The Epic Story of the Great Migrations That Made the American People* (Boston: Little, Brown and Company, 1951); O'Farrell, *Letters from Irish Australia*.
172. William Nixon Chapman (Lyttleton) to his brother (England), December 1862, private collection.
173. William Ruskin (Cromwell) to his brother, George (Scotland), 29 January 1878, William Ruskin Letters.
174. William Smith, reminiscences, 142–3.
175. O'Farrell, *Letters from Irish Australia*, 3–8; Fairburn, *The Ideal Society*. Quotation taken from ibid., 201.
176. Fitzpatrick, *Oceans of Consolation*, 617; McCarthy, *Irish Migrants*, 199.
177. Fitzpatrick, *Oceans of Consolation*, 627.

2

'A Great Many People I Know from Victoria': The Victorian Dimension of the Otago Gold Rushes

In 1852, at the age of thirteen, John Henry Watmuff and his father, Steven Watmuff, left their home in Adelaide, Australia, to join the rush to the Bendigo goldfield. The two were moderately successful at gold digging, and they were able to finance Steven's return to England in 1859 to protect the family's inheritance. Meanwhile, John Henry continued to support their family in Adelaide through gold seeking in Victoria. When news of the Otago gold rushes reached Melbourne in 1861, his younger brother, Ned, joined the throng of diggers leaving Victoria for the new diggings. When John Henry received glowing accounts from his brother at Gabriel's Gully, he decided to follow Ned to Otago. He continued to prospect there until 1864, when he gave up gold seeking and returned to Melbourne.

Shortly before sailing for Otago, John Henry Watmuff lamented in his diary that he was leaving 'so many pleasent friendships and am endeared to by so many associations ... that I shall ever regret parting with'.[1] However, his diaries show that gold seeking in Otago never constituted a clear break from his connections in Bendigo. Stories of old friendships reawakened on the goldfields filled virtually every diary entry he wrote while in Otago. Within hours of arriving in Dunedin, Watmuff joined a party of former mates from Bendigo. When the party arrived at Weatherston's, he remarked that there were 'a great many people I know from Victoria'. Another evening a few months later, he wrote that his tent 'was crowded with neighbours. Spent [the evening] very jolly singing, card playing and reading with a little gambling'.[2] At the same time as he renewed old friendships in Otago, he maintained connections with diggers and family members in Victoria. He exchanged letters monthly with former mates still working at Bendigo, making both him and his friends aware of conditions in both places.[3] Surrounded by acquaintances in Otago, exchanging letters with friends and relatives in Bendigo, and returning to Victoria after two years, Watmuff remained oriented to Victoria throughout his brief time in Otago. For Watmuff, and other gold seekers like him, the Otago gold rushes were more a series of events in Victorian than New Zealand history. For many, the Otago rushes flowed out from gold seeking in Victoria and remained firmly connected to Victoria throughout their course.

Narratives like Watmuff's are at odds with the historical memory of the Otago gold rushes. In their respective studies of the West Coast gold rushes, Philip Ross May and Lyndon Fraser both stress the flows of people and information between Victoria and New Zealand's West Coast but the relative neglect of Otago by historians leaves the connections between Otago and Victoria largely unexplored. When the Otago rushes are discussed, scholars are overwhelmingly concerned with the events' role in forming a national economy and society, thereby overlooking these trans-Tasman connections.[4] Even William Parker Morrell's and J. H. M. Salmon's magisterial studies of the nineteenth-century gold rushes are largely chronological histories of the rushes, charting the movement from Victoria to Otago and on to the West Coast. They, therefore, neglect the two-way traffic of people, goods and knowledge across the Tasman Sea and the ways in which events on one side of the Tasman Sea influenced developments on the other during the 1860s.[5] Links between Victoria and Otago are overlooked to an even greater degree in the literature on the Australian rushes, where the Otago rushes are discussed only as prospectors leave Victoria. The moment individuals left Australian shores, the Otago rushes are depicted as no longer relevant to this national narrative.[6] Implicit in these separate historiographies is the assumption that gold seekers were Australians while in Victoria and New Zealanders while in Otago. Gold seekers, however, were neither here nor there; most migrated seasonally across the Tasman Sea and remained connected to mates and relatives on both sides. It is more accurate to speak of a single trans-Tasman gold-seeking population that migrated between Melbourne and Dunedin.

This chapter counteracts these nationalising approaches by placing the Otago gold rushes within the regional Tasman World, which existed 'across bridges, or in the spaces between the ramparts of cultural formation on either side' of the Tasman Sea.[7] Its analysis builds off the previous chapter to show the ways in which transnational social networks and geographic mobility were extended to Australasia and manifested in frequent migrations between Victoria and Otago throughout the gold rushes. Here it connects to Frank Thistlethwaite's plea to analyse the ways in which mobility continued after an individual first travelled overseas.[8] As Chapters Two and Three argue, Victoria remained both a sending and receiving colony for gold seekers. Personal networks also problematise clear divisions between Otago and Victoria when individuals remained attached to two places. Some individuals in Otago dug alongside mates from the Victorian diggings while they remained connected to loved ones on the other side of the Tasman Sea.

This analysis of mobilities and networks links up with recent geographic approaches to the British Empire that map the flow of people, knowledge and commodities between colonial sites rather than exclusively from Britain and Ireland.[9] This networked perspective also reveals multiple regional centres across the British Empire. The chapter argues that throughout the early 1860s, Melbourne remained the financial hub of the Otago goldfields on the other side of the Tasman Sea. Moreover, Otago diggers relied overwhelmingly on products shipped by Melbourne merchants, and a steady two-way traffic of people and knowledge flowed in both directions between Dunedin and Melbourne. The flow of diggers and commodities had a profound impact on both societies. As newspapers in both places competed for an itinerant population of trans-Tasman gold seekers, both colonial sites 'were constituted through their transactions with one another'.[10]

TRANS-TASMAN POPULATION FLOWS

The total number of gold rush migrants from Victoria to Otago is frustratingly difficult to determine, as Victorian and Otago newspapers did not systematically mention arrivals and departures. While the expected arrival and departure dates of some thirty or forty vessels were often published in the *Argus*, *Otago Daily Times* and *Otago Witness* in a given week, not every ship advertised its departure date and few noted passenger complements. The *Passenger Lists, Victoria, AUS Outwards to Otago, New Zealand* records those who left Victoria for Otago; however, it does not distinguish migrants who travelled to Otago more than once, and the accuracy and completeness of the records are doubtful.[11] The 1863 and 1865 reports of the goldfields commissioner, included in the *Appendices to the Journal of the House of Representatives*, provide the most complete picture of migration between Otago and Victoria; however, they make no mention of ship arrivals at Bluff in 1863 and 1864, when it was the closest port to the Wakatipu goldfields. Moreover, the reports make no mention of migrant origins. Even more problematically, there is no report covering the period between 1 August 1863 and 31 July 1864, when the goldfields population peaked in Otago.

While the absolute numbers cannot therefore be determined, a rough estimate of their proportion can be made. Most gold seekers in Otago were veterans of the gold rushes in Victoria and New South Wales during the 1850s. Of the 237 autobiographies that mention gold seeking in Otago in the six-volume *Cyclopedia of New Zealand*, 184, or 78 per cent, also describe prior experience gold seeking in Australia.[12] For example, in 1863 William Edmonds arrived at the Hamiltons goldfield at the foot of the Rock and Pillar range with nine years of experience gold seeking in New South Wales and Victoria.[13] James Chandler spent seven years at Ballarat, Bendigo and Castlemaine in Victoria before he travelled out to Otago, where he continued gold seeking for another fifteen years.[14] The percentage of gold seekers from Victoria was much larger than the *Cyclopedia* recorded, as the series left unrecorded gold seekers who did not remain in New Zealand after the rushes, as well as those less successful or unwilling to pay the cost of inclusion in the subscription-based *Cyclopedia*.[15] J. H. M. Salmon is likely correct when he estimates that by 1863, 90 per cent of the gold seekers in Otago arrived from Australia, with the Victorian population predominant.[16]

News of Gabriel Read's discovery of gold on the Tuapeka in late May 1861 reached Victoria in mid-July, and by the end of the month there were three vessels in Melbourne advertising passage to Dunedin and Invercargill.[17] Most gold seekers, however, were at first probably hesitant to rush off to a distant goldfield with the memory of the failed Port Curtis rush in Queensland, Australia, four years earlier undoubtedly fresh in the minds of some. Nevertheless, by August Tuapeka fever swept across the Victorian goldfields when subsequent discoveries at Weatherston's and Waitahuna, combined with sustained yields at Gabriel's Gully, hinted at the rush's permanence. Thirty-seven vessels advertised passage to Otago in the *Argus* in late August 1861, which included 'almost every ship now in the bay'.[18] Four days later, the *Argus* remarked that hundreds had already left the colony for Otago, while hundreds more were arriving weekly from the goldfields. As Figure 2.1 indicates, the wharf at Geelong was packed with diggers, publicans and shopkeepers preparing to travel to Port Chalmers.

A month later Otago fever consumed the goldfields. The *Otago Witness* remarked that 'we cannot take up a Victorian newspaper, without finding Otago and the Otago gold diggings referred to in diverse places'. Until recently, the writer stated, Otago 'was scarcely known in Australia'.[19] Phillis Russell at Dunolly marvelled to a friend that

Figure 2.1 Individuals boarding vessels in Melbourne harbour, bound for Otago, date unknown, in *Otago Daily Times, 1861–1936, 75th Anniversary* (Dunedin: Otago Daily Times, 1936).

'this colony is now in such an upset state as every one is leaving for the *n*ew Zealand goldfields. All are going who can.'[20] The roads from Ballarat, Bendigo and the Ovens were flooded with diggers travelling to Melbourne on their way to Otago. One of these diggers was Robert McDougall, who left a claim in the Ovens district in August 1861 and travelled out to Gabriel's Gully.[21] At Moonambel, the exodus cut the selling price of mining property in half, while some shares in quartz reefs that previously sold for £100 were then unable to sell for £20.[22] The *Ballarat Star* remarked that a recent rumour of a steamer arriving in Sydney with 70,000 ounces of Otago gold led many to abandon their claims or employment and join the throng bound for Otago that was already passing through from other goldfields on the way to Melbourne.[23] Thomas Kerr joined this stream when, after seven years' digging in Victoria, he left his claim at Ballarat in 1861 and went out to the Tuapeka.[24] At Mount Maldon, a group of seventy-two diggers who were unable to finance their passages to Otago pooled their income to purchase six passage fares given out by lottery.[25] One of these diggers may have been Samuel Caudwell, who left Mount Maldon in early August for the Tuapeka.[26]

Meanwhile, diggers surged into Dunedin. Between the middle of July and the middle of October 1861, some 6,900 migrants arrived from Australia, the majority of whom travelled from Victoria.[27] The number continued to grow in the first three months of 1862, when there were 14,000 arrivals from Australia. After gold seeking for a year in Victoria, Lachlan McDonald travelled out to Waipori, where he began gold seeking early in 1862.[28]

While 11,000 gold seekers arrived from Australia in the last three months of 1861, there were only 750 departures to Australia in the same period.[29] The few departures did not spell contentment among gold seekers; rather, they were more the result of destitute and disillusioned diggers unable to return to Victoria.[30] At this time, there were 7,000 individuals on the Tuapeka diggings. If we assume an extremely conservative estimate of 1,200 Otago colonists on the Tuapeka goldfields at the same time, there were still at the very least 2,000 Victorian diggers in Dunedin who were unable or unwilling to travel to the diggings.[31] None of the newly established diggings at Weatherston's, Waitahuna, Waipori and Mount Highlay were as rich as Gabriel's Gully, where most of the payable claims were taken up by mid-October 1861. Nevertheless, diggers continued to arrive. The intention of many of these diggers probably was not to obtain a lucrative claim on an existing goldfield, as the Otago and Victorian press frequently maintained that most of the good claims were already taken up; rather, it was the expectation gleaned from the Otago press that new diggings would develop quickly in other parts of Otago.[32] If they were in the colony already, prospectors would be able to join the first wave of gold seekers, rather than arrive two or three months later when all of the good claims were already taken up. In this way, the travel time from Victoria, combined with the rapidity of an alluvial rush and the prospect of future rushes, always created a much larger gold-seeking population in Otago than the existing goldfields could maintain.

The Dunstan and Wakatipu rushes brought a second wave of gold seekers towards the end of 1862. Between August 1862, when the Dunstan rush commenced from Victoria, and August 1863, Dunedin received a net immigration of 29,830, more than triple the previous year's influx.[33] There were also many more uncounted, who arrived in the neighbouring province of Southland in 1863 and travelled north to the Wakatipu diggings. News spread through the Victorian goldfields like wildfire. While thousands of disillusioned diggers disembarked at Melbourne over the previous six months, thousands more surged into the city looking for the fastest passage to Otago. When news first reached Inglewood, 151 of the field's gold seekers rushed off to Otago in one week.[34] The *Ballarat Star* stated that the administrators of the local benevolent asylum were inundated with requests from wives, whose husbands abandoned them by rushing off to the Dunstan when news arrived.[35] A correspondent for the *Argus* remarked that, although wages were high, Bendigo Flat was deserted. Steadily paying claims were abandoned 'that the owner might be first in the rush to a distant district or colony, buoyed up by the hope of renewing there the experiences of the diggers of Bendigo in 1853'.[36] Thomas McCourt was one of these gold seekers at Inglewood, when in March 1863 he sold his share in a claim and travelled out to the Shotover River in the Lakes District.[37] The same year John Penderick travelled out with five mates to Otago, and the party spent a year digging at Campbell's Creek and Skipper's Canyon.[38] Peter Warren travelled out from Victoria with his brother in December 1862 and spent two years on the Dunstan and at Mount Ida.[39] These diggers flooded into Dunedin and Invercargill during the last few months of 1862 and the first few months of 1863. During one week in September 1862, more than 3,000 diggers arrived in Dunedin.[40]

Despite the buoyant expectations of prospectors, the Dunstan and Wakatipu were much more difficult to supply than the Tuapeka. This issue was magnified by exceptionally long and brutal winters in 1862 and 1863. In 1862 Jeremiah Eagerty, a police constable in Otago who previously served on the Victorian diggings, said he had 'never beheld more savage scenery, and [observed that] other men who have hitherto been accustomed to the flats and creeks of Australia and Tuapeka appear bewildered at their new diggings'.[41] Reports quickly reached Victoria of frostbite and diggers having to beg for bread on the way back to Dunedin.[42] When news of starvation on the Dunstan reached Ballarat, Otago fever greatly diminished.[43] One digger wrote that the scarcity of supplies and fuel and the poor returns compelled many gold seekers to retrace their steps back to Dunedin, begging at every sheep station they passed through.[44] By November 1863, the *Argus* reported that thousands of diggers in Otago were destitute and pleading the Victorian government for £150,000 to finance their return. By December, a group of Tasmanian gold seekers was also petitioning the Tasmanian government to finance their return when Otago's Provincial Government suspended government work in Dunedin.[45] The Tasmanian House of Assembly, however, was unwilling to sponsor their return when the moribund Tasmanian colony could not absorb the population.[46] The following February, the situation was little improved when George McVicar commented that he saw groups of diggers standing at street corners signing petitions to have the Victorian government charter ships to assist in their return.[47]

For most of these prospectors, their migration to Otago was a temporary sojourn during a life largely spent in Victoria. William and John

Walker only spent three years in Otago before they left the province for Victoria, eventually returning to England.[48] Thomas McCourt spent ten months in Otago before returning to Victoria.[49] Charles Robjohns was in Otago for only seven months.[50] It was not that all gold seekers necessarily retained a strong connection to Victoria. Some had only been in Victoria for a few years before migrating to Otago, and frequent mobility throughout Australasia often broke down any attachment to place on either side of the Tasman Sea.[51]

For most gold seekers, such place-based natural phenomena as geology and weather patterns in Otago guaranteed the province's connection to Victoria throughout the rushes. Gold seekers almost unanimously berated Otago for its volatile climate. John Henry Watmuff swore that Otago was 'a damned miserable country, the last God ever created & left it unfinished'.[52] For David Jones, the harshness of the environment made it an unfavourable comparison to his home in Victoria:

> I cannot think of a home here, a very uncomfortable place ... the winter is really cold, and we have to live without much fire and we see it strange to live in such a poor country after being use to live in a country where fine material is so plentiful as Victoria.[53]

As the author of one Otago guidebook published in Melbourne stated, 'new arrivals in Otago are liable to be attacked by dysentery, troublesome and lasting colds, to suffer from asthmatic and neuralgic affections, and not a few from rheumatic pains'.[54] These representations were widely circulated in Victoria through newspapers and private correspondence, and there were undoubtedly many gold seekers like George Wakefield, who wrote to his mother from Ballarat about the gold discoveries in Otago: 'Were it not for the climate, which is most inhospitable, cold and wet continually it would not be long before I was there.'[55]

Even successful prospectors often returned to Victoria seasonally when rainfall swelled rivers in the summer and blizzards crippled transportation in the winter. Phillis Russell, for example, commented in March 1862 that many gold seekers were returning to Victoria and would return to Otago the following spring.[56] Finally, Otago deposits were often shallow by comparison to Victoria, and the inability of diggers to find many gold-bearing quartz reefs or deep leads in the province guaranteed individuals' ongoing connection to Victoria. As surface deposits evaporated and the local goldfield economy became more capital intensive, many diggers returned to Victoria and those that remained tended to be less mobile.[57]

MOTIVATIONS

The arrival of thousands of diggers in Dunedin often had as much to do with economic conditions on the Victorian goldfields as the quantity of gold dug up on the other side of the Tasman Sea. Just as rushes in Victoria followed boom and bust cycles of the colonial economy, migration from Victoria to Queensland, Otago or the West Coast coincided with the contraction of the Victorian goldfield economy.[58] As David Emmons demonstrates in his study of Butte, Montana, gold seekers migrated to new fields when older diggings were worked out.[59]

In the early 1860s, the Victorian economy was in the midst of a depression. The colony had already experienced a boom in quartz mining in the mid-1850s, which led to the creation of hundreds of public mining companies in Melbourne and on the goldfields. Most of these companies had no intention of working the claims they obtained, and speculation and claim shepherding quickly set in. When the mining bubble burst in 1860, most of these companies collapsed, freezing credit, diminishing spending, and filling the colony with a glut of unsellable products that were piled up in stores and on wharfs.[60] This coincided with a drought and the arrival of some 43,000 assisted migrants that year, which combined to only intensify the economic distress.[61] When the American prospector Charles Ferguson later recounted his journey from Melbourne to Port Chalmers, he recalled that many of the diggers he travelled with from Bendigo to Otago had lost everything during the collapse of quartz mining on the Victorian diggings.[62] Andrew French was almost destitute when he rushed from Victoria to Otago in 1862.[63] As the *Mount Alexander Mail* commented in 1861, many in Victoria would rather migrate to Otago than work for 'bare tucker' in Victoria.[64]

The contrast between the expectations of prospectors and the conditions on the Victorian goldfields also influenced many to migrate to Otago. As David Goodman argues, reports of the Victorian goldfields often presented gold seeking as an easy path to financial independence, if not fantastical riches.[65] This account was closely connected to the alluvial nature of gold deposits in Victoria. Gold formed in quartz outcroppings and over centuries was eroded and carried down into streams and creeks, where it remained long after waterways evaporated or changed course. Metropolitan newspapers, guidebooks and public lectures frequently stressed gold deposits that were easy and inexpensive to prospect.[66]

These accounts encouraged many individuals who later dug in Otago to rush from Britain and Ireland to the Victorian diggings. John Lees travelled from Lancashire to Melbourne in 1853 when reports of gold discoveries in Victoria filled local newspapers.[67] A year later, Arthur Scoullar left for Victoria when stories of the diggings swirled near his home in Ayrshire, Scotland.[68] These prospectors found a field very different from the image of the one circulating in Britain and Ireland. Reports of the gold discoveries combined with the extension of government-assisted immigration schemes, funded by the rushes, to swell the colony's goldfield population.[69] While there were approximately 20,000 individuals on the goldfields in December 1851, the diggings' combined population rose to 147,000 by 1858.[70] The fields were over-rushed and an increasing number of diggers competed for increasingly rare gold. Within this context, frequent rushes became a dominant theme. In December 1854, 20,000 gold seekers rushed to Creswick, north of Ballarat, and a month later the field was virtually deserted. In one week during 1857, Ararat held 50,000 people before diggers abandoned the goldfield. The same year, 8,000 diggers joined a failed rush to Port Curtis in Queensland with little information and even fewer supplies.[71] This rush after alluvial deposits only increased towards the end of the decade as diggers continued to flood in at the same time that failed prospectors returned to Victoria. Many studies of the Australasian rushes depict the continual advance of colonisation and settlement on the goldfield frontier, but disappointment, financial decline and retreat characterised the lives of some prospectors who travelled across the Tasman Sea to Otago.[72] As Chapter Four will argue, these patterns of failure and disillusion were often manifested among gold seekers in Otago throughout the rushes.

Caution should be exercised, however, against equating migration entirely with economic necessity. As Geoffrey Serle and Susan Lawrence both show, absolute destitution was minimal on the goldfields.[73] Colonial legislation in Victoria allowed gold seekers the legal right to a block of twenty acres adjacent to their claims, on which they could build a house and farm the land. The extension of the railroad into the goldfields districts also drove down the cost of living.[74] Many diggers enjoyed a varied diet of beef, pork, vegetables, eggs and dairy.[75] Moreover, a sustained heavy rainfall early in 1863 increased gold yields throughout the goldfields at the same time that the Wakatipu rush swelled the numbers of those leaving for Otago. A writer for the *Bendigo Advertiser* lamented amid abandoned claims and derelict equipment that 'a waste is being made of what might have been a paradise'. The editorialist argued that gold seekers left because 'they wait with mouth wide open expecting the nuggets to drop into it like ripe plums'.[76]

As the author of this article argued, there were some gold rush migrants who pursued riches rather than fled poverty. Trans-Tasman migration was often a calculated decision made possible because it was a relatively small and inexpensive jump to Otago when compared to travel from Britain and Ireland to Australasia. Like Irish migration to Britain in the twentieth century, the Otago diggings' close proximity to Victoria allowed them to appeal to individuals' 'aspirations towards a higher standard of living, and not simply sheer economic necessity'.[77] Trans-Tasman migrants employed the same premeditation that earlier allowed them to choose Australasia after critically weighing information about potential destinations.[78] James Gascoigne left a claim on the Loddon paying £3 a week when the Tuapeka rush rippled through Victoria.[79] When John Henry Watmuff received two letters from mates at Gabriel's Gully, he decided to migrate to Otago, stating that 'my sole object in taking this step will be in the hope of realising a lump sum of money that I may be enabled to enter into some other pursuit that I've been engaged in so unprofitably for such a number of years'.[80] However, in contrast to Irish migrants in Britain, who pursued better wages and a higher standard of living across the Irish Sea, Victorian gold seekers migrated to a region with a more hostile terrain and climate and fewer and more costly supplies.[81] This was because the goldfields offered the possibility of wealth and a better livelihood in the future in exchange for adverse conditions in the present. Despite repeated failures, Victorian prospectors endured Otago's harsher conditions in hopes of riches that too often were deferred. As Watmuff observed shortly before sailing for Otago, 'My only regret is that I am leaving a certainty for an uncertainty.'[82] The smallness of the Tasman Sea in this regard and the volume of the flow also combined to maintain individuals' connections to acquaintances in Victoria and map Victorian social networks onto the Otago diggings.

COMMERCIAL AND PERSONAL NETWORKS

While economic conditions in Victoria encouraged migration, networks directed prospectors to Otago.[83] In his study of trans-Atlantic migration, Brinley Thomas demonstrates that British migrants travelled to the United States during periods of economic stagnation in Britain. During these periods of commercial inertia, British capital was not invested locally but instead flowed across the Atlantic. British investment in the United States stimulated American economic growth at the same time that it conveyed an image of America infused with possibilities for wealth.[84] A similar development can be discerned in the flow of gold seekers from Victoria to Otago in the early 1860s. When the Victorian goldfields were crippled by the mining collapse in 1860, the colony already possessed an extensive infrastructure to cater to the needs and wants of gold seekers within its borders. Shipping lanes, railways and an army of merchants and tradesmen facilitated the shipment of commodities and consumables to Victoria from Britain, India and around Australasia.[85] Commercial webs were extended across the Tasman during the Otago rushes and pulled the province further into this Victorian network. Supplies arriving into Melbourne from across the globe that for the last ten years had fed, clothed and entertained diggers in Victoria now were shipped from Melbourne to Dunedin by a merchant fleet.[86] In return, Otago gold was conveyed to Melbourne, where it was purchased by London agents and re-exported to Britain alongside Victorian gold.[87] All letters and newspapers from Britain and Ireland also travelled through Melbourne, so that connections between Otago residents and loved ones at home depended on this trans-Tasman link.[88] These findings echo Earl Pomeroy's and Daniel Marshall's respective arguments that San Francisco during the North American rushes became a nodal point for goldfields scattered west of the Rocky Mountains.[89]

Victorian capital and commerce flooded into the province with a rapidity that stunned Otago colonists. In 1861, shortly after Victorian gold seekers began arriving, Thomas Burns remarked that the arrival of shopkeepers, publicans and land speculators increased the price of real estate in Dunedin. 'Everyone', Burns stated, 'is a shopkeeper or owns a gin palace.'[90] Shopkeepers also followed their customers out to the diggings in central Otago, where they lined their shelves with flour from Tasmania, socks from Aberdeen, sugar from Mauritius and tea from India.[91] While on the way back to Dunedin from the Lakes District, one digger recognised many 'bakers, storekeepers, publicans and sinners' he had known at Bendigo.[92] One of these may have been Bendix Hallenstein, who left Bendigo to open a wholesale store at Queenstown in 1863. At Hamiltons in 1864, several Victorian businesses established local branches.[93] The same year, William Mears was operating his store, 'Wonders of the World', on both the Wakatipu and Dunstan goldfields alongside branches in Melbourne, New South Wales and the Victorian diggings.[94] In a 'speeded-up' society, the desire for more diggers, more commodities and more immediate news pulled Otago closer to Melbourne during the rushes.[95] An editorialist for the *Otago Daily Times* commented in 1862:

> The saving of time is the object ever kept in view – the compressing into the narrowest duration that interchange of ideas from which springs knowledge ... The railway, the steamer, and the telegraph ceaselessly toil on in their never-ending mission – the lessening the obstacles interposed by time and space. Rapidity has become the watchword of the age.[96]

Enclosing the Otago rushes within New Zealand history neglects the ways in which commercial networks stretched back to Victoria. From the province's relationship to global commercial and financial networks down to the digger, beside a campfire, reading a letter from home while drying his socks and cooking his dinner, the Otago gold rushes would be inconceivable without their links to Victoria. In a multitude of ways, the Otago goldfields existed more as a periphery of Melbourne than of Dunedin. As Phillip Ross May argues of New Zealand's West Coast later in the decade, the gold rushes made Otago a frontier of the Victorian colony during the early 1860s.[97]

While prospectors and products poured into Dunedin, letters and newspapers travelled in the opposite direction. Between 1862 and 1864, 391,780 letters were sent from Otago to Australia.[98] During the same period, some 349,715 newspapers were shipped from the province to Australia. Although the Otago government did not distinguish between the Australian colonies, most letters and newspapers were likely sent to Victoria given that most gold seekers came from that colony. Diaries from the Victorian diggings also sometimes recorded the steady flow of news from Otago. In 1861 the Ballarat prospector Frederic Ramsden noted briefly the arrival of letters from an acquaintance on the Otago diggings.[99] A year later, Charles Jarvis Coles also mentioned in his diary that he received several letters from acquaintances in Otago.[100] The flow of correspondence from Otago made trans-Tasman migration self-perpetuating when successive waves of prospectors often decided to migrate 'based on the guidance of pioneering migrants'.[101] James Gascoigne decided to rush from Castlemaine to Otago when he received a letter from his brother that was 'altogether favourable'.[102] Near the end of 1861, John Henry Watmuff travelled across the Tasman upon receipt of positive reports from his brother on the Tuapeka.[103] From Buckland Valley, Henry Morgan commented that 'the news of the gold mines in New Zealand is of the most flattering nature, both by the press and from private sources and there are a great number going there'.[104]

Framing the Otago rushes within the Tasman World also reveals a range of personal networks in Victoria that diggers abandoned or maintained while in Otago. Within the working lives of gold seekers, mining parties often were formed in Victoria before migration or were composed of diggers who had worked together previously. Rather than emerging as a pragmatic and situational response to thin settlement, as Jock Phillips argues, gold-seeking party formation drew on these Victorian networks.[105] Martin Gardner and David Rattray dug alongside each other in Ballarat before they both rushed to the Tuapeka in July 1861, where they formed a gold-seeking party with two other acquaintances from Ballarat, Alexander Don and William Rattray.[106] Henry Hawkins and Frederick Carpenter, mates and friends of twenty-eight years, prospected together at the Arrow. Robert Webb and Carl Sorrenson were mates for ten years before they joined the Otago rush in 1863.[107]

Trans-Tasman connections also extended beyond gold seeking. The binding of the gold rushes within national history often imagines the gold seeker as an itinerant loner or as part of an egalitarian masculine culture.[108] Yet by shifting our gaze back to Victoria, the gold seeker emerges as a husband or son, a brother or father. The geographically dispersed family was rooted in the experience of migration from Britain and Ireland, and most gold seekers came from families in which overseas mobility was a fact of life.[109] For some diggers who either settled down or grew up in Victoria, 'home' had slowly shifted to this colonial periphery, and many families replicated this system of family dispersion in Victoria during the Otago gold rushes. However, transience did not necessarily break down kinship bonds, as Angela McCarthy demonstrates.[110]

Susan Lawrence shows that by the early 1860s strong kinship networks had materialised on the Victorian goldfields, when earlier gold seekers encouraged subsequent waves of migrants, composed of relatives and friends.[111] The Otago rushes directed these networks across the Tasman, and many gold seekers remained connected to loved ones through correspondence and seasonal returns from Otago. The McMillan brothers, Hamilton, James and John, and John's brother-in-law rushed to Otago twice, yet remained connected to their stepfather, John McCance, of Chewton, Victoria, despite frequent mobility. For the McMillan brothers, McCance's home became the nodal point for a wide range of family migrations throughout Australasia.[112] Throughout his time in Otago, John Henry Watmuff frequently exchanged letters with his mother, siblings and cousins at Bendigo. On one occasion after he received a letter which detailed the 'most extreme poverty' of his mother and sisters in Melbourne, Watmuff lived 'nearly ... on dry bread' in order to send home £3.[113]

There were also several instances in which husbands and fathers on the Otago goldfields reneged on their responsibility to care for wives and children in Victoria. The Victorian government's lack of success in encouraging return migration from Otago undoubtedly contributed to this state of affairs. As an editorialist for the *Mount Alexander Mail* asserted:

> almost every postmaster could tell of more than one pale and anxious woman, who trembling enquires for letters from New Zealand which never come, betray an unfathomed death of hopes deferred and of silent sorrow ... while she, perhaps, is struggling with poverty to maintain her offspring, their natural guardian is rejoicing in emancipation from irksome lives and sacred duties.[114]

Whether through premeditation or failed expectations of gold seekers, there were frequent instances of abandoned wives requesting government aid.[115] In 1864 a woman at Collingwood left to care for her four children was entirely dependent on government aid when her husband did not send money for two years. The local mayor took up a collection to pay for the family's passage to Otago in order to track down the husband.[116] Wife desertion extended beyond the Victorian goldfield population. One woman in Tasmania was forced to break stones for road building in order to sustain herself and her six children, when her husband, John Scott, did not send any money for a year. The governor's wife paid for the family's passage to Otago. After the wife notified the Provincial Government, a magistrate summoned Scott from the Dunstan to appear in court, where he saw his wife and children. The digger was ordered to take care of his family or pay them a weekly allowance of £1.[117] As one doctor in Hobart noted, the town's benevolent society was unable to care for the many families left destitute by breadwinners 'having gone to New Zealand'.[118] There were likely far more cases of abandonment that went unnoticed. For most prospectors, 'the only effective imperative to act upon their familial responsibilities was internalised'.[119]

The absence of kin also affected family members in emotional ways. Especially for elderly and sick parents, the absence of children could crush one's heart. Thomas Pierson, an ageing American gold digger at Ballarat, was ill-equipped to cope with the departure of his son, Mason, for Otago, alongside his wife's declining health and his ostracism by local residents because of the American Civil War. Though his son was only away six months, Thomas' diary was filled with comments about absent letters, offering evidence that they were a poor emotional substitute when they did arrive. He remarked in his diary in January 1862:

Frances and me alone in Australia, all of our relatives in America except mason our son who is in N. Zealand about 1000 miles from here. It seems dreary – to be wandering as we wander here, so aimless dark and weary.[120]

On another occasion, he lamented, 'No bright spot to look upon nothing but sadness. Oh! That some oasis might come to our view in this our Desert life, some fragrant Savannah.'[121] Two weeks later, the situation was little improved: 'Several mails arrived from N. Zealand but they bring us no letters from Mason, which occasions us to feel very weary.'[122] For those left behind in Victoria, the Otago exodus could be a moment of impoverishment and loneliness, revealing that there were two sides to what was a trans-Tasman event.[123] An account of the gold rushes in Otago needs to emphasise the societies, families and individuals left behind, alongside the societies and cultures formed within the political boundaries of Otago.[124] As will be shown below, the impacts of the human tide that flowed to the Otago goldfields stretched beyond personal networks to upend the colony at the same time it transformed Otago. As Otago and Victorian colonists watched the flow of diggers alter their societies, the press in both places attempted to control the flow of knowledge about the goldfields.

TRANS-TASMAN PRESS NETWORKS

The Otago gold rushes, like all of the rushes in the second half of the nineteenth century, only became possible during the age of steam power when the advent of the steamship and mechanised printing press constituted a 'conquest of distance' that quickened communication and pulled distant societies closer together.[125] These technologies also mediated the role of the Victorian press during the Otago rushes. When success often depended on arriving on a field first, the gold rushes always magnified the importance of immediate and timely news. Moreover, the volatility of the rushes also necessitated continuous coverage of a goldfield. These factors combined to amplify the importance of the instantaneous and the regular because the gold seeker in Victoria could only hear echoes from the diggings a week old, the time it took for the Otago mail to arrive in Melbourne. News from the Otago goldfields in Victoria oscillated every week between feast and famine, with articles and commentary followed by a week of silence before the next steamship arrived carrying the Otago mail. Moreover, even after an individual decided to migrate to Otago, it could take upwards of two weeks to collect supplies, travel to Melbourne, obtain a passage and more recent information, before finally travelling out to the diggings. Passage by sail extended the travel time to well over a month.[126] For many gold seekers arriving on the Otago diggings, the environment they found was likely to be very different from the one upon which they first based their decision to migrate. Many gold seekers booked a return passage to Victoria almost immediately after arriving at Port Chalmers.[127]

The Tasman Sea shaped the Otago rushes in another way. When the volatility of gold seeking gave preference to the most timely knowledge, the Victorian newspapers were always at a disadvantage to the Otago press. Throughout the rushes, Victorian newspapers relied heavily on the Otago press for their coverage of the rushes and at the same time they criticised Otago papers with puffing them. The Melbourne-based *Argus* and all of the goldfield newspapers regularly copied articles from Dunedin newspapers for the most current news from Otago.[128] Moreover, Victoria was flooded with Otago newspapers: 349,715 issues were sent from Otago between 1862 and 1864.[129]

Reading cultures in Victoria could also quickly swell a rush. For most gold seekers who depended on newspapers and correspondence, gaining knowledge about Otago was a social endeavour. As Alan Atkinson observes, colonial reading was done in homes, public houses, miners' institutes, or on claims, and gold seekers often debated and discussed the merits of the Otago and Victorian diggings.[130] This is not to say that private information was not relevant; indeed, it was usually regarded by readers as more trustworthy. However, the need for rapid and regular news of gold discoveries when news was scarce gave the press a greater role in directing the flow of migrants than trans-oceanic migration, which relied overwhelmingly on personal correspondence.[131]

The difficulty with newspaper accounts from gold rush Otago was that they often did not present a single coherent message. In the first months of the Tuapeka rush, Julius Vogel's two papers, the *Otago Witness* and the *Otago Daily Times*, often gave contradictory messages to diggers when he wanted to encourage a rush to Otago – only not too big and not too soon. In August 1861, a writer for the *Witness* remarked that the Tuapeka could hold up to 60,000 diggers, and the colony could hold another 200,000 once additional goldfields were discovered.[132] Two months later, when some 7,000 migrants had arrived in the province from Victoria, the Tuapeka diggings were filled beyond capacity, and thousands of idle diggers were rambling about Dunedin when no new diggings were discovered to rival Gabriel's Gully. Under these circumstances, the editors of the *Otago Daily Times* thought it necessary 'not to encourage such an invasion by any statement that may in the least degree give an erroneous or exaggerated impression of the extent and richness of our Gold Fields'. They then went on to state that the goldfields were much smaller than the richest Victorian diggings, and that 'it is decidedly unwise for miners who are doing well in Australia to leave for Otago'. The editorial concluded by deflecting blame onto Australian merchants who were circulating 'an erroneous notion of our field'.[133] The opinion of the newspaper changed again in December 1861 when it stated that 'it is certain that Otago is now considerably under-populated'.[134]

Gold rushes always affected communities on both sides of a rush, and these inconsistent reports, and the exodus they caused, left their mark on the Victorian goldfields. Moreover, when the Victorian economy was entangled with the success of its own diggings, the impact of this Otago exodus reached far beyond the gold-seeking population. 'The fever has seized upon every one', George Wakefield told his father in September 1861 from Ballarat, and 'publicans have left their Hotels, Storekeepers their shops and in fact all who are not fixed and can raise the money are off. 8,000 have already left and I believe 80,000 or more are prepared to swell the throng.'[135] That same month, a correspondent in the *Mount Alexander Mail* warned that if the Otago diggings proved permanent, the Victorian goldfields 'will shrivel up with as rapid a decay as their growth was'.[136] Amid the exodus for the Dunstan and Wakatipu goldfields the following year, an editorialist for the *Inglewood Advertiser* warned again that Otago gold would unravel Victorian society:

> There is not a miner ... who will not be seized with an almost irresistible desire to migrate ... Bendigo, Ballarat, and the rest of the Victorian goldfields will bewail the exodus of the stalwart industrious men who will have made them prosperous. In short, we are in for it ... The 'diggers' ... will move by the thousands. The democratic element which has troubled Conservative politicians is clearing away ... it is vain attempting to control the torrent.[137]

Local developments in Victoria combined with the Dunstan and Lakes District rushes to overwhelm the Victorian economy. By December 1862, virtually all goldfield shopkeepers and publicans froze orders in Melbourne, fearing a wholesale exodus to Otago.[138] At Bendigo this was immediately preceded by a drought that stagnated mining and plummeted prices, and many stockholders sold off their livestock rather than continue to operate at a loss. When the Dunstan rush set in, prices for the scarce supply of food in Bendigo skyrocketed. Many diggers who remained on the field faced destitution when the cost of living mounted and employment evaporated.¹³⁹ 'The colony', the *Bendigo Advertiser* lamented in 1863, 'is to let.'¹⁴⁰ When the Dunstan and Lakes District rushes, drawing no more than 15,000 diggers from across Victoria, were able to cripple a goldfield with 30,000 inhabitants, they were clearly able to punch above their weight. The instability of the rushes constantly swung Victorian society between a surplus and shortage of labour. Moreover, the unpredictability of the rushes and the itinerancy of gold seekers seemed to magnify the impact on local communities of the smallest piece of information circulating about Otago. These factors magnified the role of the Victorian press in controlling and directing the flow of diggers to Otago.

In order to counteract what it deemed 'hearsay gossip, of uncertain origin and conflicting character, which has found its way into Otago papers' circulating about the Tuapeka rushes, the *Argus* dispatched a correspondent to Dunedin in September 1861.¹⁴¹ The picture of the Otago rushes the reporter presented was very different from the one filling the Otago newspapers. On the goldfields, prices were high, fuel was scarce and carriage difficult, which made gold 'hardly worth the trouble of a search'.¹⁴² On another occasion the correspondent argued that the diggings were far more populated and parties' returns were far smaller than the *Otago Daily Times* had assumed.¹⁴³ Dunedin was overflowing with diggers who, unable to return to Victoria, were employed in government labour or simply doing nothing.¹⁴⁴ *The Argus* warned that the 'greed for intelligence' among gold seekers had caused the Otago press' 'injudicious publication [of material so false] to have emanated from the father of lies'.¹⁴⁵

Alongside these press networks, the Victorian newspapers published private letters from Victorian prospectors in Otago, revealing an image of the province that contrasted strongly with those in the Otago press. As elsewhere, newspapers in Victoria were profit-making enterprises and their proprietors shared a vested interest in moulding knowledge about the rushes in a way that aligned with their own commercial interests.¹⁴⁶ In September 1861, William Mahay wrote from Dunedin that 'this is the worst place I ever was in. Everything on the diggings is very dear, and the road very bad. Tell anybody inquiring for news to stay where they are.'¹⁴⁷ The same day, *The Argus* wrote that two gold seekers had recently returned with news that hundreds of Victorian diggers were starving in Dunedin and unable to return to Victoria.¹⁴⁸ In October 1862, the *Mount Alexander Mail* published another letter from Otago, warning that many gold seekers were on the verge of starvation. The writer pleaded, 'Do not, for God's sake, advise any man to come here.'[149] In February of the following year, the *Ballarat Star* carried a letter in which a digger warned that 'there is three times the amount of population on these diggings more than newspapers state'.[150] 'Dunedin', one correspondent stated, 'is a very wretched place ... The streets are crowded with men looking the perfect pictures of misery.'[151] An even greater evil, a gold seeker argued, were its colonists: 'Maoris in open warfare would not matter, but to have to put up with religious Scotchmen is too much.'[152] Another group of diggers put it more bluntly: 'Those chaps are asses.'[153] *The Witness* fought back. In October 1861, it stated that it was the Victorian rather than the Otago press that manipulated gold seekers with misinformation:

> The extraordinary effect of our Gold Fields is to be found in the tone and style of the [Victorian] press, which has endeavoured to pooh-pooh the whole affair ... endeavouring to persuade its readers that the state of Otago is so frightful, that no one should venture to go there; comparing it to the Port Curtis rush ... Now the fact is that we have avoided, as far as it is possible, giving any exaggerated reports. We have carefully weeded the information that has been given us ... and any stories of extraordinary finds which were not fully confirmed by the most satisfactory evidence we have invariably omitted.[154]

Six months later the situation was little improved. In an article entitled 'Otago v. *The Argus*', a writer for the *Otago Witness* argued that above all the *Argus* desired 'to depreciate Otago in the eyes of the world. Pretending to take a friendly interest in the progress of the new gold country ... the *Argus* yet lets no occasion slip that offers the le[a]st opportunity for disparaging its resources or throwing doubt upon the permanence of its prosperity.'[155] In 1863 the *Daily Telegraph* argued that all those who returned to Victoria were 'drunk and disorderly [and] hate a well-run police' and the Victorian press was willing to publish their accounts 'no matter how reliable'.[156] The paper stressed confidence, however, that 'the thousand and one letters from the scrum of those who have visited these shores – the persistent exaggeration in editorials, and the "write to order" misrepresentations of "Our Own Correspondent", have failed to cover with disfavour the Gold Fields of this Province'.[157] On another occasion in 1861, the *Otago Daily Times* contended that 'the Victorian journals indulge in a lot of absurd attempts to run Otago down. According to them our goldfields are unproductive, of no extent, and not likely to be long-lived. The more gold there is found, the more vehemently they repeat their assertions.'[158]

The one thing that the Otago and Victorian newspapers could agree on was the power of the press to determine the movements of gold seekers. As Aled Jones and Mark Hampton argue, nineteenth-century newspaper editors shared a confidence in their ability to shape understanding of the world.[159] Time and again editors in Victoria and Otago found that confidence deserved. An immediate rush to Otago often followed the publication of new finds or higher yields in newspapers. In 1862, upon publishing news about gold found on the Molyneux that arrived in the Otago mail, the *Bendigo Advertiser* stated that 'the rush [to the Dunstan] is as certain to set in this day as the sun is to rise'.[160] In 1861 Charles Clifford rushed to Gabriel's Gully upon reading about the discovery in the *Otago Witness*.[161] William Wright and John Martin wrote in 1862 that the *Otago Daily Times* duped them into believing payable gold was widespread on the Dunstan. On at least one occasion, newspaper editors held back knowledge. In December 1861, one Dunedin colonist complained that the Victorian press refused to publish his favourable letter about Otago. He believed that 'had it comprised a series of disasters, deaths, starvations, etc., it would of course have been published with "comments", and a separate paragraph to draw attention to it.'[162]

In a way, this exchange was not simply an intercolonial debate, but a trans-Tasman one; editors and press correspondents in Otago often travelled from Victoria with prospectors rushing after gold. Julius Vogel, who previously served as the editor of the *Maryborough and Dunolly Advertiser* and the *Inglewood and Sandy Creek Advertiser*, also recruited most of his staff from Victoria.[163] The paper constantly jockeyed with Victorian periodicals for the attention of the trans-Tasman group of gold seekers who migrated between Victoria and Otago. When the Victorian and Otago press helped to shape the flow of information about the goldfields, the Otago rushes always existed at any moment in the spaces between these two accounts.

CONCLUSION

The Otago rushes depended on public knowledge of the rushes circulated in Victoria, which placed the events between the accounts contained in the Victorian and Otago press. In his study of European migration, Dirk Hoerder observes that most images of emigrant destinations circulating in sending communities tended to be positive, when those who wrote home were often the successful or those wanting to justify their decision to migrate.[164] In Victoria, however, the proximity of the Otago diggings and the continual flow of migrants across the Tasman flooded the colony with both negative and positive accounts from Otago, giving the prospective digger a multitude of contradictory images of the Otago goldfields. Gold seekers struggled to make sense of this cacophony of information as the rushes overwhelmed societies in both Otago and Victoria, and yet many 'wanted so much to believe that their normal scepticism dropped away'.[165] While there were many prospectors who criticised the Otago press for puffing its goldfields, thousands of diggers abandoned claims the moment favourable news of Otago arrived. The 'new, the exceptional, or the large [always captured] the imagination' of diggers and lent the province its 'magnetic qualities'.[166] Despite negative accounts in the Victorian press, many prospectors in Victoria were more willing to believe the Otago newspapers that the province's interior was a thirty-mile-wide goldfield, on which a million diggers could support themselves by simply picking gold up off the ground.[167]

When the flow of knowledge from Otago to Victoria fuelled migration, these trans-Tasman networks became self-perpetuating. Moreover, the migration of consumers extended Victorian commercial networks to Otago, where a web of shipping firms, carters and shopkeepers transported goods from Melbourne and sold them to Victorians on river flats and in crevices across central Otago. Meanwhile, the volume of the population flows allowed Victorian goldfield networks to be mapped onto Otago at the same time that the province's relative proximity to loved ones and acquaintances in Victoria allowed individuals to maintain relationships that were 'neither here nor there, but in both [localities] simultaneously'.[168] The Otago rushes were in many ways an event in Victorian history.

Chapters One and Two have built upon the work of transnational and migration historians to show the ways in which the Otago gold rushes extended beyond New Zealand shores. However, as stated in the introduction, there is a danger of simply mapping cultures and networks onto an 'empty' landscape. The Otago gold rushes were shaped as much by local environments and daily interactions as the networks that extended to Britain, Ireland and Victoria. Chapters Three and Four, therefore, move beneath the nation to analyse the patterns of work and leisure from a local perspective.

NOTES

1. John Henry Watmuff, diary, book 2, p. 252: 5 December 1862, private collection.
2. Ibid., 13 April 1862, book 2, p. 320.
3. Watmuff exchanged monthly correspondences with John Halley and

Henry Vikerman, who both were employed by the Nelson Reef Company at Bendigo. Upon describing the gloomy contents of the letters, Watmuff frequently restated that he would remain in Otago, as it provided him with the best financial prospects. See, for example, ibid., 29 March 1862, book 2, p. 315; 20 April 1862, book 2, p. 320.

4. See Stevan Eldred-Grigg, *Diggers, Hatters and Whores: The Story of the New Zealand Gold Rushes* (Auckland: Random House, 2008); Miles Fairburn, *The Ideal Society and Its Enemies: The Foundation of Modern New Zealand Society, 1850–1900* (Auckland: Auckland University Press, 1989); Jock Phillips, *A Man's Country?: The Image of the Pakeha Male, a History*, 2nd edn (Auckland: Penguin Books, 1996); Jock Phillips and Terry Hearn, *Settlers: New Zealand Immigrants from England, Ireland and Scotland, 1800–1945* (Auckland: Auckland University Press, 2008).

5. William Parker Morrell, *The Gold Rushes* (London: Macmillian Company, 1941); J. H. M. Salmon, *A History of Goldmining in New Zealand* (Wellington: Government Printer, 1963).

6. See, for example, Geoffrey Serle, *The Golden Age: A History of the Colony of Victoria, 1851–1861* (Melbourne: Melbourne University Press, 1963), 228; Geoffrey Blainey, *The Rush That Never Ended: A History of Australian Mining*, 4th edn (Melbourne: Melbourne University Press, 1993), 59; Anthony Edward Dingle, *The Victorians: Settling* (McMahons Point: Fairfax, Syme and Weldon Associates, 1984), 99. For a discussion of the historiography of the Australian gold rushes, see Iain McCalman, Alexander Cook and Andrew Reeves, 'Introduction', in Iain McCalman, Alexander Cook and Andrew Reeves (eds), *Gold: Forgotten Histories and Lost Objects of Australia* (Cambridge: Cambridge University Press, 2001), 1–22.

7. Philippa Mein Smith, 'The Tasman World', in Giselle Byrnes (ed.), *The New Oxford History of New Zealand* (Melbourne: Oxford University Press, 2009), 297.

8. Frank Thistlethwaite, 'Migration from Europe Overseas in the 19th and 20th Centuries', in Rudolph J. Vecoli and Suzanne M. Sinke (eds), *A Century of European Migration, 1830–1930* (Urbana: University of Illinois Press, 1991), 31.

9. Alan Lester, 'Imperial Circuits and Networks: Geographies of the British Empire', *History Compass* 4, no. 1 (2006): 124–41; David Lambert and Alan Lester, 'Introduction: Imperial Spaces, Imperial Subjects', in David Lambert and Alan Lester (eds), *Colonial Lives Across the British Empire: Imperial Careering in the Long Nineteenth Century* (Cambridge University Press, 2006), 1–31.

10. Alan Lester, 'British Settler Discourse and the Circuits of Empire', *History Workshop Journal* 54 (2002): 25.

11. For a discussion of these sources, see Jock Phillips and Terry Hearn,

'The Provincial and Gold-rush Years, 1853–70', *New Zealand History Online*, accessed 4 February 2018, 81, http://www.nzhistory.net.nz/files/documents/peopling3.pdf

12. *The Cyclopedia of New Zealand: Otago and Southland Provincial Districts* (Christchurch: Horace J. Weeks, 1903); *The Cyclopedia of New Zealand: Wellington Provincial District* (Wellington: The Cyclopedia Company, 1897); *The Cyclopedia of New Zealand: Auckland Provincial District* (Christchurch: The Cyclopedia Company, 1902); *The Cyclopedia of New Zealand: Canterbury Provincial District* (Christchurch: The Cyclopedia Company, 1903); *The Cyclopedia of New Zealand: Nelson, Marlborough and Westland Provincial Districts* (Christchurch: Horace J. Weeks, 1903); *Cyclopedia of New Zealand: Taranaki, Hawke's Bay and Wellington Provincial Districts* (Christchurch: Horace J. Weeks, 1908).
13. *CNZ: Otago*, 602.
14. *CNZ: Nelson*, 146.
15. For example, Frederick Clark was gold mining in Victoria for six years before he left for the Otago goldfields in 1862, where he spent nine months before returning to Victoria. See *The Cyclopedia of Victoria*, vol. 2 (Melbourne: F. W. Niven and Co., 1904), 384. Robert Clark briefly tried his luck at Gabriel's Gully before he returned to gold mining at Ballarat. See David Potts, 'Clark, Robert (1841–1883)', *Australian Dictionary of Biography*, vol. 3 (Melbourne: Melbourne University Press, 1969), 407–8.
16. J. H. M. Salmon, *Gold-mining in New Zealand* (Wellington: R. E. Owen, 1963), 101.
17. *Argus*, 30 July 1861.
18. *Argus*, 20 August 1861.
19. *Otago Witness*, 14 September 1861.
20. Phillis Russell (Bet Bet, Dunolly, Victoria) to Edwin Smith, 20 September 1861, 20 September 1861, Edwin Smith Letters, SLV, MS 14189.
21. *CNZ: Otago*, 317.
22. *Mount Alexander Mail*, 28 August 1861.
23. *Ballarat Star*, 2 September 1861.
24. *CNZ: Nelson*, 412.
25. *Tarrangower Times and Maldon District Advertiser*, 27 August 1861.
26. *CNZ: Otago*, 641.
27. *Otago Witness*, 12 October 1861.
28. Lachlan McDonald (Waipori) to his brother, Donald McDonald (Scotland), 2 May 1862, OSM, DC-2810.
29. *Otago Witness*, 12 October 1861, 4. Although no data exists for the early 1862 migrants, the numbers were probably slightly larger.
30. See *Colonist*, 27 September 1861, 4 October 1861, 15 November 1861; W. G. Fail, 'Mr. W. G. Fail's First Year's Experience in New Zealand. Delivered at Old Identities Meeting, March 23 1916', OSM, DC-2153.

31. The estimate of New Zealand gold seekers is derived from the Tuapeka goldfields population in mid-July. See *Otago Witness*, 20 July 1861, 4. The overwhelming majority of these gold seekers were colonists from Otago, Southland and Canterbury. There were most likely more New Zealand colonists on the goldfields by mid-October, further inflating the number of idle Victorian gold seekers.
32. *Otago Daily Times*, 7 April 1862, 20 December 1862, 5 February 1863, 3 July 1863; *Colonist*, 6 November 1862.
33. The net immigration total from the Australian colonies between 31 July 1861 and 31 July 1862 was 10,445. There was no tabulation of arrivals exclusively from Victoria. 'Report on the Otago Goldfields of New Zealand', *Appendix to the Journal of the House of Representatives*, 1863, D-6, 10–11.
34. *Otago Daily Times*, 27 September 1862, 5.
35. *Ballarat Star*, 8 September 1862, 4.
36. *Argus*, 12 August 1862.
37. Thomas McCourt, diary, LDM, N-2377.
38. John Penderick, diary, LDM, N-1901.
39. Peter Warren, diary, OSM, no call number.
40. *Otago Daily Times*, 27 September 1862.
41. *Otago Daily Times*, 1 September 1862.
42. *Mount Alexander Mail*, 6 October 1862, 3 November 1862.
43. *Melbourne Age*, 16 September 1862.
44. *Argus*, 1 June 1863.
45. Roger Kellaway, 'Tasmania and the Otago Gold Rush, 1861–1865', *Papers and Proceedings. Tasmanian Historical Research Association* 46, no. 4 (1999): 219.
46. Roger Kellaway, 'Immigration from New Zealand: The Tasmanian Select Committee of 1864', *New Zealand Geographical Society Conference Proceedings, 1999* (2000): 174.
47. George McVicar (Dunedin) to his brother (Russell, South Australia), 16 February 1864, OSM, no call number.
48. William and John George Walker Letters, OSM, C-128.
49. Thomas McCourt, diary, LDM, N 2377.
50. Charles J. D. Robjohns, diary, ATL, MS-Papers-4913.
51. See, for example, Lachlan McDonald Letters, OSM, DC-2810; John George and William Walker Letters, OSM, C-128.
52. John Henry Watmuff, diary, 9 February 1862 [2/301], private collection.
53. David Jones (Otago) to his family (Cefn Cirbwr, South Wales), 12 May 1862, ATL, MS Papers 6249.
54. Sigismund Wekey, *Otago as It Is, Its Gold-Mines and Natural Resources: Hand-book for Merchants, Capitalists, and the General Public, and a Guide to Intending Emigrants* (Melbourne: F. F. Baillière, 1862), 27.
55. George Wakefield (Ballarat) to his mother (England), 23 February 1863,

SLV, MS-6331; *Mount Alexander Mail*, 21 August 1861; *Bendigo Advertiser*, 11 September 1862.
56. Phillis Russell (Bet Bet, Victoria) to Edwin Smith, 21 March 1862, SLV, MS 14189.
57. Philip Ross May, *The West Coast Gold Rushes*, 2nd edn (Christchurch: Pegasus Press, 1967), 106.
58. Geoffrey Blainey, 'A Theory of Mineral Discovery: Australia in the Nineteenth Century', *Economic History Review* 23 (1970): 298–313.
59. David M. Emmons, *The Butte Irish: Class and Ethnicity in an American Mining Town, 1875–1925* (Champaign: University of Illinois Press, 1989), 18.
60. Serle, *The Golden Age*, 225–8.
61. Ibid., 241.
62. Charles D. Ferguson, *The Experiences of a Forty-Niner During Thirty-Four Years' Residence in California and Australia* (Cleveland: Williams Publishing Company, 1888), 153.
63. William Crawford Walker, diary, 20 September 1862, SLV, MS 11485.
64. *Mount Alexander Mail*, 9 September 1861.
65. David Goodman, *Gold Seeking: Victoria and California in the 1850s* (Stanford: Stanford University Press, 1994), especially 46–64.
66. See, for example, *Daily News*, 28 August 1852; *Lloyd's Weekly Newspaper*, 22 February 1852; *Caledonian Mercury*, 4 September 1851; G. Butler Earp, *The Gold Colonies of Australia, and Gold Seeker's Manual* (London: Routledge, 1853); James Bonwick, *Notes of a Gold Digger and Gold Diggers' Guide* (Melbourne: R. Connebee, 1852); Godfrey Charles Mundy, *Our Antipodes: Or, Residence and Rambles in the Australasian Colonies with a Glimpse of the Gold Fields*, vol. 3, 2nd edn (London: Richard Bentley, 1852). For a discussion of the rush from Britain to Victoria, see Serle, *The Golden Age*, Chapter 2; R. A. Stafford, 'Preventing the "Curse of California": Advice for English Emigrants to the Australian Goldfields', *Historical Records of Australian Science* 7, no. 3 (1987): 215–30.
67. Biographical information, John Lees Letters, SLV, MS-10083.
68. Arthur Scoullar, reminiscences, OSM, DC-3028.
69. See Robin Haines, *Emigration and the Labouring Poor: Australian Recruitment in Britain and Ireland: 1831–1860* (New York: St Martin's Press, 1997). The Victorian rushes had a similar effect on New Zealand immigration schemes in the 1850s, which in turn brought out migrants who would later dig for gold in Otago. The population influx and gold yields in Victoria combined to drive up both demand and prices for grain, which combined to stimulate an immense growth in agriculture in New Zealand that both encouraged the Provincial Government to recruit more agricultural labourers and provide them with the funding to do so. In 1854 the province exported 1,603 bushels of grain. Over the next two

years, the province shipped some 39,000 bushels, most of which went to the Victorian goldfields. *Statistics New Zealand*, 1853–6 (Wellington: Government Printer, 1858), table 35. Also see *Otago Witness*, 6 June 1857 and Erik Olssen, *A History of Otago* (Dunedin: John McIndoe, 1984), 46.

70. Serle, *The Golden Age*, 388.
71. Blainey, *The Rush That Never Ended*, 36–41, 57–8; Serle, *The Golden Age*, 217–20; Sue Palmer-Gard, 'Canoona Gold Fields – boom or Bust in 66 Days', *CQ University Library*, 2–3, accessed 1 July 2011, http://library-resources.cqu.edu.au/cqcollection/manuscripts/short-manuscripts/canoona.pdf; Morrell, *The Gold Rushes*, 215–39.
72. See, for example, Dingle, *The Victorians: Settling*, 39–57; Eldred-Grigg, *Diggers, Hatters and Whores*; Salmon, *A History of Goldmining*, 12; Geoffrey Blainey, 'The Momentous Gold Rushes', *Australian Economic History Review* 50, no. 2 (2010): 209–16; Kerry Cardell and Cliff Cumming (eds), *A World Turned Upside Down: Cultural Change on Australia's Goldfields 1851–2001* (Canberra: Australian National University Press, 2001). One notable exception is May, *The West Coast Gold Rushes*.
73. Serle, *The Golden Age*, 228; Susan Lawrence, 'After the Gold Rush: Material Culture and Settlement on Victoria's Central Goldfields', in Iain McCalman, Alexander Cook and Andrew Reeves (eds), *Gold: Forgotten Histories and Lost Objects of Australia* (Cambridge: Cambridge University Press, 2001), 262.
74. Serle, *The Golden Age*, 228.
75. Lawrence, 'After the Gold Rush', 262.
76. *Bendigo Advertiser*, 28 January 1863. Also see *Bendigo Advertiser*, 1 October 1861, 15 October 1861, 2 December 1862; *Inglewood Advertiser*, 9 December 1862; *Mount Alexander Mail*, 21 August 1861.
77. Enda Delaney, *Demography, State and Society: Irish Migration to Britain, 1921–1971* (Liverpool: Liverpool University Press, 2000), 289.
78. Eric Richards, 'An Australian Map of British and Irish Literacy in 1841', *Population Studies* 53, no. 3 (1999): 356–8, doi:10.1080/00324720308091; Angela McCarthy, *Irish Migrants in New Zealand, 1840–1937:'The Desired Haven'* (Woodbridge: Boydell Press, 2005), 2–3, 70–80; Lyndon Fraser, *Castles of Gold: A History of New Zealand's West Coast Irish* (Dunedin: Otago University Press, 2007), 16–17.
79. Gascoigne, 'Adventures of a Norfolk Boy', unpaginated.
80. Watmuff, diary, 2 December 1861 [2/251]. Also see Thomas Armstrong (Melbourne), 27 August 1869, SLV, MS-12164; William Jackson Barry, *Past and Present, and Men of the Times* (Wellington: McKee and Gamble, 1897), 145–6.
81. Delaney, *Demography, State and Society*, 289–92.
82. Watmuff, diary, 2 December 1861 [2/251]. Also see Archibald Henderson (Patea) to his niece, 2 December 1869, Archibald Henderson Letters,

OSM, DC-2399; John Lees (Melbourne) to his wife (Oldham, Lancashire), 21 January 1862, John Lees Letters, SLV, MS 10083; Watmuff, diary, 27 December 1863 [4/44]. This point will be further discussed in Chapter Four.
83. For an excellent discussion of the need to cross-integrate the structures and freedoms of migration, see Nancy L. Green, 'The Comparative Method and Poststructural Structuralism: New Perspectives for Migration Studies', *Journal of American Ethnic History* 13, no. 4 (1994): 3–22.
84. Brinley Thomas, *Migration and Economic Growth: A Study of Great Britain and the Atlantic Economy* (Cambridge: Cambridge University Press, 1973), 111.
85. Serle, *The Golden Age*, 229–41.
86. In 1862 the *Hobart Town Mercury* complained that Tasmania's inability to establish a direct steam service to Dunedin allowed Melbourne merchants to buy up Tasmanian flour intended for sale in Otago and re-export it more cheaply to Dunedin. See *Otago Daily Times*, 9 January 1862. At Hobart, this frustration was intensified by the migration of many of the town's merchants to Otago. See Kellaway, 'Immigration from New Zealand: The Tasmanian Select Committee of 1864', 173–4. For products imported and sold on the diggings, see *Otago Daily Times*, 3 January 1862, 6 July 1863; Day Book of Bendix Hallenstein, OSM, DC-1430.
87. Otago colonists frequently attributed the lack of a rush from Britain and Ireland to the lack of a direct gold shipment to Britain. See, for example, *Otago Daily Times*, 20 May 1863.
88. *Otago Daily Times*, 1 January 1862.
89. Earl Pomeroy, *The Pacific Slope: A History of California, Oregon, Washington, Idaho, Utah, and Nevada*, 3rd edn (Reno: University of Nevada Press, 2003), xviii; Daniel Patrick Marshall, 'Claiming the Land: Indians, Goldseekers, and the Rush to British Columbia' (PhD thesis, University of British Columbia, 2000), 8–18.
90. Thomas Burns, *Early Otago and Genesis of Dunedin: Letters of Rev. T. Burns, D. D., 1848–1865* (Dunedin: R. J. Stark and Co., 1916), part 5. Also see Wekey, *Otago*, viii–ix.
91. *Otago Daily Times*, 3 January 1862, 6 July 1863, Day Book of Bendix Hallenstein.
92. *Bendigo Advertiser*, 10 March 1863.
93. *Otago Daily Times*, 19 March 1864; 16 May 1864.
94. Ibid., 16 May 1864.
95. Aled Jones, *Powers of the Press: Newspapers, Power and the Public in Nineteenth Century England* (Aldershot: Scolar Press, 1996), 5.
96. Ibid., 1 January 1862.
97. May, *The West Coast Gold Rushes*, 125.

98. 'Reports of the Postal Superintendent of New Zealand', *AJHR*, 1863–1865, D1-D2.
99. Frederic Ramsden, diary, 17 September 1861, SLV, MS 12522.
100. C. J. Coles, diary, 5 September 1861, 22 March 1862, 24 March 1862, SLV, MS-12398.
101. McCarthy, *Irish Migrants*, 2–3.
102. James Gascoigne, 'Adventures of a Norfolk Boy', OSM, DC-0483, unpaginated.
103. Watmuff, diary, 20 October 1816 (2/240), 27 October 1861 (2/241), 2 December 1861 (2/250).
104. Henry Morgan, diary, 1 February 1863, NLA, M848M.
105. Phillips, *A Man's Country*, 27–8.
106. Alexander Don, *Early Central Otago; A Bathurst Miner's Reminiscences* (Dunedin: Otago Daily Times, 1932), 2–4.
107. Eldred-Grigg, *Diggers, Hatters and Whores*, 282.
108. Fairburn, *The Ideal Society*; Eldred-Grigg, *Diggers, Hatters and Whores*; John Milton Hutchins, *Diggers, Constables and Bushrangers: The New Zealand Gold Rushes as a Frontier Experience, 1852–1878* (Lakewood: Avrooman-Apfelwald Press, 2010); Phillips, *A Man's Country*.
109. David Fitzpatrick, *Irish Emigration, 1801–1921* (Dundalk: Economic and Social History Society of Ireland, 1984), 30; Eric Richards, *Britannia's Children: Emigration from England, Scotland, Wales and Ireland Since 1600* (Hambledon and London: Continuum International Publishing Group, 2004), 13–14, 298–9; McCarthy, *Irish Migrants*, 189; Colin Pooley and Jean Turnbull, *Migration And Mobility In Britain Since The Eighteenth Century* (London: Routledge, 1998), 180–213.
110. McCarthy, *Irish Migrants*, 188.
111. Lawrence, 'After the Gold Rush', 253.
112. David Fitzpatrick, *Oceans of Consolation: Personal Accounts of the Irish Migration to Australia* (Ithaca and London: Cornell University Press, 1995), 187–229. The Victorian prospector, Charles Jarvis Coles, also received letters from acquaintances and family members on the Otago goldfields. See Charles Jarvis Coles, diary, 5 September 1861, 22 March 1862, 24 March 1862, SLV, MS-10869.
113. See, for example, Watmuff, diary, 27 July 1862 [2/359-360]. Also see 20 October 1861 [2/241]; 21 February 1862 [2/306]; 16 March 1862 [2/311]; 23 March 1862 [2/312]; 5 April 1862 [2/317]; 23 August 1862 [2/371]; 31 August 1862 [2/374]; 3 November 1862 [3/26]; 9 November 1862 [3/28]; 30 November 1862 [3/35]; 7 December 1862 [3/37]; 21 December 1862 [3/41]; 18 January 1863 [3/52]; 25 January 1863 [3/53]; 1 February 1863 [3/57]; 27 February 1863 [3/65]; 27 April 1863 [3/90]; 24 May 1863 [3/99]; 28 June 1863 [3/124]; 27 July 1863 [4/6]; 22 November 1863 [4/31].
114. *Mount Alexander Mail*, 8 January 1863.

115. *Mount Alexander Mail*, 27 December 1862, 10 March 1863; *Otago Daily Times*, 7 January 1863; *Daily Telegraph*, 19 November 1863.
116. *Argus*, 28 May 1864.
117. *Daily Telegraph*, 19 November 1863. It is unclear if Scott ever paid for the care of his wife and children.
118. Kellaway, 'Tasmania and the Otago Gold Rush, 1861–1865', 172.
119. Fitzpatrick, *Oceans of Consolation*, 503.
120. Thomas Pierson, diary, 1 January 1862, SLV, MS-11646.
121. Ibid., 27 January 1862.
122. Ibid., 16 February 1862.
123. See D. H. Akenson, 'Reading the Texts of Rural Immigrants: Letters from the Irish in Australia, New Zealand, and North America', *Canadian Papers of Rural History* 7 (1990): 402.
124. For a study of correspondences between husbands and wives during the gold rushes, see Brian Roberts, *American Alchemy: The California Gold Rush and Middle-Class Culture* (Chapel Hill: University of North Carolina Press, 2000), especially 69–92.
125. Cole Harris, *The Resettlement of British Columbia: Essays on Colonialism and Geographical Change* (Vancouver: University of British Columbia Press, 2011), 162.
126. See, for example, Peter Warren, diary; Watmuff, diary; Charles J. D. Robjohns, diary; John Penderick, diary.
127. Andrew Bools, *The Wonders of Providence and Grace, as Illustrated in the Life of the Author, While Doing Business in Deep Waters, in Travels on Sea and Land, and over the Gold Fields of Australia and New Zealand* (London: Frederick Kirby, 1890), 71.
128. See, for example, *Mount Alexander Mail*, 13 September 1861, 8 September 1862; *Inglewood Advertiser*, 9 September 1862, 28 October 1862; *Bendigo Advertiser*, 30 October 1862.
129. 'Annual Report of the Postmaster General of New Zealand', *AJHR*, 1863–1865, D-1.
130. Alan Atkinson, *Europeans in Australia* (Melbourne and New York: Oxford University Press, 1997), 242.
131. On migration and private correspondences, see McCarthy, *Irish Migrants*; Fitzpatrick, *Oceans of Consolation*; Angela McCarthy (ed.), *A Global Clan: Scottish Migrant Networks and Identities Since the Eighteenth Century* (London: Tauris Academic Studies, 2006); Eric Richards, Richard Reid and David Fitzpatrick (eds), *Visible Immigrants: Neglected Sources for the History of Australian Immigration*, 1989.
132. *Otago Witness*, 26 August 1861, republished in *Argus*, 9 September 1861.
133. Ibid., 12 October 1861.
134. *Otago Daily Times*, 20 December 1861.
135. George Wakefield (Ballarat, Victoria) to his father (England), 23 September 1861, George Wakefield Letters, SLV, MS 6331.

136. *Mount Alexander Mail*, 9 September 1861.
137. *Inglewood Advertiser*, 9 September 1862.
138. *Bendigo Advertiser*, 6 December 1862.
139. Ibid., 12 March 1863.
140. As cited in the *Otago Daily Times*, 13 February 1863.
141. *Argus*, 24 September 1861.
142. Ibid., 22 October 1861.
143. Ibid., 5 April 1862.
144. Ibid., 22 October 1861, 26 June 1862.
145. Ibid., 28 October 1861.
146. Mark Hampton, *Visions of the Press in Britain: 1850–1950* (Urbana: University of Illinois Press, 2004), 43–4.
147. Ibid., 28 September 1861.
148. Ibid.
149. *Mount Alexander Mail*, 11 October 1862.
150. *Ballarat Star*, republished in *Daily Telegraph*, 10 February 1863.
151. *Bendigo Advertiser*, 17 October 1861.
152. Ibid., 2 October 1861.
153. Ibid., 25 November 1862. Because these letters were clipped (or composed) by the newspaper's editors, the intended private audience is unclear.
154. *Otago Witness*, 12 October 1861.
155. Ibid., 7 April 1862, 5.
156. *Daily Telegraph*, 10 February 1863.
157. Ibid.
158. *Otago Daily Times*, 11 December 1861.
159. Jones, *Powers of the Press*, 6; Hampton, *Visions of the Press in Britain*, 19–39.
160. *Bendigo Advertiser*, 8 September 1862.
161. *Argus*, 30 October 1861.
162. *Otago Daily Times*, 18 December 1861.
163. Raewyn Dalziel, *Julius Vogel: Business Politician* (Auckland: Auckland University Press, 1986), 23–30.
164. Dirk Hoerder, 'Introduction. From Dreams to Possibilities: The Secularization of Hope and the Quest for Independence', in Dirk Hoerder and Horst Rössler (eds), *Distant Magnets: Expectations and Realities in the Immigrant Experience, 1840–1930* (New York and London: Holmes and Meier, 1993), 1–32.
165. Patricia Nelson Limerick, *The Legacy of Conquest: The Unbroken Past of the American West* (New York and London: W. W. Norton and Company, 1987), 44.
166. Ibid., 5.
167. *Otago Daily Times*, 1 September 1862. Also see *Otago Daily Times*, 15 April 1862, 17 May 1862, 10 November 1862, 9 January 1863; *Colonist*, 27 September 1861.

168. David A. Gerber, *Authors of Their Lives: The Personal Correspondence of British Immigrants to North America in the Nineteenth Century* (New York: New York University Press, 2006), 8.

3

Work and Environments

In an essay charting the trans-Tasman connections between Otago and Victoria during the nineteenth century, Erik Olssen astutely notes that 'those who came to New Zealand often had the benefit of Australian experience and usually tried to learn from Australian mistakes'.[1] Olssen's comment is confirmed by the previous chapter, which explored the various ways in which the Otago rushes grew out of the Victorian rushes of the previous decade and remained connected to Victoria throughout their course. While acknowledging these origins and connections, it is important to recognise that the Otago gold rushes were not simply appendages of the Victorian goldfields, in which Victorian cultures and identities were universally mapped onto what was an empty and meaningless landscape. This chapter will argue that Victorian gold seekers in Otago may have arrived with 'Australian experience', but they sometimes found these experiences ill-suited to local environments.

The intention here is not simply to analyse the transnational and the local as separate parts of the Otago gold rushes. Historians of the gold rushes often choose between a transnational or local lens. David Goodman and Douglas Fetherling stress the flows and networks that linked multiple goldfields and made gold rushes in the nineteenth century 'instructive in their unremarkableness'.[2] In contrast to these transnational and global histories, Miles Fairburn and Jock Phillips ignore Imperial and Australasian scales when they argue that gold rush societies were shaped exclusively by unique environments in New Zealand.[3] Chapters Three and Four of this book emphasise what William Cronon describes as the 'dialectical' relationships between individuals – and the networks and practices they brought with them – and the ecologies they found in Otago as they looked for gold.[4] At the same time that diggers remade environments in Dunedin and across central Otago by their arrival and work, their social networks and cultures were also changed by nature and the transformations wrought upon it by gold seeking. Moreover, the economic, the cultural and the social were always entangled with each other and ecologies in the gullies and flats where individuals hunted for gold.[5] As Kathryn Morse demonstrates in her study of the stampede to the Klondike, gold was just a single mineral among the mass of materials individuals found, and yet it embodied all of gold seekers' dreams of wealth and independence, precisely because their society valued it as money.[6] These cultural meanings of gold sometimes were inseparable from social networks connecting individuals to loved ones in Victoria, Britain or Ireland, because some individuals dug for gold in order to provide for family members. Finally, the natural properties of gold and the natural environments in which it was found always necessitated cooperation between diggers and sometimes also resulted in conflict.[7] Gold seeking, therefore, entangled local social networks with the cultures, economics and ecologies of the rushes. The volatility of natural environments always threatened to upend gold seeking and its associated economies, cultures and networks.

While stressing the relevance of networks and cultures from Britain, Ireland and Victoria, this chapter also emphasises cultural formation as an ongoing process that occurred in a specific locality. Cultural historians of the gold rushes usually analyse gold rush societies as a frontier of either the eastern United States or Britain, stressing the ways in which 'Old World' culturally defined meanings of 'reproductive' and 'productive' work were thrown into disarray in the early years of a gold rush. Susan Lee Johnson and Brian Roberts both argue that the digger's negotiation between eastern American culturally defined meanings of work and local economies created a 'crisis of representation' for white diggers on the Californian goldfields.[8] In his study of gold rush Victoria, David Goodman likewise calls for an 'edgier history' of the gold rushes that centres on these moments of disorder and alarm when British cultures were upended by the scramble for gold.[9] While these approaches do much to problematise monolithic characterisations of gold seekers as pioneer settlers, they provide only a snapshot of the first experiences of a rush, which leaves little room for understanding the ways in which the extraordinary became ordinary in the everyday lives of prospectors over the months and years on the diggings.[10] By shifting the lens away from the 'East–West' and 'metropole–colony' binaries implicit in this body of literature, this study follows Earl Pomeroy's argument that gold rushes are better understood within regional and sequential frameworks than national scaffoldings that changed very little between rushes.[11] This analysis links up with Philip Ross May's and Lyndon Fraser's claims that Victorian 'structural factors' remained central to social formation on the West Coast goldfields.[12] Work and leisure cultures in Otago, therefore, reveal the ongoing process of identity and cultural formation that was extended to – and further shaped by – new social and natural environments on 'second-wave' goldfields. In contrast to studies on the Californian and Victorian rushes, this chapter discusses a population of diggers who had long become acclimatised to goldfield life through daily work routines stretched over years.[13]

These structures, technologies and experiences of gold seeking reiterated time and again the pervasiveness of what Barbara Rosenwein describes as 'emotional communities' that were formed through the daily face-to-face interactions between individuals at a particular place.[14] However, these communities were not formed exclusively by environments on the goldfields, as Jock Phillips argues.[15] Rather, they were equally shaped by prior networks and experiences in Victoria. These Victorian foundations preconditioned individuals to respond to obstacles presented by nature, whether clearing a paddock or turning the course of a river, in ways that repeatedly stressed the importance of social networks on the diggings.

This chapter is divided into six sections. The first section discusses the cultural meanings that individuals ascribed to gold and the reasons they dug for it. It reveals that for individuals who rushed to Otago, the decision to prospect for gold was often an economic choice grounded in a desire to provide for family members or as a means of eventual land ownership. The chapter then maps the work of travelling to the diggings from Victoria. The analysis underscores the ways in which the rushes transformed landscapes in Dunedin and central Otago and how these transformations influenced the lives of prospectors as well as their perception of Otago. The following two sections look at the environments on the goldfields. The changes wrought upon landscapes where individuals looked for gold had an unintended transnational dimension to them. The mass of diggers and the tools prospectors employed remade central Otago in the image of Victoria in the early 1850s. However, nature always exerted its power over the rushes when success in digging depended on local climates and weather patterns. The two concluding sections of the chapter detail the ways in which individuals relied on experiences, technologies and social networks from Victoria to combat these new environments in Otago. This discussion casts doubt on Miles Fairburn's insistence that the gold rushes were atomising events.[16] While generally agreeing with Jock Phillips' conclusion about social bonding on the goldfields, the chapter attributes this not exclusively to 'New Zealand' conditions but to the interactions between Victorian practices and networks and Otago environments.[17]

MOTIVATIONS

Gold, and the work done to obtain it, was closely connected to the dreams and ambitions individuals associated with it. Most historians of the nineteenth-century gold rushes understand the search for gold as a mythic quest for independence from the tyranny of modernity.[18] Studying the British Columbian gold rush, Adele Perry contends that the gold rushes allowed individuals an opportunity to flee the constricting 'temperate, disciplined and domestic masculinity' that gained hegemony in Britain and America during the second half of the nineteenth century. On the diggings, prospectors 'refashioned definitions of manliness and civilisation [in an environment] where a reinvigorated vision of white manhood could flourish'.[19] Similarly, Brian Roberts draws on California gold seeker diaries and correspondence to argue that the gold rushes were an act of 'rebellion against certain middle-class values' of respectability and repression, while still allowing their middle-class participants to retain class privileges and identity.[20] In his study on the New Zealand rushes, J. H. M. Salmon contends that the 'gold rushes were at once a protest against the restrictive forces of the old world, and an extension in individualistic terms of its aggressive, acquisitive spirit'.[21]

Some diggers in Otago were attracted by the gold-seeking lifestyle. While on the Dunstan, John George Walker, the son of a Freeman of London, told a friend that 'it is very jolly to live in one's own house with no rates and taxes and independant of everybody'.[22] For others, the excitement and the 'rush' of the rushes became their own end.[23] James Booth joined the rushes because he was 'bent on adventure'.[24] Diggers at John Garrett's hotel huddled around tables recounting stories of excitement, near riches and near deaths.[25] Charles Ferguson found that stories like these made gold seeking 'so infatuating [that it was] almost impossible for one to be cured ... or keep out of [digging]'.[26] Harry Enniss, a 'hot brained wild & most reckless devil', joined the rushes for adventure after he was expelled from the University of Dublin.[27] In his first weeks in Otago, Alexander McKay also saw novelty in being a '<u>new chum</u>' on the diggings, setting off in search of riches while dressed like 'the beggars at home'.[28]

Other historians stress economic motivations over flight from cultural norms. As the Californian historian Kevin Starr demonstrates, diggers recorded few moments of self-conscious reflection; rather, 'anxious to strike it rich, having risked their lives to do so, [gold seekers] wasted little time in asking who they were'.[29] Much of the literature about the Victorian goldfields confirms Starr's conclusion.[30] Geoffrey Serle argues that gold seekers arrived in Victoria with little more than a desire to '"get on", up and out of the ruck'.[31] In her study of Scottish Highland prospectors in Victoria, Donna Hellier shows that most migrated to Victoria to avoid destitution rather than redefine 'manliness and civilisation'.[32]

The surviving personal accounts from the Otago diggings support Starr's and Serle's claims by emphasising economic motivations in letters, diaries and reminiscences. Most gold seekers were migrants and the children of migrants who left Britain and Ireland during the first half of the nineteenth century in response to economic transformations which made tenancies redundant and cottage industries obsolete.[33] As they shovelled and swirled tons of earth, diggers understood gold seeking as a means to land ownership. When Horatio Hartley discovered gold in the Molyneux River, sparking the Dunstan rush, he declined an enlarged prospecting claim on the new field, instead using his money to purchase land in Canterbury where he began farming.[34] Hunched inside a tent on the banks of the Kawarau River, Daniel Calwell wrote to his brother, Davis, in 1862: 'I shold like very well to have a Block of Land somewhere or other and setle on it.'[35] At the same time that diggers wrote home about dreams of owning a farm, they clamoured in public meetings and in the press for pastoral runs to be opened up to permanent settlement. In 1865 gold seekers successfully petitioned for the extension of goldfield leases from ten acres to fifty acres, and the following year those who held leases were able to purchase their holdings outright.[36] Moreover, there were many gold seekers who transitioned into farming as surface deposits began to evaporate in Otago. After twelve years gold seeking in California, Victoria and Otago, James Gascoigne purchased land on the Tuapeka and settled into dairy farming.[37] Other gold seekers took to farming elsewhere. Capital and diggers from Otago and the West Coast diggings largely drove the farming boom on the North Island in the 1880s.[38] One of these diggers-turned-farmers was Archibald Henderson, who purchased a farm at Patea after prospecting in Otago and on the West Coast.[39]

Moreover, gold seeking was rarely a life's vocation. Stevan Eldred-Grigg notes that the army of diggers who moved between gold seeking and waged work, and later shifted seamlessly out of digging into other occupations, was always larger than the number who never left the diggings.[40] Some individuals understood gold seeking as a temporary employment little different from waged work. John Brown dug up £150 with his mates in three months on the Tuapeka before he returned to his farm in the Pelorus Valley.[41] The squatter Edmund Bowler noted a steady flow of diggers employed temporarily on his runs.[42] Other prospectors left the diggings for the sea. Thomas Armstrong prospected in Otago for six months before he took up employment on a sailing vessel, trading around Australasia and with Hong Kong.[43] William Chapman was on the Otago diggings for six months until he shifted to Port Cooper, where he purchased a schooner and began trading along the New Zealand coast.[44]

For other gold seekers, the search for gold was interwoven with links to communities on the other side of the world. As Chapters One and Two illustrated, many gold seekers remained connected to the communities and loved ones they left behind in Britain, Ireland or Victoria. Everyday routines of shovelling and washing dirt were closely connected to the desire to be providers. Diggers' wives and daughters may often have been absent on the diggings, but they were present in the letters diggers penned home or carried on them. In 1863 John Love's frozen corpse was found buried under a snowdrift on the Old Man Range with several letters from his wife and pictures of her and their children in Glasgow.[45] Francis Joseph Mapleson travelled to Otago in order to provide for his family in Braybrook, Victoria.[46] For John Lees it was these translocal connections that paradoxically inhibited him from returning to his family. In his letters to his wife in Oldham, England, Lees frequently reiterates his need to return home in riches, rather than face the scorn of gossipy neighbours.[47] As Chapter Two explained, there were also others who saw the rushes as an opportunity to abandon these relationships and responsibilities.

Many gold seekers likely arrived in Otago with rosy ideas of easy wealth and exciting adventures, but they quickly discovered that nature had a way of taking the glitter out of gold digging. Such romanticised views of prospecting often obscured the uncomfortable realities of life during the rushes. Gold seeking in Otago meant throwing supplies over one's shoulder, trudging through muddy bogs and over rocky mountains, labouring knee-deep in water under a scorching sun in the summer and near-continual darkness in the winter, only to return to damp tents to rest under a thin blanket with little more than manuka scrub for bedding.[48] These tactile experiences of looking for gold in Otago made prospectors acutely aware of the power of nature to shape the gold rushes.

RUSHING TO RICHES, FINDING SQUALOR

Mobility was central to the gold rushes when work routines were often characterised by failure and migration in search of better prospects. Itinerancy during the rushes, however, did not exist in strong contrast to a sedentary life off the goldfields. Rather than a phenomenon unique to the gold rushes, mobility was simply a fact of life for individuals growing up in the nineteenth century.[49] As Chapter One showed, mobility on the goldfields grew out of enduring migration practices in Britain and Ireland. Moreover, employment in colonial Australasia was often a series of short-term contracts, which induced frequent mobility. Gold rush mobility, therefore, flowed from previous practices within Britain, Ireland and the Australasian colonies.

Gold seeking for most diggers began across the Tasman, where Otago fever ripped through the Victorian diggings. As Chapter Two documented, glowing accounts flooded into the colony from diggers and newspapers in Otago, inducing many to travel to the province. There were also others who arrived from neighbouring colonies or directly from Britain or Ireland. When these migrants arrived in Port Chalmers they found a cacophony of noise and chaos. The harbour was 'chocked full of vessels' unable to depart when their crews deserted (see Figure 3.1).[50] A fleet of rickety and 'dirty, greasy boats' weaved between ships, and their captains offered passengers transport to Dunedin.[51] Meanwhile, an army of draymen competed for the passengers and luggage being unloaded at the port.

When gold seekers arrived in Dunedin they found a scene of squalor and destitution, in strong contrast to the glowing accounts circulating in Victoria. Ironically, the filth they found was of their own making. As in all gold rush societies, the desire for wealth paradoxically created squalor. Local infrastructures were overwhelmed by the arrival of thousands of individuals, which in turn transplanted many harmful characteristics of urban environments in the Old World.[52] The Victorian army similarly transformed Dunedin from a struggling town into an instant city, yet the city lacked the infrastructure to keep pace with the arrival of diggers. The British traveller, B. A. Heywood, described the city as 'prematurely grown', in which a sudden traffic was thrown upon it.[53] Many streets in Dunedin became muddy quagmires.[54] Business fronts were simply 'masses of mud', and many of the thoroughfares throughout the city were impassable as muddy swamps.[55] Manuka twigs and bark were tied together and laid across the streets to provide a semblance of pavement.[56] Blood and carcasses were thrown out of slaughtering

Figure 3.1 Rattray Street, Dunedin, 1862. Early Dunedin, Meluish – Burton – Muir & Moodie, ATL, O.030516. Otago Harbour is in the background, filled with ships carrying goods and gold seekers from Port Chalmers to Dunedin.

houses and into the streets, and at least one colonist complained that the smell of decaying flesh and organs filled the neighbourhoods around Walker Street.[57] Heaps of fish were piled up outside the Town Board office.[58] Hundreds of horses imported from Victoria filled the town with tons of dung. James Hector estimated that 20,000 tons of excrement were dumped annually into the streets and cesspools of Dunedin.[59] This became such a problem that by September 1862 the government employed labourers to shovel the manure and cart it to the junction of Anderson Bay and the Main South Road.[60] There were probably many gold seekers who questioned their decision to prospect in Otago when the road from Anderson Bay to the diggings was literally marked by a mountain of shit. This excrement combined with vomit and trash and collected in marshes of 'dark putrid mud ... in the progress of decomposition', most noticeably in the Northeast Valley, Anderson Bay and the land bordering Knox Church.[61] In the summer it baked in the sun and the smell wafted into homes and shops throughout town.[62] Along Princes Street, the stench was so rank that several storekeepers and publicans shut up shop because of infections and headaches from it.[63] For the arriving Victorian prospectors, the town seemed to be built not on gold but on garbage.

This sewage created by prospectors infested the city and spread sickness and disease among gold miners and colonists. 'There is poison in Dunedin', the *Times* thundered in 1862, 'in the air, in the water, and in the ground'.[64] The following year, Lauder Lindsay, the former resident physician of the City Cholera Hospital in Edinburgh, warned that the arrival of prospectors had transformed Dunedin from a 'straggling village' into a 'crowded town', resulting in scenes of disease and death 'familiar in our large overcrowded cities at home'.[65] Clean water and drainage were rare.[66] Intestinal worms, rheumatism, measles, typhus and a range of other diseases infected the city.[67] It certainly did not help that the Dunedin Hospital was built adjacent to a large cesspool.[68]

Gold had lured many diggers to Dunedin, but its absence now kept them there. In 1861 over 1,000 individuals signed a petition to the Otago Provincial Government asking for employment at 6s–7s per day.[69] This request was refused, although a year later the Provincial Government advertised work at 5s per day cutting away the side of Bell Hill (see Figure 3.2). Prospectors, who rushed to dig for gold and now shovelled mud in Dunedin, fumed at these low wages when many had been making 50s per week in wages as quartz miners in Victoria.[70] As one prospector from Bendigo complained, gold miners 'are not wanted, and to them no crumbs of comfort are held out; no means of sustenance; only the cold shoulder'.[71] Despite such complaints, the Provincial Government employed 450 'destitute and distressed' gold seekers in three weeks and turned down requests from scores more.[72]

Prospectors who could not obtain work, and many who could, crammed into tiny and wretched huts and tents crowded together in 'digger camps' around the town (see Figure 3.3).[73] This replicated earlier urban environments across the Tasman Sea. In the first few years of the Victorian rushes, the colonial government established a canvas town in South Melbourne, where living conditions were so deplorable that 'young wives and young mothers wept through the night, hungry and cold, deploring the day that they ever left Old England, and comfortable homes'.[74] This pattern was replicated in Otago. In 1862 Dr Lindsay noted in Dunedin that many people in these camps lived in conditions more deplorable than the Scottish Highlands and Islands or the worst Edinburgh slums. Upon visiting a child suffering from typhus, the doctor found the boy housed in a public house made of caked mud and stuffed beyond capacity with men, women and children.[75] In 1863 a magistrate visiting a tented digger ghetto in Dunedin had never seen such 'filth, squalor and misery accumulated in one spot'.[76]

For many gold seekers, the Otago rushes ended here with the purchase of a return ticket to Melbourne.[77] For those who continued on to the diggings, the first task was to roll up one's 'swag' – a small blanket or bag which contained the digger's worldly goods. Charles Money filled his with food, tobacco, sewing materials, a shovel and a tin dish, tying it all over his shoulder with a few blades of flax.[78] James Gascoigne carried 87 pounds of supplies on his back as he sloshed through mud and filth for ninety kilometres from Dunedin to Gabriel's Gully.[79] Charles Robjohn's

Figure 3.2 Bell Hill excavations, 1863. Toitū Otago Settlers Museum, no reference number.

Figure 3.3 View looking over Maclaggan Street, Dunedin, with Rattray Street in the foreground and the digger camp above Stafford Street on the hill in the upper left of the photograph, 1862. ATL, Dunedin Album 1, PA1-0-143-06.

back ached as he trudged with this pack through the Tuapeka, where 'the ground was so sliply [*slippery*] that for every 3 steps forward you went 2 back'.[80] Not everyone was well equipped for prospecting. One prospective digger on the road to the goldfields was seen carrying only a pickaxe, shovel, hatbox and umbrella.[81]

TRAVELLING TO THE DIGGINGS

When diggers left Dunedin for the goldfields, they found an empty landscape in strong contrast to the din and activity of the provincial capital.

Reflecting on his journey to the Dunstan, John George Walker told his mother that 'the land is the most sterile place I ever saw'.[82] To Andrew Bools, the hills and gullies formed an endless maze that stretched to the horizon in every direction.[83] William Turnbull Smith remarked in his diary that there was 'nothing but white grass and dust flying' for miles surrounding the Dunstan.[84] During a prospecting trip above the Kawarau River, Harry Dight fumed that 'people must be damned mad, that would come a mile to see such a damned rocky, mountainous, wear your-soul-out kind of place'.[85]

Yet everywhere there was evidence of 20,000 pairs of feet travelling over the same ground. While gold seekers were fairly ordinary in their itinerancy, the volume and speed of the exodus across lands little known to European migrants were unrivalled in the nineteenth century. Ten years earlier, the rush to the Victorian diggings had transformed the roads from Melbourne into quagmires that were filled with the skeletons and corpses of horses and bullocks that sank into the mud.[86] In the first few months of the Tuapeka rush, the 'straggling, undisciplined army' of diggers and draymen similarly transformed the lands adjacent to Lake Waihola and the Waipori River into a morass of mud, debris and carcasses.[87] George O'Halloran realised he was near the Tuapeka diggings when streams began flowing with 'pea soup colour'.[88] The following year the road from the Tuapeka to the Dunstan was marked by the corpses of bullocks decaying in the hot summer sun.[89] Gold seekers also left their imprint on inland sheep stations. James Murison commented that the usual calm at the Puketoi Station on the Maniototo Plains was broken in the first weeks of the Dunstan rush by the clatter and bustle of the digger army surging through the sheep run.[90] Many of these diggers left these stations ravaged, carrying off doors and fence posts for mining equipment and sheep for food.[91]

As gold seekers rushed to the diggings, they struggled against natural disadvantages in Otago's topography which made travel more difficult than in Victoria. In the early 1860s, many of the Victorian goldfields were connected to Melbourne by rail.[92] The first legs of the journey from Victoria to Otago often relied on steam power, which made transportation reliant on money and technology rather than animal and human muscle. Diggers stuffed into railway cars travelling from the Victorian goldfields to Melbourne or Geelong before boarding steamships bound for Otago.[93] As William Cronon argues, the railroad constituted a 'liberation from geography' when individuals could travel more quickly without having to struggle against steep gradients, muddy roads and harsh climates.[94] When prospectors arrived in Dunedin and rushed out to the diggings, they stepped back in time, finding themselves more reliant on human and animal power as they struggled to travel over a landscape that often impeded easy movement. 'This island wants hammering out flat', one digger complained.[95] Roads to the diggings were erected along rivers and through gullies that became muddy quagmires immediately following a heavy rainfall.[96] Commerce and migration to and from the diggings thus 'followed the hot-cold, wet-dry cycles of all temperature climates [and] fluctuated widely from season to season'.[97] It was in this context that Otago colonists frequently stressed the importance of roads as they fought against the environment to secure and retain gold seekers. And time and again, it was clear that nature was winning.[98]

CONDITIONS ON THE DIGGINGS

Upon arriving on a goldfield, diggers sometimes commented on the contrast of this 'beehive of commotion' with the seemingly endless network of hills and mountains surrounding it.[99] Gullies that weeks before were silent were now filled with the sight of calico tents glistening in the sunlight and the din of shovel in gravel and pick on rock. As night followed day, the scene was lit up with billowing smoke from campfires and the flickering glow of calico illuminated by candlelight.[100]

Yet beneath this panoramic beauty the landscape bore proof of thousands of individuals consumed by the pursuit of a metal because their society told them it was valuable. Wherever gold seekers went in the nineteenth century, natural environments were transformed by the human desire for gold. A mass of diggers in pursuit of a single mineral moulded alluvial ecosystems into sites of human industry, thereby making 'it difficult for nature itself to produce anything besides gold'.[101] Diggers in Otago came from goldfields in Victoria where the landscape was covered with craters from prospecting attempts and the streams were clogged with debris and silt.[102] From the beginning of the rushes until their end, gold seekers ripped open the earth and tossed aside tons of dirt, reshaping Otago landscapes into mirrors of their Victorian precedents. When William Smith arrived at Gabriel's Gully early in the rush, the field was still covered in grass, and he was astonished how a few weeks later 'there was no grass to be seen, as all the ground was turned over'.[103] A year after Smith arrived, the gully was covered with craters marked only by equipment and mounds of discarded earth, as depicted in Figure 3.4. On the Wakatipu the following year, reports of diggers falling down similar holes appeared weekly in the local newspaper. One digger dropped into a forty-foot shaft at Arthur's Point while on

Figure 3.4 Gabriel's Gully, 1861, Meluish. Hocken Collections, Reader Access File, 'gold mining'.

his way back to his camp one Sunday evening.[104] A week later another prospector on the Shotover fell twenty feet and split his head open on rocks at the bottom of the paddock.[105] In 1865 one digger described how the Dunstan was littered with 'great masses of excavated earth tumbled about & lying in mounds in all directions'.[106]

Diggers also had to contend with mud when rain, gold and men all converged at the same localities. Rainfall, which centuries before carried gold down into gullies, now soaked those same gullies that were swarmed by prospectors. As one gold seeker at Gabriel's Gully later recalled, diggers frequently worked ankle- or knee-deep in muddy quagmires.[107] MacLeod Orbell slept on a bed of soaked grass and manuka bark, which sank down every night into the muddy ground.[108] In November 1863, rainfall transformed the West Taieri goldfield into a 'slough of despond', though there were still a 'beery individual or two [who were] seen . . . enjoying this sea of liquid mud, with quite as much gusto as though they were luxuriating in a bath of tepid milk'.[109] As depicted in Figure 3.5, gold seekers frequently perched their camps on the side of hills in order to leave the richest ground exposed. The earth

Figure 3.5 Gabriel's Gully, 1862, taken by Frank Arnold Coxhead. Hocken Collections, P08-083.

on which these individuals relaxed, ate and slept sometimes slipped away, sliding their camp down the hill. One night in July 1863 on the Wakatipu, rainfall became deadly when John Bell and his mate were buried under a landslip.[110]

Other times it was what mixed with the mud that proved lethal. Virtually all of the problems with sewage and sanitation in Dunedin during the rushes migrated with diggers to goldfields that before had scarcely known human habitation. Prospector and merchant dumped their rubbish behind claim or shop.[111] In the summer this refuse baked under the hot sun and during a shower seeped into streams and water races that overflowed onto prospecting claims. Sickness quickly followed. The muck led to an outbreak of diarrhoea on the Tuapeka a month into the rush.[112] Hamilton McIlrath developed a fever while on the same goldfield, which caused 'the hair nearly [to come] off my head'.[113] Another man fumed that contaminated water caused diggers' hands to swell and the only relief was rubbing them with warm bullock dung.[114] In 1862 a correspondent stressing the need for a local hospital at Weatherston's described the field's deterioration:

I am sorry to say that a kind of ague or low fever has been very prevalent on the goldfields, especially at Weatherston's. Unfortunately, the site of the township of Weatherston's is little better than a swamp, and the filth which must necessarily accumulate from the collection of such a large number of men, is retained on the spot. As a necessary consequence noxious gases are evolved [and] the number of deaths from low fever have been numerous.[115]

As Stevan Eldred-Grigg notes, these sicknesses accompanied prospectors as they travelled between diggings.[116] The problems with trash and disease became so severe at Queenstown that an Improvement Committee and a Hospital Committee were established to keep the township clean and to provide for sick diggers.[117] Rheumatism and respiratory diseases were prevalent on every goldfield when individuals worked all day in water and at night slept in damp clothes on wet ground.[118] Thomas Langford's rheumatism became so severe that he took a 'powerful opiate' which 'stupefied him' enough to be arrested by Dunedin constables.[119] Again, such pollution and disease followed Victorian precedents. Across the Tasman Sea, 'the absence of any sanitary arrangements, the frequently polluted water ... and the stinking butchers' tents and slaughter-houses' spread dysentery and other diseases throughout the diggings.[120]

All this filth and rubbish brought rats. Rodents rushed to the diggings where they feasted on the trash that surrounded diggers. Most were far more successful than human prospectors. Stories circulated in Dunedin and on the diggings that there were 'rats in Hundreds as big as cats running on these ranges'.[121] John Penderick believed they survived by feasting on the corpses of diggers who died while travelling over the Carrick and Old Man Ranges.[122] When rivers froze in the winter, rats scurried into tents where there were 'often as many as 30 running about at a time'.[123] In one accommodation tent on the way to the Dunstan diggings, John and William Walker found it impossible to sleep when they heard rats scramble throughout the tent and watched them crawl over other diggers who were asleep.[124] One prospector near the Molyneux River was attacked by rats while he was in bed suffering from rheumatism. When the disease immobilised his arms, the rats gorged on his nose before he was able to frighten them away by screaming.[125] Another prospector was so 'terribly frightened' of rats that he slept inside a bag every night.[126]

Individuals took a variety of approaches to solving the rodent problem. One knife-wielding butcher in the upper Dunstan township slew sixty rats on one Saturday in 1864.[127] Another individual with a similar skill set was Queenstown's self-proclaimed 'rat-catcher', who paraded his services in the town's streets, 'hoisting up numerous specimens' for whomever passed by.[128] Fred Smith, however, had a more opportunistic response when he caught sixty rats for a 'rat pit' he established at his hotel.[129] It is perhaps understandable, then, that some diggers considered a tomcat to be the most useful domestic appliance.[130]

This filth and squalor that diggers lived in was compounded by the frequent rise and fall of the water levels throughout central Otago. Heavy rainfall or heatwaves that melted snow in the mountains would frequently flood claims, carrying off sluice boxes and tossing up crates and wheels. The ensuing drop in the waterline would leave a trail of timber, machinery and clothes, interspersed with dead rats and faecal matter, coagulating into a black, putrid sludge that covered the gold buried in the riverbank.[131] It was here in these gullies and streams that individuals set to work, viewing gold seeking as a path to riches at the same time that they wallowed in mud and filth, suffered sicknesses and dodged rats.

NATURE'S INFLUENCE

Gold seekers came to know nature through the bodily effects of their work: aching backs, sore feet, creaking joints and blistered feet.[132] If gold seekers could agree on anything as they fought with nature to obtain riches, it was that the most important – and often the most fragile – tool for gold extraction was human muscle. David Jones grumbled to his family in Wales that he often spent a day shovelling dirt only to spend the next half day washing it.[133] Daniel Calwell told his brother in Victoria that his back became so bad from digging that he was 'hardly able to get out of the tente for a weake at a strech [stretch]'.[134] Yet, because many prospectors had worked for wages in Victoria before travelling to Otago, the tangible connection between work and reward – the glittering of a few gold flakes in the bottom of a tin dish – fired the determination of prospectors across Otago, giving a 'single-minded intensity [to] those at work'.[135]

The Otago gold rushes, however, were about natural as well as human labour. The geological 'work' of the gold rushes predated human settlement in the region. Natural processes occurring over millennia formed and located gold in central Otago long before gold seekers prospected for it in a few short years during the middle of the nineteenth century. Gold in the earth's crust originated in outer space from exploded supernovas, and it later collected with other metals into meteors that bombarded the earth's crust four billion years ago.[136] Over millennia, this gold shifted, heated and cooled within the earth's crust. It surged through faults some two million years ago with superheated water that evaporated, leaving behind minerals that crystallised into quartz. Again, natural processes pushed these masses towards the surface as part of the network of hills and mountains in central Otago. Gold then was eroded by wind and water, and it collected in the bottom of rivers and creeks that simultaneously were carving out valleys and gullies throughout the region.[137] Gold lay dormant in central Otago until a few short years in the middle of the nineteenth century, when individuals rushed to the region because their society, half a world away, valued it as currency.

As diggers began prospecting for gold in Otago, they trusted nature to cooperate, yet time and again they felt betrayed when nature 'behaved according to its own rules and not theirs'.[138] Like in Victoria, patterns of work on Otago's goldfields were always dictated by natural cycles of light and dark, hot and cold, rain and drought, at a time when work in Britain was increasingly associated with the organisation of time in human-made environments.[139] As Kathryn Morse and Andrew Isenberg argue of the North American rushes, the course of gold rushes always depended on these natural environments at least as much as they did on human desire and industry.[140] Moreover, the volatility of weather patterns and the differences in topography within Otago made the gold rushes extremely uncertain events.

When the Tuapeka district was first rushed in 1861, gold deposits were very similar to those in Victoria at the beginning of its rushes. In this context, prospectors on the Tuapeka relied on gold-extraction methods they had learned in Victoria. They would strip the top layer of sediment and wash gold-bearing dirt with water, which would carry away lighter materials, leaving behind the gold.[141] After Horatio Hartley and Christopher Reilly's sensational finds in the Kawarau and Molyneux rivers, gold seekers migrated to the Dunstan goldfield in central Otago. Upon arrival, they found an environment that differed significantly from Victoria and the Tuapeka. The historian John Salmon notes that central Otago 'is one where nature knows no compromise'.[142] The region is covered by a series of hills and mountains which increase in size as they push westward. Narrow valleys trap heat in the summer and snowdrifts in the winter. The high peaks to the west prevent most moisture from reaching the region, and the arid and rocky landscape in central Otago is unable to absorb most rainfall in the summer and autumn and snow thawed at the beginning of spring. The runoff of rain and melted snow collects in a multitude of streams that flow into the three main rivers in the region: the Molyneux, the Manuherikia and the Kawarau. A downpour could quickly swell streams and rivers, submerging claims under metres of water, or a dry spell could lower water levels and expose rich alluvial deposits. Moreover, the region's weather patterns are extremely volatile, which only intensifies these changes in water level. A heavy snowfall followed by a rise in temperature could melt snow in the mountains and very quickly flood alluvial claims across central Otago.[143]

These landscapes and climates made gold seeking an extremely erratic occupation, and they constantly induced mobility when successful gold seeking depended on factors as fickle as how much rain fell the night before or how much snow melted in the mountains. When Hartley and Reilly dug up their eighty-seven pounds of gold on the Dunstan, they did so during a winter in which the Kawarau and Molyneux were at their lowest points over the decade. By the time news of their discovery reached Dunedin and the Tuapeka in August, the snow in the mountains had already begun to thaw, covering virtually all of the payable ground along the river. Many of the first parties on the field began shepherding claims that were in fact under water, and most gold seekers were simply waiting for the water level to retreat. As the English gold seeker John George Walker told his mother in 1863, 'an immense number of men have been doing nothing for months past but just live on the banks of the river and wait for it to go down'.[144] One of these men was Thomas Andrew, who told his brother and sister from the banks of the Molyneux, 'We are . . . waiting for the river to fall as far down as what it did last winter. We will have a good chance to make something but it will just depend on what sort of winter it is.'[145] Another was William Smith, who watched the river at the Lower Township surge thirty feet above a claim in which he had just purchased a £50 share.[146] As the geographer James Forrest demonstrates, in the dual contexts of flooded claims and overpopulated goldfields, diggers in Otago regularly took part in a series of summer rushes in nearby flats and creeks, while they returned to abandoned river claims in the winter months.[147] These environmental dynamics counteract Stevan Eldred-Grigg's contention that the mobility of gold seekers arose out of an innate restlessness rather than environmental contexts.[148]

As diggers pushed farther west into the Wakatipu basin, more extreme topographies and climates were even more at odds with individuals' Victorian experience, magnifying the rushes' volatility. Steeper grades and narrower gorges carved out by the Shotover River meant higher and more changeable water levels (see Figure 3.6). Meanwhile, the more treacherous terrain also meant that goldfields like Moke Creek and

Figure 3.6 Shotover River, date and author unknown. Hocken Collections, Reader Access File, 'gold mining'.

Skipper's Canyon were easily cut off from Queenstown during floods and blizzards.[149] While gold seekers on the Tuapeka had constantly bemoaned the muddiness of the field, diggers on the Dunstan and Wakatipu had to contend with steeper grades and rockier terrain that could quickly flood canyons rushed by diggers.

The low water levels during the winter months also tended to encourage gold seeking during the most dangerous season of the year. As a correspondent for the *Otago Daily Times* stated in February 1863, prospectors on the Dunstan were 'as thoroughly determined to make the attempt of realising in the brief hour the results of a lifetime', even though everyone agreed that some would die before spring.[150] That July, John Penderick was snowed in on a claim at Pomahaka Creek, where he worried that 'we shall soon have to eat some roasted rats'.[151] Another problem was that no one knew exactly when seasons would change and for how long. A freak snowstorm in October 1862 cut off supply to Campbell's Gully, and two hundred diggers there, buried under a metre of snow, were forced to survive on snow and roots that caused diarrhoea and vomiting.[152] An unexpectedly heavy rainfall at the Lakes District in August of the following year drowned thirty-seven gold seekers in three days, and diggers on the Dunstan who sat idly on their flooded claims watched at least one body float by on its way to the sea.[153]

Too little water could be detrimental. There were also many forms of gold extraction that required a continual supply of water. The development of sluicing claims on the Dunstan depended on high water levels in the Kawarau and Molyneux rivers.[154] At the Hogburn, dry spells evaporated water races and froze cradles and long toms. This dried up credit and induced many prospectors to abandon the goldfield. Some diggers with wives and children were unable to migrate and their families were reduced to destitution.[155]

There were also more hazardous effects of dry spells. In Victoria during the 1850s, prospectors frequently burned away scrub and grass to clear ground for prospecting.[156] Bush fires on the Victorian diggings were frequent when dry northerly winds and dense vegetation combined to 'brew a deadly chemistry of air and fuel'.[157] While the sparseness of vegetation in central Otago lessened the threat of bushfire in the province, the centrality of fire in goldfield life meant that bushfires still occurred occasionally. Throughout the rushes, gold seekers depended on fire for light, heat and fuel for cooking. After a cold day of wading knee-deep in water, fire was a welcome relief and a means of drying one's clothes. For diggers who worked from dawn to dusk, it also provided them with the ability to count and distribute gold, write letters, read a newspaper or novel, or simply relax. This became especially important for diggers working in isolated gullies on the Dunstan and Wakatipu diggings, some of which never received sunlight in the dead of winter. However, in such circumstances, these valleys also functioned as open vents that funnelled wind. Essentially the same topography that caused gold deposits to gather in the bottom of gullies also sometimes transformed those gullies into furnaces, and the collection of wind and gold proved a lethal cocktail. John Moffatt awoke one night to find the ridges above his claim ablaze, and he spent the next several hours protecting the claim from the onrush of the flames.[158] Another digger at Skipper's Canyon was awoken by his dog when a bush fire engulfed the hillside and was rapidly approaching his camp.[159] Fire was central to goldfield life, whether for cooking, warmth or relaxation; yet even in the coldest months it was not always welcomed.

More than any other hardship, diggers from sunny Victoria complained about the cold in Otago. Because the temperatures in Victoria rarely fell below freezing, few diggers had experience in winter prospecting before their arrival in Otago. The fall in water levels during the winter in Otago often induced diggers to remain in the province during the harshest time of the year. Rivers froze over and strong winds created snowdrifts which would resemble 'the waves of the sea', covering prospecting holes into which diggers would frequently fall.[160] When John Penderick was lost in a thick fog on the way back to Campbell's Gully, he waded knee-deep in snow for hours until he found his camp.[161] John Moffatt had to thaw his boots over a fire when they were too stiff to put on.[162] Moreover, again in contrast to Victoria, the land in Otago near the goldfields lacked enough firewood to meet the needs of the population that rushed across it. When wood was absent on the Tuapeka, William Smith had to use cow dung for fuel.[163] In 1862 J. H. Watmuff noted that the roots growing in rocky crevices were the only source of fuel on the Dunstan.[164] A year later, the absence of fuel forced a desperate Thomas McCourt to burn his bedding in order to boil a pot of tea.[165] All across the diggings, gold seekers struggled to keep warm as they wrote in their diaries and letters home about the frigid conditions on their claims. In 1862 John Brown told his parents that he left the Tuapeka after a brief and disastrous period digging when 'the whether [was] bad stormey and we*a*t and we wair [*were*] *h*allways exploaring for gold, camping in whet from one plases [*place*] to another'.[166] Two years later, William Jones told his sister in Bangor, Wales, that 'this place is not fit to be liven in tents. The wethere is to [*too*] severe. There is a great many popel lainress with colds fever [*word illegible*] and rumate ... and [*word illegible*] been freis [*freezing*] to death.'[167] John Moffatt spent more time discussing the location of firewood than gold deposits.[168] Even the Otago prospector, Lachlan McDonald, who first left the harsh conditions on the Isle of Tiree in the Scottish Hebrides for Victoria, thought it was easier to work on 'the slopes of Beinn-Cheanu-a-Mhara' than Waipori in winter.[169] All this cold was intensified by living under thin canvas that could not retain heat. For David Jones the contrast between frigid Otago and sunny Victoria was easily apparent:

> The winter is really cold, and we have to live without much fire and we see it strange to live in such a poor country after being use to live in a country where fine material is so plentiful as Victoria, therefore this county is not going to win my regard, but I intend to stay this winter as much as I know at present.[170]

Yet, despite the harsh terrain, the frigid climate and the scarcity of firewood, diggers continued to come, forsaking for a period the relative comfort of Victoria in hopes of riches won in Otago.

VICTORIAN PRACTICES AND OTAGO ENVIRONMENTS

When the 'productive' work of gold seeking was always given prominence over domestic tasks like cooking and shopping, the cultures that crystallised in these hills and gullies had much to do with these natural environments and the tools and muscle diggers employed to cleave gold from the interior of this province. Moreover, the methods of gold recovery that individuals transplanted from Victoria or adopted in response to local conditions required cooperation between gold seekers, making work practices profoundly social.

As stated above, gold deposits on the Tuapeka resembled those found on most of the goldfields in Victoria from which prospectors migrated. In the first year of the rush, the procurable gold on the Tuapeka was eroded from adjacent hills and spurs and buried in dried-up streams under metres of sediment. Gold seekers relied on one basic characteristic of gold: its weight. Because gold was heavier than almost every material it was found with, it was more resistant to water currents and tended to collect at the bottom of hills when other eroded materials were carried downstream. Most prospectors similarly used water flow to separate gold from lighter materials. In this, knowledge of gold seeking did not simply migrate only from Victoria but travelled with gold seekers who rushed across North America and the Pacific Ocean throughout the second half of the century. From Georgia in 1828 to the Klondike in 1898, the basic methods of gold sifting at the beginning of a rush changed very little on Australasian and North American goldfields.[171] Moreover, when these methods of gold collection depended upon cooperation among a small group of prospectors, pre-existing social structures were transplanted in Otago. Even among those who migrated alone or left a prospecting party, very few diggers ever worked alone when both custom and environment required cooperation between prospectors.

On the Tuapeka in 1861, prospecting parties would first dig for 'colour', which might indicate a larger gold deposit. If gold was found in sufficient quantities, a party would peg off its claim and seek legal protection for the ground from the local warden. The party would then clear a paddock. Once the gold-bearing dirt was exposed, one or two diggers would shovel it into a bucket, which would be counterbalanced and attached to a pole. Another member of the party would pull up a bucket and cart it to a stream where a fourth digger submerged the gold-bearing dirt in a pan and sifted out the soil, leaving behind the gold in the bottom of the pan.[172] The following year, gold seekers on the

Tuapeka increasingly used two tools from California and Victoria – the cradle and the long tom – to more efficiently wash gold-bearing dirt.

While the basic tools of gold sifting – the pan, cradle and long tom – always remained constant, the particular means of gold discovery depended on geology, topography and proximity to water. In their respective studies of the Victorian gold rushes, Geoffrey Serle and Geoffrey Blainey argue that when surface deposits diminished, gold-seeking parties frequently pooled their capital and manpower into cooperative mining companies in order to extract gold that was more difficult to obtain.[173] This social practice of cooperation was also manifested during the Otago gold rushes. As diggers migrated to the Dunstan, Wakatipu and Upper Taieri goldfields, they discovered new environments that required new methods for locating gold. On these newer fields, deposits often resembled those in California or British Columbia, where gold collected in the bottom of streams and could only be prospected during dry seasons when the water level was low. Diggers frequently pooled their capital to turn the course of a river in order to prospect its bed. A party that turned six hundred yards of the Arrow River began prospecting the riverbed early in 1863.[174] The same year, another party purchased five hundred bags of sand to turn the course of the Shotover River.[175] At the Shotover, parties constructed dams made from crates filled with gravel and laced together with rope. They were then plugged with scrub and braced by poles which were fastened with bullock hide.[176]

Moreover, Otago diggers had to contend with a greater scarcity of water than in Victoria. As gold seekers grappled with inconsistent water levels on the Dunstan and Wakatipu goldfields and depleted deposits at the Tuapeka, prospectors fanned out into adjacent gullies farther from water sources. Gold recovery techniques then began to evolve as diggers became more dependent on the conveyance of water over greater distances. Because water had been much more available on the Victorian diggings, gold seekers instead drew on Californian precedents as they responded to local environments. Especially on the southern Californian diggings, where water was unprocurable for most of the year, some prospectors found greater wealth in supplying water to diggers than looking for gold themselves.[177] At Weatherston's on the Tuapeka, diggers contracted carters to convey gold-bearing dirt to nearby streams at a costly 5s per cartload. When the wealth of a claim was only relative to the cost of extracting and washing the gold-bearing dirt, conflicts quickly arose between diggers and carters over the price of a load.[178] In order to lower the cost of washing (and make a substantial profit), James Gascoigne, a digger with Californian experience, spent £14,000 with his mates erecting a water race, which conveyed water directly to a claim and reduced the cost to £1–5 per day, based on its use.[179]

As water became more procurable, a natural consequence was the transition to other forms of washing. Parties came to rely on a sluice box, which was a twenty-foot wooden chute lined with a tussock with a porous board placed loosely on top. A steady flow of water would carry wash dirt over the board and the gold would fall through the holes and into the tussock. Gold was extracted from the tussock by rocking the debris left behind and the tussock would be burned and the ashes rocked for any remaining gold.[180] Sluicing could be a very expensive operation and gold-seeking parties sometimes consolidated into companies in order to utilise their combined capital and muscle. Near the end of 1863, the Waitahuna Sluicing Company cut a fourteen-mile race to bring water to their sluicing claim and burrowed two hundred yards through a dividing range.[181] By this point the sounds of cradles rocking and water splashing from gold pans was muffled across the Tuapeka by the din of water rushing through water races and sluice heads.

As prospectors travelled across central Otago in search of gold, they were faced with ecological conditions that were different from those experienced in Victoria. Yet the ways in which diggers responded to these new environments repeatedly relied upon previous experiences in and social practices from Victoria. Identities and societies, therefore, were not simply the products of environmental conditions in Otago; rather, both were processes that drew upon Victorian precedents and contemporary Otago environments.

COMMUNITIES AND CONFLICTS

When success in gold seeking often depended on cooperation, prospecting parties were sometimes extremely organised. From the moment a party arrived on a field, they set about like clockwork, dividing tasks like gathering firewood or tussock, cooking, or setting out for supplies.[182] They were also often formed spontaneously. One party was formed in an Invercargill pub one evening in 1863 by ten diggers intent on prospecting in Fiordland. The group purchased a vessel, which they christened the 'Nugget', and sailed up the west coast of the South Island. Along the way, they divided tasks based upon the skills of each of the mates. A carpenter, joiner and tentmaker in the ship's complement regularly performed repairs on the vessel, while other diggers spent their time hunting, fishing and cooking. One digger caught a shark, from which he produced oil for a binnacle lamp, while another digger salted cod the party also caught. The diary ends after failed prospecting ventures around Milford Sound, and the party sailed up the West Coast to the Haast River.[183] Few parties probably possessed this same degree of organisation, but all personal accounts of the rushes indicate that diggers always depended on each other for success in gold seeking.[184]

Bonds between gold seekers were not always simply relationships of utility. Stevan Eldred-Grigg and Jock Phillips both argue that the daily slog of shovelling and panning dirt and the absence of women together created strong bonds between diggers who worked together.[185] The responses of diggers to death, injury and sickness from the Otago diggings support these scholars' claims of strong bonds between digging partners. An analysis of individuals' responses to personal tragedy is especially illuminating because goldfield society, like every society, 'gauges and assesses itself in some way by its system of death'.[186]

A gold seeker, weakened by malnutrition and labours, still risked death and injury in order to stake out lucrative claims. Diggers on the Shotover always faced the threat of landslips when they camped below soft-rock slate that was prone to landslips.[187] One digger named Jarvis was crushed beneath a rockfall while working on his claim in 1863.[188] It took fifty diggers twenty minutes to dig out Joseph Cooper when he was buried on his claim.[189] The toes fell off another digger's foot that was crushed on a sluicing claim on the Kawarau in 1864.[190] River crossings were especially dangerous. Near Maori Point, a hollowed-out tree was used to convey diggers across the Shotover River.[191] One digger drowned when his boat toppled in the Kawarau River.[192]

Such events of injury and death were frequently witnessed by mates whose lives were twisted together by daily routines of work and leisure and shared experiences of excitement and disappointment. From the riverbank Bengt Frykberg watched hopelessly as his son drowned before his eyes.[193] When one prospector on the way to the Arrow fell down a chasm, his mates watched him die slowly over thirty hours, unable to reach him.[194] After a flood on the Wakatipu in 1863, William Naylor was forced to identify the decaying corpse of his deceased mate, John Donoghue.[195]

Prospectors often went to great lengths to care for sick and injured mates. When John Moffatt's party heard that their mate was taken ill with diarrhoea at Arrowtown, they immediately left their claim at Twelve Mile to care for him.[196] When a Danish prospector, Charles Morgan, was crushed by a boulder at Kawarau Gorge in December 1863, his mates carried him twenty-three miles to the Dunstan hospital, where he died five days later.[197] When, two months later, a digger was crushed to death on his claim, his mates carried him to the cemetery because they did not have enough money to pay for a proper burial.[198]

The fragility of life on the goldfields helped to establish a sense of community beyond the mining party, as miners were apt to care for strangers with whom they competed for gold. The gold rushes created a 'collective return to primary experience' for prospectors who together and individually struggled against nature to secure gold, who trudged over mountains with heavy swags thrown over their backs or waded in rivers in the dead of winter, risking everything for a few specks of gold.[199] Prospectors who rushed over ranges or prospected along riverbanks sometimes found corpses of other individuals who perished in pursuit of gold. Especially after floods, diggers watched decaying corpses float by their claims while they swirled gold on the riverbanks.[200] The bodies lining gully floors which diggers passed on the road from Invercargill to Wakatipu provided a jarring contrast to the golden riches that filled many travellers' thoughts.[201] Within this context, prospectors laid down gold and coin for the care and burial of individuals they did not know. In the first few months of the Tuapeka rush, many diggers generously donated to establish a hospital on the diggings for the care of diggers suffering from fractures or rheumatism.[202] When a party of Māori diggers came across an isolated hut on the Shotover River full of bedridden diggers, suffering from scurvy, relief committees were established at Arthur's Point, Arrowtown and Frankton, collecting over £175 for their care.[203] After John Love and George Hyde died during a blizzard atop the Old Man Range in 1863, a funeral procession in the Lower Township, widely attended by diggers, shopkeepers and publicans, escorted his body to the local cemetery.[204] There were certainly limits to this charity. When James Strachan noticed that there were less than two dozen people at another funeral for a man who died at Waitahuna, he commented that 'so indifferent does the rush after gold make people'.[205] Nevertheless, contemporary newspapers and personal accounts from the diggings push against Miles Fairburn's argument that social bonding on the goldfields was 'gravely deficient'.[206]

Close relationships between diggers also sometimes created problems. Most moments of friction surfaced between diggers with different ideas of how much work was enough and when to do it. William Martin complained that although his party made £64 per day, most of his mates worked little and spent the party's earnings on liquor.[207] John Henry Watmuff grumbled in his diary that his two mates disappeared for three days on a spree, leaving him to work alone on their claim.[208] Two diggers in MacLeod Orbell's prospecting party were so 'utterly useless' that they were made to do the cooking.[209] Occasionally, conflicts turned violent. Thomas Whitehead and David Stewart came to blows when Whitehead accused his mate of stealing his cash. After a scuffle, Whitehead picked up an axe and hacked his skull, splitting it six inches and spilling out his brains.[210] Near Conroy's diggings, Daniel Clifford may have murdered his mate for a similar reason.[211] Theft could also occur between diggers who worked together. When a gold seeker named 'Burnett' fell into gambling debt, he began stealing gold from his party's collective purse.[212] However, such violence and theft within gold-seeking parties were rare. As Jock Phillips argues, 'loyalty and protection' characterised the relationship between mates who shared trials and joys.[213] Even when warm sentiment was absent between diggers, the lack of anonymity within prospecting groups usually dissuaded all but the most desperate.

Beyond the gold-seeking party, crime was more common when the speed of the rushes and the itinerancy of their participants more easily concealed offenders. Theft occurred often enough when hundreds of pounds of gold lay across central Otago under mattresses, in pockets and in unlocked boxes. The eccentric Henry Garrett and seven associates robbed fifteen gold-laden travellers on the Waipori Road in 1861.[214] There were also several hold-ups on the Hogburn and Taieri goldfields in 1863. When constables came across a group of bushrangers camping near the Taieri Road, the affair turned violent when one officer was stabbed through the mouth and tongue with a pair of scissors.[215] When one thief robbed a digger named Bailey at gunpoint, he left with a bow and a sincere apology.[216]

Pickpocketing, hidden by darkness or clouded by booze, was even more common. More than a few diggers who passed out in public houses and on streets complained that they woke up a few ounces lighter. Money and a miner's right were stolen from William Trudgen one evening after he passed out in a public house on the Dunstan. A watch was lifted from an intoxicated James Dallas by a watchmaker who invited him, very drunk, back to his house.[217] On the Wakatipu, John Walton stole cash from the pocket of William Williams after the latter passed out on the side of the road.[218]

Sometimes these crimes turned violent. In 1863 one packer known as Yorkie was beaten with a pickaxe so severely that he was beyond recognition.[219] In the winter of 1862, John Fratson murdered Andrew Wilson, this time with a razor, axe and blunt object. Fratson then tossed the body into the Molyneux, where it was found in advanced decomposition weeks later. The head and neck bore numerous axe marks and the coroner noted during the inquest that he had 'never seen such butchery'.[220] There were likely other crimes committed in remote gullies across Otago. The body of one gold seeker floated for six days in a river in the Lakes District in 1863. The skull was crushed with a blunt object, there were fourteen cuts on the face, numerous kick wounds and the scalp was removed.[221]

In spite of these occurrences, murder was rare. Claim jumping, however, especially in the first weeks of a rush, was common. In newspapers and personal accounts, physical scuffles over claims were sometimes described in ethnic terms when ethnic identification rarely surfaced elsewhere on the diggings. The Irish especially were labelled as offenders. A two-hour fight erupted on Boxing Day 1861 between two groups of Cornish and Irish prospectors.[222] William Smith's party was forced off their claim by a group of Irish diggers: 'It was a case of club law and the survival of the fittest', he later remembered.[223] John Henry Watmuff and his mates got into a scuffle with 'a wild lot of Irishmen with a few Spaniards and Italians'.[224] One resident of the Wakatipu district believed that the Irish population formed a secret society, 'with headquarters, scouts, spies and heads to direct various movements', which orchestrated a coordinated conspiracy for jumping claims on the goldfields.[225] While ethnic conflict remained marginal on the goldfields, as demonstrated by Lyndon Fraser, diggers sometimes fell back on cultural stereotypes of the Irish as they fought with each other for gold located in nature.[226]

Despite the sensationalised accounts in the newspapers and more recent scholarship, murders and armed robberies were scarce on the diggings apart from the first weeks of a rush, as demonstrated by Wayne Angus and Marianne van der Voorn.[227] It may be true, as Tom Brooking contends, that gold miners in Otago had a greater interest than their Victorian and Californian counterparts in community building and maintaining order because they were usually older than participants in earlier rushes.[228] Alternatively, as Erik Olssen argues, the relative pervasiveness of order on the diggings could have been attributed to effective management of the goldfields by the Provincial Government.[229] While a thorough analysis of crime is beyond the scope of this chapter, more work certainly needs to be done before a clearer image of lawlessness on the Otago diggings can be drawn.[230]

As surface deposits began to evaporate, most diggers did not resort to crime but instead pooled their resources to prospect more difficult claims, thereby extending social networks from a small group of three or four diggers to a larger party of ten or more members. This shift towards larger gold-seeking parties mirrored developments in Victoria. In the early 1850s, most diggers in Victoria operated in small prospecting parties, but by the end of the decade many either worked in cooperative companies or were employed by a mining company.[231] The practice of forming cooperative companies was transplanted almost seamlessly in Otago. In January 1862, the Waitahuna Mining Association was formed at a public meeting to prospect for deep sinking prospects.[232] A month later, twenty-eight men established the Ballarat Sluicing Company to turn the course of the Waipori River.[233] By March there was also a joint stock company mining for coal near Gabriel's Gully.[234] Companies became even more prevalent on the Dunstan, where a huge amount of capital was invested to turn the course of rivers. In December 1862, the Grand Junction Company and the Manuherikia Company were formed to prospect near Fraser's River.[235] Four months later, the Nil Desperandum Gold Mining Company was also established by fifty-four diggers to turn the river nine miles above the Lower Township.[236] Within a month of the Arrow River rush, a joint stock company was formed by fifty prospectors to systematically prospect the flat adjacent the river.[237]

In a largely open society, communities and conflicts on the goldfields rarely broke along ethnic lines. Newspapers occasionally referenced mining parties by ethnicity, but first-hand accounts of the rushes indicate that these were likely migrants from the same neighbourhood or family.[238] There is no evidence in the diaries, letters or reminiscences of prospectors seeking out members of their ethnic group. Prospectors usually sought out mates based on kinship or expediency. Apart from the occasional row over a mining claim – such as a brawl between Irish and Cornish miners in 1863 – conflicts often were not ethnic in nature.[239]

Drawing on Victorian experiences, goldfield communities often crystalised around practical concerns like water conveyance, mining claims and road construction, all of which instilled a strong sense of localism on the goldfields. Gold seeking, whether in North America or Australasia, was a heavily regulated occupation, as colonies, states and territories attempted – often unsuccessfully – to keep gold and gold miners from departing. The regulation of the goldfields also politicised mining communities. Several scholars argue that prospectors in the California hills and the Rocky Mountains displayed a penchant for political organising.[240] On the Victorian goldfields, this political culture drew heavily from Chartism in Britain. Geoffrey Serle and David Goodman both observe that Victorian prospectors often came from the ranks of Chartists in Britain or were at least sympathetic to the movement's political organisation.[241] Miners sympathetic to Chartism were among those who joined the Victorian rush to Otago. Chartism on the Otago goldfields entangled the social, economic, environmental and political aspects of the rushes. As miners arrived with Victorian experiences and fought with nature to secure gold, they complained about the Provincial Government's corrupt management of the goldfields. In doing so, they identified 'a political solution to distress and a political diagnosis of its causes'.[242]

Prospectors in Otago criticised what they saw as an unethical and unjust management of the goldfields. In 1862 the province repealed the gold miners' ability to vote for the province's superintendent and increased the period of residency required to vote from three to six months. Moreover, while new electoral seats were established, their number did not reflect the number of residents on the goldfields, and the time it took to travel to the place of registration made it impractical for miners.[243] In order to maintain law and order, as well as effectively manage the goldfields, the Provincial Government installed a goldfields commissioner, who in turn appointed wardens as administrators and judicial officials on each goldfield. Without adequate political representation or input on the management of the goldfields, gold miners demanded that 'the mines ought not to be considered merely as a source of wealth to Dunedin, the miners ought to be considered [for] they have equal right to good legislation with any other class of the community'.[244] They criticised the Provincial Government as 'large landowners in Dunedin' who trivialised gold seekers as a means of wealth rather than contributors to the province through their labour.[245]

In the midst of perceived injustice, gold seekers consistently stressed their allegiance to the Crown and the colonial government, as well as petitioning, which was their 'only constitutional method of obtaining redress'.[246] A multitude of public meetings were held on almost every field and a mass of petitions were submitted every year to the Provincial Government.[247] In an economy that depended on the easy and cheap movement of people, knowledge and supplies, the loudest outcry was usually over the state of the roads to the diggings.[248] In 1863 the miners of the Lakes District submitted a petition to the governor, requesting his direct oversight of the goldfields due to the mismanagement of the goldfields by the province. The size of the petition became a particular source of pride for the gold-mining community. It was not simply a list of complaints against the Provincial Government; rather, it manifested for its signatories 'a unified (popular body), confronting the corrupt authority in power, and demanding a restoration of the people's rights'.[249] Moreover, as James Vernon notes, newspapers became a central vehicle for portraying an active local political culture that resembled the procedure, language and behaviour of the British Parliament.[250] Minutes and notices of public meetings were printed in the newspapers, speeches were transcribed, and comments were made by correspondents who 'never saw or attended a more orderly meeting'.[251] Editorials deployed constitutional rhetoric that framed local political issues within the language of ancient rights and the 'characteristic of the Anglo-Saxon'.[252] Petitions and newspapers 'both symbolically and practically ... endowed the politically excluded with a sense of dignity and agency denied them by the official political process'.[253]

All this is not to argue that the social sphere possessed absolute community cohesion. Arguments between parties often erupted on claims and in courtrooms. Yet the ways in which diggers transformed landscapes also helped to shape social relations. Throughout the gold rushes and across every goldfield, diggers allied themselves with individuals with whom they pooled their earnings, or shared interests or methods of prospecting. In June 1863, a group of gold seekers on the Arrow River sued a party of Italian prospectors for damages when the Italians' water race flooded adjacent claims.[254] On the Tuapeka, parties working in the gullies frequently protested against terrace prospectors who hurled their tailings into the gully, covering claims and clogging waterways.[255] Moreover, nature created its own havoc in digging communities, resulting in ensuing social conflict. Warden's Court hearings often followed the changes in water levels. A rise in rivers would wipe away boundaries between claims. Diggers packed into the courthouse on the Tuapeka in 1862 when a flood wiped out most claim markers across the district.[256] The following year, two gold seekers sued for damages in Arrowtown when a flood demolished another party's dam and submerged their claim under water.[257] When the Molyneux fell rapidly early in 1863, prospectors rushed to the Warden's Court to secure claims along the river's edge.[258] What is important here to note is that in almost every way that diggers fought, they reasserted the centrality of the social, allying with some diggers as they fought with others. The evidence that litigation and fisticuffs were more often between parties than between individuals casts doubt on Miles Fairburn's assertion that conflict necessarily inferred atomisation.[259]

CONCLUSION

As the environmental historian Arthur McEvoy forcefully argues, studies that do not analyse the 'inter-embeddedness and reciprocal constitution' of ecology, production, culture and society run the risk of only telling part of the story and thereby misidentifying historical causes.[260] This chapter has explored the importance of these multiple characteristics of place in determining the shape and course of the Otago gold rushes. The chapter has also conceived of place spatially, stressing the ways in which cultures, networks and societies in Otago cannot be separated from their Victorian roots. Here the findings of this chapter align closely with Lyndon Fraser's and Philip Ross May's analysis on the interplay between Victorian origins and local social and economic dynamics on the West Coast goldfields.[261] These local conditions and Victorian paths were always entangled when individuals responded to new environments in Otago by drawing on Victorian experiences and social structures that repeatedly emphasised cooperation and community cohesion.

Just as the social, the cultural, the economic and the environmental cannot be separated, work and leisure were mutually constitutive on the diggings. Like the ways in which gold seekers worked, the ways in which they played directed social life inward at the relationships and communities they were forming in these gullies and flats of central Otago. Yet, again like work practices, these modes of leisure drew from cultures and networks in Victoria and the United Kingdom. This will be the subject of the following chapter.

NOTES

1. Erik Olssen, 'Lands of Sheep and Gold: The Australian Dimension to the New Zealand Past', in Keith Sinclair (ed.), *Tasman Relations: New Zealand and Australia, 1788–1988* (Auckland: University of Auckland Press, 1987), 36.
2. David Goodman, *Gold Seeking: Victoria and California in the 1850s* (Stanford: Stanford University Press, 1994), xiii; Douglas Fetherling, *The Gold Crusades: A Social History of Gold Rushes, 1849–1929* (Toronto: University of Toronto Press, 1997). Also see Jeremy Mouat, 'After California: Later Gold Rushes of the Pacific Basin', in Kenneth N. Owens (ed.), *Riches for All: The California Gold Rush and the World* (Lincoln, NE and London: University of Nebraska Press, 2002), 263–95; William Parker Morrell, *The Gold Rushes* (London: Macmillan Company, 1941); Donald Denoon, Philippa Mein Smith and Marivic Wyndham, *A History of Australia, New Zealand and the Pacific: The Formation of Identities*

(Oxford and Malden: Blackwell Publishers, 2000), 140–58; John Milton Hutchins, *Diggers, Constables and Bushrangers: The New Zealand Gold Rushes as a Frontier Experience, 1852–1878* (Lakewood: Avrooman-Apfelwald Press, 2010); Stevan Eldred-Grigg, *Diggers, Hatters and Whores: The Story of the New Zealand Gold Rushes* (Auckland: Random House, 2008).

3. Miles Fairburn, *The Ideal Society and Its Enemies: The Foundation of Modern New Zealand Society, 1850–1900* (Auckland: Auckland University Press, 1989); Jock Phillips, *A Man's Country?: The Image of the Pakeha Male, a History*, 2nd edn (Auckland: Penguin Books, 1996).
4. William Cronon, *Changes in the Land: Indians, Colonists, and the Ecology of New England* (New York: Hill and Wang, 2003), 13.
5. I am influenced here by Arthur F. McEvoy, 'Towards an Interactive Theory of Nature and Culture: Ecology, Production and Cognition in the California Fishing Industry', in Donald Worster (ed.), *The Ends of the Earth: Perspectives on Modern Environmental History* (New York: Cambridge University Press, 1988), 211–29.
6. Kathryn Morse, *The Nature of Gold: An Environmental History of the Klondike Gold Rush* (Seattle: University of Washington Press, 2003), 6–8.
7. I am here influenced by Richard White, *The Organic Machine: The Remaking of the Columbia River* (New York: Macmillan, 2011), ix–x.
8. Quotation is from Susan Lee Johnson, *Roaring Camp: The Social World of the California Gold Rush* (New York: W. W. Norton and Company, 2000), 103. Also see Brian Roberts, *American Alchemy: The California Gold Rush and Middle-Class Culture* (Chapel Hill: University of North Carolina Press, 2000).
9. David Goodman, 'Making an Edgier History of Gold', in Iain McCalman, Alexander Cook, and Andrew Reeves (eds), *Gold: Forgotten Histories and Lost Objects of Australia* (Cambridge: Cambridge University Press, 2001), 23.
10. Paula Mitchell Marks, *Precious Dust: The American Gold Rush Era, 1848–1900* (New York: William Morrow and Co., 1994); Kevin Starr, *Americans and the California Dream, 1850–1915* (New York: Oxford University Press, 1973); Goodman, *Gold Seeking*; H. W. Brands, *The Age of Gold: The California Gold Rush and the New American Dream* (New York: Doubleday, 2002); Geoffrey Serle, *The Golden Age: A History of the Colony of Victoria, 1851–1861* (Melbourne: Melbourne University Press, 1963); Ralph Mann, *After the Gold Rush: Society in Grass Valley and Nevada City, California, 1849–1870* (Palo Alto: Stanford University Press, 1982).
11. Earl Pomeroy, *The Pacific Slope: A History of California, Oregon, Washington, Idaho, Utah, and Nevada*, 3rd edn (Reno: University of Nevada Press, 2003), 50–1.
12. Lyndon Fraser, *Castles of Gold: A History of New Zealand's West Coast*

Irish (Dunedin: Otago University Press, 2007), 77–8. Also see Philip Ross May, *The West Coast Gold Rushes*, 2nd edn (Christchurch: Pegasus Press, 1967), especially 121–5.

13. This argument follows from Phillip Gleason's conception of identity as a lifelong process despite frequent mobility. See Philip Gleason, 'Identifying Identity: A Semantic History', *The Journal of American History* 69, no. 4 (1983): especially 913–14, 917.
14. Barbara Rosenwein, 'Worrying About Emotions in History', *American Historical Review* 107, no. 3 (2002): 842.
15. Phillips, *A Man's Country*, 10–37.
16. Fairburn, *The Ideal Society*.
17. Phillips, *A Man's Country*.
18. Goodman, *Gold Seeking*; Fetherling, *The Gold Crusades*; Morrell, *The Gold Rushes*; Roberts, *American Alchemy*; Marks, *Precious Dust*; Eldred-Grigg, *Diggers, Hatters and Whores*.
19. Adele Perry, *On the Edge of Empire: Gender, Race, and the Making of British Columbia, 1849–1871* (Toronto: University of Toronto Press, 2001), 38.
20. Roberts, *American Alchemy*, 7. Also see Johnson, *Roaring Camp*; Marks, *Precious Dust*; Fetherling, *The Gold Crusades*.
21. J. H. M. Salmon, *A History of Goldmining in New Zealand* (Wellington: Government Printer, 1963), 17–18.
22. John George Walker (Dunstan) to 'Fred', 4 January 1863, Walker Letters.
23. Marks, *Precious Dust*, 171.
24. Robert B. Booth, *Five Years in New Zealand* (London: J. G. Hammond and Co., 1912), 55.
25. John Garrett (Dunedin) to his brother, Joseph Garrett, 31 October 1862, OSM, DC 2670.
26. Charles D. Ferguson, *The Experiences of a Forty-Niner During Thirty-Four Years' Residence in California and Australia* (Cleveland, OH: Williams Publishing Company, 1888), 157.
27. Watmuff, diary, 18 January 1863 [3/51].
28. Alexander McKay (Hamiltons, Otago) to his brother, Robert McKay (Carsphairn, Scotland), 10 April 1864, Alexander McKay papers, ATL, MS-Papers 4409-1.
29. Starr, *Americans and the California Dream, 1850–1915*, 50.
30. Perry, *On the Edge of Empire*; Roberts, *American Alchemy*; Johnson, *Roaring Camp*; Marks, *Precious Dust*; Patricia Nelson Limerick, *The Legacy of Conquest: The Unbroken Past of the American West* (New York and London: W. W. Norton and Company, 1987).
31. Serle, *The Golden Age*, 374.
32. Donna Hellier, '"The Humblies": Scottish Highland Migration into Nineteenth Century Victoria', in Patricia Grimshaw, Chris McConville and Ellen McEwen (eds), *Families in Colonial Australia* (Sydney: Unwin

Hyman, 1985), 10. For similar conclusions, see Geoffrey Blainey, *The Rush That Never Ended: A History of Australian Mining*, 4th edn (Melbourne: Melbourne University Press, 1993); Chris McConville, 'The Victorian Irish: Emigrants and Families, 1851–91', in Patricia Grimshaw, Chris McConville and Ellen McEwen (eds), *Families in Colonial Australia* (Sydney: Allen and Unwin, 1985), 1–8; Barry McGowan, 'The Working Miners of Southern New South Wales: Adaptability, Class and Identity', *Australasian Mining History Journal* 1, no. 1 (2003): 95–109.

33. Fraser, *Castles of Gold*, 37; Terry Hearn, 'Scots Miners in the Goldfields, 1861–1870', in Tom Brooking and Jennie Coleman (eds), *The Heather and the Fern: Scottish Migration and New Zealand Settlement* (Dunedin: Otago University Press, 2003), 67–86.
34. *Otago Daily Times*, 13 November 1862.
35. Daniel Calwell (Kawarau Junction, Otago) to Davis Calwell (Victoria), 17 March 1862, SLV, MS 11492. Also see Hamilton McIlrath (Rangiora, Canterbury) to his father, mother and brothers (Balloo, Ireland), 12 August 1862; Angela Hannah McCarthy, in '"Seas May Divide": Irish Migration to New Zealand as Portrayed in Personal Correspondence, 1840–1937' (PhD thesis, Trinity College, Dublin, 2000), 207; Andrew Roy (Southland) to his sister (Catharine Roy), 26 September 1863, Andrew Roy Letters, OSM, DC-0683; Archibald Henderson (Dunedin) to his brother and sister (Scotland), 4 November 1860, Archibald Henderson Letters, OSM, DC-2399; David Jones (Otago) to his family (Wales), 10 August 1862, Jones Family Letters, ATL, MS-Papers-6249.
36. Salmon, *A History of Goldmining*, 108–10.
37. James Gascoigne, 'Adventures of a Norfolk Boy', OSM, DC-0483.
38. James Belich, *Reforging Paradise: A History of the New Zealanders from the 1880s to the Year 2000* (Auckland: Penguin Press, 2001), 71.
39. Archibald Henderson (Patea) to his niece (Scotland?), 2 December 1869, OSM, DC 2399.
40. Eldred-Grigg, *Diggers, Hatters and Whores*, 216–17.
41. John Brown (Pelorus Valley, Marlborough) to his parents (unknown), 21 September 1862, Brown family papers, ATL, MS-Papers-8869-2.
42. Edmund Bowler, diary, see for example 7 February 1863, OSM, C-012.
43. Thomas Armstrong (Melbourne) to his sister, Eliza (England?), 27 August 1869, Thomas Armstrong Letter, SLV, MS 12164.
44. William Chapman (Lyttleton) to his brother, December 1862, private collection.
45. *Otago Daily Times*, 8 December 1863.
46. Francis Joseph Mapleson (Dunedin) to his wife, Susan Mapleson (Braybrook, Victoria), 20 March 1862, Susan Mapleson (Braybrook) to Francis Joseph Mapleson (Dunedin), 20 March 1863, Francis Joseph Mapleson Letters, SLV, MS 10869.
47. John Lees (Melbourne) to his wife (Oldham, England), 21 January 1862;

John Lees (Waitahuna) to his wife (Oldham), 10 May 1862; John Lees Letters, SLV, MS 10083.
48. Cf. Marks, *Precious Dust*, 172.
49. David Fitzpatrick, *Irish Emigration, 1801–1921* (Dundalk: Economic and Social History Society of Ireland, 1984); Colin Pooley and Jean Turnbull, *Migration And Mobility In Britain Since The Eighteenth Century* (London: Routledge, 1998); John Bodnar, *The Transplanted: A History of Immigrants in Urban America* (Bloomington: Indiana University Press, 1985).
50. George O'Halloran, autobiography, ATL, MS-Papers-1345/1, 13.
51. Sigismund Wekey, *Otago as It Is, Its Gold-Mines and Natural Resources: Hand-book for Merchants, Capitalists, and the General Public, and a Guide to Intending Emigrants* (Melbourne: F. F. Baillière, 1862), 68.
52. See Duane A. Smith, *Rocky Mountain Mining Camps: The Urban Frontier* (Bloomington: Indiana University Press, 1967), 149–53; Marks, *Precious Dust*, 202–5; Graeme Davison, 'Gold Rush Melbourne', in Iain McCalman, Alexander Cook and Andrew Reeves (eds), *Gold: Forgotten Histories and Lost Objects of Australia* (Cambridge: Cambridge University Press, 2001), 53, 62–4; Limerick, *The Legacy of Conquest*, 42; A. H. McLintock, *The History of Otago* (Dunedin: Otago Centennial Historical Publications, 1949), 473.
53. B. A. Heywood, *A Vacation Tour at the Antipodes, through Victoria, Tasmania, New South Wales, Queensland and New Zealand in 1861–1862* (London: Longman, Green, Longman, Roberts, and Green, 1863), 162, 166.
54. E. R. Chudleigh, *Diary of E. R. Chudleigh, 1841–1920: Settler in New Zealand* (Christchurch: Cadsonbury Publications, 2003), 43.
55. *Otago Daily Times*, 12 December 1861.
56. G. M. Hassing, *Pages from the Memory Log of G. M. Hassing: Sailor, Pioneer, Schoolmaster* (Invercargill: Southland Times Company, 1930), 135.
57. *Colonist*, 4 October 1861.
58. *Daily Telegraph*, 24 December 1863.
59. Erik Olssen, *A History of Otago* (Dunedin: John McIndoe, 1984), 82.
60. *Colonist*, 27 September 1862.
61. Ibid.
62. *Daily Telegraph*, 24 December 1863.
63. *Colonist*, 27 September 1862.
64. *Otago Daily Times*, 6 May 1862.
65. Ibid.
66. *Otago Daily Times*, 27 March 1862, 8 April 1862.
67. Ibid., 20 March 1862; 27 March 1862; *Colonist*, 27 September 1862.
68. *Otago Daily Times*, 6 November 1862.
69. *Colonist*, 18 October 1861.

70. Charles Fahey, 'Labour and Trade Unionism in Victorian Goldmining: Bendigo, 1861–1915', in Iain McCalman, Alexander Cook and Andrew Reeves (eds), *Gold: Forgotten Histories and Lost Objects of Australia* (Cambridge: Cambridge University Press, 2001), 72.
71. *Bendigo Advertiser*, 15 October 1861.
72. *Otago Daily Times*, 3 October 1862, 9 October 1862, 16 October 1862, 28 October 1862. Also see *Daily Telegraph*, 16 December 1863, 25 December 1863.
73. *Colonist*, 4 August 1862; Olssen, *A History of Otago*, 82.
74. Davison, 'Gold Rush Melbourne', 60.
75. *Colonist*, 27 September 1862.
76. Olssen, *A History of Otago*, 82.
77. Andrew Bools, *The Wonders of Providence and Grace, as Illustrated in the Life of the Author, While Doing Business in Deep Waters, in Travels on Sea and Land, and over the Gold Fields of Australia and New Zealand* (London: Frederick Kirby, 1890), 71.
78. C. L. Money, *Knocking About in New Zealand* (Melbourne: Samuel Mullen, 1871), 23.
79. Gascoigne, 'Adventures of a Norfolk Boy', 68.
80. Charles J. D. Robjohns, diary, 30 May 1864, ATL, MS-Papers-4913.
81. *Otago Daily Times*, 10 February 1863.
82. John George Walker (Dunstan) to his mother (London), 25 December 1862, OSM, C-128.
83. Bools, *The Wonders of Providence*, 77.
84. William Turnbull Smith, diary, 28 January 1863, HC, MS-578-B.
85. John Henry Watmuff, diary, 12 October 1862, private collection, 3/21.
86. Warwick Frost, 'The Environmental Impacts of the Victorian Gold Rushes: Miners' Accounts During the First Five Years', *Australian Economic History Review* 53, no. 1 (2013): 77–8.
87. Salmon, *A History of Goldmining*, 57.
88. George O'Halloran, autobiography, 9, ATL, MS-Papers-1345/1.
89. John George Walker (Dunstan) to his mother (London), 25 December 1862, Walker Letters.
90. In two days several hundred diggers passed through the sheep station, with some 350 spending the night. See 'Diary of James Murison, Puketoi Station, Maniototo Plains', 23 August 1862 and 23 August 1862, OSM, C-191.
91. Henry Walton reminiscences, in *Gabriel's Gully Jubilee: Reminiscences of the Early Gold Mining Days* (Dunedin: Otago Daily Times, 1911), 12.
92. Geoffrey Blainey, *A History of Victoria* (Cambridge: Cambridge University Press, 2013), 52.
93. See, for example, *Otago Daily Times*, 14 September 1861; *Argus*, 23 December 1861; *Bendigo Advertiser*, 22 August 1861, 8 September 1862, 23 January 1863.

94. William Cronon, *Nature's Metropolis: Chicago and the Great West* (New York: W. W. Norton and Company, 1991), 74.
95. Olssen, *A History of Otago*, 59.
96. *Otago Daily Times*, 23 November 1863, 17 November 1863; Salmon, *A History of Goldmining*, 57.
97. Cronon, *Nature's Metropolis*, 57.
98. *Otago Daily Times*, 6 December 1861, 16 December 1861, 24 December 1861, 4 January 1862, 20 January 1862, 1 February 1862, 25 March 1862, 7 April 1862, 29 April 1862, 14 June 1862, 13 August 1862; *Colonist*, 11 August 1862, 13 August 1862, 5 September 1862, 11 September 1862, 23 September 1862, 23 January 1863, 28 August 1863; *Otago Witness*, 3 August 1861, 10 August 1861, 24 August 1861, 16 December 1861; *Southland Times*, 16 December 1862, 9 January 1863, 16 January 1863.
99. William Smith, 'Reminiscences of a long and active life by an old colonist', 65, OSM, C-101. Also see J. C. Bremner, 'The memories of the early diggings', OSM, DC-0986.
100. *Gabriel's Gully Jubilee: Reminiscences of the Early Gold Mining Days*, 13; O'Halloran, autobiography, 9. Similar comments were also frequently made from the North American and Victorian goldfields. See Serle, *The Golden Age*, 71–2; Elliott West, *The Contested Plains: Indians, Goldseekers, and the Rush to Colorado* (Lawrence: University of Kansas Press, 1998), 158–63; Isenberg, *Mining California* (New York: Macmillan, 2010), 3–4; Malcolm J. Rohrbough, *Days of Gold: The California Gold Rush and the American Nation* (Berkeley: University of California Press, 1998), 55–66; Keith D. Lilley, '"One Immense Gold Field!" British Imaginings of the Australian Gold Rushes, 1851–59', *Landscape Research* 27, no. 1 (2002): 67–80.
101. Morse, *The Nature of Gold*, 92.
102. Frost, 'The Environmental Impacts of the Victorian Gold Rushes', 82; Don Garden, 'Catalyst or Cataclysm?: Gold Mining and the Environment', *Victorian Historical Journal (1987)* 72, nos. 1–2 (September 2001): 29–30; Donald Stuart Garden, *Australia, New Zealand, and the Pacific: An Environmental History* (Santa Barbara, CA: ABC-CLIO, 2005), 83.
103. Smith, reminiscences, 65.
104. *Lake Wakatip Mail*, 10 June 1863.
105. Ibid., 17 June 1863.
106. Allan Houston, diary, 1865, HC, Misc-MS-1413.
107. *Gabriel's Gully Jubilee*, 19.
108. Macleod Clement Orbell, reminiscences, OSM, C084, 74.
109. *Daily Telegraph*, 24 November 1863.
110. *Lake Wakatip Mail*, 18 July 1863. Also see *Otago Daily Times*, 20 November 1862, 22 June 1863, 27 July 1863, 28 July 1863, 3 August 1863; *Colonist*, 18 September 1863.
111. *Otago Daily Times*, 22 February 1864.

112. *Colonist*, 16 July 1861.
113. Hamilton McIlrath (Rangiora) to his father, mother and siblings (County Down, Ireland), 12 August 1862, 'McIlrath Correspondence', in Angela McCarthy, '"Seas May Divide": Irish Migration to New Zealand as Portrayed in Personal Correspondences, 1840–1937', vol. 2 (PhD thesis, Trinity College, Dublin, 2000), 207. Many thanks to Angela McCarthy for providing transcripts of these letters.
114. *Colonist*, 27 September 1861.
115. *Otago Daily Times*, 19 March 1862.
116. Eldred-Grigg, *Diggers, Hatters and Whores*, 303.
117. Wayne R. Angus, 'Queenstown 1862–1864: The Genesis of a Goldfields Community' (BA (Hons), University of Otago, 1987), 37–45.
118. *Otago Daily Times*, 13 October 1862, 11 August 1863, 9 October 1863,
119. Ibid., 20 August 1662. Langford's case was dismissed on these grounds.
120. Serle, *The Golden Age*, 80.
121. D. and G. McVicar (Dunedin) to their brother (Russell, South Australia), 16 February 1864, OSM, no call number.
122. John Penderick, diary, 19 October 1863, LDM, N-1901.
123. John Henry Watmuff, diary, 7 June 1862 [2/340], private collection.
124. John George Walker (Upper Dunstan) to his mother, Ann Thorogood (London), 25 December 1862, OSM, C-128. For a similar account of rats, see Thomas McCourt, diary, 7 April 1863, 14 August 1863, LDM, N-2377.
125. John George Walker (Lower Dunstan) to his mother, Ann Thorogood (London), 10 May 1863, ibid.
126. Watmuff, diary, 7 June 1862 [2/340].
127. *Otago Daily Times*, 27 May 1864.
128. *Colonist*, 29 May 1863.
129. *Lake Wakatip Mail*, 25 July 1863.
130. Cf. *Otago Daily Times*, 1 September 1862, 18 May 1863.
131. *Lake Wakatip Mail*, 24 June 1863; 11 July 1863;
132. Morse, *The Nature of Gold: An Environmental History of the Klondike Gold Rush*, 89.
133. David Jones (Otago) to his family (Cefn Cribwr, South Wales), 12 June 1862, ATL, MS-Papers-6249.
134. Daniel Calwell (Molyneux River) to his brother, Davis Calwell (Victoria), 1 November 1863, SLV, MS-11492.
135. Blainey, *The Rush That Never Ended*, 31–6; Serle, *The Golden Age*, 75–6. Quotation taken from Rohrbough, *Days of Gold*, 124.
136. Matthias Willbold, Tim Elliott and Stephen Moorbath, 'The Tungsten Isotopic Composition of the Earth's Mantle before the Terminal Bombardment', *Nature* 477, no. 7363 (2011): 195.
137. Terence J. Hearn, 'Land, Water and Gold in Central Otago, 1861–1921:

Some Aspects of Resource Use Policy and Conflict' (PhD thesis, University of Otago, 1981), 80–3.
138. Limerick, *The Legacy of Conquest*, 42.
139. E. P. Thompson, 'Time, Work-discipline and Industrial Capitalism', *Past & Present* 38 (1967): 56–97.
140. Morse, *The Nature of Gold: An Environmental History of the Klondike Gold Rush*, 94–106; Isenberg, *Mining California*, 4–8.
141. Salmon, *A History of Goldmining*, 65–6; Anthony Edward Dingle, *The Victorians: Settling* (McMahons Point: Fairfax, Syme and Weldon Associates, 1984), 41–2.
142. Salmon, *A History of Goldmining*, 76.
143. *Lake Wakatip Mail*, 6 June 1863, 24 June 1863, 11 July 1863, 25 July 1863.
144. John George Walker to his mother, 5 April 1863.
145. Thomas Andrew (Molyneux River) to his brother and sister (Crossgate, Fifeshire, Scotland?), 1 February 1863, ATL, MS-Papers-4802.
146. William Smith, reminiscences, 77, OSM, C101.
147. James Forrest, 'Population and Settlement on the Otago Goldfields, 1861–1870', *New Zealand Geographer* 17, no. 1 (1961): 67–8. Also see Olssen, *A History of Otago*, 59.
148. Eldred-Grigg, *Diggers, Hatters and Whores*, 217–21.
149. *Lake Wakatip Mail*, 5 July 1863, 15 August 1863.
150. *Otago Daily Times*, 5 February 1863.
151. John Penderick, diary, 22 July 1863, LDM, N-1901.
152. *Otago Daily Times*, 21 August 1863. Also see *Lake Wakatip Mail*, 22 August 1863, 10 October 1863, 14 October 1863, 30 December 1863, 2 January 1864.
153. *Lake Wakatip Mail*, 1 August 1863; John McLay, 'Waikouaiti and Dunedin in 1850', OSM, DC-0112, 69–70.
154. *Colonist*, 11 September 1863.
155. Bremner, reminiscences, OSM, DC-0986.
156. Warwick Frost, 'The Environmental Impacts of the Victorian Gold Rushes: Miners' Accounts During the First Five Years', *Australian Economic History Review* 53, no. 1 (2013): 79–80.
157. Christine Hansen and Tom Griffiths, *Living with Fire: People, Nature and History in Steels Creek* (Collingwood: CSIRO Publishing, 2012), 31–6, 73–5.
158. Moffatt, diary, 21 September 1863, OSM, C-0204.
159. *Lake Wakatip Mail*, 3 June 1863.
160. McCourt, diary, 7 April 1863, LDM, N-2377.
161. Penderick, 15 June 1863, LDM, N-1901.
162. Moffatt, diary, 12 September 1863.
163. Smith, reminiscences, 67. Also see letter from unknown gold seeker (Waitahuna) to his sister (unknown location), 10 November 1861, ATL,

MS-Papers-10252; Vincent Pyke, *History of the Early Gold Discoveries in Otago* (Dunedin: Otago Daily Times and Witness Newspapers, 1887), 103; Watmuff, diary, 26 October 1862 (3/26), private collection.
164. Watmuff, 30 November 1862 [3/35].
165. Thomas McCourt, diary, 18 July 1863.
166. John Brown (Pelorus, Marlborough) to his parents, 21 September 1862, ATL, MS-Papers 8869-2.
167. William Jones (Port Chalmers) to his sister, Mrs Richards (Bangor, Wales), 17 April 1864, ATL, MS-Papers-10303.
168. Moffatt, diary, 11 September 1863, 15 September 1863, 18 September 1863, 26 September 1863, 27 September 1863, 29 September 1863, 8 October 1863.
169. Lachlan Macdonald (Otago) to Donald Macdonald (Scotland), 30 August 1863. The mountain Lachlan refers to is likely Beinn Ceann a' Mhara on the western edge of the Isle of Tiree, where Lachlan likely lived before migrating to Australasia.
170. David Jones (Otago) to his family, 12 May 1862, ATL, MS-Papers-6249. Also see David Jones (Otago) to his family, 12 June 1862.
171. David Williams, *The Georgia Gold Rush: Twenty-Niners, Cherokees, and Gold Fever* (Columbia: University of South Carolina Press, 1993), 66–8; Pomeroy, *The Pacific Slope: A History of California, Oregon, Washington, Idaho, Utah, and Nevada*, 47–51; Morrell, *The Gold Rushes*.
172. Salmon, *A History of Goldmining*, 65.
173. Serle, *The Golden Age*, 374; Blainey, *The Rush That Never Ended*, 65.
174. *Otago Daily Times*, 30 January 1863.
175. *Lake Wakatip Mail*, 10 June 1863.
176. *Lancashire Gazette*, 23 January 1864. Also see *Otago Daily Times*, 28 November 1862, 10 March 1863.
177. Rodman W. Paul, *California Gold: The Beginning of Mining in the Far West* (Cambridge, MA: Harvard University Press, 1947), 113–14.
178. Gascoigne, 'Adventures of a Norfolk Boy', 71.
179. Ibid., 71–3; *Otago Daily Times*, 28 November 1862.
180. Orbell, reminiscences, 73.
181. *Otago Daily Times*, 13 October 1863.
182. Martin reminiscences.
183. Thomas Williamson, diary, OSM, DC-2073.
184. See, for example, Peter Warren, diary; Martin, reminiscences; Moffatt, diary; Penderick, diary; McCourt, diary; Watmuff, diary.
185. Phillips, *A Man's Country*, 17–23; Eldred-Grigg, *Diggers, Hatters and Whores*, 282–4.
186. Patricia Jalland, *Death in the Victorian Family* (Oxford: Oxford University Press, 1996), 1.
187. *Otago Daily Times*, 18 April 1911.
188. *Lake Wakatip Mail*, 27 May 1863.

189. Ibid., 3 June 1863.
190. *Daily Telegraph*, 21 January 1864.
191. *Lake Wakatip Mail*, 10 June 1863.
192. *Otago Daily Times*, 28 November 1862. Also see *Otago Daily Times*, 16 November 1861; Alexander Don, *Early Central Otago; A Bathurst Miner's Reminiscences* (Dunedin: Otago Daily Times, 1932), 12.
193. Bengt Frykberg (Lawrence) to Nils Frykberg (Sweden), 1864, HC, Misc-MS-1931.
194. Watmuff, diary, 11 January 1863 [3/48].
195. *Lake Wakatip Mail*, 22 August 1863.
196. John Moffatt, diary, 13 October 1863–17 October 1863, OSM, C-0204. Moffatt was caring for his mate at Arrowtown when the diary ended on 17 October.
197. *Lake Wakatip Mail*, 19 December 1863.
198. *Daily Telegraph*, 4 February 1864. Also see *Otago Daily Times*, 5 February 1862, 11 March 1863, 9 November 1863.
199. Starr, *Americans and the California Dream, 1850–1915*, 51.
200. McLay, 69–70; *Otago Daily Times*, 31 December 1862; *Lake Wakatip Mail*, 18 July 1863, 19 September 1863, 8 October 1863.
201. *Lake Wakatip Mail*, 4 February 1863.
202. *Otago Daily Times*, 31 December 1861.
203. Ibid., 11 August 1863.
204. Ibid., 8 December 1863.
205. Strachan, reminiscences, 21.
206. Fairburn, *The Ideal Society*, 11.
207. Ibid.
208. John Henry Watmuff, diary, 15 March 1863 [3/69].
209. MacLeod Orbell, reminiscences, 74.
210. Eldred-Grigg, *Diggers, Hatters and Whores*, 256.
211. *Otago Daily Times*, 9 February 1863. Also see ibid., 255–6.
212. Martin, reminiscences.
213. Phillips, *A Man's Country*, 27.
214. Salmon, *A History of Goldmining*, 72–3.
215. *Lake Wakatip Mail*, 21 November 1863.
216. Ibid., 17 June 1863. Also see *Lake Wakatipu Mail*, 27 May 1863, 24 June 1863, 22 August 1863; *Otago Daily Times*, 27 February 1862, 19 April 1862, 20 January 1863.
217. Ibid., 9 May 1862.
218. Ibid., 10 February 1863.
219. Ibid., 26 March 1863.
220. *Colonist*, 21 July 1862.
221. *Lake Wakatip Mail*, 29 August 1863.
222. *Otago Daily Times*, 1 January 1862.
223. Smith, reminiscences, 64.

224. John Henry Watmuff, diary, 8 June 1862 [2/346].
225. *Otago Daily Times*, 21 January 1863. Also see *Otago Daily Times*, 26 January 1863, 6 February 1863.
226. Fraser, *Castles of Gold*, especially 59–70.
227. Angus, 'Queenstown'; Marianne Van der Voorn, 'The Police Department on the Otago Goldfields, Dunstan 1861–1864' (BA (Hons), University of Otago, 1979). Also see Salmon, *A History of Goldmining*, 114–15. Two studies that perpetuate these earlier images of lawlessness on the Otago diggings are Eldred-Grigg, *Diggers, Hatters and Whores*; Hutchins, *Diggers, Constables and Bushrangers*.
228. Tom Brooking, 'Gold in Otago: Digging for a New Perspective', in Richard Stedman (ed.), *A Golden Opportunity: Proceedings of the New Zealand Society of Genealogists Annual Conference* (Dunedin: New Zealand Society of Genealogists, 2011), 18.
229. Olssen, 'Lands of Sheep and Gold', 42–3.
230. The difficulty of comparing the Otago rushes with other goldfields is even more problematic because of the incomplete and inconsistent literature on crime during the Californian and Victorian rushes. The leading historian of the Victorian gold rushes argues that gold seekers were characterised by 'traditional restraints' and a 'fraternal spirit' between diggers. See Serle, *The Golden Age*, 374. There have been no quantitative studies of violence during the Victorian rushes. Concerning the North American literature, most studies draw on diaries and correspondence to emphasise the role of racial antagonism and vigilantism during the rushes. See, for example, Johnson, *Roaring Camp*, 185–234; James A. Sandos, '"Because He Is a Liar and a Thief": Conquering the Residents of "Old" California, 1850–1880', in *Rooted in Barbarous Soil: People, Culture and Community in Gold Rush California* (Berkeley: University of California Press, 2000), 86–112; Rohrbough, *Days of Gold*, 216–29; Marks, *Precious Dust*, 247–307; Albert L. Hurtado, *Indian Survival on the California Frontier* (New Haven, CT: Yale University Press, 1988), 100–24. However, the two leading historians of the violence in the American West both argue that stereotypes of lawlessness in the region are overstated. Rates of interpersonal violence were similar to other regions of the country, and the federal government was most often the instigator of bloodshed. See Robert R. Dykstra, 'Quantifying the Wild West: The Problematic Statistics of Frontier Violence', *The Western Historical Quarterly* 40, no. 3 (2009): 321–47; Michael A. Bellesiles, 'Western Violence', in William Deverell (ed.), *A Companion to the American West* (Malden: Blackwell Publishing, 2007), 162–78. More work on the Victorian and North American rushes certainly needs to be done before a clear comparison with Otago can be made.
231. Serle, *The Golden Age*, 73, 220–2.
232. *Otago Daily Times*, 4 January 1862.

233. Ibid., 4 February 1862.
234. Ibid., 25 March 1862.
235. Ibid., 23 December 1862, 26 January 1863.
236. Ibid., 10 March 1863.
237. Ibid., 30 January 1863.
238. For example, see *Otago Daily Times*, 3 February 1863.
239. *Otago Daily Times*, 1 January 1862. Also see *Otago Daily Times*, 31 May 1862, 6 October 1862, 2 February 1863, 27 February 1863.
240. Paul, *California Gold*, 212–26; Smith, *Rocky Mountain Mining Camps*, 187–90.
241. David Goodman, 'Gold Fields/Golden Fields: The Language of Agrarianism and the Victorian Gold Rush', *Australian Historical Studies* 23, no. 90 (1988): 32–3; Serle, *The Golden Age*, 110–13, 183–4.
242. Gareth Stedman Jones, *Language of Class: Studies in English Working Class History, 1832–1982* (Cambridge: Cambridge University Press, 1983), 94–6.
243. John Angus, 'Populism, Parochialism and Public Works: Politics on the Otago Goldfields from the 1860s to the 1880s', in Lloyd Carpenter and Lyndon Fraser (eds), *Rushing for Gold: Life and Commerce on the Goldfields of New Zealand and Australia* (Dunedin: Otago University Press, 2016), 73–4.
244. *Lake Wakatip Mail*, 31 October 1863. Also see *Lake Wakatip Mail*, 23 December 1863.
245. *Lake Wakatip Mail*, 11 November 1863. Also see *Lake Wakatip Mail*, 10 October 1863.
246. *Lake Wakatip Mail*, 18 November 1863.
247. *Otago Daily Times*, 5 December 1861, 20 December 1861, 31 December 1861, 18 January 1862, 27 February 1862, 8 March 1862, 14 June 1862, 6 August 1862, 28 November 1862, 6 February 1863. Also see Angus, 'Queenstown', 29–34.
248. See, for example, *Otago Daily Times*, 27 February 1862, 12 April 1862, 14 June 1862, 26 November 1862, 29 December 1862, 10 February 1863, 9 March 1863, 30 April 1863; *Lake Wakatip Mail*, 2 May 1863, 16 May 1863, 17 June 1863, 29 June 1863, 5 July 1863, 26 September 1863.
249. James Vernon, *Politics and the People: A Study in English Political Culture, c. 1815–1867* (Cambridge: Cambridge Unversity Press, 1993), 146.
250. Ibid.
251. *Lake Wakatip Mail*, 5 December 1863.
252. Ibid., 24 October 1863. For a discussion of medievalism in Chartist rhetoric, see Jones, *Language of Class*, 124–6.
253. Vernon, *Politics and the People*, 205.
254. *Lake Wakatip Mail*, 6 June 1863. Also see *Lake Wakatip Mail*, 4 July

1863, 11 July 1863, 18 July 1863, 9 September 1863, 26 September 1863, 30 September 1863, 9 December 1863. The *Otago Daily Times* rarely published the reports of the Warden's Court unless it involved murder or robbery. This accounts for the exclusive reliance on the *Lake Wakatip Mail*'s narratives of the Lakes District courts proceedings. An excellent source for future research is the Tuapeka Warden's Court minutes located at Archives New Zealand, Dunedin branch.

255. *Otago Daily Times*, 13 August 1862, 15 August 1862, 28 November 1862, 1 December 1862, 8 December 1862, 10 December 1862, 17 December 1862, 29 December 1862, 11 August 1863. For a similar conflict at Moke Creek and Moonlight in the Lakes District, see ibid., 5 February 1863.
256. *Otago Daily Times*, 16 May 1862.
257. *Lake Wakatip Mail*, 27 June 1863.
258. *Otago Daily Times*, 3 February 1863.
259. Fairburn, *The Ideal Society*, 227.
260. McEvoy, 'Towards an Interactive Theory', 229.
261. Fraser, *Castles of Gold*, 77–8; May, *The West Coast Gold Rushes*, 121–5.

4

Leisure Sites and Cultures

In the midst of trials and tribulations, aching muscles and blistered feet, gold seekers always found time for leisure. For most, leisure stood in binary opposition to work. There was a clear beginning and end to the workday, and Sunday was always looked forward to as a time of relaxation and rejuvenation. Diggers who worked together for ten hours a day would spend their downtime together, relaxing at their camp or in a local public house.

All gold seekers sought diversion from their work, and yet work on the goldfields never truly ended. When the Industrial Revolution in Britain and the United States stressed time discipline and created clear delineations between labour and leisure, diggers found themselves thrown into pre-industrial patterns on the goldfields that entangled the two practices.[1] Whenever the digger put down his shovel or put aside his sluice box, there was a publican holding a tumbler of brandy or a shopkeeper with a bag of flour, plying his trade. It was therefore much more than the allure of gold that moulded culture on the diggings. Almost every means by which miners sought diversions from the drudgery of gold digging was paid for by the gold won from the ground on which miners slept, ate, worked and played, entangling leisure practices with both natural environments and economics on the goldfields. Gold was exchanged for the bottle of whisky prospectors passed around the campfire after a long day of work. It was what diggers were willing to give up for a five-minute conversation or dance with a hotel's barmaid. It was the cost of ten minutes of respite during the workday to read a newspaper or smoke a pipe. Like work routines, the ways in which diggers relaxed were often social experiences.

These modes of leisure often centred on communication. In his seminal work, *Communication as Culture*, James Carey argues that communication is culturally informing when it 'comprises the ambience of all human existence'.[2] Cultural formation on the goldfields, therefore, never ended when diggers who worked together all day also conversed or sang together around campfires or in public houses after a long day on their claim. Moreover, these communication forms also extended beyond the prospecting party. As they read local newspapers, participated in public debates or attended musical or theatrical performances, a particular image of the societies they were building on the goldfields emerged.[3]

The intention here is not to present local cultures and transnational networks in conflict with one another. Like work practices, leisure was often entangled with networks elsewhere. Many diggers spent their downtime with brothers and cousins with whom they worked on the Otago goldfields. Others pored over letters from relatives overseas. Still others recollected loved ones as they listened to sentimental ballads in public houses. Just as work practices linked local environments and societies with transnational models and networks, leisure practices entangled communities in Otago with networks and cultures in Victoria and the United Kingdom.

This chapter builds upon the previous chapter to show the ways in which leisure practices animated gold rush cultures alongside work routines. It begins with a discussion of reading and writing practices on the goldfields, especially highlighting the role of the newspaper in describing the local community. There follows a discussion of the public house as the primary social space on the goldfields, and through a case study of Charles Thatcher, the ways in which public house entertainments were concerned overwhelmingly with local communities. The chapter concludes with a discussion of the goldfield courthouse, which gave the gold seeker a voyeuristic gaze into the dysfunction of other individuals who helped to define the local community. The chapter argues that diggers constantly drew upon cultural models from Britain and Ireland and from the Victorian goldfields, but directed these forms inward on the local community that they helped to define. As such, the nineteenth-century gold rushes are ill-suited to the national narratives within which they are most often understood.

READING AND WRITING

Leisure was woven into the daily lives of gold seekers throughout the rushes, when individuals with aching backs and sore limbs sought relaxation and rejuvenation after a long day on a claim. In *Days of*

Gold, Malcolm Rohrbough draws on gold seeker diaries and correspondence to argue that Californian diggers were often too wearied during the work week to partake in any form of leisure other than the 'leisure of exhaustion'.[4] However, personal accounts from the Otago diggings often record long hours sharing grog and stories with mates around a campfire after the workday. George Hassing and his mining party often spent their evenings singing and playing the cornet until after midnight.[5] Robert Booth and his mates sang songs, lit pipes and told stories until they were on the verge of passing out.[6] In 1864 the sounds of singing and laughter also echoed nightly from camps through the main gully on the Hamiltons goldfield.[7] This contrast between accounts from California and Otago is difficult to reconcile. For most prospectors discussed by Rohrbough, their time in California was their first participation in a gold rush, and they possibly found the backbreaking work overwhelming. In contrast, most letters and diaries from the Otago diggings were written by gold seekers who had already become acclimated to prospecting work during years spent in Victoria. This argument is difficult to substantiate when there is no comparable study on the Victorian rushes that relies heavily on private correspondence and diaries.

There were also many gold seekers in Otago who found enough energy to pen a diary entry after a long day of work. The numerous newspaper advertisements within the province for annual diary books indicate that there were many individuals interested in composition.[8] One of the most zealous diarists was John Henry Watmuff, who wrote some 90,000 words in his diary during his three-year career prospecting in Otago.[9] There were probably few gold seekers who possessed Watmuff's determination to document daily events, but there were many diggers who often took time to pen a few lines about the day's activities. One evening, an exhausted and depressed Peter Warren wrote only: 'Heavy fall of snow & a storm, no Gold today.'[10] All the diaries located for this book are most often concerned with the everyday routines of work and leisure, repeated constantly, and rooted in a particular locality.[11]

There were probably even more gold seekers who regularly composed letters for loved ones. Some 180,000 letters were sent overseas from Otago annually between 1861 and 1864, and one shopkeeper at Queenstown sold nineteen reams of letter paper and some 2,000 envelopes during a two-month span early in 1864.[12] One of these letters sent home from Otago was written in 1863 by John George Walker, who complained to his mother about the toil of gold digging but was still able to compose an eight-page letter.[13] As Chapter One showed, such correspondence connected the individual to a particular network of social relations within Britain and Ireland or across the Empire.

Other gold seekers relaxed by candlelight with a book or newspaper after a long day of work.[14] As the book historian John Traue contends, the Otago rushes occurred amid the rising curve of modernity during the second half of the nineteenth century, and diggers arrived in the province with an understanding of reading material as a basic necessity of life.[15] Diggers frequently spent their gold on literature when any personal possession beyond a blanket or prospecting equipment was considered a luxury. One digger carried around a two-volume set of historical biographies by Lord Macaulay.[16] During the rushes, public houses sometimes provided reading material for their patrons, and stores often carried newspapers and novels which were either sold or loaned to their customers.[17] When prospectors began leaving for the West Coast or returning to Victoria in 1864, the remaining population on the diggings shifted to a more settled state, leading to the establishment of reading rooms and lending libraries. On the Tuapeka alone, subscription libraries were founded at Lawrence, Waipori and Weatherston's.[18]

Few prospectors described their reading preferences, and those who did often connected literature to the culture of self-improvement which was evolving in Britain during the nineteenth century. W. T. Smith took copious notes in his diary on essays he read about weather patterns and ocean currents.[19] The self-educated John Henry Watmuff read widely from Shakespeare, Machiavelli and Milton, as well as various works on European history.[20] As diggers like Smith and Watmuff dug for the gold they hoped would provide them with economic freedom, they shared the belief of some members of the working class in Britain that knowledge was an 'essential precondition for the pursuit of freedom'.[21] Watmuff's copious diary, which describes his understanding and purpose of work and leisure, provides a valuable window into how some prospectors viewed labour and leisure on the goldfields. Watmuff valued gold seeking as materially enabling, yet he believed that the occupation was morally 'degrading to the searcher, [was] half unhumanising & wholly [unsettled] him'.[22] Faced with the 'degrading' and 'unhumanising' realities of prospecting, Watmuff saw reading and writing as 'moral necessities of life'.[23] Watmuff was likely atypical. Few prospectors possessed his zeal for writing and belief in the moral benefits of literature. This is confirmed by Robin Marks' research on the Lawrence Athenaeum. As Marks demonstrates, between 1865 and 1874, the period immediately following the rushes, subscribers to the Athenaeum's lending library overwhelmingly preferred fiction, despite the library committee's large collection of non-fiction.[24] Most books read on the diggings were likely popular novels, or 'wretched trash' as John George Walker called them.[25]

The most widely read material throughout the rushes was always the newspaper. In Victoria newspaper proprietors quickly found a lucrative market on the diggings. When Melbourne's leading newspaper, the *Argus*, began retailing on the diggings, the paper's circulation increased five-fold.[26] Victorian diggers brought with them a strong practice of newspaper reading. Within a few months of the Dunstan rush in Otago, a weekly handwritten newspaper was circulated at the diggings, and by 1863 the fortnightly *Dunstan News* had been established at the Upper Junction.[27] Within two months of the Arrow River rush, the *Lake Wakatip Mail* was also established at Queenstown. The following year, the *Tuapeka Recorder* was founded at Lawrence. The most widely circulated paper on the diggings throughout the rushes, however, was always the *Otago Witness*, which from 1861 existed as a digest of the *Otago Daily Times* for the goldfields and country districts.[28] The establishment of the rival *Daily Telegraph* in 1863 similarly transformed the *Otago Colonist* into a weekly digest marketed to the goldfields.

Gold rush newspapers document the ways in which the global and the local became entangled in the patterns of leisure on the goldfields. At the same time that prospectors celebrated their independence they depended on newspapers, like letters, for knowledge of the communities they left in the United Kingdom and Australasia as well as for broader global developments.[29] Newspapers flooded onto the goldfields from Britain, Ireland and Victoria throughout the rushes. In the three years between 1862 and 1864, some 700,000 newspapers arrived in the province from overseas destinations.[30] Moreover, as Tony Ballantyne argues, the pages of the newspapers 'were an important vehicle that brought the world to the district'.[31] Almost every issue of local newspapers contained material copied from overseas papers. Copious coverage was always given to European and American affairs, especially the Lancashire relief efforts and the American Civil War.[32] Rather than being motivated by the need to fill empty space, as one gold rush historian argues, editors sought to profit from this borderless quality of news consumption.[33]

If newspapers often contained global affairs, they were also saturated with local news. The American communication historian, James Carey, argues that local newspapers were an important social tool in frontier communities, 'where strangers came together and had to negotiate a world out of diverse and conflicting cultural resources'.[34] In his work on the press in late nineteenth-century Otago, Tony Ballantyne similarly argues that colonial newspapers must be placed 'in a specific set of social and political relationships' at a particular locality.[35] In other work, Ballantyne shows that newspapers in Otago convey 'an image of rich social life' and were overwhelmingly concerned with such local institutions as road boards, town councils and education committees, which had an ongoing and everyday impact on their readers' lives.[36] A reading of gold rush newspapers confirms these observations. The *Lake Wakatip Mail* contained regular coverage of local balls, committees and meetings, as well as local gold yields.[37] Both the *Witness* and the *Colonist* staffed a local reporter on all of the major diggings, providing for their audiences an account of the previous week's news.[38] Moreover, prospectors who dug for gold all day also read the newspaper in the evening for knowledge about gold deposits elsewhere, as well as the future course of the rushes.[39]

These social and economic descriptions of the goldfields were not objective presentations when colonial newspapers were 'first and foremost commercial enterprises'.[40] Such economic and political contexts must also be emphasised. The *Daily Times'* editor, Julius Vogel, allied the paper with the Dunedin commercial community, which he depended on for advertising. Moreover, he held that economic growth was the surest way to social development, and he continually stressed the economic and social benefits of the rushes at the same time that he contested criticisms that they worsened the moral state of the province.[41]

The interests of Vogel closely intersected with the ambitions of local correspondents on each goldfield. The most important correspondent was George Brodie, who served as the *Daily Times'* correspondent on the Tuapeka and later the Dunstan. In both locations, he simultaneously operated an auction business and financed water races and prospecting ventures.[42] On the Dunstan he also established the goldfield newspaper, the *Dunstan Times*, serving as the founding editor.[43] Moreover, he became a prominent figure in both Tuapeka and Dunstan social life and frequently acted as the political voice of the goldfield community in Otago.[44] These commercial interests infused his representation of the Otago goldfields. In his reports from the Tuapeka, he argued that several quartz lodes would soon be discovered and that the multitude of diggers fleeing from the diggings in 1862 intended to return the following season.[45] However, as John Henry Watmuff recorded in his diary that same autumn, prospecting proved a failure for most parties, and he was keenly looking forward to leaving 'the damned country'.[46] From the Dunstan, Brodie also highlighted social developments. In December 1862, he remarked that the Upper Township now boasted a mile-long main street, theatres and concert rooms, and hotels; it was filled with iron and stone buildings, which indicated that local gold deposits were rich enough to retain a large population of diggers.[47]

Goldfield newspapers, therefore, became central because of their skill in 'establishing a network of relationships' between the Otago community and 'a spectrum of content producers', whether editing or reporting staff, merchants, court officials or provincial administrators.[48] This structure created communication webs through which news and information were transmitted back to the editorial staff and clipped and sold to a reading public. Commercial columns explained current business in light of gold returns and correspondence from individual goldfields. Shipping columns and Melbourne correspondence combined to chart the flow of Victorian gold seekers to Otago.[49] These flows were explained in other columns. Magistrate court summaries offered narratives of interactions between recent arrivals and the local community.[50] Town board meetings highlighted the bearing of this influx on the town's infrastructure.[51] Alongside this news were placed reports of lectures, meetings and entertainments that were more an effect of the rushes than a reaction to them. Such events were widely patronised by Victorians, held in public houses owned by the Victorians, and funded by wealth generated by Victorians digging for gold in central Otago. Published letters to the editor were sprinkled throughout the newspaper, weighing the importance of an article here, disagreeing with a conclusion there. When the financial successes of merchants, reporters and newspaper proprietors depended on attracting and retaining a large population of gold seekers, the accounts diggers read of the rushes were infused with optimism.

Reading such local news provided individuals with a lens through which to understand the communities they were forming in the gullies and on the river flats of central Otago. More than that, reading was what James Carey calls a 'dramatic' act, in which one engages with a particular portrayal of the world in a newspaper.[52] As the reader made his way through the paper he was faced with a continual shift of roles or dramatic forces. Amid the instability and fluidity of the rushes, the newspaper provided continuity and consistency, when its content changed very little. A lead article about the Māori Wars in the North Island called on his patriotism to support the war. A report about increased gold returns made him hopeful about his future livelihood on the diggings. A story of a constable single-handedly capturing a band of bushrangers filled him with excitement. A murder case evoked antagonism, resentment and fear. When diggers put down their shovels and cradles, the work of the rushes continued as newspaper editors conveyed a cohesive picture of the goldfield community to their local audience.

THE GOLDFIELD PUBLIC HOUSE

While gold seekers often found time to relax with a letter or newspaper during the week, the weekend usually provided the opportunity to visit commercialised entertainment spaces in the rapidly forming digging townships. New Zealand scholars have frequently treated goldfield leisure as synonymous with the 'spree'. Jock Phillips characterises the spree as the defining ritual of masculine culture on the goldfields, while Miles Fairburn sees its infrequency as evidence of insufficient social bonding.[53] It was also the word diggers sometimes used to describe a distinct trip into town for the sole purpose of pleasure, and it is vital to understanding how miners chose to spend their leisure time.[54]

A spree implied a distinct commercialised space. It always took place in a township, and usually involved public houses (usually in the plural). While the word 'spree' had its genesis on the California goldfields, the event occurred against the backdrop of increasing urbanisation in nineteenth-century Britain and the United States and the goldfields' ambiguous relationship with the urban environment. Goldfields were paradoxically both urban and frontier spaces – highly dense populations surrounded by and interspersed across a wide, expansive landscape. This was partially attributed to the gold rush economy. Because individuals were more inclined to look for gold where others had found it, and because gold deposits usually were larger than the size of a mining claim, mining parties tended to congregate in tightly compacted populations. 'Urban' also implied, however, the gold seeker's conception of leisure as a 'necessity' that was evolving in industrialising Britain and filtering into the colonies.[55] In the ways diggers relaxed across Otago, they remained firmly connected to Britain and these metropolitan cultures took on particular local salience on the Otago goldfields. In the words of the American historian Patricia Limerick, gold seekers had a habit of 'celebrating independence while relying on a vital connection to the outside world'.[56] Letters and newspapers flowed into makeshift post offices, composed of a sheet of calico hung over a few poles and staked to the ground. Publicans sold Holloway pills, 'Spanish liquorice' and 'Aberdeen socks' in storehouses constructed with a few dozen boards hammered together. Calico-and-weatherboard drinking establishments sprang up, taking cues from the gin palaces of London and filled with diggers enjoying farces and melodramas from the London stage.

On Sundays, the usual day of a spree, gold rush townships were crowded, loud and sometimes rowdy places. A cacophony of sights, sounds and smells imposed themselves on the senses of the digger, while merchants, publicans and bellhops all tried their best to secure the gold in his pocket.[57] In 1861 Charles Money visited a store, which consisted of a calico sheet thrown over a pole. Inside, a makeshift table was made from old brandy and gin cases, on top of which were heaped sides of bacon, butter, tobacco, bread, cheese and various pickled fishes.[58] There are scant first-hand accounts of a spree on the Otago goldfields, the primary evidence being magistrate court records, usually because an individual was robbed after he became drunk. The only personal description of a spree located for this study was by John Henry Watmuff, who constantly used his diary as a sort of moral gauge similar to the spiritual autobiographies prevalent in industrial Britain.[59] His diary is filled with descriptions of the literature he read, topics he discussed in the local debating society at Weatherston's and the uplifting scenery of central Otago. All this was often juxtaposed against the mental and moral depravity he saw around him on the diggings, as well as his own weekly visits to 'free and easies' and 'gambling hells'. Recalling a recent spree at Weatherston's, Watmuff wrote:

> Spent the evening recklessly. Visiting every place of amusement (dancing, fighting, rowing, doing everything of the most wild and discreditable character.) Regular dens they are, every variety of character are to be met at them ... I never in my life attended so many places of amusement & saw so much life (of rather a questionable character I must admit) on so little money ... I never drink & yet I've free ingress & egress into every place on Weatherston's, Dance rooms, Singing Saloons, Gambling Hells, & Billiard and Bowling alleys I never play, but enjoy myself studying the various shades of characters one meets at these places.[60]

To Watmuff the spree emerged as a moment of ambiguity. He continually distanced himself from the 'character' of more hedonistic diggers at the same time he was repeatedly drawn into the public houses they frequented. This aligns with Brian Roberts' account of the California rushes. According to Roberts, the rushes allowed the digger the power to redefine himself between the poles of licence and sensuality and the moral constraints of the society he left.[61] However, as this scene illustrates, there were many other gold seekers who had no reservations about such 'wild and discreditable' lifestyles.

Alcohol was central to the spree. Jock Phillips writes that 'drinking was without a doubt the most important and defining ritual of the male community', and diggers routinely crowded into public houses where they drank to the point of passing out.[62] He suggests they did so for three reasons. Firstly, they tried to escape the mental anguish brought on by the dangers and difficulties of gold seeking. Secondly, in a lonely environment largely devoid of women, the pub was an opportunity for socialisation. Thirdly, drinking was a celebration of masculine culture, devoid of feminine morals.[63] In a similar manner, Miles Fairburn sees frontier drinking as a reflex against loneliness and atomisation. Both Phillips and Fairburn attribute high levels of alcohol drinking to the frontier environment in New Zealand.[64]

Lost in all this is that the gold-digging boozer hardly had his drinking debut in Otago. During the Victorian gold rushes, the drinking patterns of diggers who slogged for weeks before experiencing 'sudden changes in fortune' were often characterised by 'work and burst'.[65] Moreover, colonists in Otago understood drunkenness as a foreign evil that was transplanted from Victoria into their society by the gold rushes.[66] In July 1861, a colonist drew on this characterisation of gold rush society when he wrote to the *Otago Witness*, warning that grog selling resulting from the gold rushes would result in many deaths and destitute wives and orphans in the colony.[67] When Otago settlers began digging in Gabriel's Gully, they instituted a ban on liquor sales on the goldfields, fearing Otago would follow a similar course as California and Victoria.[68] To many Dunedin settlers during the 1860s, the gold seeker was a drunkard long before he ever touched Otago soil.

To what extent was the gold seeker a drunkard? There was certainly a degree of truth to this claim. Stevan Eldred-Grigg estimates that in 1862 and 1863 Otago imported enough liquor for every man, woman and child to consume twenty-three litres of spirits.[69] Newspapers reveal several instances of alcohol-induced sickness and death on Otago's goldfields. In November 1862, James Campbell died in his tent at Clyde from alcohol poisoning.[70] The following September a group of diggers found an individual known only as 'Stockings' lying face down in mud outside a public house on the Hogburn diggings. He died from alcohol poisoning two hours later and was described at the inquest as a 'notorious character and had scarcely been sober for the last month'.[71] Two months later the decaying body of Bryan Redmond was found on the shore of Lake Wakatipu, and his death was also attributed to habitual drunkenness.[72]

Caution should be stressed against equating drunkenness with frontier atomisation. Estimated liquor consumption is extremely difficult to gauge when Otago's population numbers were in constant flux. Moreover, this tells us little about drinking practices on the goldfields. There is no evidence that thousands or even hundreds died from alcohol poisoning. Moreover, as Greg Ryan demonstrates, high consumption of liquor did not necessarily mean that individuals drank to get drunk, especially when the scarcity of clean water and the difficulty of transporting and storing beer and wine on the goldfields often made liquor a drink of necessity.[73] There were many gold seekers like John Henry Watmuff and William Martin who rarely touched a drop.[74] Frank Harbottle wrote that while he 'went on a spree and got jolly well tight' with two diggers one night, it was 'the only time I was ever senseless in my life'.[75] The antipathy towards extending liquor licensing in Dunedin and on the goldfields was wedded to a perception that the rushes were an urban phenomenon and would contaminate their new Wakefieldian society with old-world urban vices. Among the diggers arriving from Victoria there were many who were equally hostile to drinking cultures. It was precisely the fact that drink was so deeply embedded in British society, rather than the effect of atomisation, that colonial gold seekers protested so vehemently against the granting of liquor licensing.[76] Likewise, Otago colonists' perceptions of British drinking culture cannot be assumed to be accurate any more than a prohibitionist portrayal of alcohol drinking fifty years later. Most accounts of goldfield drinking rely on newspaper and court records, both of which give inordinate attention to the transgressor or the outlier. We need, instead, to understand what alcohol meant to those who consumed it.[77]

Goldfield drinking was an acceptable form of social bonding that grew out of and mimicked British and Irish drinking cultures, rather than a desperate grasping for social interaction by atomised individuals. It was a reflection of social cohesion rather than evidence of its lack. The public house on the Otago goldfields had its genesis in the transformation of social drinking practices in Britain and Ireland during the first half of the nineteenth century. In 1830 the Beerhouse Act allowed any householder in Britain to convert his premises into a beer shop upon payment of two guineas to the local magistrate. The intention was to shift consumption from gin to beer and ale, and it resulted in the immediate and vast proliferation of public houses across Britain. By 1838, 45,717 new beer shops had been opened across Britain. In towns where there had previously been one public house there were often six.[78] In Ireland, the greater difficulty of procuring a liquor licence meant the drinking customs relied more heavily on illegal whisky distilling than in Britain. While liquor production and consumption in Ireland was more frequently done at home than in Britain, Richard Stivers demonstrates that the local public house in Ireland, whether licit or illicit, still remained the primary meeting and recreational place in the local community.[79] Within this context, the local pub or tavern represented a key meeting place and recreation centre for the local community in both Britain and Ireland.[80]

As leisure became increasingly commercialised in Britain from the 1830s onward, the drinking establishment was transformed. In the early nineteenth century, it was modelled after the family home, in which customers were served as if a family guest. During the expansion of drinking establishments from the 1830s, these small taverns slowly gave way to larger public houses. Chairs and tables were removed to maximise the number of customers, and high ceilings and wall mirrors were used to give the illusion of space. Female staff were hired to sell drinks behind the newly constructed bar, which provided a physical as well as symbolic distance from the customer. Some barmaids were also hired to sing ballads, and professional or semi-professional musical troupes and singers were hired to provide entertainment to paying customers.[81] In this environment, alcohol was only one commodity in a multi-dimensional entertainment experience public houses sold, and drinking habits cannot be easily separated from socialisation and other forms of commercialised leisure.

This model was copied in Victoria during the 1850s. From very early on in the rushes, publicans competed with each other by offering diggers a multi-faceted leisure experience. Bars were constructed, behind which attractive barmaids served drinks with a smile. Tables were arranged around the edges of the room, allowing for dancing, either stag or with a barmaid, who would then encourage her dance partner to buy a drink at the bar. Many publicans built adjoining theatres and hired touring companies to perform musical concerts and melodrama and vaudeville performances. In the second half of the 1850s, the transformation of the mining economy splintered Victorian drinking culture into two groups. As the goldfields industrialised, wealth was increasingly consolidated in the hands of capitalists and shareholders of larger mining companies. Several public houses sprang up catering to this high-end clientele with ballroom dancing, opera and classical performances. Meanwhile, public houses that had catered to the individual miner in the first few years of the rushes found it increasingly difficult to compete for his declining income. Sly grog shops proliferated in the second half of the decade even more than they had in the first years of the rushes, and some establishments resorted to fermenting their own spirits with tobacco.[82]

By mid-century the public house in Britain, Ireland and Victoria was firmly established as a local meeting place and as a space for commercialised leisure – a model that publicans in Otago continually drew upon in marketing their establishments. The most successful publican during the gold rushes was Shadrach Jones. Jones migrated from England in the 1840s and operated a stable and auction house at Bendigo before he travelled to Dunedin in October 1861. Once in Dunedin, he shifted his business interest to entertainment when he purchased the Provincial Hotel and an adjacent horse bazaar between Stafford and High streets. In the bazaar Jones built a collapsible stage and a removable partition, which transformed the bazaar at night into a theatre 'with almost the rapidity of a pantomime scene'.[83] He then spent £14,000 on renovations to the hotel, building a public bar and several upstairs private bars staffed with barmaids.[84] The hotel opened a few days before Christmas with a boxing match and several dramas and farces that were also showing in London.[85] On Boxing Day, over five hundred diggers and colonists attended several impromptu 'English sports' held in the bazaar, as well as a performance by the San Francisco Minstrels, a theatre troupe that was serendipitously touring New Zealand at the time.[86] Around New Year in 1862, the games were expanded over two days and Jones – an English migrant – marketed them to Dunedin's Scottish community as the first Caledonian Games in the province. A 'Highland fling', open to the public and attended by gold seekers and colonists, was held at the end of each day's competitions.[87] Two months later, Jones organised Otago's first horse race, modelled after the newly established Melbourne Cup and strategically named the Provincial Cup. Jones followed the races with a series of farcical dramas held in the Princess' theatre, which earlier in the day had been the race stables.[88] In addition to entertainment, Jones was able to establish the Provincial as the primary point of communication and transit to and from the diggings by contracting the Cobb and Company carriages to operate out of the hotel.[89] In effect, Jones was able to establish the Provincial Hotel as a one-stop shop for gold seekers in Otago, blending the Victorian and Otago cultural worlds together. A digger leaving Victoria for Otago in May 1862 could have attended a performance of the pantomime *Maid and the Magpie* at the Royal Hotel in Ballarat with mates as a final farewell, arrived in Dunedin the following month and visited the Provincial Hotel, where he connected with former mates, found letters from a mate on the Dunstan, booked carriage there and watched another performance of the same pantomime.

This duplication of British and Irish drinking spaces was intended 'to create a unique and familiar atmosphere that would recall similar places back home' – to provide continuity and familiarity during gold rush societies that were always in a state of flux.[90] For publicans, this longing for the familiar became an economic tool to attract potential patrons by drawing on metropolitan and Victorian drinking cultures to meet local social needs.

THE GOLDFIELD THEATRE

Despite publicans' creative inducements to drink, diggers frequently lamented the dearth of entertainment. Thomas McCourt wrote in his diary that 'nothing was doing' or that 'no amusements' were to be found.[91] John Penderick similarly commented that there was often very little to do even in the townships.[92] Much like the claims on which they dug for gold, the public house often did not live up to their expectations.

The editor of the *Lake Wakatip Mail* remarked that in the absence of entertainments in the Lakes District, the theatre provided a well sought-after diversion from the daily grind on the goldfields.[93] As Peter Kuch demonstrates, the theatre was one of the most popular forms of entertainment in the British World during the second half of the nineteenth century.[94] Like the public house, the goldfield theatre drew on Victorian precedents of fashioning the local theatre after metropolitan models. The injection of wealth into Victoria during the colony's rushes stimulated a 'desire for a vibrant and diverse performance culture'.[95]

Theatre in the first few years of the Victorian rush was little more than a branch of the liquor industry. In an attempt to expand entertainment and attract customers, publicans attached theatres to their public houses, where concerts, melodramas and vaudevilles were performed.[96] This practice was replicated on the Otago goldfields, where theatre was inseparable from public houses. After a long work week, diggers and merchants would funnel into a small, flimsy weatherboard structure. Lighting would usually be poor and would be refracted in a haze of tobacco smoke that enveloped the room and made singing all but impossible.[97] The smells of tobacco, sweat, dirt and liquor lingered. A din of conversations throughout the room between miners swapping yarns or flirting with barmaids provided the background noise.[98] This was the context in which miners forgot their backaches and headaches and listened to songs and ballads, perhaps drifting back to memories of home or forward to dreams of the future. Drawing on the music-hall tradition in London and broadside balladry from other parts of the United Kingdom, goldfield theatre fit largely into two genres: the farce or comedy; and the sentimental or melodramatic. These genres are examined through a case study of Charles Thatcher, who was the most successful and influential performer during the Otago gold rushes.

Charles Thatcher was born in 1830 in England, where he was involved in theatrical orchestras from an early age. He was particularly influenced by the repertoire and style of music-hall singers and would draw on their style of performance throughout his career. He arrived in Victoria in 1852 and after a brief bout at gold seeking joined the Royal Victoria Theatre, Bendigo, where he sang between acts. He became extremely popular and by 1854 attracted large crowds to his performances at the Shamrock Hotel, Bendigo. Early in 1862, Thatcher was recruited by Shadrach Jones to sing nightly at the Provincial Hotel in Dunedin, where he would regularly draw audiences of six hundred. He travelled to Queenstown in February 1863, where he performed until August 1863, when he departed for Victoria.[99] He returned again to New Zealand in December 1863, performing in Invercargill, Queenstown and Dunedin before following the diggers to the West Coast in 1865.

The chief attraction of Thatcher was his unrivalled ability to deploy satire and exaggerate personalities in order to provide a new and fresh account of the local community to his audience. In doing so, he drew on shared experiences and stereotypes that both informed and validated the collective identity of gold seekers. Furthermore, like British music-hall performers, his acts were visual affairs. Like any performer, Thatcher constantly had to compete for the attention of his audience, which was otherwise engaged in eating, drinking, conversing, lounging, smoking, flirting or daydreaming. In combating this, he performed techniques such as moving frequently between singing and shouting, and ad-libbing between verses directly with the audience.[100] As Alexander Bathgate recalled, this prose was usually coarse and vulgar, which made the entertainment 'hardly one to which one could take a lady', although it undoubtedly kept the attention of many of his male patrons.[101] He also composed sentimental ballads, set to well-known tunes, which were sung by his wife, Annie Vitelli. Finally, and most important to his success, Thatcher was able to adapt his own locally drawn lyrics to traditional British and Irish music-hall songs and ballads, effectively imbuing metropolitan tunes with local meaning. While most contemporary Otago performers simply repeated songs derived from the London stage or broadside ballads from the United States, Britain and Ireland, Thatcher's songs were charged with local meaning that reflected back on the society of his listeners.[102]

Thatcher's early Otago songs described the gold rush community by contrasting it with Otago's early settlers. In his first and most famous song, entitled *The Old Identity*, Thatcher mocked E. B. Cargill for his call to preserve the Free Church character of Otago amid the influx of Victorian diggers. To Cargill, who witnessed Victorian fever grip the Otago settlement in its early years, the gold rushes were cataclysmic to society.[103] During a session of the Provincial Council in 1861, he insisted that Otago colonists should endeavour to 'preserve their old identity' amid an influx of gold seekers from Victoria.[104] Thatcher employed satire to twist this term's meaning, drawing a contrast between the backwardness of Otago settlers and the progress that gold and gold diggers represented:

> Mr Cargill in the Council
> >   Made such a funny speech;–
> He got up and he stated
> >   That it devolved on each
> Of all the early dwellers
> >   To preserve safe as could be,
> Amid the Victorian influx,
> >   The Old Identity . . .
>
> Still cherish barbarism–
> >   Stick to Dunedin mud,
> And with your eight-years' leases
> >   Chouse the Victorian blood;
> Still dress your ancient Postman
> >   In the style we daily see–
> His costume is essential
> >   To the Old Identity.[105]

Thatcher crystallised and popularised the term of 'Old Identity'. It quickly became part of the vernacular of the Otago rushes in Victoria and Otago. It could be seen in the articles and letters to the editor of the *Otago Daily Times*, *Lake Wakatip Mail* and *Melbourne Argus*, among other newspapers, and in diaries, correspondence and memoirs, defining both gold miner and colonist in binary opposition.[106] On one occasion, when Alexander Bathgate was on a ship leaving Port Chalmers filled with diggers bound for Hokitika, an old man with a violin and a female harpist were playing on-board the ship for diggers. Upon request, the pair played *The Old Identity* from memory and were greeted with uproarious applause and generous donations.[107] While the term 'Old Identity' came in memoirs to mean a quiet and decorous life that was momentarily upset by a group of wild and fun-loving Victorians, its early meaning was one of mockery and derision, interspersed with coarse prose.

When Thatcher travelled to Queenstown, he continued to use his 'Old Identity' songs as his core repertoire, finding it easily translatable to the goldfields. Moreover, he began composing sentimental songs that characterised gold as a coloniser, again stressing the differences between the progressive gold seeker and the backward colonist in Otago. In 1863 Thatcher sang to gold seekers sitting in the Theatre Royal on the shores of Lake Wakatipu about the community they formed a year before:

> Gold's a wonderful thing, what a change it can make,
> Who'd have thought we should ever have come to this Lake;
> Like magic there springs up a populous town,
> And hundreds to get gold are here settling down . . .
>
> No Queenstown was formed with its noisy hotels,
> And no restaurants with their loud dinner bells;
> No Port Chalmers boats could be seen on the Lake
> But the ducks had it all to themselves, no mistake!
> No bellman here shouted as he walked along–
> That Thatcher was going to sing a new song;
> If you told Thatcher then here his time he would spend,
> He'd have thought you were booked for the fam'd Yarra Bend.[108]

In 1865, while the clamour of the rushes departed the province with diggers travelling to the West Coast, Thatcher also brought his audience back to the memory of Dunedin engulfed by the rush:

> The light of other days burns dim,
> And in the shade is case;
> You'll own I'm right, if you will just
> Look back upon the past.
> Its glories now are faded–
> And all of you must know,
> That time aint what they used to was
> About three years ago
>
> Gabriel's then was all the rage,
> And diggers came to town–
> And in the public houses here
> They knocked the money down.
> The steamers came with thousands,
> And the money used to flow;
> And Shadrach did a nipping stroke.
> About three years ago.[109]

In 1862 he looked back on the decline of the Victorian goldfields that pushed many to Otago, while still longing for continuity:

> As the sun of Victoria begins to decline
> Let's hope that the star of Otago may shine;
> There's gold in the hills, boys, so let's work away,
> There's enough to support us for many a day.

In these songs, Thatcher charged the everyday monotony of digging for gold with transcendent meaning. As gold seekers packed into public houses in Dunedin and on the goldfields, Thatcher described how, in muddy gullies and on flooded claim, their aching backs and blistered feet had brought civilisation to this backward settlement of the 'Old Identity'. Moreover, Thatcher used dramatic contrast to highlight the gold rushes as events in constant flux. The moment the gold seeker shifted his gaze forwards or backwards, the rushes disappeared or transformed. Prospectors in Queenstown could reflect on the rapid progression of civilisation to the shores of Lake Wakatipu, undoubtedly strengthened by *The Old Identity*, which would be sung wherever Thatcher performed. And yet, in *Three Years Ago*, sung while thousands of Otago miners were departing for the West Coast, the gold rushes were ultimately unstable.

Thatcher also deployed the sentimental ballad to bring recollections to his audience of a wife or sweetheart left behind, or perhaps dreams of a future marriage. The sentimental ballad was always sung by a woman, and Thatcher's compositions were sung by his wife Madam Vitalli. The feminine character of the sentimental ballad is instrumental to understanding its popularity when female vocalists were often more loudly applauded than their male counterparts.[110] Commenting on the British public house, Peter Bailey argues that in the pub 'sexuality was a natural resource rather than a natural enemy'.[111] Historians of the gold rushes have often said that the absence of women automatically led the gold seeker into the dance hall and the brothel.[112] As Susan Lee Johnson notes, however, this erroneously assumes a 'volcanic theory of male sexuality – that men will be men, and that being a man means experiencing insistent desire that will be satisfied, one way or another'.[113] This is not to say that many did not seek after Eros as fervently as they did gold. The two hundred prostitutes in Dunedin during the gold rushes clearly show that many did.[114] However, for many gold seekers the attractiveness of female singers was far more nuanced than merely sexual desire.

If women were scarce on the diggings, they pervaded the thoughts of gold seekers. John Henry Watmuff frequently drifted in his diary back to past romances, tinged with anxiety about whether the women still loved him.[115] For others, thoughts would float back to sisters, mothers and wives. Andrew Roy always carried letters from his sister and mother with him wherever he went.[116] When John Love died in a blizzard on the Old Man Range in 1863, the only possessions he had on him were a few letters and photographs of his wife and child in Glasgow.[117]

As Sandra Quick shows, the female singer in the goldfield public house was commoditised to fill all these roles of mother, sister and lover.[118] Singers were expected to entertain with their beauty and their voice and to invoke memories of sweethearts and mothers and earlier, calmer times. Time and again these performers were applauded by audiences and newspapers to the degree that they conformed to representations of 'sweet-girl entertainment'.[119] Kate Grant, in Arrowtown, was praised by the *Lake Wakatip Mail* for her role as Lisette in the play *The Swiss Cottage*, and 'caused roars of laughter as the hoyden Good-for-nothing-Nan – throwing herself completely into the fun and spirit of the piece and avoiding entirely those clap-trap vulgarities which occasionally disfigure the performance of the character'.[120] Madame Vitelli received high praise as well for her performance of *That Young Man in Victoria*, which was written by her husband to the eighteenth-century Irish sentimental ballad, *One Bottle More*:

> I came out here three months ago unto this land of gold,
> That wages here rules very high, in Melbourne I was told.
> So I left Collingwood for good, and bid farewell, you see,
> To a young man in Victoria that's sticking up to me.[121]

Amid the smell of sweat and liquor and the haze of tobacco smoke, the voice and image of Vitelli singing would have been sharply discordant with the goldfield public house. However, it is precisely in their discordance that performances like these were so popular on the Otago goldfields. Scenes like this made the public house valuable in gold rush communities precisely because they recalled memories of kith and kin living elsewhere, rather than simply shaping a distinctive national identity.[122]

At the same time that Thatcher pulled his readers back to the families and communities they had left in the United Kingdom or Australasia, he also directed their gaze inward on the community they were forming in the dusty corners of the antipodean frontier. In doing so, he informed diggers' relationships by representing and distorting events, conflicts and personalities in a distinct locality. Many of Thatcher's Queenstown songs were sensationalist, and he took every opportunity to mock an individual or expose a scandal. One of Thatcher's first subjects was the Invercargill gold receiver, Thomas Jackson, who was unable to find many prospectors willing to sell him their gold when the Otago Provincial Council would not allow the Southland gold escort to enter Otago. When in one song Thatcher called him 'a potato merchant' who stored crops in an iron safe, Jackson sued him for slander. The case caused a sensation, with two hundred visitors crowded in and around the courthouse listening to the proceedings.[123] While the case was being heard, Thatcher took notes about the courthouse for a song he performed a few days later:

> ... there's a towel and wash-bowl close handy,
> And a saddle hangs there by the door;
> On the shelf half a bottle of brandy,
> And an old leather trunk on the floor.
> A pair of gold scales, getting rusty,
> That really should have a good wipe,
> And a Bible so shabby and dusty,
> And on it a dirty old pipe ...
>
> By the traps then a pris'ner is brought in,
> Our great Gold Receiver is there,
> Opposite Manders, who is reporting,
> And at one another they glare.
> A trap was sworn there, and by thunder
> In his right hand the volume he took,
> Not the Bible – for he made a blunder,
> And kissed an old cookery book.[124]

THE GOLDFIELD COURT

Thatcher was not the only individual who saw entertainment in the goldfield court. Gold seekers poured into courthouses across the goldfields where, like the goldfield public house and theatre, local cultures crystallised as individuals sought diversions from their frequent labour. The goldfield court, where publicans attempted to dodge liquor restrictions and gold seekers bickered with one another, was vital to individuals framing their hastily formed society in Otago. In one sense, the local courts became a key way in which metropolitan notions of race, gender and labour were contested and moulded by local conditions.[125] However, acknowledging the social basis for cultural formation, this section approaches these court cases from the perspective of the local community, rather than metropolitan cultures.

The courts were not simply a site where the state named and categorised what was what and who was who. It was entertainment. In her study of scandal in colonial Cape Town and Sydney, Kirsten McKenzie contends that gossip 'forges bonds within a community as participants use it to reassert their shared values'.[126] Similarly, the court became an important means for individuals to define their society. Values like respectability, honesty and industry that were batted around in the courtroom were not metaphysical speculations, but descriptions of people with whom residents drank, fought and gossiped. For many, this small local community constituted their social world. This is not to say that communication with loved ones back home was inconsequential; the tide of letters sent from Otago to Victoria and the United Kingdom, and the vehement calls for more post offices, clearly indicate otherwise.[127] Nevertheless, while thoughts of home surfaced throughout the day, the preoccupations with daily routine on the goldfields – swirling a pan and looking forward to a warm fire – remained ever-present. Furthermore, these daily cycles of work and play were charged with social meaning, as relationships crystallised over a bottle of whisky or disintegrated over a claim boundary.

The courthouse, the forward guard of colonial governance, was quite literally paper-thin. More times than not it was, in the words of Thatcher, 'a shabby little tent' that was unable to keep out the rain.[128] A gust of wind could easily blow the case notes out the door or even topple the whole structure. A correspondent at Waitahuna noted that the post office, which was crammed between a 'pill shop' and a general store, was soaked after every rain and was easily blown over by a heavy wind.[129] A year into the Tuapeka rush, a correspondent for the *Otago Daily Times* wrote about the goldfield's courthouse, known as the 'crow's nest' for its position atop the Blue Spur overlooking Gabriel's Gully:

> The present dilapidated tent in which justice is administered is a disgrace to the Government which allows it to remain. A tent about 12 x 16 [feet], by no means waterproof, and on hot days so steaming from the crowd that throng the precincts, as frequently to cause people who are compelled to stay in Court, to become ill. Only the other day a man, while giving evidence fainted from the suffocating heat and smell of the place.[130]

On any given day the courthouse would be crowded with about twenty litigants and witnesses and an additional few dozen miners and merchants, glimpsing in as spectators.[131] A correspondent for the *Otago Daily Times* complained when a new courthouse was built in Lawrence that it was too small to accommodate the fifty to sixty spectators who would be sitting in on the hearings on any given day.[132] Litigants fought with and shouted at each other while they were waiting for their cases to be heard.[133] This scene of chaos probably attracted several miners rambling about the township. Alfred Elvery, a digger at Moke Creek, was one of many who dropped in at the court one day to kill time while he was in Queenstown.[134] Many more read about the court cases in the newspapers. The *Lake Wakatip Mail* and the *Otago Daily Times* both carried extensive descriptions of court sessions, on some days running even longer than the paper's lead article. The goldfield courthouse would also be a meeting point for miners to congregate outside. On one occasion a man was brought in and tried for using coarse language among a crowd outside the courthouse.[135] For others still it might be a cosy spot for a post-drinking nap. One man fell asleep drunk on the doorstep of the court shortly after he was fined for failing to pay medical bills. He was dragged in, tried again and sent to the gaol.[136]

The courtroom was a sign of the dissonance of goldfield society, a jarring reminder that it was both a manifestation of the state and a sign of the state's incongruence with goldfield life. Even more than that, the court was a spectacle, a point of gossip and an occasion for a voyeuristic gaze into the anti-social behaviour of those who helped to define social space. As such, the court became an important lens for the public to understand the paradoxes and inconsistencies of gold rush culture. Diggers elbowed their way into the Dunedin police court, where they heard claims of respectability ushered forth in defence of binge drinking. While on a spree one night in 1862, Andrew Stephen walked out the front door of a brothel carrying a prostitute's dressing wardrobe. The next day, when the 'tall, dashing woman, fashionably dressed' accused him in court, his only defence was that he had 'always stuck to teetotalism', but let himself go one night and now could not remember a thing.[137]

Others piled into a tent staked into the ground forty metres from the Arrow River in 1863, where they saw gender thrown into disarray when distinctions between the prostitute and the helpmeet were blurred. The scene went something like this. Constable Lynch introduced the defendant to the magistrate (and the audience) as Florence Halliday, a well-known 'common prostitute' at the Arrow who was making a repeat appearance for drunkenness and abusive language. She was charged for riding wildly through town drunk at one in the morning and threatening to horsewhip a certain Mrs King, the wife of a publican. Halliday interrupted Lynch at this point, shouting across the courtroom: 'Well, I never! You are a nice fellow, to tell such lies. I was only "a little on", your Worship.' In contrast to Halliday, Mrs King was held up by Sergeant Lynch as 'a hard working respectable woman', although the local newspaper also indicated that she had been convicted four days previously for breaking into a shop in Queenstown and beating and kicking a certain Mrs Abbott.[138] Lynch then went on to describe how after threatening King, Halliday backed her horse into a knot of 'gentlemen' and shouted 'Kick the bastards!' She next rode up and down the street cursing the inhabitants of every store. At this point in the proceedings, a Mrs Watson was called to the witness stand to give her deposition:

> I am a married woman on the Arrow. My husband is a miner. After having gone to bed with my husband two hours earlier, we were woken up by hearing obscene language shouted outside our tent. I could not think it applied to me until I heard my name mentioned. She called me most obscene names, and swore awfully. I heard her afterwards, a long way up the street blackguarding everybody.

'That's a good one!" Halliday blurted out. 'Wasn't you with me on the Dunstan, and in the same position, and what are you now?' At this point Watson shouted back, 'I've never seen you before in my life! I would not dare ever socialising with such a low and dirty woman as you!' The case was hastily concluded by the magistrate with a fine of £5 imposed on Halliday, who paid it, gave a scowl to Lynch and went on her way.[139]

For the individual drawn into the courtroom to see the dysfunction of other members of the community, this spectacle was likely a sought-after diversion from the daily slog of digging, shovelling and washing. It was as good a performance and as good an entertainment as the most well-produced theatrical production in the Golden Age Hotel across the street from the courthouse. More than that, it was culturally informing. The goldfield court did not simply perform a judicial function; it also manifested the fragile and ongoing process of creating a 'symbolic order' out of the incongruences and inconsistencies of goldfield society.[140] The content of these cases changed very little. There was the drunkard (often impaired during the proceedings) and the pickpocket, the brawling diggers and the squabbling prostitutes, the crooked publican and the quack doctor.[141] Yet, despite these reiterations of goldfield types, spectators found court observation intrinsically satisfying, not for the information it provided but rather its dramatic portrayal of contending forces in their local community.[142]

CONCLUSION

This chapter has shown that in a society that centred on gold extraction, the 'work' of cultural formation continued after diggers walked off their claims. This was especially the case because individuals valued their time away from work almost as much as the precious metal that brought them to Otago. Moreover, relaxation and entertainment were profoundly social; whether reading a newspaper, visiting a public house or watching court proceedings, the variety of ways in which diggers spent their free time constantly presented them with an account of the community they were creating on the colonial frontier.

Thus far, this book has centred on the lives of British and Irish prospectors. In presenting this narrative, the intention has not been to treat the Otago gold rushes as 'white' events along a path towards national maturation as a 'neo-Britain' in the South Pacific. The analysis has strongly pushed against a trans-Tasman amnesia that forgets the shared histories of events and societies on either side of the Tasman Sea. This decentring of the nation also casts a clearer focus on Chinese prospectors, who were not marginal participants in a New Zealand event but part of the same transnational processes that repeatedly brought out individuals to Otago. The following chapter investigates the networks, societies and cultures of Chinese prospectors in Otago.

NOTES

1. Susan Lee Johnson, *Roaring Camp: The Social World of the California Gold Rush* (New York: W. W. Norton and Company, 2000), 142. Also see E. P. Thompson, 'Time, Work-discipline and Industrial Capitalism', *Past & Present* 38 (1967): 90.
2. James W. Carey, *Communication as Culture: Essays on Media and Society* (Boston: Unwin Hyman, 1989), 24.
3. Ibid., 21–5.
4. Malcolm J. Rohrbough, *Days of Gold: The California Gold Rush and the American Nation* (Berkeley: University of California Press, 1998), 146.
5. G. M. Hassing, *Pages from the Memory Log of G. M. Hassing: Sailor, Pioneer, Schoolmaster* (Invercargill: Southland Times Company, 1930), 35, 45.
6. Robert B. Booth, *Five Years in New Zealand* (London: J. G. Hammond and Co., 1912), 57.
7. *Otago Daily Times*, 11 May 1864.
8. See, for example, *Otago Daily Times*, 5 November 1862, 3 December

1862, 22 January 1863, 31 January 1863, 19 November 1863, 15 December 1863.
9. John Henry Watmuff, diary, 10 January 1862 [2/284]–4 January 1864 [4/51], private collection.
10. Peter Warren, diary, 30 April 1863, OSM, no call number.
11. See, for example, James Coutts Crawford, diary, ATL, MS-Papers-1001-012; Thomas McCourt, LDM, N-2377; John Moffat, diary, OSM, C-0204; John Penderick, diary, LDM, N-1901; Charles J. D. Robjohns, diary, ATL, MS-Papers-4913; Peter Warren, diary, OSM [no call number]; Thomas Williamson, diary, OSM, DC-2073; John Rodgers, diary, private collection.
12. Day Book of Bendix Hallenstein, 28 March–24 May 1864, OSM, DC-1430; 'Letters sent Overseas from Otago, 1861–1864' and 'Letters received from Overseas to Otago, 1861–1864', Reports on the Postal Service of New Zealand, *Appendices to the Journals of the House of Representatives*, 1862, D-2, 4; ibid., D-2, 20–1; ibid., 1864, D-1a, 12, 14; ibid., 1865, D-1, 10.
13. John George Walker (Dunstan) to his mother, Anne Walker (London), 25 January 1863, Walker Letters. Also see Penderick, diary, 8 July 1863, 11 July 1863.
14. *Colonist*, 13 December 1861.
15. J. E. Traue, 'Reading as a "Necessity of Life" on the Tuapeka Goldfields in Nineteenth-century New Zealand', *Library History* 23, no. 1 (2007): 41–8; J. E. Traue, 'The Public Library Explosion in Colonial New Zealand', *Libraries and the Cultural Record* 42, no. 2 (2007): 151–64. Also see Dulcie Gillespie-Needham, 'The Colonial and His Books: A Study of Reading in Nineteenth Century New Zealand' (PhD thesis, Victoria University of Wellington, 1971).
16. John Henry Watmuff, diary, 16 March 1862 [2/311]. Macaulay's essays were published in the *Edinburgh Review* between 1825 and 1844 and were later published in book form. See Thomas Babington Macaulay, *Critical and Historical Essays* (London: Longman, Brown, Green and Longmans, 1843).
17. *Lake Wakatip Mail*, 2 January 1864.
18. Traue, 'Reading as a "Necessity of Life"', 41–2. Also see J. E. Traue, 'Fiction, Public Libraries and the Reading Public in Colonial New Zealand', *Bulletin of the Bibliographical Society of Australia and New Zealand* 28, no. 4 (2004): 84–93; J. E. Traue, 'The Public Library Explosion in Colonial New Zealand', *Libraries and the Cultural Record* 42, no. 2 (2007): 151–64; Robin Marks, 'The Lawrence Athenaeum and Miners' Institute: a Fragment of Goldfields History' (MA thesis, University of Otago, 1973); Wayne R. Angus, 'Queenstown 1862–1864: The Genesis of a Goldfields Community' (BA (Hons), University of Otago, 1987).
19. W. T. Smith, diary, 28 August 1863, HC, MS-578-B.

20. Watmuff, diary, 16 November 1862 [3/32].
21. David Vincent, *Bread, Knowledge and Freedom: A Study of Nineteenth-Century Working Class Autobiography* (London: Europa Publications, 1981), 109.
22. Watmuff, diary, 12–13 September 1863 [3/7]. Also see ibid., 4 May 1862 [2/326]; 1 February 1863 [3/57]; 27 December 1863 [4/43].
23. Vincent, *Bread, Knowledge and Freedom*, 172.
24. Marks, 'The Lawrence Athenaeum', 160–5. For similar findings, also see Tony Ballantyne, 'Placing Literary Culture: Books and Civic Culture in Milton', *Journal of New Zealand Literature* 28, no. 2 (2010): 92–3; Lydia Wevers, *Reading on the Farm: Victorian Fiction and the Colonial World* (Wellington: Victoria University of Wellington Press, 2010), 31; Gillespie-Needham, 'The Colonial and His Books', 364.
25. Gillespie-Needham, 'The Colonial and His Books', chapter 18; John George Walker (Dunstan) to his mother, Anne Walker (London), 4 March 1863, Walker Letters.
26. Alan Atkinson, *Europeans in Australia* (Melbourne and New York: Oxford University Press, 1997), 234.
27. Hassing, *Memory Log*, 58.
28. Patrick Day, *The Making of the New Zealand Press: A Study of the Organizational and Political Concerns of New Zealand Newspaper Controllers, 1840–1880* (Wellington: Victoria University Press, 1990), 113.
29. See Patricia Nelson Limerick, *The Legacy of Conquest: The Unbroken Past of the American West* (New York and London: W. W. Norton and Company, 1987), 18.
30. 'Newspapers received from Overseas Destinations', *AJHR*, 1863, D-2, 22; ibid., 1864, D-1a, 13; ibid., 1865, D-1, 10. On the arrival of newspapers from overseas, also see Hassing, *Pages from the Memory Log of G. M. Hassing: Sailor, Pioneer, Schoolmaster*, 43; 'Simple Diary of an Unsuccessful Digger', *Christchurch Star*, 27 August 1931; Watmuff, diary, 21 December 1862 [3/41], 25 January 1863 [3/54].
31. Tony Ballantyne, 'On Place, Space and Mobility', *New Zealand Journal of History* 45, no. 1 (2011): 62.
32. *Otago Daily Times*, 3 December 1861, 27 January 1862, 31 January 1862, 20 February 1862, 5 March 1862, 26 April 1862, 20 June 1862, 8 August 1862, 22 August 1862, 14 November 1862, 17 November 1862, 6 December 1862, 27 December 1862, 23 February 1863, 14 April 1863, 29 April 1863.
33. Rohrbough, *Days of Gold*, 25.
34. James W. Carey, 'The Chicago School and the History of Mass Communication Research', in *James Carey: A Critical Reader* (Minneapolis and London: University of Minnesota Press, 1997), 27. Also see Carey, *Communication as Culture*, 18–23.

35. Ballantyne, 'Placing Literary Culture', 83.
36. Tony Ballantyne, 'Reading the Newspaper in Colonial Otago', *Journal of New Zealand Studies* 12 (2011): 52; Tony Ballantyne, 'Thinking Local: Knowledge, Sociability and Community in Gore's Intellectual Life, 1875–1914', *New Zealand Journal of History* 44, no. 2 (2010): 145. Many thanks to Tony Ballantyne for alerting me to his articles and Carey's work.
37. *Lake Wakatip Mail*, 2 May 1863, 20 May 1863, 3 June 1863, 15 August 1863, 28 August 1863, 25 November 1863, 5 December 1863, 23 December 1863.
38. See, for example, *Otago Daily Times*, 5 December 1861, 20 December 1861, 23 December 1861, 4 January 1862, 18 January 1862, 20 January 1862, 27 February 1862, 4 April 1862, 29 September 1862, 29 October 1862, 2 December 1862, 20 December 1862, 29 December 1862, 8 February 1863, 14 March 1863, 16 April 1863, 2 July 1863, 5 October 1863, 7 October 1863, 13 October 1863, 4 March 1864, 30 July 1864; *Colonist*, 16 January 1863, 27 November 1863.
39. Watmuff, diary, 22 February 1863 [3/63].
40. Kenton Scott Storey, '"What Will They Say in England?" Violence, Anxiety, and the Persistence of Humanitarianism in Vancouver Island and New Zealand, 1853–1862' (PhD thesis, University of Otago, 2011), 21.
41. Raewyn Dalziel, 'Vogel, Julius – Biography', *Dictionary of New Zealand Biography*, Te Ara – the Encyclopedia of New Zealand, URL: http://www.TeAra.govt.nz/en/biographies/1v4/1, accessed 22 March 2016. While the *Colonist* and *Daily Telegraph* similarly stressed the economic benefits of the rushes, they lamented what they saw as the weakening of the social and moral fabric of the settlement. See *Colonist*, 24 January 1862, 14 July 1862, 27 August 1862, 10 September 1862, 29 December 1862, 12 November 1863; *Daily Telegraph*, 22 January 1863, 19 December 1863, 5 January 1864.
42. *Otago Daily Times*, 23 January 1862, 18 March 1862, 23 January 1863, 25 January 1863, 5 November 1872; *Daily Telegraph*, 21 April 1863.
43. *Otago Daily Times*, 23 January 1862, 18 March 1862, 23 January 1863, 25 January 1863, 5 November 1872; *Daily Telegraph*, 21 April 1863.
44. In 1862 Brodie was elected at the top of the ballot to the short-lived Weatherston's Mining Board, of which he served as chairman until its dissolution. In 1863 he was elected unopposed as one of two goldfields representatives in the New Zealand House of Representatives, serving until 1865. That same year he was also one of four goldfield representatives elected to the Provincial Council, a position he held until the dissolution of the Provincial Council in 1866. Throughout his time on the Tuapeka and the Dunstan, Brodie also chaired several ad hoc committees and led numerous delegations to the government petitioning for

reform on the goldfields. *Otago Daily Times*, 15 May 1862, 1 November 1862, 5 November 1862, 21 January 1863, 26 January 1863, 27 July 1863.
45. Ibid., 14 December 1861, 17 December 1861, 20 January 1862.
46. Watmuff, diary, 25 May 1862 [2/330]. Also see 9 February 1862 [2/302], 8 June 1862 [3/340], 13 July 1862 [2/353].
47. *Otago Daily Times*, 12 December 1862, 11 November 1863, 2 February 1864, 10 February 1864, 12 February 1864, 24 February 1864, 29 February 1864, 6 April 1864, 11 April 1864.
48. John Nerone, 'Newspapers and the Public Sphere', in Scott E. Casper et al. (eds), *A History of the Book in America*, vol. 3 (Chapel Hill: University of North Carolina Press, 2007), 232. Also see Ballantyne, 'Reading the Newspaper'; James W. Carey, 'Communications and Economics', in *James Carey: A Critical Reader* (Minneapolis and London: University of Minnesota Press, 1997), 60–75.
49. *Otago Daily Times*, 12 November 1862, 10 January 1863, 30 January 1863.
50. Ibid., 9 May 1862, 12 December 1862, 15 May 1863.
51. Ibid., 24 September 1862, 27 November 1862, 19 November 1862, 12 November 1863, 25 June 1863.
52. Carey, *Communication as Culture*, 20.
53. Miles Fairburn, *The Ideal Society and Its Enemies: The Foundation of Modern New Zealand Society, 1850–1900* (Auckland: Auckland University Press, 1989), 144–7, 200–4; Jock Phillips, *A Man's Country?: The Image of the Pakeha Male, a History*, 2nd edn (Auckland: Penguin Books, 1996), 35–6.
54. Watmuff, diary, 24 August 1862 [2/370].
55. Robert Phelps, '"All Hands Have Gone Downtown": Urban Places in Gold Rush California', in Kevin Starr and Richard J. Orsi (eds), *Rooted in Barbarous Soil: People, Culture and Community in Gold Rush California* (Berkeley: University of California Press, 2000), 115.
56. Limerick, *The Legacy of Conquest*, 18.
57. *Colonist*, 1 May 1864.
58. C. L. Money, *Knocking About in New Zealand* (Melbourne: Samuel Mullen, 1871), 12.
59. Vincent, *Bread, Knowledge and Freedom*, 14–15.
60. Watmuff, diary, 13 April 1862 [2/320-2/322].
61. Brian Roberts, *American Alchemy: The California Gold Rush and Middle-Class Culture* (Chapel Hill: University of North Carolina Press, 2000), 9–13.
62. Phillips, *A Man's Country*, 36.
63. Ibid., 35–7, 47–59.
64. Ibid., 32–8, quote from p. 36; Fairburn, *The Ideal Society and Its Enemies*, 203–16. For a similar portrayal, see Stevan Eldred-Grigg, *Diggers, Hatters*

and Whores: The Story of the New Zealand Gold Rushes (Auckland: Random House, 2008), 284–92.
65. Russell Ward, *The Australian Legend* (Melbourne: Oxford University Press, 1958), 122.
66. This connection between the gold rushes and drunkenness was often assumed in Britain and the Australasian colonies. See David Goodman, *Gold Seeking: Victoria and California in the 1850s* (Stanford: Stanford University Press, 1994), 173–6, 197–8; R. A. Stafford, 'Preventing the "Curse of California": Advice for English Emigrants to the Australian Goldfields', *Historical Records of Australian Science* 7, no. 3 (1987): 215–30.
67. *Otago Witness*, 13 July 1861. Also see *Colonist*, 19 July 1861, 9 August 1861, 16 August 1861.
68. See ibid., 13 July 1861; 20 July 1861. Also see A. H. McLintock, *The History of Otago* (Dunedin: Otago Centennial Historical Publications, 1949), 456. In a similar manner, Victorian gold seekers instituted a ban on liquor sales in the first two years of the Victorian gold rushes. See Geoffrey Blainey, *The Rush That Never Ended: A History of Australian Mining*, 4th edn (Melbourne: Melbourne University Press, 1993), 41.
69. Eldred-Grigg, *Diggers, Hatters and Whores*, 286.
70. *Otago Daily Times*, 28 November 1862, 5.
71. *Lake Wakatip Mail*, 19 September 1863, 6.
72. Ibid., 11 November 1863, 4.
73. Greg Ryan, 'Drink and the Historians: Sober Reflections on Alcohol in New Zealand 1840–1914', *New Zealand Journal of History* 44, no. 1 (2010): 39–42.
74. John Henry Watmuff, diary; William Martin, reminiscences, HC, MS-0203.
75. Frank Harbottle, reminiscences, HC, Misc-MS-1654, 32.
76. See McLintock, *The History of Otago*, Chapter 4. Also see Fairburn, *The Ideal Society and Its Enemies*, 62–73.
77. Ryan, 'Drink and the Historians', 35.
78. John Burnett, *Liquid Pleasures: A Social History of Drinks in Modern Britain* (London and New York: Routledge, 1999), 120–1.
79. Richard Stivers, *Hair of the Dog: Irish Drinking and Its American Stereotype*, 2nd edn (New York: Continuum, 2000), 10–22.
80. Brian Harrison, *Drink and the Victorians: The Temperance Question in England, 1815–1872*, 2nd edn (Staffordshire: Keele University Press, 1994), 302–41.
81. Peter Bailey, 'Parasexuality and Glamour: The Victorian Barmaid as Cultural Prototype', *Gender & History* 2, no. 2 (1990): 148–72; Peter Bailey, 'Conspiracies of Meaning: Music-Hall and the Knowingness of Popular Culture', *Past and Present* 144 (1994): 138–70.
82. Geoffrey Serle, *The Golden Age: A History of the Colony of Victoria,*

1851–1861 (Melbourne: Melbourne University Press, 1963), 362–6; Michael Cannon, *Melbourne after the Gold Rush* (Main Ridge: Loch Haven Books, 1993), 306–39.
83. *Otago Witness*, 15 February 1862.
84. James Strachan, reminiscences, HC, MS-563, 10.
85. *Otago Daily Times*, 23 December 1861.
86. Ibid., 26 December 1861.
87. Ibid., 1 January 1862, 1 January 1863.
88. Ibid., 25 March 1862.
89. For description of diggers loitering about the Provincial for news, see *Otago Daily Times*, 10 February 1863.
90. Elliott West, *The Saloon on the Rocky Mountain Mining Frontier* (Lincoln: University of Nebraska Press, 1996), 146.
91. McCourt, diary, 11 April 1863, 13 April 1863, 6 May 1863, 3 August 1863.
92. Penderick, 13 March 1863.
93. *Lake Wakatip Mail*, 26 December 1863.
94. Peter Kuch, 'The Irish and the Australasian Colonial Stage: Confrontation and Compromise', *Australasian Journal of Irish Studies* 10 (2010): 105–6.
95. Richard Fotheringham, 'Theatre from 1788 to the 1960s', in Elizabeth Webby (ed.), *The Cambridge Companion to Australian Literature* (Cambridge: Cambridge University Press, 2000), 140.
96. Serle, *The Golden Age*, 362–3.
97. *Lake Wakatip Mail*, 14 October 1863, 4.
98. Ibid.
99. Robert H. B. Hoskins, 'Thatcher, Charles Robert', from the *Dictionary of New Zealand Biography, Te Ara – the Encyclopedia of New Zealand*, updated 30 October 2012, http://www.TeAra.govt.nz/en/biographies/1t91/thatcher-charles-robert, accessed 3 July 2013.
100. Cf. Bailey, 'Conspiracies of Meaning', 143.
101. 'Reminiscences of the Inimitable Thatcher', *Otago Witness*, 27 August 1896, 52.
102. *Lake Wakatip Mail*, 30 September 1863, 3 October 1863, 7 October 1863, 10 October 1863, 14 October 1863.
103. Erik Olssen, *A History of Otago* (Dunedin: John McIndoe, 1984), 56–7.
104. Alexander Bathgate, Colonial Experiences or Sketches of People and Places in the Province of Otago, New Zealand (Glasgow: James Maclehose, 1874), 26.
105. Charles Thatcher, *Thatcher's Dunedin Songster, Containing the Popular Local Songs as Written and Sung by Him at the Theatre Royal, Commercial Hotel*, vol. 1 (Dunedin: Daily Times Office, 1862), 1–2.
106. For uses of 'Old Identity' and its opposite, 'New Iniquity', see *Otago Daily Times*, 15 April 1862, 28 June 1862, 29 September 1862, 9 February

1863; *Lake Wakatip Mail*, 23 June 1863, 22 August 1863, 9 September 1863, 25 November 1863; Watmuff, diary, 23 March 1862 [2/313]; Henry Walton reminiscences, in *Gabriel's Gully Jubilee: Reminiscences of the Early Gold Mining Days* (Dunedin: Otago Daily Times, 1911), 17.
107. 'Reminiscences of the Inimitable Thatcher', *Otago Witness*, 27 August 1896.
108. Charles Thatcher, 'Olden Days at Lake Wakatipu', in Robert Hoskins, *Goldfield Balladeer: The Life and Times of the Celebrated Charles R. Thatcher* (Auckland: HarperCollins, 1997), 171. Yarra Bend was a mental asylum in Victoria that operated between 1848 and 1925.
109. Charles Thatcher, *Thatcher's Otago Songster, Containing Many of the Popular Local Songs, as Written and Sung by Him at the Corinthian Hall, Dunedin*, vol. 1 (Dunedin: Joseph Mackay, 1865), 15.
110. See, for example, *Otago Daily Times*, 8 October 1863, 12 February 1864.
111. Peter Bailey, *Popular Culture and Performance in the Victorian City* (Cambridge: Cambridge University Press, 1998), 152.
112. Paula Mitchell Marks, *Precious Dust: The American Gold Rush Era, 1848–1900* (New York: William Morrow and Co., 1994), 336–8; Rohrbough, *Days of Gold*, 91–6; Roberts, *American Alchemy*, 226.
113. Susan Lee Johnson, '"My Own Private Life": Toward a History of Desire in Gold Rush California', in *Rooted in Barbarous Soil: People, Culture and Community in Gold Rush California* (Berkeley: University of California Press, 2000), 323. In the New Zealand context, see Phillips, *A Man's Country*, 36–8; Eldred-Grigg, *Diggers, Hatters and Whores*, 370–99. For an excellent discussion of the limitations of deterministic impressions of the gender ratio in colonial New Zealand, see Charlotte McDonald, 'Too Many Men and Too Few Women: Gender's "fatal Impact" in Nineteenth-century Colonies', in *The Gendered Kiwi* (Auckland: Auckland University Press, 1999), especially 32–3.
114. Terry Hearn, 'Review of *Diggers, Hatters & Whores: The Story of the New Zealand Gold Rushes*', *New Zealand Journal of History* 43, no. 1 (2009): 77–9.
115. John Henry Watmuff, diary, 2 February 1862 (2/300): 'Today I wrote Agnes Rakowski a valentine from New Zealand. Very like what an enthusiastic lover might write to his mistress. I trust she will not take it as its meant. Oh! Vanity. I am ashamed of the small quantity I possess, & yet I'd sooner hear from or see Isa King for an hour, than live a month with Miss R.'
116. Andrew Roy (Hokitika) to his mother and father (Glendevon, Scotland), 19 December 1865, Andrew Roy Letters, OSM, DC-0683.
117. *Otago Daily Times*, 8 December 1863.
118. Sandra Quick, '"The Colonial Helpmeet Takes a Dram": Women

Participants in the Central Otago Goldfields Liquor Industry, 1861–1901' (MA thesis, University of Otago, 1997), 81.
119. Ibid., 80.
120. Ibid., 80–2. *The Swiss Cottage* was a farce written by Thomas Haynes Bayly (1797–1839), among the most popular English songwriters and playwrights during the nineteenth century. See John W. Cousins, *Short Biographical Dictionary of English Literature* (London: J. M. Dent and Sons, 1910), Project Gutenberg, http://www.gutenberg.org/files/13240/13240-8.txt (accessed 13 December 2012).
121. Thatcher, *Thatcher's Dunedin Songster, Containing the Popular Local Songs as Written and Sung by Him at the Theatre Royal, Commercial Hotel*, No. 1: 10–11.
122. Phillips, *A Man's Country*, 35–6. For a discussion of the links between the goldfield public house and communities and families living elsewhere, see West, *The Saloon*, 146.
123. *Otago Daily Times*, 21 April 1863, 30 August 1863.
124. Charles Thatcher, 'Queenstown Police Court', in Hoskins, *Goldfield Balladeer*, 64.
125. See Adele Perry, *On the Edge of Empire: Gender, Race, and the Making of British Columbia, 1849–1871* (Toronto: University of Toronto Press, 2001); Lindsay Proudfoot and Dianne Hall, *Imperial Spaces: Placing the Irish and Scots in Colonial Australia* (Manchester and New York: Manchester University Press, 2011).
126. Kirsten McKenzie, *Scandal in the Colonies: Sydney and Cape Town, 1820–1850* (Melbourne: Melbourne University Press, 2004), 34.
127. *Otago Daily Times*, 11 December 1861, 23 December 1861, 24 December 1861, 15 January 1862, 20 January 1862, 29 January 1862, 11 March 1862, 27 June 1862, 7 August 1862, 13 August 1862, 27 September 1862, 13 November 1862, 26 November 1862, 29 December 1862, 17 January 1863, 2 April 1863, 1 May 1863, 6 May 1863, 20 May 1863, 22 May 1863, 10 September 1863, 30 October 1863.
128. Charles Thatcher, 'Nocturnal Session of the Arrow Court', in Hoskins, *Goldfield Balladeer*, 67–8.
129. *Otago Daily Times*, 2 April 1863.
130. Ibid. Also see 18 January 1862, 6 May 1862.
131. *Colonist*, 22 August 1862; *Otago Daily Times*, 30 April 1863, 31 August 1864.
132. *Otago Daily Times*, 27 August 1862.
133. *Lake Wakatip Mail*, 24 June 1863.
134. Ibid., 26 September 1863.
135. Ibid., 21 October 1863.
136. Ibid., 9 January 1864.
137. *Otago Daily Times*, 15 January 1863.
138. *Lake Wakatip Mail*, 27 June 1863.

139. *Lake Wakatip Mail*, 27 June 1863.
140. Carey, *Communication as Culture*, 19.
141. *Lake Wakatip Mail*, 3 June 1863, 13 June 1863; *Otago Daily Times*, 27 February 1862.
142. Carey, *Communication as Culture*, 21–2.

5

'We Return Home in Glory':
Chinese Networks and Gold Seeking in Otago

The Chinese in nineteenth-century New Zealand are often neglected by historians as marginal participants in a national history centred on Māori–Pakeha relations. Although the histories of the New Zealand gold rushes decentre this bi-national narrative, they rarely yield greater acknowledgement of Chinese prospectors. Miles Fairburn and Jock Phillips construct their narratives of gold rush societies without reference to the Chinese. They also do not analyse the ways in which European colonial identities were shaped by engagements with Chinese prospectors on the goldfields.[1] Studies that discuss the Chinese in Otago also rarely take Chinese perspectives seriously, typically focusing instead on European colonial responses to their arrival.[2] Similarly, among the body of unpublished theses on the Otago rushes completed in the last forty years, there is only one study that analyses the experiences and identities of Chinese prospectors.[3] When the Chinese always hovered on the margins of national development in New Zealand, they remain relevant in this literature primarily for their role in forming a stronger sense of nationalism among European prospectors – those who stayed and became 'New Zealanders'.

Lost in this distinction between white 'New Zealand' gold miners and Chinese sojourners is that ever-transient European prospectors sit only awkwardly in a historiography that treats the Otago rushes as New Zealand events and the prospectors as settlers. The European goldfields population in the early 1860s was often more transient than Chinese miners, who began arriving in the province in the late 1860s. Few also ever identified themselves with the colony during what was usually a brief stay in Otago. This book has so far shifted perspective away from the nation to local and transnational scales of the European rushes. Such an approach also brings Chinese prospectors into clearer focus.

By pushing against the national genealogies of the rushes, this chapter locates Chinese societies and cultures in Otago at the intersection of transnational networks and local environments and social structures.

In doing so, this study aligns closely with James Ng's path-breaking work on the Chinese in Otago.[4] It identifies especially the pervasiveness of transnational networks that connected Chinese prospectors in Otago to family members in China and scattered throughout the Chinese diaspora. Similar to European migrants discussed in Chapter Two, most Chinese prospectors relied on family and community networks to organise and finance their migration. The chapter also affirms Yong Chen's argument that Chinese identities in white societies did not emerge only from experiences of antipathy but were also created through transnational networks connecting individuals to home villages and family members in China, much like their British and Irish counterparts.[5] Moreover, as Adam McKeown argues in his study of Chinese migrants in Peru, Chicago and Hawaii, Chinese identities must also be grounded in the ideas, rituals and practices that migrants brought with them and replicated in their new homes.[6]

The chapter also assesses European colonists' perceptions of and interactions with Chinese migrants. James Ng and Stevan Eldred-Grigg are among the few scholars to treat the Chinese with any more than a passing reference; however, both understand European–Chinese relations largely through the lens of apparently axiomatic racism.[7] Similarly, Miles Fairburn, James Belich and Laurie Guy entirely neglect Chinese agency by discussing Chinese migrants only as victims of European colonial racism.[8] However, as George M. Fredrickson explains, historical approaches to race relations should seek to explain the contexts and processes through which discrimination crystallised, rather than 'make moral judgments' on past societies.[9] Stressing both local and global contexts that gave rise to anti-Chinese sentiment, this chapter confirms Marilyn Lake and Henry Reynolds' conclusion that anti-Chinese antagonism 'was born in [colonists'] apprehension of imminent loss'.[10] As Erik Olssen demonstrates, waged gold miners and labourers clamoured loudest against Chinese immigration when they feared competition for work.[11] Responses to the arrival of Chinese prospectors in Otago often broke along class lines: while labourers adamantly opposed the Chinese in the province, merchants and industrialists favoured an influx of Chinese consumers and workers as European diggers returned to Victoria or rushed to the West Coast. Chinese identities in Otago crystallised through the combinations of these colonial experiences and individuals' transnational connections to home.

This chapter is divided into three parts. The first section adopts the geographic approach of earlier chapters to analyse Chinese gold seeking in Otago during the nineteenth century. It locates the Chinese experience at the intersection of transnational networks, which connected the Chinese prospector to his neighbours and family members at a particular village in southeast China, and local societies and cultures in Otago, where identities were shaped and boundaries were defined. Much like the British and Irish prospectors discussed in Chapter Two, these transnational and local networks and identities were entangled through the routines of work and leisure in the dusty corners of Otago and Southland. Connections to home depended on gold won from the ground or lost in the gambling house. Local Chinese cultures and networks framed Chinese interactions with each other and Europeans as they were impacted by such engagements, as well as local economic conditions.

The second section of the chapter surveys Chinese cultural practices on the goldfields. The core social unit for Chinese prospectors was the extended family, which also connected the individual to a particular village in China populated with relatives. When migration was often a family decision, gold seekers were expected to send remittances to loved ones in China, yet many prospectors were unable to contribute significantly to their family's wealth. Moreover, many diggers spent their earnings on opium and gambling rather than send money home. Because cultural practices required diggers to send remittances along with correspondence, the lack of remittances often fractured family connections. Despite the disintegration of transnational networks, Chinese prospectors maintained strong attachments to home through religious rituals, seasonal celebrations and food cultures.

The third part of this chapter critically assesses the interactions between the Chinese and European populations in Dunedin and on the goldfields. Debates in Otago about Chinese immigration were entangled with local and global scales that both helped to nationalise concerns about Chinese prospectors and structure those concerns within class debates. However, it also stresses imperial scales by framing these local anxieties within Australasian fears of the British government catering to Chinese imperial desires to open Australia and New Zealand to large-scale Chinese immigration, as demonstrated by Persia Crawford Campbell.[12] Moreover, these local and global fears were fuelled by transnational press networks when the telegraphic cable allowed individuals to read accounts of anti-Chinese riots in Australia and California. When fears of China colonising New Zealand with its millions of migrants were always present, such external events were often more important in framing contemporary understanding than local developments.

By organising Chinese gold seekers within a separate chapter, the intention is not to quarantine them as marginal participants in a Pakeha history. Rather, it highlights the different economic, social and political climates that facilitated the arrival of the Chinese and framed their experiences in Otago. Moreover, the chapter reveals the impacts of the transforming of Otago's economy to factory production and capital-intensive forms of gold extraction on class identity and the importance of Chinese arrivals to shaping colonial anxiety of the province becoming a Chinese dependency. Under the threat of Chinese immigration, earlier waves of European gold seekers were remembered not as the Victorian Iniquity, but as New Zealand settlers, set in strong contrast to the 'Chinese hordes' which threatened to transform the province from a Better Britain into a Chinese satellite. In reality, however, the Victorian prospector was often no less a sojourner than the Chinese.

LOCATING CHINESE GOLD SEEKING

Virtually all Chinese emigrants during the nineteenth century originated in an area of ten thousand square kilometres in the Pearl River Delta in Guangdong.[13] Otago received a small trickle from this stream, less than 1 per cent between 1860 and 1900.[14] The 'roll of the Chinese in New Zealand', compiled by Alexander Don, a Presbyterian missionary to the Chinese in Otago, provides probably the most complete picture of the origins of the Chinese in any Pacific Rim settler society. One historian goes so far as to call this text a 'Doomsday Book' for New Zealand Chinese.[15] The roll book contains the names, and from 1896 the village and district origins, of 3,159 Chinese in Otago whom Don visited on his annual missionary tours between 1883 and 1913. Although Don's roll records the Chinese population in Otago after it dwindled from its peak in 1873, the book still presents the most reliable source of the Otago Chinese. Moreover, many of the later arrivals were likely to have been repeat immigrants, because a £10 poll tax on first-time Chinese immigrants, and its increase to £100 in 1888, meant that many of the annual arrivals were repeat migrants who did not have to pay the tax. An analysis of Don's roll by the New Zealand historian Charles Sedgwick reveals that 2,104 (67 per cent) came from 165 villages in the Panyu district, mostly the Upper Panyu district just north of Guangzhou, the capital of Guangdong. Another 432 (14 per cent) came from 42 villages in the neighbouring district of Zengcheng and 411 (13 per cent) originated from 285 villages in Siyi. The final 5 per cent of the documented Chinese came from other counties scattered across Guangdong.[16] What follows is a brief overview of the local contexts in the region of Guangdong which helped to facilitate and direct migration to Otago.

Developments within the Pearl River Delta encouraged emigration from Guangdong. During the eighteenth and nineteenth centuries the region underwent a gradual shift away from subsistence farming towards textile production and cash crops like sugar and tobacco, which required fewer people to work the land. When the early Qing dynasty restricted all Chinese trade with Europe to flow through Guangzhou under the 'Canton system', a new Guangdong merchant class was created with extensive experience interacting with Europeans. Merchants contracted families in the surrounding districts to harvest silk and weave cotton and flax, which was sold throughout China and to European merchants in Guangzhou.[17] When the Opium Wars (1839–42 and 1856–60) opened additional ports in China and ceded Hong Kong to Britain, European products flooded Chinese markets. Increased competition from overseas textiles devalued local products and lowered wages. Moreover, trade from other regions shifted to other ports, leading to economic stagnation.[18]

Alongside these economic contractions, the Pearl River Delta was gripped by frequent political unrest. A series of rebellions spread through the region due to the state's weakened status after the Opium Wars. While Guangdong did not experience much of the carnage from the Taiping Rebellion (1851–64) that killed twenty million across China, the unrest caused by the war destabilised the region enough to inspire the Red Turban Revolt (1854) that besieged Guangzhou. Government reprisals were even more disastrous when the emperor ordered the beheading of some 70,000 rebels and supporters, many of whom supported the revolution under duress.[19] Even more devastating was a series of local wars two years later over arable land in Guangdong that erupted between the native Poonti and the Hakka, an itinerant group that arrived from northern China. The conflict, which continued intermittently until 1867, left 200,000 dead in the province.[20] These causes alone, however, cannot explain the emigration, especially when the outflow continued to grow in the late nineteenth century as economic and social stability returned to the region. Moreover, other regions of China were experiencing similar and at times even more destructive warfare and feuds.[21] An account of Chinese migration also needs to take into account the structures and networks which facilitated and directed migration abroad to Otago.

Chinese emigration was closely linked to European penetration into China and the growth of markets and economic networks throughout the Pacific. From the sixteenth century, Portuguese and Spanish merchants began trading North American maize and potatoes in exchange for Chinese silk, and the Pearl River Delta became deeply embedded in global commercial networks. This global trade had profound impacts on local economic structures, because both crops could be grown on rocky soil, thereby providing a nourishing food source that did not compete with rice and wheat, which required more fertile land. This stimulated a population explosion from the seventeenth to the nineteenth centuries, which helped to spur emigration.[22] As the population in the region continued to grow, families began sending their sons abroad in order to diversify their sources of income. At the beginning of the nineteenth century, there were over 250,000 Guangdong migrants living in Indonesia and a Chinatown in Mexico City was already 250 years old.[23] By mid-century, Guangdong migrants began leaving in large numbers for the goldfields in European settler societies across the Pacific. In 1852, four years into the California gold rushes, there were 25,000 (10 per cent of the state's population) Chinese in California. By 1857 the same number of Chinese migrants had reached Victoria, Australia.[24] Otago always drew a much smaller number of Chinese than either California or Victoria – in 1871 fewer than 4,000 Chinese were living in the province.[25]

As Philip Kuhn shows, nearly all Chinese migration after 1842 flowed through British shipping lanes that were based in Hong Kong.[26] By the time the gold rushes began, Hong Kong and Guangzhou both possessed a local Chinese merchant community operating closely with British agents. The London firm John Swire and Company established the China Navigation Company in 1872, with Butterfield and Swire as a local syndicate; it operated four merchant vessels carrying migrants, tea and Chinese commodities to Sydney, Melbourne and Dunedin.[27] Several Hong Kong financial firms, known as *jinshanzhuang*, also arranged the passage of Chinese migrants under a credit-ticket system, in which the gold seeker agreed to exchange a certain amount of gold annually for three years for the cost of a fare.[28] With the security of collateral, the firm might also extend a loan to a family looking to finance their son's emigration. Ah Kow and another Chinese prospector from the same town financed their passage to Otago with a £13 loan from a Chinese firm on 25 per cent annual interest.[29] Such firms also were an important link for migrants to home, as they were the primary facilitators of correspondence and remittances between emigrants and native villages in Guangdong.[30] Mercantile networks were, therefore, an important means by which the migrant both left his home and remained connected through correspondence and material culture. These networks were also interwoven with British imperial organisation. Chinese firms negotiated the transportation of goods and people with British merchants who unloaded their goods and people in Dunedin and Invercargill. In exchange, return migrants and remittances were shipped back to Hong Kong, where Guangzhou firms arranged letters to be delivered in home villages to family members.[31]

The networks that facilitated migration also extended beneath British imperial structures to community and family groups. Chinese sons growing up in a sojourner village, or *qiaoxiang* (literally, 'native place'), were prepared throughout childhood for the expectation of leaving home. Over generations, the local economy of a *qiaoxiang* was maintained almost entirely by remittances sent home. Emigration had often begun generations earlier, but by the mid-nineteenth century emigration from these villages had become a way of life. For example, one quarter of the population living in Taishan county by 1900 had lived overseas and there were many more from the region who emigrated but never returned.[32] Throughout the second half of the nineteenth century, the shortage of labour in these villages caused by emigration was filled by migrants arriving from other more depressed regions of China.[33]

While there were some individuals who emigrated to escape an unwanted marriage, seek adventure or avoid conscription, emigration was most often a family decision.[34] Mobility became the primary means through which a family was able to sustain itself or better its circumstances. A family would develop a diversified portfolio by having their sons pursue different financial prospects. This formation grew out of older practices of internal migration, in which a son would migrate to the city to find work. He would marry a woman from his native village, who would reside with his family. Through periodic visits home, he would hope to father children by her. This practice changed very little with the advent of overseas migration. One son might remain on the family farm, selling produce in a local market. Another might pursue a business venture or government position in Guangzhou, while a third might work as a labourer in Peru or Hawaii or seek his riches on the goldfields of North America or Australasia.[35] Ideally, all sons would only live on the bare essentials and send all other surplus money back to the father, who would disperse it according to need. One historian of the Chinese in the United States goes so far as to say the desire to send money home 'was what gave meaning to Chinese Americans' existence and their labour in the New World'.[36] The expectation of remittances was so strong that, as

Alexander Don commented, 'of ten letters between Otago Chinese and their family back home, nine concern money'.[37] Home correspondents who eagerly awaited money from Otago gold seekers referred to a letter with remittances as a *gum san*, or 'gold letter', while they called a letter without a *húng san*, or 'empty letter.'[38] Essentially, the economies of a handful of villages on the Pearl River Delta became inseparable from hundreds of local economies scattered, as one Chinese newspaper commented, 'to the four corners of the earth'.[39]

Families on the Pearl River Delta often took an active role in arranging the marriages of their family members in Otago. Many Chinese gold seekers in Otago were either married or betrothed to women in the village, who would live with their husband's family in his absence.[40] Otago and Guangdong members of the family usually expected that the prospector would return home after a few years to establish himself in farming or a business in his local village; however, the local tradition of seasonal migration in China and the infrequency of miners returning home probably meant that many understood a longer sojourn was possible. One gold miner on the Nevis, who had been in Otago for twelve years, told Don that his family had arranged his betrothal to a woman from his village, but he did not have enough money to return to China for the marriage.[41]

When Pearl River Delta residents depended almost entirely on remittances and correspondence from emigrant sons, the Otago Chinese camp in Lawrence or Round Hill would often appear closer and more present in everyday life in a *qiaoxiang* village than the neighbouring village in Upper Panyu, which may have spoken a different dialect or originated from a different lineage. It was not simply a two-way traffic between *qiaoxiang* and overseas Chinese communities in Otago. Native place networks also connected the Chinese gold miner in Otago with his clansmen in North America, Indonesia, Micronesia and southeast Asia, as well as Australasia.[42] A Chinese man in Otago thumbing through a list of Hong Kong and San Francisco subscribers who paid for the removal of a deceased Chinese migrant's remains from California to China could, therefore, remark with pride that his clansmen were among the most generous donors.[43] However, much like European migrant groups, these wider connections to diasporic communities cannot rightly be considered global, for their awareness of the 'global' rarely extended beyond a close-knit group of kin transplanted to particular locales around the Pacific.[44]

GUANGDONG CULTURES ON THE GOLDFIELDS

In 1890 Alexander Don, upon returning from one of his annual missionary tours among the Chinese in Otago, wrote in the *New Zealand Presbyterian* that

> many writers about the Chinese . . . seemed to have started with the *theorem*, The Chinese are a very peculiar people, and to have written to prove this. Thus *caricatures*, not pictures of the Chinese, have been produced. The quantity of inaccurate information, and the want of real information, about the Chinese, is extraordinary. Any atrocity, or curiosity, or absurdity, or enormity, appearing in the newspapers, has only to be credited to China to be believed.[45]

Don believed that the chief obstacle to the acceptance of the Chinese in Otago was the inability – or unwillingness – of Europeans to understand the Chinese on their own terms. His narratives in the Presbyterian journals of his mission trips to the Chinese communities in the province were an attempt to break down resistance to the Chinese in the colony by allowing Europeans a humanising glimpse into Chinese society. The historian must be equally mindful of Don's caution. As Roger Daniels argues in his study of Asian migrants in the United States, the Chinese 'have been celebrated more for what happened to them than for what they have accomplished'.[46] In order to understand the formation of Chinese society on the goldfields, we must first understand the cultural imprints and diasporic networks that framed their interactions in these spaces and animated their connections to home. Otherwise, we run the risk of only defining them, like so many colonial commentators, in oppositional terms to the imagined ideal society. This is not to say that all Chinese universally accepted the same system of beliefs any more than all Catholic Irish diggers recited their rosaries by candlelight every week. Nevertheless, Chinese culture touched all aspects of social life in China and was transplanted to Otago. An individual might react against this system or abandon it, but its pervasiveness among the Chinese on the goldfields never made it irrelevant.

Despite extended absences from home villages, individuals retained a strong connection to family members in China. The core unit of Chinese social life in the nineteenth century was the extended family. An eclectic mix of Chinese religious beliefs held that life and the afterlife and the material and the immaterial constantly overlapped in everyday life. When a man died he would be worshipped and given offerings by his descendants, which would provide for his happiness in the afterlife.

In exchange, the ancestor would watch over his family, granting them success in their endeavours and protection from wandering ghosts. This filial piety was extended to the living patriarch of the family, who was said to have direct authority down from the ancestors. Any personal honour or embarrassment affected the family as a whole, which shared a collective identity by descent from the ancestor.[47] At the risk of oversimplification, identity and happiness both in the present life and the next life were deeply linked to participation in a family unit and the fathering of sons.

While this system was subscribed to in varying degrees, the desire to maintain connections with family members in Guangdong, provide for their welfare, and return to the ancestral home and establish a family was frequently mentioned by Chinese gold seekers in Otago, even after thirty years' residence in the province.[48] Chinese prospectors who wrote home were, like British and Irish gold seekers, 'inspired not by fear of sanctions but by adherence to a code of obligations and entitlements'.[49] Local contexts placed a severe strain on these transnational networks. Because the family was a geographically dispersed unit and correspondence often depended on remittances, relationships frequently depended on how much gold was won in the ground and how much was lost in gambling and opium houses. James Ng estimates that 20 per cent of the Otago Chinese were addicted to opium in 1890.[50] In this context, gold letters were infrequent if sent at all, and many gold seekers would rather not write than send an empty letter. As one Chinese man told Don,

> We Chinese you know will not write unless we have money to send. If you wrote me wanting money and I had none to send I would not reply. So in writing to China, without money we will not write home.[51]

This statement cannot be taken as necessarily indicative of intention, because the individual could have had money but chose not to send it home. Nevertheless, it reveals that remittance remained important for individuals even if they chose not to send money home.

In 1894 a pair of brothers told Don that they had not written home during the twelve years they had been in Otago because neither had enough money to send home.[52] Another digger, 'Glorious Dignity', did not send a letter home for seventeen years because he did not have money to send.[53] One old man at Tuapeka was only able to send £7 to family in China in sixteen years.[54] Mr Ip, who migrated to Otago to retrieve his family's fortune when his father died, told Don seven years later that he was unable to send any money home and lost all contact with his family.[55]

These silences would lead to recriminations from family members at home. One Guangdong miner at Riverton, for example, received an abrupt letter from his father, stating, 'Most important, most urgent: Send some money.'[56] Both letters and silences, therefore, bear testament to the fractured relationships between the Chinese in Otago and their kin at home. As letters flooded in from home, describing destitution and asking for money, and the absence of letters spoke of even greater tragedy, many miners frequently lamented their inability to assist their kin. Tears streamed down the face of one miner as the result of receiving a letter from his destitute and lonely mother and his inability to aid and comfort her.[57]

Don frequently commented that gambling, opium and prostitution caused greater destitution in more Chinese diggers than anything else. Like remittances, money spent on leisure often depended on how much gold was won in the ground. Gambling houses and brothels sprang up at Alexandra in the spring of 1891 when the Molyneux River was low; in a span of a few months, entertainment houses ballooned from one saloon and one fan-tan house to three saloons and two fan-tan houses, and there were three prostitutes working among the Chinese.[58] When the population peaked at Round Hill in 1881, most of the thirty buildings in the Chinese settlement were opium or gambling houses.[59]

Gambling in Guangdong had a very different meaning than in European society. According to Chinese religion, an individual's happiness was dependent on a combination of *ming* (fate) and *yun* (luck). Moreover, there was no clear separation for some Chinese between a mining claim and a pakapu ticket[60] or a fan-tan table.[61] Both were partially predestined by fate. Don noted that the most commonly heard sayings on the diggings were that 'nothing follows man's own calculations' or 'wife, wealth, children, pay, all are predestined'.[62] One miner Don asked about his prospects of returning home, replied, 'It is hard to say; it may be God's will.'[63] Some miners attempted to foresee their successes and failures through fortune tellers and dream almanacs. 'Cherished' was ostracised by the miners at Pigburn, who believed him to be cursed when a 'life-reckoner' predicted his death within a year.[64] Chinese almanacs, which circulated widely throughout the diggings, contained among other things a catalogue of dream interpretations. For instance, being attacked by a spirit in a dream foretold ill fortune, but being attacked by a dead man meant prosperity in a current endeavour.[65] However, by soliciting aid from gods, ghosts and ancestors, an individual could determine his luck on a claim or in a gambling house. Moreover, subscribers to Confucian thought held that the Chinese printed word was sacred and possessed the ability to create reality, rather than merely describe it. In one hut Don found an idol with the word 'happiness' pasted on the wall above it, with the inscription, 'YELLOW METAL GREAT COME'.[66] In a Chinese temple at Round Hill was written: 'Let us rejoice that on this day, with a full myriads guineas, we have met happily, pleasure and profit in becoming wealthy. So along with our fellows we return in glory home.'[67] Several owners of gambling houses used this meaning of print to draw in crowds by posting above their doorway, 'Enter the house of slaughter' – an encouragement to share in the swindling of victims' money.[68]

Kinship also melded into wider clan loyalties on the goldfields, as individuals who emigrated from the same region and traced their lineages back to a common ancestor dug alongside each other on the goldfields. These clan allegiances also required financial obligation, which further mitigated against the sending home of remittances. Subscription lists were widely circulated and pledged to for a variety of local needs, including care for the sick and aged, building of temples, participation in festivals and rituals, and the disinterment and shipment of 'former men', the remains of Chinese migrants, to China. Sometimes familial obligations extended to all Chinese who left from a single *qiaoxiang*, for villages frequently traced their origin back to a common ancestor, erasing distinctions between translocal and local.[69] In 1882 the Poonti community at Riverton and Round Hill contributed £78 for the return passage of three elderly clansmen, £800 for exhumations of deceased clansmen and £30 to £40 for the care of a fellow clansman.[70] Everyday practicalities also stressed clan loyalties at the expense of kinship, when gold seekers relied on clan affiliation to secure credit on the goldfields for purchasing food and supplies or witnesses in court cases.[71] Living on the margins of colonial society, some Chinese residents also worried at the cost of being abandoned by clansmen. In 1883 a man travelling from Riverton on his way to the hospital had to lodge with another clan at Round Hill because his clan shunned him when he did not contribute towards the recent exhumations. In a quivering voice he told Don he worried that his clansmen would disown his body if he died, leaving his soul forgotten and cut off from his homeland.[72]

Seasonal celebrations formed another connection to home. As Adam McKeown argues, myths presented the Chinese overseas with a timeless order that connected individuals back to native places and, like genealogies, stressed continuity through time.[73] Rituals rooted the individual in a local community at home through communal celebration, although an ocean away. More than all this, ritual celebrations were a much sought-after diversion from the drudgery and monotony of gold seeking. The most widely attended celebration, both in Guangdong and on the goldfields, was the Chinese New Year, when all clan bickering and internal conflicts would be forgotten. Debts were settled and all began the year afresh. Chinese residents covered their doors and walls with paper inscriptions that told the dreams for the coming year. In the evening they would gather for a feast, after which miners would pour into gambling houses where they smoked opium and played dominoes, cards, fan-tan or pakapu.[74] During the Autumnal Equinox, local Chinese merchants imported moon cakes, made of pork fat, sugar, melon seeds, olive seeds and almonds and enclosed in a crust, from Hong Kong. The Dragon Boat Festival, which commemorated the death of the poet and minister, Qu Yuan, was celebrated annually by feasting for a day on rice, fowl, pork and Chinese preserves.[75]

Finally, connections to home among the Chinese sometimes extended beyond translocal ties to a sense of Chinese nationalism. Experiences of exclusion in host societies often forged a stronger national identity among Chinese migrants; however, they also arose out of the ideas and cultures that individuals brought with them. As Adam McKeown illustrates, the Chinese imperial state constantly sought to exert its influence over its subjects through an effective bureaucracy, a common written language and the performance of ritual, while at the same time allowing regional and local religions and cultures to coexist throughout the empire. Moreover, Guangdong enjoyed a special relationship with the state because it was the country's primary trading centre with Britain and the other colonial powers. Governmental policies frequently favoured local elites when 'the material interests of Cantonese elites existed comfortably with the bureaucratic order'.[76]

Some Guangdong migrants in Otago stressed this pride in the Chinese empire. One Chinese man at Naseby kept a Chinese 'Map of the World' which he referred to often. In the map, China dominates both hemispheres and is surrounded by 'some petty barbarian states and islands'.[77] Chinese gold miners frequently sought news about Chinese national affairs from Don during his tours, and they relied heavily on Chinese-language newspapers that circulated widely on the goldfields.[78] Prospectors were overwhelmingly concerned with the political and military affairs of China, which the newspapers presented in very glowing terms. In 1895 Don commented that the Chinese population in Otago was overwhelmingly preoccupied with the Sino-Japanese War engulfing north China. Many prospectors scoffed at accounts of the war in the Otago press – one gold miner stating after hearing of a Japanese victory that 'the idea of the great Chinese Empire yielding to the Dwarfs is ridiculous'.[79] Another Chinese resident said that he read that the combined forces of sixteen nations invaded China, but 'the number of slain foreigners [mounted] well into the tens of thousands'.[80] For many of these miners from China, their nationalism was more the result of emigration than any Imperial policy within Guangdong, and they proudly conveyed their knowledge of home to Don. As 'Harmony' stated, 'we in the colonies know more about [the Sino-Japanese War] than the people in China do ... While your foreign newspapers make so much ado about it, our country folk and villagers do not even know that there is a quarrel at all.'[81] For gold seekers who remained in Otago for decades at a time, China remained the centre of civilisation in conversations with the Presbyterian missionary. To these same migrants, Otago was by contrast a land without civilisation, populated only by barbarians. The lack of immersion of the Chinese in Otago society, therefore, had more to do with the strength of translocal bonds than exclusion from colonial society.

Connection to home meant a variety of things for the Chinese in Otago. An individual might remain attached to home through participation in rituals and festivals or purchase food imported from his home district, or through association on the goldfields with members of the same clan or from the same *qiaoxiang*. Even if he held allegiance to his family to be sacrosanct, he depended on clan loyalties to secure food, supplies and local support to send gold home, which of course required more money. As gold deposits decreased and prospects for return more remote, Chinese gold seekers often opted for the immediate and local advantages of clan loyalty over the increasingly distant *qiaoxiang* expectations.

As the three-year sojourn turned into thirteen and then thirty years, connections to loved ones at home disintegrated. The most frequent request from family members was for their sons to return home. The sister-in-law of 'Sea-Possessing' wrote in 1905 after a long period of silence:

> The family is extremely poor and distressed, with no one to attend to the graves. Therefore now this word is sent praying my noble brother-in-law to return home at once.[82]

The same year, two brothers digging in Otago, 'Cassia Foundation' and 'Cassia Forest', received a letter from their mother saying that their father had just died and that she and their brothers at home were in abject poverty. She begged her two sons to return home immediately and 'see your mother's face' before she became 'like a candle in the wind', adding that 'although you two men of wealth amass a myriad sovereigns, I fear you will drink bitter regret into your souls'.[83] While her sons' emigration may have been a family strategy, their continued absence meant the forsaking of filial duty to become 'men of wealth'. Meanwhile, back in Guangdong, wives and fiancées remained dependent on the families of the men they were supposed to marry, many of whom never returned. In 1900, when most of the last remaining Chinese prospectors were into their seventies, Don remarked that 'many a young wife has seen her husband leave, to return rich in five years: six and eight times have passed, and he has not come; his parents are dead, and she is alone – the last ray of hope lost in gloom long years back. And while she has turned to lead yonder he has turned to clay here.'[84] Three years later one of these diggers, 'Perfect man', wrote home after a long period of silence only to find out all of his family members had died in the intervening years.[85]

While remittances were an important object of gold seeking, and many spent freely on local petitions and amusements, the ultimate intention was to secure enough gold to return home wealthy. As dreams of quick wealth slowly vanished over decades in the dusty gullies of Otago and Southland, many miners spoke of their overriding desire to return home. When Invercargill was aflame with anti-Chinese agitation, one exasperated miner told Don, 'I wish the Government would drive us out, and give us our passage money to go back to China.'[86]

Death away from home was considered a tragedy by many because happiness in the next life depended on filial devotion from kin.[87] An individual who was unable to return to China would have no one to provide for him in the next life – a cruel twist of fate when many left out of filial devotion. Even worse would be to be buried abroad, forgotten and separated from kin and clan. In light of this tragedy, Chinese clans in Otago frequently subscribed for the removal of the sick or elderly back to their home villages in Guangdong.[88] On other occasions, the Chinese community in Otago financed the disinterment and shipment of 'former men' to China for burial. The Poon Fah Association, established by Panyu and Hua Chinese, exhumed more than seven hundred bodies across New Zealand between 1883 and 1902, costing £5000, which was paid for by the New Zealand Chinese.[89]

While Chinese migrants considered dying in New Zealand a tragedy, the greater fear was dying in the open ocean, where the body would be lost and forgotten forever. It would never be able to find its home in an ancestral grave, where it could be worshipped and remembered by later generations at the family altar. The soul of such a body would become a tortured ghost wandering throughout the world with no attachment to the world of the living.[90]

Despairing of returning home in riches, some miners instead chose to return home after death. Suicide was common among Chinese on the goldfields when they were unable to pay debts or send money home to aid distressed family members. Suicide was probably seen by some as a way of going home, where one could be reunited with family members, both living and dead, if clan members would pay for the return passage. Ten per cent of Chinese deaths investigated by inquest in New South Wales after 1854 were suicides.[91] While there is no comparable statistical evidence of Chinese suicides in Otago, newspapers and cemetery records hint impressionistically at its presence among the Chinese in the province. In 1884 one Chinese man in Otago was found dangling from a ridgepole in his hut.[92] In 1902 Ah Gee also committed suicide at Arrowtown by hanging himself. The *Otago Witness* noted that he had visited the cemetery every day for the past few months and become increasingly deranged.[93] Another Chinese prospector who may have attempted to return home in death was sixty-eight year-old Ah Kip, who hanged himself in his hut in 1904.[94]

CHINESE–EUROPEAN INTERACTIONS

Throughout their time in Otago, the Chinese were the object of widespread antipathy from colonists who sought to push them off New Zealand shores. Colonists in Dunedin and on the goldfields wrote letter after letter calling for the exclusion of the Chinese from Otago.[95] This hostility towards the Chinese sometimes flowed into action. When a Chinese party settled at the Upper Nevis in 1866, the Europeans working nearby rose up en masse and attacked the Chinese camp at night, driving them 'in a state of fear and trembling, half drowned' from the goldfield.[96] In 1868 a group of European miners at Hamiltons brutally 'cuffed and kicked' a miner named Ah Pack, before they cut off his cue, or ponytail, and nailed him into a wooden barrel, rolling him about town. The *Otago Witness* fumed that the miner 'was so ill-treated and frightened that he was driven in terror, and the melancholy sequel is his admission to the Lunatic Asylum'.[97] On another occasion, an old Chinese man was beaten and his head shaved, while another miner was tied hand and foot in a cave while his clothes were torched. When another Chinese man went missing shortly after, a group of Europeans faked his death with a charred sheep corpse, with a shaved head and dressed in Chinese clothes.[98]

Historians of New Zealand too often fall back on seemingly self-evident terms like 'racism' to depict European interactions with the Chinese similar to those described above.[99] The desire to distance the past from a more tolerant present, therefore, ironically runs the risk of 'othering' nineteenth-century Pakeha at the same time it criticises colonists for doing so to the Chinese. As Brian Moloughney and John Stenhouse warn, the 'Victorian Pakeha are these days in danger of becoming the modern scholar's incomprehensible, diabolical Other'.[100] Moreover, analysis needs to push both beyond and beneath the nation to show the relevance of both imperial and local dynamics that fostered racial antagonism. It is not enough to say simply, as Michael King and James Belich do, that the Chinese were excluded by virtue of their race, which would undermine the 'Better Britain' that colonists were attempting to create in Otago.[101] The following discussion instead stresses the Imperial and the local social circumstances that created cultural anxieties at a certain historical moment in a particular locality.

Anti-Chinese sentiment in Otago was often rooted in European fears that New Zealand would soon be overrun by China, with its 64 million inhabitants.[102] One European miner in Otago feared that 'the Chinese being numerically the greatest nation of the world ... could scatter their thousands over the face of the world, and still make no appreciable effect upon the myriads of the Chinese Empire'.[103] In 1888 the *Tuapeka Times* reprinted an article in the Auckland *Weekly News*, warning Australia that its colonies needed the protection of the British fleet from a Chinese invasion:

> the ironclads of China could blow the paltry fort of Port Jackson to eternal smash; her eighteen knot cruisers could sweep the Australian seas of shipping and lay Sydney in ashes, and her transports could land a force from her millions of armed soldiers to which the forces and reserves of Australia would not give a bite apiece; while at every port and inlet of North Australia they could disembark a swarm of settlers from China's three hundred and fifty millions, which would spread over the continent like lotus, and eat up every green thing in the land.[104]

This anxiety of the 'Chinese Empire' was especially heightened in Otago because the apparent smallness of the province made it much less able to cope with a 'Mongolian horde' than Victoria, New South Wales or California, which also received Chinese migrants. Because Otago's Chinese population was never above 4,200, while the European goldfields population had peaked at over 26,000, anti-Chinese agitation was directed at the prospect of future floods rather than actual conditions in the colony.[105]

Paranoia that Chinese immigration would overwhelm Otago's colonial population was magnified by many European colonists' belief that the British government was sacrificing its antipodean colonies for trade alliances with China. At the Convention of Peking in 1860, which ended the Second Opium War, the Chinese government agreed to allow Chinese migrants to make contracts with British shipping firms operating out of Hong Kong.[106] In Australia, several attempts to prohibit Chinese immigration by the colonial governments were vetoed by the British government, which favoured the boon Chinese migration offered to British shipping firms in Hong Kong. Persia Crawford shows that many colonists in New Zealand feared Chinese migrants would soon also swarm their societies when the Imperial government appeared to cast off the Australasian colonies for commercial interests in China.[107] This aligns with Moloughney and Stenhouse's argument that historians must treat colonial anxieties about Chinese imperialism seriously, rather than see them only 'as an embarrassing reminder of the unfounded racism associated with the idea of a "yellow peril"'.[108]

Press networks connecting the province to California, British Columbia and Australia only intensified the impacts of these Imperial developments. Colonists who watched unrest in San Francisco, Melbourne and Sydney feared that anarchy elsewhere would soon be established in Otago. As argued in Chapter Two, the gold rushes integrated Otago into a trans-Tasman social and economic world. The trans-Tasman submarine cable, which was completed in 1876, intensified this process.[109] Newspaper readers throughout the goldfields now could read about developments in Victoria, New South Wales or Queensland as they happened. In this context, local developments were profoundly affected by what was happening around the Pacific.[110]

Dunedin and goldfield newspapers were saturated with reports of Chinese and anti-Chinese agitation in Australia and North America from the late 1860s that fed sinophobia in Otago.[111] The coverage of Chinese migration and the ensuing unrest in Australia and California reached a peak in 1888 when, paradoxically, the Chinese population of Otago was in decline.[112] The *Tuapeka Times* reported that daily arrivals of Chinese in Victoria and New South Wales were leading to widespread unrest in Melbourne and Sydney, while anti-Chinese meetings were being held throughout New Zealand as colonists feared the Chinese migration would soon shift across the Tasman.[113] The *Otago Daily Times* meanwhile reported that a mob of five thousand colonists marched on the Parliament house, demanding the termination of the Chinese influx. When the premier refused to meet with the protestors, the mob invaded and clashed with police constables.[114] From California, Jacob Terry, an *Otago Daily Times* correspondent, pleaded with Otago colonists to prevent Chinese immigration, warning that otherwise, they would regret their 'heedless neglect . . . Prevention is at all times better than the cure.'[115]

Many white residents also believed the fate of the colony was intimately linked to those of Australia and California. Colonists, who acutely followed Chinese developments around the Pacific Rim, worried that Chinese migrants who were restricted from the United States and Australia would overwhelm the relatively small colony of New Zealand. In 1878 a 'working man' warned that barriers must be erected against Chinese immigration, because the recent poll tax enacted in Queensland would direct the Chinese population to Otago shores.[116] Unless some decisive action was taken, 'another working man' continued, 'we will waken some morning to find that we are in a Chinese Colony instead of a British one'.[117] This anxiety reached fever pitch in 1888 when Chinese migrants were barred from arriving in the United States and Australia. Panic quickly set in when a ship carrying two hundred Chinese from Hong Kong was refused entry in Australia and began travelling to Riverton, Southland. Public meetings were held across the colony to petition the government to prohibit the Chinese arrivals and raise the poll tax. As the ship approached Invercargill, a vigilance committee was established to march on Riverton and prevent the passengers from disembarking by any means necessary. One colonist said all should be prepared to use force as they 'might have to kill a Chinaman or two', insisting they should not be too cowardly to follow the example of New South Wales and Victoria. Another shouted that 'the colony was near its death, and the finishing blow would be the introduction of Chinese'.[118] In the context of this alarm, the New Zealand government passed the Chinese Immigrants Bill (1888), which only allowed one Chinese immigrant for every 100 tons of weight of the vessel.[119]

Many not only saw the future state of Otago in the reports they read from Sydney or San Francisco; Otago was also at the mercy of the other Pacific Rim settler colonies. When Otago colonists read accounts of Chinese immigration in Victoria and California, they repeatedly stressed the importance of national boundaries that excluded the Chinese from their society. As Marilyn Lake and Henry Reynolds argue in their study of race relations along the Pacific Rim, 'The project of whiteness was thus a paradoxical politics, at once transnational in its inspiration and identifications but nationalist in its methods and goals.'[120]

The trouble was that there was no clear consensus about what these developments around the Pacific meant. Some colonists shifted the blame in California away from the Chinese towards the inherent lawlessness of American society. One colonist wrote to the *Otago Daily Times* that Californian anarchy had more to do with men there always settling their arguments with a six- shooter than with Chinese immigration.[121] While discussing an editorial in the California-based *Oakland Transcript* calling for the killing of Chinese in California, the *Mount Ida Chronicle* called the newspaper the most 'purely idiotic newspaper permitted by a public unconscious' and recommended for 'the good people of Oakland to soak the head of this editor in a bucket of buttermilk; the vacuum inside his skull is becoming unpleasantly warm.'[122]

These debates intersected with nascent class-consciousness that began to emerge in Otago during the Long Depression of the 1880s. Several factors contributed to this change. Low returns in agriculture encouraged Otago's elite to invest in manufacturing, shipping and coal mining, transforming Dunedin into the most industrial city in New Zealand.[123] When this industrialisation made obsolete the cottage industries that predominated in the early 1860s, a strong working-class identity began to emerge. Labourers lived in newly created low-income housing developments near factories and shipping yards, where they worked 'together in large numbers and relative isolation from other social groups'.[124]

Meanwhile, the goldfields were also transforming. While most gold seekers left for the West Coast or returned to Victoria, those that remained shifted from independent surface panning to waged work in river dredging and more capital-intensive forms of sluicing. Mining parties consolidated into larger mining companies, which by the 1880s were increasingly run by a board of trustees in London, Dunedin or Melbourne and employed the gold seeker on wages. Central Otago became the industrialised goldfields that, ironically, many gold seekers first fled when they left Victoria in the early 1860s. As diggers shifted into waged labour and became less transient, many took to subsistence farming as a way to shield themselves and their families from uncertain wages gold mining.[125] The growing agricultural interests of gold seekers collided with those of squatters, who after the rushes sought to expand their holdings in central Otago.[126]

In this increasingly divided society, responses to Chinese immigration were framed by class issues and usually broke along occupational and class lines. Factory workers and waged gold miners opposed the arrival of Chinese labourers, with whom they would compete for work contracts, while merchants and factory owners favoured more customers and cheap labour. In a letter to the *Otago Daily Times*, one labourer fumed that Chinese workers would transform Otago into a classed society:

> A semi-slave labour, such as the Chinese, and free labour cannot exist together. The one is compelled to succumb to the other. In no country where Chinese, Coolies and labour of that sort has been introduced, is free white labour able to exist.[127]

Another 'working man' thundered that

> there is a numerous class of people in these Colonies who would be glad of the presence of an inferior race, as then they could dispense with the services of insolent whites, as they are pleased to designate their poorer fellow-countrymen.[128]

European miners also complained about the effects of Chinese immigration. One miner wrote that 'it degrades working-men in their own eyes to be sent to work among a mob of Chinamen; it makes them feel as if they were the off-scourings of the earth.'[129] It should be noted that labourers in Otago depicted European immigrants, as well as Chinese arrivals, as enemies of the ideal society. As Keith Sinclair notes, urban trade unions in New Zealand sought the prohibition of all labour immigration, both Chinese and assisted Europeans, because greater competition for work would lower wages and make the colony a rigidly classed society.[130]

Meanwhile, other colonists lauded the Chinese as consumers and hard workers, in contrast to depictions of European labourers as ever indolent and always intoxicated. One writer in the *Otago Daily Times* described the Chinese as greater consumers of colonial products than the European miner.[131] In 1870 a colonist asserted again that the Chinese were not indolent, but more frugal, more industrious, and not always drunk like European labourers.[132] The same year another colonist recommended that the hundreds of European 'loafers' rambling about Dunedin complaining about immigration should imitate the Chinese, who rarely complained and were not prone to drunkenness.[133] Another colonist grumbled that Europeans should be more like the Chinese, who did not hold unemployment meetings and demanded that government be created for them at high wages, adding that 'men who set capital free and promote profitable industry enrich a country, whatever they may think fit to do with their earnings in the end'.[134]

Understandings of Chinese immigration did not simply emerge out of a newly articulated working-class identity, but were an important part of establishing that identity. As Erik Olssen astutely notes of Dunedin labourers, 'The Chinese urban presence ... played a crucial role in creating a working class conscious of its own interests.'[135] Chinese gold seekers in Otago helped to reimagine the Victorian gold-seeking interloper into a permanent settler. Ironically, the most vocal critics of Chinese immigration were themselves often members of the 'New Iniquity', as earlier Otago settlers called them in the 1860s. When Victorian prospectors poured into Otago in the early 1860s, some colonists feared that the gold rushes would destroy the province. Early in 1863, the *Colonist* warned that the gold seeker's 'lust for new rushes' would unravel the provincial economy, and transform the settlement into a home only for the 'roving gold delver'.[136] At the beginning of the Dunstan rush the previous year, E. B. Cargill similarly feared that the impending exodus of the sojourning gold miners would drain the province of its wealth and saddle it with debt after their departure.[137]

Debates about the itinerancy of gold seekers remained after the 1860s. However, Victorian prospectors were transformed from the enemy of the ideal society in the early 1860s to one of its strongest defenders over the next two decades. At this time, European gold seekers formed an important part of a larger working class in Otago that was the loudest critic of the Chinese prospectors' attachments beyond New Zealand and disinterest in settling in the province – criticisms that had been frequently directed at European prospectors in the early 1860s. One European miner, allying himself to earlier language against the gold rushes, warned that the European gold seeker, now a permanent settler with wife and family, would be unable to compete with single itinerant Chinese prospectors:

> This province is at present gorged with [Chinese gold seekers] to its utmost ... The goldfields are presently in a quiet and settled state. The roughs and rowdies have gone on to the West Coast or left the colony. The goldfields are now populated by men with families and households. There is not enough gold to hold a larger population, and Europeans have large families and are unable to prospect ... Gold digging is a thing of the past as far as a money-making occupation, and how is it to be imagined that all these Chinese are to be employed? ... Because they do not have families, they are able to prospect and move around easily. The European meanwhile is more tied to land and has to provide for his family, while the Chinese only worries about himself.[138]

Another European gold seeker asserted that white diggers could rightfully claim Otago's gold as an 'inheritance' by birthright as Englishmen, while the Chinese were an alien race unwelcomed in colonial society.[139] A miner at Mount Ida described the Chinese as 'a bad lot, bad colonists, bad men, and real harpies, whose work contains the worm of destruction, in it'.[140] The strongest condemnation came in 1871 from the president of the Arrow Miners' Association: 'We are free men, they are slaves! We are Christians, they are heathens!! We are Britons, they are Mongolians!!!'[141]

On at least one occasion, criticisms of the Chinese combined with – rather than replaced – earlier colonial anxieties of Victorian gold seekers. In a debate about Chinese immigration in the Otago Provincial Council in 1865, John Bathgate, the interim Chief Commissioner of Dunedin, also drew on earlier anxieties about the European rushes. As the lone opponent of Chinese immigration in the Council, he warned that the province would repeat the same mistakes of the early 1860s. Bathgate cautioned that gold seekers, whether European or Chinese, were not settlers. He warned that the Chinese migrant, 'or any other, [came] to destroy acres of land, and then walk off to another country to spend their gains'. A governmental policy that pursued short-term wealth, Bathgate reasoned, would always see that wealth leave the province in the pockets of departing gold seekers.[142] Through understanding the 'Chinese question' alongside earlier debates about the impact of the gold rushes on colonial society, it becomes evident that racialised discourses sometimes hid earlier debates about what constituted the ideal society and how gold seeking, whether European or Chinese, either contributed to or undermined it.

While gold seeker and merchant bickered about what materially benefited the province, not all impressions of the Chinese came from economic utility. The Presbyterian Church, for example, vociferously argued the need for Christian charity towards the Chinese. This is not to say that church leaders did not dread the impact of Chinese immigration. As Susan Chivers demonstrates, evangelisation often blended with self-preservation.[143] The *Evangelist*, the journal of the Presbyterian Church in Otago, feared that the arrival of Chinese would 'be most disastrous to the morality and religion of the rising generation'.[144] However, Presbyterian theology also held that all human events were guided by Divine Providence. In 1867 Revd D. M. Stuart told the congregation of the Otago Bible Society that while the Chinese posed a great danger to the foundations of law, religion and education in the province, their arrival was preordained by God and, therefore, colonists were called on to spread the gospel to the Chinese population.[145] The Presbyterian Church in Otago often humanised Chinese gold seekers as a way to encourage colonists to evangelise them. Revd Dr Roseby toured Otago giving his popular lecture on his Chinese experiences entitled

'The Flowerly Land, or China and the Chinese', with all charitable donations providing for famine relief in China.[146] The clearest windows into Otago's Chinese society were Revd Alexander Don's published reports of his annual mission tour to the Otago goldfields. As one study notes, Don's narratives of his circuits were written 'against the backdrop of an emerging settler nationalism ... and the consolidation of the nation-state as a key focus for political and cultural life'.[147] Because some colonists attempted to alienate the Chinese as outsiders of the national project, Don repeatedly described the tears and sufferings, the joys and celebrations of Chinese prospectors in order to convey the humanity of these diggers who many colonists understood only as the 'Yellow Peril'.[148]

Close relationships between Chinese and Europeans were forged through interactions on the goldfields. Sometimes these emerged out of the empathy of European prospectors who worked alongside Chinese diggers. In 1871 Frederick Barrell described a group of Chinese gold seekers he met on the road to Queenstown: 'Poor devils ... They were near perished with the cold, some of them being barefooted.'[149] In 1867 a group of European miners circulated a petition on the diggings and in Dunedin begging mercy for Chinese prospectors convicted of the murder of another European digger, Benjamin Harbord.[150] In 1891 a group of Chinese at Cardrona presented a framed inscription in crimson on a blue silk background to a European shopkeeper as a wedding present. The inscription read, 'as the husband sings may the wife follow', meaning may the wife sing treble to her husband's bass.[151] In a 1948 interview about her childhood in Arrowtown, Anne Hamilton remembered that the local Chinese residents were 'very nice, very quite nice and friendly you know'.[152] As Liping Zhu shows in her study of the Chinese on the Rocky Mountain goldfields, such accounts of charity and cooperation need to be stressed alongside colonial antipathy to show a fuller and more varied picture of colonial reactions to Chinese gold seekers.[153]

CONCLUSION

This chapter has briefly analysed Chinese gold seeking in Otago through a discussion of local networks and structures that spurred emigration from Guangdong and directed it to Otago. It reveals similarities between Chinese migrant networks and British and Irish connections discussed in Chapter One. Chinese and European prospectors both relied on family and community networks to finance and facilitate overseas migration, and they often transplanted in Otago as migrants dug for gold among relatives and neighbours. Much like the British and Irish gold seekers, Chinese prospectors in Otago relied on newspapers, remittances and letters to maintain connections to home, while an inability to send money sometimes frayed these links to neighbours and relatives at home. These kinship networks constituted the primary social world for these gold seekers, who most often worked and played alongside other clan members in Otago. Despite the intention to return home after a few years, the extended absence from home substantially weakened the relationships between these individuals and their family members in China. Despite the infrequency of correspondence with loved ones, most Chinese diggers retained a firm connection to home through ritual and commemoration, which connected individuals back to China. Eventually, most did return home, often after an absence of a decade or more. Those who remained in New Zealand retained a strong mental connection to home that long outlasted any prospect of return. Both the Chinese diggers who eventually left New Zealand shores and the few that remained never regarded themselves as New Zealanders or saw themselves contributing to the making of the nation. The Chinese did not understand their experiences as helping to make a national identity or heritage in New Zealand, but as part of a transnationally dispersed family, which might have sons in Otago, Manila, Honolulu and Lima at the same time. The separation of the Chinese population from the Europeans in Otago was not simply the result of atomisation or exclusion from European society; rather, it was often an indication of the strength of these Chinese networks and cultures.

Despite similarities between Chinese and European networks and itinerancy, Otago colonists described the Chinese population in the province as sojourners who inhibited the development of the ideal society. The ongoing presence of Chinese residents became 'symbolically central' for white colonists and gold seekers, who fought over what type of society they were creating in Otago.[154] These debates about Chinese immigration were framed by a newly emerging nationalism in New Zealand. Within these dual contexts, white gold seekers who remained in the province after the European rushes ended began to characterise themselves not as Victorian prospectors but as New Zealand pioneers, in strong contrast to itinerant Chinese diggers whose networks and mobility did not differ substantially from their Victorian precedents. Chinese prospectors, therefore, became an important facilitator of a memory of the European rushes that differed significantly from how they occurred in the early 1860s. The following chapter discusses the reminiscences Otago diggers penned about their experiences during the rushes and their participation in the public semi-centennial celebrations in the early twentieth century.

NOTES

1. Miles Fairburn, *The Ideal Society and Its Enemies: The Foundation of Modern New Zealand Society, 1850–1900* (Auckland: Auckland University Press, 1989); Jock Phillips, *A Man's Country?: The Image of the Pakeha Male, a History*, 2nd edn (Auckland: Penguin Books, 1996).
2. Philip Ross May, *The West Coast Gold Rushes*, 2nd edn (Christchurch: Pegasus Press, 1967), 298–9; J. H. M. Salmon, *A History of Goldmining in New Zealand* (Wellington: Government Printer, 1963), 111–14; William Parker Morrell, *The Gold Rushes* (London: Macmillan Company, 1941), 271; John Milton Hutchins, *Diggers, Constables and Bushrangers: The New Zealand Gold Rushes as a Frontier Experience, 1852–1878* (Lakewood: Avrooman-Apfelwald Press, 2010), 128–35. The only study that attempts to analyse the experiences of Chinese prospectors is Stevan Eldred-Grigg, *Diggers, Hatters and Whores: The Story of the New Zealand Gold Rushes* (Auckland: Random House, 2008), 423–58.
3. Susan Chivers, 'Religion, Ethnicity and Race: The Mission of the Otago Church to the Chinese, 1860–1950' (MA thesis, University of Otago, 1992).
4. James Ng, *Windows on a Chinese Past*, vol. 1 (Dunedin: Otago Heritage Books, 1993).
5. Yong Chen, 'Understanding Chinese American Transnationalism During the Early Twentieth Century: An Economic Perspective', in Sucheng Chan (ed.), *Chinese American Transnationalism: The Flow of People, Resources, and Ideas Between China and America During the Exclusion Era* (Philadelphia: Temple University Press, 2006), 160.
6. Adam McKeown, *Chinese Migrant Networks and Cultural Change: Peru, Chicago, Hawaii, 1900–1936* (Chicago and London: University of Chicago Press, 2001), especially 61–135.
7. Ng, *Windows*, 1:85–205; Eldred-Grigg, *Diggers, Hatters and Whores*, 431–8, 450–5.
8. Miles Fairburn, *Nearly Out of Heart and Hope: The Puzzle of a Colonial Labourer's Diary* (Auckland: University of Auckland Press, 1995), 19; James Belich, *Reforging Paradise: A History of the New Zealanders from the 1880s to the Year 2000* (Auckland: Penguin Press, 2001), 123; Laurie Guy, *Shaping Godzone: Public Issues and Church Voices in New Zealand* (Wellington: Victoria University Press, 2011).
9. George M. Fredrickson, *White Supremacy: A Comparative Study of American and South African History* (Oxford: Oxford University Press, 1982), xii.
10. Marilyn Lake and Henry Reynolds, *Drawing the Global Colour Line:*

White Men's Countries and the Question of Racial Equality (Melbourne: Melbourne University Press, 2008), 2.
11. Erik Olssen, *A History of Otago* (Dunedin: John McIndoe, 1984), 105–6.
12. Persia Crawford Campbell, 'Chinese Emigration to Canada, Australia, and New Zealand', in Anthony Reid (ed.), *The Chinese Diaspora in the Pacific* (Aldershot: Ashgate, 2008), 209–34.
13. McKeown, *Chinese Migrant Networks*, 62.
14. Ng, *Windows*, 1:156. The nineteenth-century Chinese-New Zealand population peaked in 1881 at five thousand but most had migrated to Wellington or Dunedin. H. D. Min-hsi Chan, 'Qiaoxiang and the Diversity of Chinese Settlement in Australia and New Zealand', in Tan Chee-Beng (ed.), *Chinese Transnational Networks* (Abingdon and New York: Routledge, 2007), 154.
15. Chan, 'Qiaoxiang', 158.
16. Charles P. Sedgwick, 'The Politics of Survival: A Social History of the Chinese in New Zealand' (PhD thesis, University of Canterbury, 1982), 60.
17. June Mei, 'Socioeconomic Origins of Emigration: Guangdong to California, 1850–1882', *Modern China* 5 (1979): 168–9.
18. Ibid., 170–2.
19. Frederic E. Wakeman, *Strangers at the Gate: Social Disorder in South China, 1839–1861* (Berkeley: University of California Press, 1966), 149–50; Madeline Y. Hsu, *Dreaming of Gold, Dreaming of Home: Transnationalism and Migration Between the United States and South China, 1882–1943* (Stanford: Stanford University Press, 2000), 25–7. On the Taiping Rebellion, see Jonathan D. Spence, *God's Chinese Son: The Taiping Heavenly Kingdom of Hong Xiuquan* (New York and London: W. W. Norton, 1996).
20. Philip A. Kuhn, *Chinese Among Others: Emigration in Modern Times* (Lanham, MD: Rowman and Littlefield Publishers, 2008), 39; Hsu, *Dreaming of Gold*, 27.
21. Adam McKeown, 'Conceptualising Chinese Diasporas', *Journal of Asian Studies* 58, no. 2 (1999): 314.
22. Adam McKeown, 'Global Migration, 1846–1940', *Journal of World History* 15 (2004): 155–89.
23. Liping Zhu, *A Chinaman's Chance: The Chinese on the Rocky Mountain Mining Frontier* (Niwot: University of Colorado Press, 1997), 8–10.
24. Kuhn, *Chinese Among Others*, 141–3.
25. 'Interim Report of the Chinese Immigration Committee', *AJHR*, 1872, H-5, 23.
26. Kuhn, *Chinese Among Others*, 112–13.
27. William Tai Yuen, *The Origins of China's Awareness of New Zealand, 1674–1911* (Auckland: University of Auckland Press, 2005), 45.
28. John Ah Tong, a native of Guangzhou, told the Select Committee on

Chinese Immigration in 1871 that most Chinese came out under these conditions. 'Interim report of the Chinese immigration committee', 1872, H-5, 4.
29. *New Zealand Presbyterian*, 1 July 1884, 2.
30. Michael Williams, 'Hong Kong and the Pearl River Delta Qiaoxiamg', *Modern Asian Studies* 38 (2004): 257–82; Madeline Hsu, 'Trading with Gold Mountain: Jinshanzhuang and Networks of Kinship and Native Place', in Sucheng Chan (ed.), *Chinese Americans: The Flow of People, Resources, and Ideas Between China and America During the Exclusion Era* (Philadelphia: Temple University Press, 2006), 22.
31. Tony Ballantyne and Brian Moloughney, 'Asia in Murihiku: Towards a Transnational History of a Colonial Culture', in Tony Ballantyne and Brian Moloughney (eds), *Disputed Histories: Imagining New Zealand's Pasts* (Dunedin: Otago University Press, 2006), 65–92; Hsu, 'Trading with Gold Mountain'; McKeown, 'Conceptualising Chinese Diasporas'; Williams, 'Hong Kong and the Pearl River Delta Qiaoxiamg'.
32. Hsu, *Dreaming of Gold*, 31.
33. Lynn Pann, 'The concept of *qiaoxiang*', in Lynn Pann (ed.), *The Encyclopedia of the Chinese Overseas*, 27–30.
34. One example of a Chinese gold seeker leaving independent of family consent was a man in Bendigo Gully named 'dog', who ran away to join the circus in a nearby district in Guangdong. He travelled throughout Europe and the United States, before he broke his leg performing in Melbourne. He then took up gold mining and went out to New Zealand in 1867. On another occasion, the miner named 'Child of Peace' told Don that his son in China recently stole all of the family treasure and left for British Columbia. *New Zealand Presbyterian*, 1 March 1888, 166; Alexander Don, *Annual Inland Tour among Otago Chinese, 1900–1901*, 51–2. Also see Daniel Kulp, *Country Life in South China: The Sociology of Familism* (Taipei: Ching-Wu Publishing, 1966), 184.
35. Brian Moloughney and John Stenhouse, '"Drug-besotten, Sin-begotten Fiends of Filth": New Zealanders and the Oriental Other, 1850–1920', *New Zealand Journal of History* 33 (1999): 55; McKeown, *Chinese Migrant Networks*, 70.
36. Chen, 'Understanding Chinese', 163.
37. *The Christian Outlook*, 22 May 1897.
38. Alexander Don, *Annual Inland Tour among Otago Chinese, 1900–1901*, 25.
39. *Taishan Gazetteer* 8, 1893, 6b, as cited in Hsu, *Dreaming of Gold*, 31.
40. *The Christian Outlook*, 26 June 1897; *New Zealand Presbyterian*, 2 April 1883, 1 September 1884, 1 February 1888, 1 May 1889, 1 April 1895, 1 June 1893.
41. *The Christian Outlook*, 1 September 1894.
42. McKeown, *Chinese Migrant Networks*, 10–20.

43. *New Zealand Presbyterian*, 1 January 1883, 127.
44. See Stephen Vertovec, 'Conceiving and Researching Transnationalism'," *Ethnic and Racial Studies* 22, no. 2 (1999): 455–6.
45. *New Zealand Presbyterian*, 1 November 1890, 86; Wakeman, *Strangers at the Gate: Social Disorder in South China, 1839–1861*, 132–58.
46. Roger Daniels, *Asian America: Chinese and Japanese in the United States Since 1850* (Seattle: University of Washington Press, 1988), 2.
47. Lynn Pann, 'Chinese religion', idem., ed., *The Encyclopedia of the Chinese Overseas*, 43; McKeown, *Chinese Migrant Networks*, 104–7.
48. Alexander Don, *Annual Inland Tour among Otago Chinese, 1900–1901* (Hocken Pamphlets, vol. 184), 39; idem., *Annual Inland Tour Among Chinese in Otago, New Zealand. 1905–1906*, 37; *The Christian Outlook*, 1 September 1894, 4 May 1895; *New Zealand Presbyterian*, 2 October 1882, 1 January 1885, 1 April 1890, 1 November 1890, 2 March 1891.
49. David Fitzpatrick, *Oceans of Consolation: Personal Accounts of the Irish Migration to Australia* (Ithaca, NY and London: Cornell University Press, 1995), 503.
50. Ng, *Windows*, 1:99.
51. *New Zealand Presbyterian*, 2 November 1885, 86.
52. *The Christian Outlook*, 1 September 1894, 339.
53. Don, *Annual Inland Tour among Otago Chinese, 1900–1901*, 25.
54. *New Zealand Presbyterian*, 1 August 1888, 26.
55. Ibid., 1 February 1884, 148.
56. Ibid., 1 November 1884, 85.
57. Ibid., 1 November 1890, 86.
58. Ibid., 1 April 1892, 186.
59. Ibid., 1 July 1882, 6.
60. Pakapu was a common lottery game on the Pacific Rim goldfields, in which players would receive a ticket with ten rows of Chinese characters. The player whose ticket most resembled the master ticket won a prize.
61. A gambling game in which players guess the number of beans, rocks or other items placed under a bowl by the banker.
62. *New Zealand Presbyterian*, 1 April 1885, 183.
63. Ibid., 2 March 1891, 166.
64. *The Christian Outlook*, 3 August 1895, 324.
65. Ibid., 1 September 1894, 339.
66. Ibid., 1 September 1894, 339.
67. Ibid., 4 May 1895, 167.
68. See, for example, *New Zealand Presbyterian*, 1 March 1890, 164.
69. Sedgwick, 'The Politics of Survival: A Social History of the Chinese in New Zealand', 64.
70. *New Zealand Presbyterian*, 1 October 1883, 66. There were numerous examples of Chinese miners financing the return of fellow clansmen. A

few examples are *New Zealand Presbyterian*, 1 January 1883, 127; 1 August 1883, 24; 1 December 1893, 106.
71. *New Zealand Presbyterian*, 2 March 1891, 166; 1 April 1891, 186; 25 May 1895, 196.
72. *New Zealand Presbyterian*, 1 October 1883, 68.
73. McKeown, *Chinese Migrant Networks*, 118–20.
74. *New Zealand Presbyterian*, 2 April 1883, 184; 1 February 1884, 162; 1 May 1885, 204; 1 June 1885, 224; 1 August 1888, 26.
75. See, for example, *New Zealand Presbyterian*, 1 August 1883, 25.
76. McKeown, *Chinese Migrant Networks*, 101–3. Quotation taken from p. 102.
77. *New Zealand Presbyterian*, 2 May 1892. Also see 1 February 1883, 2 August 1886.
78. See, for example, *New Zealand Presbyterian*, 1 December 1883, 1 July 1889, 1 November 1890.
79. *The Christian Outlook*, 25 May 1895.
80. Ibid., 11 May 1895, 27 July 1895, 10 August 1895, 24 August 1895, 7 September 1895.
81. Ibid., 27 July 1895.
82. Alexander Don, *Annual Inland Tour Among Chinese in Otago, New Zealand, 1905–1906*, 17.
83. Ibid., 22.
84. *The Christian Outlook*, 22 May 1897, 203.
85. Ibid., 22 May 1897, 203.
86. *New Zealand Presbyterian*, 1 November 1882, 87.
87. Ng, *Windows*, 1:64–6.
88. *New Zealand Presbyterian*, 1 January 1883, 127; 1 August 1883, 24; 1 December 1893, 106.
89. Ng, *Windows*, 1:66.
90. *New Zealand Presbyterian*, 1 August 1883, 24.
91. Valerie Lovejoy, 'Chinese in Late Nineteenth-Century Bendigo: Their Local and Translocal Lives in "This Strangers' Country"', *Australian Historical Studies* 42, no. 1 (2011): 45–61.
92. *New Zealand Presbyterian*, 1 April 1884, 183.
93. *Otago Witness*, 15 October 1902, 31.
94. Ibid., 15 June 1904, 32; Cardrona cemetery registry, plot 26.
95. Some examples are *Otago Daily Times*, 10 April 1865, 5 April 1871, 17 August 1871; *Tuapeka Times*, 3 August 1871, 11 June 1881; *Mount Ida Chronicle*, 10 October 1878.
96. *Dunstan Times*, 23 November 1866.
97. *Otago Witness*, 8 February 1868.
98. Ibid., 5 June 1897, 227.
99. Eldred-Grigg, *Diggers, Hatters and Whores*, 451–5; James Belich, *Making Peoples: A History of the New Zealanders from Polynesian Settlement*

to the End of the Nineteenth Century (Auckland: Penguin Books, 1996), 317–18; James Ng, *Windows on a Chinese Past*, vol. 2 (Dunedin: Otago Heritage Books, 1993), 136–53. For a discussion on this point, see Moloughney and Stenhouse, 'Drug-besotten, Sin-begotten'," 44–5.
100. Moloughney and Stenhouse, 'Drug-besotten, Sin-begotten', 50.
101. Michael King, *The Penguin History of New Zealand* (Rosedale: Penguin Books, 2003), 175; Belich, *Reforging Paradise*, 123. Also see, for example, Ng, *Windows*, vol. 2; Guy, *Shaping Godzone*, Chapter 4; Eldred-Grigg, *Diggers, Hatters and Whores*, Chapter 12.
102. Moloughney and Stenhouse, 'Drug-besotten, Sin-begotten', 51.
103. *Otago Daily Times*, 5 April 1871, 3.
104. *Tuapeka Times*, 25 April 1888, 2.
105. The Chinese population in Otago peaked at 4,159 in 1871 before falling gradually to 1,200 in 1901. See Ng, *Windows*, 1:156. For the European population of the goldfields during the rushes in the early 1860s, see James Forrest, 'Population and Settlement on the Otago Goldfields, 1861–1870', *New Zealand Geographer* 17, no. 1 (1961): 69.
106. Kuhn, *Chinese Among Others*, 137. Before the Convention of Peking, the Chinese government did not officially allow overseas migration.
107. Campbell, 'Chinese Emigration'," 230–4.
108. Moloughney and Stenhouse, 'Drug-besotten, Sin-begotten', 51.
109. Ross Eaman, *Historical Dictionary of Journalism* (Lanham, MD: Scarecrow Press, 2009), xxviii.
110. Rollo Arnold, *New Zealand's Burning: The Settlers' World in the Mid-1880s* (Wellington: Victoria University of Wellington Press, 1994), 220–34; Tony Ballantyne, 'Thinking Local: Knowledge, Sociability and Community in Gore's Intellectual Life, 1875–1914', *New Zealand Journal of History* 44, no. 2 (2010): 144–8.
111. *Otago Witness*, 8 February 1868, 25 September 1869, 20 August 1870, 15 July 1871, 20 March 1875; *Otago Daily Times*, 28 September 1869, 11 April 1870, 15 August 1870; *Bruce Herald*, 27 May 1873, 11 November 1868; *North Otago Times*, 14 October 1873.
112. *Tuapeka Times*, 25 April 1888, 6 June 1888, 12 December 1888; *Otago Daily Times*, 21 March 1888, 17 May 1888, 11 July 1888, 5 October 1888.
113. *Tuapeka Times*, 4 June 1881. Also see *Tuapeka Times*, 25 April 1888, 2.
114. *Otago Daily Times*, 5 May 1888, 2.
115. *Tuapeka Times*, 23 April 1879, 4.
116. Ibid., 24 July 1878, 3.
117. Ibid., 3 July 1878, 3.
118. *Southland Times*, 7 May 1888, 2.
119. Campbell, 'Chinese Emigration', 232.
120. Lake and Reynolds, *Drawing the Global Colour Line*, 4.
121. *Otago Daily Times*, 20 March 1882, 4. Also see ibid., 24 August 1870, 4.

122. *Mount Ida Chronicle*, 8 September 1871, 3.
123. Olssen, *A History of Otago*, 91.
124. Ibid., 105.
125. Salmon, *A History of Goldmining*, 108.
126. Ibid., 108–9; Terence J. Hearn, 'Land, Water and Gold in Central Otago, 1861–1921: Some Aspects of Resource Use Policy and Conflict' (PhD thesis, University of Otago, 1981), 29–33, 75–9.
127. *Otago Daily Times*, 18 July 1871, 3.
128. Ibid., 19 April 1872, 3.
129. *Tuapeka Times*, 26 June 1878, 3.
130. Keith Sinclair, *A History of New Zealand*, 3rd edn (London: Allen Lane, 1980), 166–8.
131. *Otago Daily Times*, 21 August 1867.
132. Ibid., 24 August 1870.
133. Ibid., 14 September 1870.
134. Ibid., 8 June 1881.
135. Olssen, *A History of Otago*, 105–6. Also see Erik Olssen, *Building a New World: Work, Politics and Society in Caversham, 1880s–1920s* (Auckland: Auckland University Press, 1995), 44.
136. *Colonist*, 3 July 1862, 2 January 1863.
137. *Otago Daily Times*, 3 October 1862. Also see *Otago Witness*, 25 May 1861.
138. *Tuapeka Times*, 28 September 1871, 5.
139. Ibid., 3 August 1871, 6. Like most individuals, the miner did not distinguish between English and other European ethnicities.
140. *Mount Ida Chronicle*, 10 October 1878, 4.
141. *Otago Daily Times*, 17 August 1871.
142. Ibid., 21 September 1865, 6.
143. Chivers, 'Religion, Ethnicity and Race', 22.
144. *Evangelist*, 1 January 1870, as cited in ibid.
145. *Otago Daily Times*, 18 September 1867, 4.
146. *Otago Daily Times*, 17 August 1878, 11.
147. Brian Moloughney, Tony Ballantyne and David Hood, 'After Gold: Reconstructing Chinese Communities, 1896–1913', in Henry Johnson and Brian Moloughney (eds), *Asia in the Making of New Zealand* (Auckland: Auckland University Press, 2006), 74.
148. See, for example, Alexander Don, 'Annual Inland Tour among Otago Chinese, 1900–1901', HC, pamphlets, vol. 184, 12; *The Christian Outlook*, 4 May 1895; *The New Zealand Presbyterian*, 1 December 1882, 1 January 1883, 1 October 1883, 1 November 1884, 1 May 1889.
149. Frederick Barrell, diary, 1871, 8, HC, DU484.3B37B827.
150. *Otago Witness*, 11 October 1867.
151. *New Zealand Presbyterian*, 2 March 1891, 167.

152. Anne Elizabeth Hamilton (Arrowtown), Oral History Transcripts, 1948, LDM, MU 1080-3.
153. Zhu, *A Chinaman's Chance*, especially 3–4, 161–8.
154. Olssen, *Building a New World*, 44.

6

'Monuments of Industry'? The Otago Gold Rushes in Public and Private Memory

In May 1911, fifty years after Gabriel Read's discovery of gold that sparked the Otago gold rushes, Gabriel's Gully was once again teeming with life. A few days before the commencement of the Gabriel's Gully Semi-Centennial Jubilee, the Lawrence correspondent for the *Otago Daily Times* remarked that 'the old gully, now almost silent and deserted,

Figure 6.1 Former gold seekers assembled outside the Lawrence Presbyterian Church, Gabriel's Gully Semi-Centennial Jubilee, 1911, photographer unknown. HC, c/nE4340/8.

is to ring with voices of old miners who half a century ago swept into it from regions beyond, and tore at its bosom for the gold that lay concealed beneath'.[1] Over three hundred gold seekers, who in 1861 first dug for riches in Tuapeka's 'bosom', returned again during the twilight of their years. Flanked by wives, children and grandchildren, they filed out of train carriages and into Lawrence to reconnect with former mates and reminisce about shared experiences in this hamlet of Otago.

The celebrations were opened with an interdenominational service held in Lawrence's Presbyterian Church, where Revd James Chisholm, himself among the 'first adventurers at Gabriel's Gully',[2] meditated on the spirit of Gabriel Read as an exemplar of Otago's diggers. Chisholm explained to the congregation that Read understood himself as 'an agent of an overruling Providence' that used gold as a tool to bring 'early pioneers . . . of great rectitude' to Otago, where their piety was matched only by their orderliness and perseverance. These diggers, Chisholm argued, provided a model for future generations. He concluded his sermon by hoping that 'this discovery of earthly treasure be a milestone on the way for lots of heavenly treasure'.[3] The gold rushes, according to Chisholm, were providentially bestowed on the province by the hand of God to bring about the establishment of a Christian community. The gold seeker then, whether consciously or unconsciously, was a divine tool used for the betterment of the provincial community. In this context, the digger was to be emulated for his industry, perseverance and piety. Such memories, set against the backdrop of early twentieth-century New Zealand nationalism, reinterpreted Victorian prospectors as settlers who colonised and Christianised New Zealand, rather than itinerant diggers who left the colony as eagerly as they entered it, as this book has so far argued.

This chapter discusses the memories of the Otago gold rushes in the late nineteenth and early twentieth centuries. It begins by discussing the public and private recollections of the Otago rushes in New Zealand. The first section analyses the public memories of the Otago gold rushes surrounding the semi-centennial celebrations on the Tuapeka in 1911. These jubilee celebrations stressed the gold rushes as a period of national maturation, forgetting the Victorian dimension to the rushes and replacing the 'digger' with the 'pioneer' and the 'settler'. Public debates about the legacy of the rushes surrounded the jubilee, as colonists argued about whether the digger epitomised the perseverance and industry of New Zealand colonists or legitimised contemporary alcoholism that was undermining the creation of New Zealand as an ideal society. Nevertheless, in both arguments, the nation still remained central as debates swirled about what *type* of nation the gold rushes had helped to create, forgetting the trans-Tasman dimension of the rushes.

The next section examines private memories of the Otago rushes among gold seekers who remained in New Zealand. It draws on six autobiographies published by their authors in book form, seventy-four reminiscences published in Otago newspapers, nineteen unpublished autobiographies and reminiscences, and twenty-eight brief oral histories compiled for a local study of the Taieri District and a history of the New Zealand gold rushes.[4] Every autobiographer who remained in New Zealand described himself as a pioneer or settler, connecting himself to the pre-gold rush stream that in the 1860s defined itself in oppositional terms to the Victorian diggers. Hindsight re-presented the influx of the New Iniquity as a moment of comedy rather than tragedy, as all were assured that social order would eventually prevail and the scarcity of wealth would once again become the regulator of society.[5] As European gold seekers celebrated their role in community formation, Chinese gold seekers hovered on the margins of both colonial society and colonial memories that excluded them from this genealogy of the gold rushes.

The chapter then turns to a discussion of memory making (and forgetting) of the Otago rushes outside of New Zealand. It first analyses the memories of prospectors who later travelled to Britain or the United States. Most of these recollections presented gold seeking as either a period of moral depravity or as part of a suspense-filled odyssey around the world. In both types of accounts, the authors never understood themselves as New Zealanders and the language of social progress is clearly absent. In Australia, a trans-Tasman memory remained in the decade following the rushes in the 1870s; however, by the 1900s, connections between Otago and Victoria during the rushes were largely forgotten on both sides of the Tasman Sea.

This study draws on recent work on the role of memory in cultural and identity formation. Several historians analyse the place of memory in New Zealand culture in the late nineteenth and early twentieth centuries. Much of this literature either focuses on the role of writing in 'cultural colonisation' of Māori and natural landscapes, or the pioneering myths about the founding of the provinces.[6] Chris Hilliard demonstrates that academic historical writing between 1920 and 1940 presented a national genealogy of New Zealand centred on the transplantation of metropolitan cultures and the marginalisation of Māori subjects.[7] Peter Gibbons argues that literature also allowed Pakeha the ability 'to domesticate the incorrigible wilderness' in New Zealand by depicting it as a land devoid of history that could be tamed through colonisation and settlement.[8] Other scholars, studying autobiographies and jubilee celebrations in the late nineteenth century, argue that such memory-making devices were 'genealogies of communities striving for a sense of legitimacy in a recently settled land'.[9]

In contrast, there has been little written on the memories of the gold rushes in New Zealand despite the reliance of historians on autobiographies for conclusions about the rushes. Scholars rarely discuss these sources critically, instead treating them only as evidence of societies and cultures in Otago during the early 1860s. Miles Fairburn, for example, mines autobiographies written in the 1870s and beyond to describe colonial society in the early 1860s without any discussion of the reliability of the autobiography as a source of understanding atomisation.[10] Stevan Eldred-Grigg makes broader use of contemporary newspapers, diaries and letters, but treats each as an accurate representation of the past, thereby ignoring the biases of each type of source.[11] Even Jock Phillips, who sets out to describe the 'ideas, stereotypes and images' of Pakeha masculinity, uses reminiscences to present a picture of how masculinity existed rather than how it was remembered.[12] However, these studies end up telling us more about New Zealand at the end of the nineteenth century, when authors wrote down their memories, than colonial society in the 1850s and 1860s.

Autobiographies certainly provide a lens into social history, as ably demonstrated by John Burnett.[13] This book has utilised reminiscences for evidence about social networks and weekly routines on the goldfields.[14] However, as Sidone Smith writes, 'autobiography is always, multiply, storytelling [and] driven by its own fictive conventions about beginnings, middles and ends'.[15] Following Smith, this chapter stresses the narrative dimension of reminiscences by analysing autobiographical writing as cultural practice rather than simply recording the past. This is not to say that autobiographers did not think they were writing social history. As Nan Hackett shows in her study of British working-class autobiographies, writers usually compiled their memories because they believed that 'their viewpoints and even the events in which they had participated would otherwise go unrecorded'.[16] Otago gold seekers often commented that they wrote down their memories in order to record their lives at the request of children, grandchildren and all New Zealanders.[17] However, the most real part of autobiography was the 'spirit brooding over the recollected material'.[18] This chapter also recognises the ways in which personal and collective memories 'interpenetrate' each other, as demonstrated by Susan Crane.[19] As individuals believed that they were writing social history, their recollections were shaped by contemporary social environments. However, memory making was never an exclusively collective phenomenon, when 'all narratives, all sites, all texts remain objects until they are "read" or referred to by individuals thinking historically'.[20]

Certain qualifications must be made about the selectiveness of the autobiographies discussed in this chapter. Autobiographers probably do not represent the general population of gold seekers. As Liam Harte argues in his study of Irish autobiographies in Britain, reminiscences are '*extra*-ordinary, even idiosyncratic, literature [from a] minority of migrants – those who were privileged, fortunate or determined enough to break the silence'.[21] The failed or the atomised individual was unlikely to put their memories on paper for posterity, a fact that highly colours Jock Phillip's use of autobiographies to depict strong social bonding on the goldfields.[22] Even more importantly, recollections of the gold rushes were largely composed by prospectors who remained in New Zealand after the gold rushes waned. Interestingly, this selectiveness was often an important precondition for many diggers to eventually pen their memories – their experiences were seen as an important contribution to a larger social identity with which they still identified.

NEW ZEALAND MEMORIES

Social memories: the Gabriel's Gully Semi-Centennial Jubilee

Public commemoration of the Tuapeka rush in the 1911 Semi-Centennial Jubilee at Lawrence was an important means through which the rushes were cemented as foundational events in Otago history. By 1911 the gold rush had long since passed from Lawrence. Gone were the brothels and grog shanties. In their place were schools and churches. An abstinence society was formed in the town in 1870 and by 1911 alcohol sales had been banned throughout the town. That this town would be the location of a celebration commemorating the overrunning of Otago by the New Iniquity shows just how much the memory of the rushes changed in fifty short years. The week of the jubilee, all the shops along Ross Street were decked with streamers and flags and a banner was hung across the street, as residents waited eagerly for the arrivals of what once were termed the Victorian hordes, but now were in the words of James Carroll, acting premier, 'the pioneers of the country'.[23] Three hundred diggers, accompanied by family members and other visitors, swelled the population of the town to over two thousand.[24]

The formal jubilee began with a procession of key figures from the rushes. The march began with the 'venerable old couple', George Munro and his wife. Munro guided Gabriel Read on his prospecting expedition when he first found payable gold. Following them was a group representing a party of prospectors, fitted out with crimson-red shirts, 'wide-awake' hats and moleskin trousers, and carrying the carcass of a wild pig. Next came Jock Graham, a rather eccentric bugle-wielding postman who somehow found his way into nearly all the reminiscences about the rushes. Following Graham was the central feature of the celebration: the procession of three hundred 'pioneer miners' from 1861 and 1862 (see Figure 6.2). Next came a re-enactment of the gold escort and Major Croker, the first warden of Tuapeka. Taking up the rear were the Lawrence School Cadets, the local fire brigade and lodges, and the Tuapeka Mounted Rifles. This procession presented a linear genealogy of the Tuapeka district from the first gold discoveries down to the present day, which seemed to have been a natural result of the gold rushes. Absent in the procession were the Chinese gold seekers, who were excluded from what was remembered as a white colonising event. The parade was followed by a series of speeches from visiting delegates and local legislators before an evening of songs and farces, a torchlight procession and fireworks display. The rest of the week, old diggers participated in several sports and banquets before the celebrations ended.

Figure 6.2 Gabriel's Gully Semi-Centennial Jubilee Procession, 1911, photographer unknown. HC, c/nE4033/16.

The Gabriel's Gully jubilee was about honouring the gold seekers who opened up central Otago, flooded Dunedin banks with capital and ballooned the province's population. The Otago gold seekers were described as those who brought about 'the first great progressive event in the history' of the South Island.[25] In the words of Carroll, the gold seekers were the 'young, courageous, and adventurous spirits, who ... had become the pioneers of the country, and who had left behind their monuments of industry and enterprise, as well as descendants to still mould the present and future destiny'.[26] According to the rhetoric, this was an event honouring the gold seekers as pioneers and settlers – men who fought battles, made sacrifices, endured hardships and won victories. Through their endurance and 'pluck' they forged a community out of dust, dirt and gold and established themselves as settlers, taking an active role in the developing of the local community and economy that proved a foundation of national greatness of which they could be proud.

This model of pioneer commemoration was a common feature in frontier societies developing around the turn of the twentieth century. As David Glassberg and Malcolm Rohrbough show, local residents held celebrations honouring the founding generations in a multitude of counties in the American Midwest and California.[27] In Australia, too, colonists formed organisations to celebrate and commemorate the accomplishments of pioneer forefathers.[28] Fiona Hamilton remarks that many New Zealand provinces planned public commemorative jubilees in the last decade of the nineteenth century, which celebrated the industriousness and fortitude of 'pioneer' settlers.[29] A provincial semi-centennial jubilee celebration was held in Otago in 1898. As Seán Brosnahan observes, the organisers of the celebration portrayed the current prosperity as a legacy of pioneers, despite Otago's modest achievements before the gold rushes.[30] Fractiousness among the settlers was downplayed as the organisers presented the pioneers as a single unified whole that would be a valuable model to subsequent generations. The Otago Early Settlers' Association was created out of this celebration to archive and remember the contributions of their pioneer settlers to Otago society.[31] The 1898 jubilee organisers identified pioneers as anyone arriving in Otago before the gold rushes. Entirely absent in the 1898 jubilee is any mention of the gold rushes, yet ironically, the Gabriel's Gully Jubilee thirteen years later applied identical language to describe the gold seekers as pioneer settlers who made Otago.

The 1911 jubilee occurred against the backdrop of an emerging interest among local residents in the historical roots of the Otago settlement. This historicity had its basis in the 1898 provincial jubilee and the establishment of the Otago Early Settlers Museum.[32] By 1911 the colonial press played a vital role in emphasising social memory to local residents, creating a shared past connected to a series of values elevated in the present.[33] The editors of the *Evening Star* remarked that the Otago diggers were

> splendid fellows, inured to the simple life, full of pluck and indomitable, and ... they supplied the element of enterprise which when fused with the grim perseverance and patience of the old identities formed the distinctive Otago character.[34]

The *Evening Star* even listed the names of miners who participated in the parade under the title 'The Old Identities', which during the gold rushes was used to describe the colonists in clear contrast to gold seekers.[35] The *Otago Daily Times*, under its managing director, George Fenwick, played an especially important role in shaping a shared past. Erik Olssen writes that Fenwick possessed a 'respect for learning and creativity, a tone of high seriousness and a certain moral strength', and his paper actively encouraged colonists to submit reminiscences about local history. In the six months leading up to the jubilee commemoration, the *Times* published letters from former prospectors about their experiences on the Tuapeka. Fenwick later compiled the reminiscences into a pamphlet printed at the newspaper's office (see Figure 6.3). The

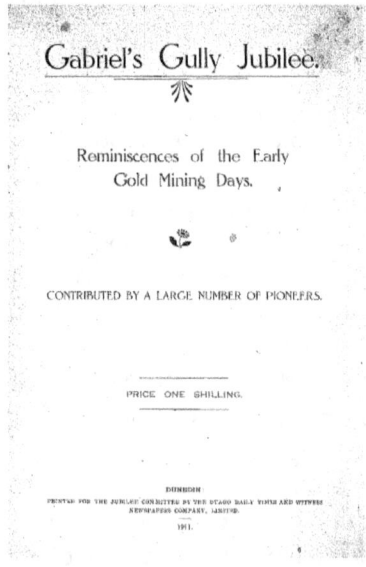

Figure 6.3 Gabriel's Gully Jubilee pamphlet, *Otago Daily Times*, 1911.

booklet stressed to its readers the strength of character and moral fibre of the pioneer diggers who had elevated the province 'from the position of a comparatively unknown settlement to the foremost rank among the provinces of New Zealand'.[36]

In the pages of the *Otago Daily Times* and *The Evening Star*, the 'distinctive Otago character', as described by the *Times*, was the result of the fusing of the Old Identities and the New Iniquity into a single society.[37] What emerges from this account is not an alternative genealogy to the 1898 'settlerism', but an attempt to fit the gold seeker into this model and, therefore, present a cohesive past to create a cohesive present. Such an account shows the importance of social genealogy as a tool used to understand contemporary social environments, as well as the weight of the pioneer myth in Otago society at the turn of the twentieth century.

The 1911 jubilee also dulled conflict on the goldfields. Few of the reminiscences surrounding the jubilee and none of the speeches given at it make any mention of claim jumping, fighting or litigation between mates or parties or between gold seekers employing different forms of gold extraction. James Chisholm stated that 'the honest men were in a decided majority'.[38] A former digger recalled that 'there was no quarrelling or fault-finding' among his mates or with any other parties.[39] Accounts of social upheaval are also softened by the passage of time; when conflict and turmoil are touched on by gold rush participants, they are most often 'vulgar factions' that are depicted more as comedy than tragedy.[40] We should, however, be cautious of assuming this as evidence of intentional omission or deceit. The passage of time allowed individuals to reassign degrees of importance to past events in a way that would have been impossible at the time.[41] The story was finished. The battles were fought and won. Gold did not topple society. The labourer returned to his work and the husband to his wife. The passing of fifty years was also probably significant enough to cool the tempers of many of these old men who once fought over gold.

While gold rush society was described by jubilee organisers as a model of cohesion, the melding of the Old Identity and New Iniquity did not sit easily with some. The ascendancy of the Liberal government in the late nineteenth century depended heavily on the support of rural electors who clamoured for the breaking up of large freeholds and the extension of government land leases.[42] Former gold seekers, many of whom earlier had clamoured for the elimination of pastoral runs in Otago, formed a key bloc for this leasehold class.[43] Moreover, elderly gold seekers were among those who most profited from the passage of the Old Age Pension Act passed by the Seddon government in 1898.[44] When Seddon became ill in 1911, James Carroll, the Native Minister in Seddon's cabinet and acting premier, wrote a letter to be read at the jubilee. He told prospectors that they had 'become the pioneers of the country . . . who had left behind monuments of industry and enterprise, as well as descendants to still mould the present and future destiny' of the nation.[45] Roderick McKenzie, the Minister of Mines and the general government's representative at the celebration, offered less diplomatic praise:

> They were men who made New Zealand, and without trenching upon policies in any way he wished them to understand that Otago had made New Zealand a Liberal country . . . If it had not been for the discovery of gold New Zealand would have been a large sheep station . . . Nothing that this country could do was too good for them.

He then assured the audience that if Seddon had been here, 'he would rise to the occasion much better than anyone else, [because] it was a gathering such as this that he would open his heart to'. This led to an uproar of applause from the crowd.[46] As a show of good faith, McKenzie concluded his speech by stating that the recently established Miners' Relief Fund would provide additional financial support to elderly miners and their families.

Others saw the gold seeker as an instrument of equality, whose egalitarianism provided the model for establishing a 'better Britain' of the southern seas. In the next speech, William Burnett, the mayor of Dunedin, attempted to soften McKenzie's rancour directed at squatters. Burnett had owned shares in the Waikaia and Wendon sheep stations from 1865 and later served as the manager of the Hawkdun Station near St Bathans.[47] In his speech he reminded his audience that the squatters had done much to assist gold seekers when they first arrived on the goldfields, and – at least – they were 'not nearly as bad as the squatters of Victoria'. He told his listeners that 'they had all left the Home Country for this land to better themselves in life, [and] they should forget everything referring to class distinction and put their shoulders together and defend this noble country'.[48] Rather than bickering among themselves, they 'must allow no foreign foe to come here . . . They were Empire builders, and, therefore let them keep together and work together, held together by the silken band of love.'[49] Amid the South African wars and the panic of the 'yellow peril', New Zealanders had greater external enemies. In both McKenzie's and Burnett's accounts, the gold seekers were held up as paragons of New Zealand identity; the problem was identifying whether that meant a society built on small farmers leasing government-owned land or a harmonious society of separate classes. Memories of the rushes became inseparable from contemporary political debates.

While speakers argued about what nation the gold seekers had helped to build, all presenters agreed that the diggers possessed moral virtues that should be emulated in the rising generation. Erik Olssen writes that Otago's social elites often held up the pioneering generation of settlers for their industriousness and moral fibre as a way to combat what was seen as indolence and drunkenness among Dunedin's workers. Like the provincial jubilee, the gold rush jubilee was partially intended to cultivate in the rising generation personal virtues that would lead to prosperity within the local community. The celebrations included several speeches for children by politicians and prospectors about the importance of civic virtues and patriotism. James Allan, a local Member of Parliament, told an audience of children at the Lawrence High School grounds that the gold seekers 'were men of whom they should be proud and emulate'.[50] In another address to the assembled children, Mayor Burnett argued that Otago gold seekers possessed a fierce 'loyalty to Queen and country' and that their interests 'and the interests of all present were bound up with the affairs of the Empire' that had brought freedom to New Zealand.[51]

Not everyone, though, believed that the gold diggers should be imitated. The early twentieth century saw a concerted attack on drunkenness throughout New Zealand. James Belich speculates that the loss of the Tasman world and the end of 'progressive colonisation' led to an identity crisis in New Zealand that resulted in the myth of a 'better Britain', guided by morality, agriculture and steady settlement.[52] An important ideological strand in the creation of an ideal society, therefore, held alcohol as the enemy, which corrupted the minds and wills of young and old alike. Old stereotypes of drunken diggers died hard when the stereotyped so easily confirmed them in print. Gold seekers loved to swap stories in the pages of the *Otago Daily Times* about their alcohol-induced exploits while digging for gold. In a letter to the *Times*, George Calder recollected how he, then fifteen years old, and his mates offered to help a drayman convey liquor illegally to the Dunstan, but in the process drank most of the contents of the dray. It was probably not the best copyediting to place memories of heavy drinking in the newspaper alongside the 'Temperance Column', which catalogued the moral and social dangers of alcohol consumption (see Figure 6.4). Moreover, these were not always empty boasts of former adventures found in the

Figure 6.4 *Otago Daily Times*, 2 March 1911.

bottom of a glass. The Old Age Pension and Miner's Pension Acts both stipulated that payments would be forfeited if the recipient was found drunk. Belich comments that this was a common enough occurrence for constables to make regular raids of public houses for pensioners.[53] This all, of course, had an impact on what people thought about holding up the gold seeker to the youth for emulation. The association of the gold digger with the calm and virtuous settler, therefore, did not fit neatly in the minds of observers concerned with the danger of alcohol and its associated transience, assault and drunkenness. This tension over the memory of the rushes became even more strained when diggers returned with memories of sly grog shanties and weekend sprees to a town that had recently outlawed the sale of all alcohol.

Against the backdrop of the temperance debate, the editors of *The Evening Star* found it noteworthy in the context of a meeting of eighty-year-olds in a dry town to quote a constable stating that 'not only were there no arrests, but they did not see one man under the influence'.[54] Two days later, G. B. Nicholls, the secretary of the Dunedin Temperance Council, followed up the article by stating he was thoroughly surprised that there had been no arrests when there certainly were some individuals who brought liquor to the event. Rather than a testament to the sobriety of the diggers, the peacefulness of the elderly diggers showed the efficiency of the no-licence system.[55] This resulted in a flurry of letters to the newspaper arguing about the sobriety of gold seekers in the 1860s and the present day. One individual recognised the stereotype at the same time he disowned it, when he accused Nicholls for not judging 'men by their record rather than their professions'. Another letter, written by 'Sixty-Niner', stated that 'fifty years ago young New Zealanders were a strictly sober lot, and drinking was practically unknown among them'. Now, because of prohibition, the author argued, 'our police records, our keg gangs, our sly grog-shops [and] our perjury cases [in a dry district]' all bear witness to the inefficiency of prohibition.[56] Prohibition, not alcohol, then became the social enemy. The Lawrence correspondent, seeing the kettle simmer, felt inclined to chime in:

> One of the veterans, aged eighty-two, asked if his present hale and hearty condition was not ascribable to his abstinence, answered with a laugh that in his time he had drunk enough beer and whisky to float the Great Eastern.[57]

What is surprising, however, is not resistance to the commemoration of the rushes but its apparent lack. This was the only negative comment that appeared surrounding the rushes, despite the strength of the prohibition movement, the social and legislative attacks on crew cultures, the common stereotype of the boozing digger and its clear confirmation in print by former gold seekers. This inconsistency indicates how entrenched the gold rushes were in the pioneer myth after fifty short years.

Private memories: gold seeker reminiscences

While personal reminiscences shaped collective memory, private recollection also depended on larger social contexts. As former diggers pondered over letters from other participants in the rushes fifty years ago, personal acts of memory making and documentation often took place within social contexts, stimulated by recollections of other individuals who helped to constitute social space.[58] This aligns with Susan Crane's claim that 'collective memory maintains the lived experience of individuals within groups . . . because that individual experience is never remembered without reference to a shared context'.[59]

Otago gold seeker autobiographies were firmly entrenched in a transnational literary canon of 'pioneer' reminiscences that existed in Australia, New Zealand and the United States. Around the end of the nineteenth century, many residents of local communities in these nations believed that the frontiers were, in the words of Frederick Jackson Turner, closed and the pioneering days had indeed ended.[60] In this climate, local residents began to compile reminiscences from pioneer settlers as a means of holding onto local memory. In the United States, Malcolm Rohrbough writes, a plethora of autobiographies were published during the late nineteenth century as part of commissioned county histories. These always documented the hard work and perseverance of their pioneering settlers. Almost every volume was littered with experiences in the California gold rushes, which became the quintessence of adventure and courage for this generation.[61] Writing on Australia, Tom Griffiths demonstrates that former Victorian prospectors began to write their autobiographies in the 1880s and 1890s, when 'they marvelled at the changes they had initiated and observed, and worried about what would be lost with their deaths'.[62] In New Zealand, enough settler autobiographies were published in the late nineteenth and early twentieth centuries that Fiona Hamilton remarks, 'pioneer reminiscences were a contemporary genre by the twentieth century'.[63]

The content of Otago gold seeker autobiographies collectively had 'a generic quality; they described remarkably similar experiences and were written with similar tone'.[64] The language of adventure, hard work and youthfulness permeated autobiographies. Narratives changed very little from one volume to the next. They were filled with stories of tramping through blizzards, food by the fire, loud and bustling townships surrounded by a silent wilderness, and all the highs and lows of digging for gold.[65] James Gascoigne titled his unpublished reminiscences 'The Adventures of a Norfolk Boy', with a subheading listing his different occupations and the lands he visited.[66] William Smith simply called his the 'Reminiscences of a Long and Active Life by an Old Colonist'.[67] George Collier, who arrived on the Tuapeka in 1861, remembered how 'like many other young colonials he had adventure in his blood'.[68]

Layered on top of these representations of the gold rushes were preoccupations with contemporary social interactions in a local community. Historians of the American gold rushes frequently emphasise the ways in which autobiographers understood the rushes as national events that left an indelible mark on national identity.[69] Writing on the autobiographies of pioneer settlers in New Zealand, Fiona Hamilton argues instead that most accounts did not provide 'a base for a sense of national cohesion' when they often were composed as part of provincial anniversaries and were overwhelmingly concerned with local rather than national history. Evidence from Otago gold seeker reminiscences generally confirms

Hamilton's conclusion, although diggers sometimes generalised about a New Zealand identity from their personal experiences.

What was remembered and forgotten about the gold rushes depended on practices of local memory consumption in Otago. Most accounts were written by prospectors who settled in Otago and penned their memories either at the request of jubilee organisers, family members or neighbours interested in the foundation of their communities. In 1911 the *Otago Daily Times* published seventy-seven collections of reminiscences that were requested by the organisers of the Gabriel's Gully Jubilee.[70] The same year the Maniototo Early Settlers' Association requested John Bremner to compose his reminiscences about his experiences at the Mount Ida goldfield. Bremner's autobiography was published in the *Mount Ida Chronicle* over five weekly instalments.[71] The Otago Early Settlers' Association played an especially important role in the documentation of the Otago rushes as part of a history of the province. William Ayson's autobiography grew out of a request by the Secretary of the Otago Early Settlers' Association.[72] In 1916 W. G. Fail delivered a public lecture sponsored by the Association about his experiences in the Otago rushes.[73] The Association's museum, the Otago Early Settlers Museum, also became a major repository for gold seeker reminiscences, including a collection of nineteen oral histories deposited by Margaret Shaw for a local history of the Taieri district.[74] This social enquiry by a community into a local past often shaped personal memory.

Writing for a local audience, most autobiographies were concerned with local history set in clear contrast to the present. Authors lived during the period of modernity, in which, as Sylviane Agacinski argues, more drastic social, economic and technological changes occurred over a shorter period of time than any previous period in history.[75] Christopher Shaw and Malcolm Chase contend that this condition intensifies nostalgia when 'the qualitative distance between us and the past widens'.[76] There were few events in the nineteenth century that brought greater changes to local communities more quickly than the gold rushes. Memories, therefore, represented an attempt, both by writers and readers, to hold onto a rapidly vanishing past which seemed more distant because of the intensity of the transformations that it wrought upon societies and environments. Gold seekers' memory making was done in the context of burgeoning towns and the rapidly transforming landscape of the goldfields. The landscapes that during the rushes had so clearly dictated daily and seasonal labour patterns on the diggings were now barely recognisable. Hillsides where claims were once dug and friendships were once made – or unmade – were washed away by thirty years of sluicing.

Tailings from dredges and quartz-crushing batteries covered creek beds where hopes so many times died or were restored. The jarring craters of the first years disappeared under a rubble of debris. Calico townships, bustling with optimism and opulence, vanished with the dreams of wealth that fuelled them, or were transformed into unrecognisable townships with marching bands, Caledonian Societies and fire brigades, almost as fast as they sprang up. Dunedin around the turn of the twentieth century was no longer a quaint, if backwards settlement where, as several autobiographers informed their readers, the jailer threatened to lock the prisoners out if they were not in at night; it was now a bustling commercial and industrial centre that financed the expansion of agriculture in the North Island and was an important link in trade with Britain.[77] Some autobiographers lamented this change. Amid the celebrations surrounding the Gabriel's Gully Jubilee in 1911, Richard Hay complained that the younger generation lacked the 'pluck and energy' that he believed so clearly defined his generation.[78] After fifty years' residence in New Zealand, MacLeod Orbell lamented that it was impossible for recent immigrants, 'surrounded as they are with every comfort and convenience', to understand the hardships and 'heroic bravery' of the previous generation, who 'practically [laid] the foundation by opening up the country and building upon it'.[79] For former gold seekers, reminiscences were a means 'to stop time, to block the work of forgetting'.[80]

Yet recollection was not only a desire to hold onto a past that was slipping away. As Fiona Hamilton writes of New Zealand settlers more generally, gold seekers in Otago 'perceived themselves arriving in a land without history, although they were (and still are) also obsessed with their historicity'.[81] Autobiographers did not simply dwell on the past but drew their readers forward to the present moment, thereby mapping out a genealogy of local communities. Progress is as much the defining feature of these accounts as the frozen past. Many of the narratives follow the author through their experiences gold seeking and into a settled community after the rushes. Often, writers viewed their autobiographies as an instrumental part of their community's local memory. John Bremner, a shopkeeper at Mount Ida, recalled the introduction of 'civilisation' after the rushes: diggers settled down and established businesses; 'happy bachelors fell victim to the trouble' of marriage; churches and lodges were built; newspapers, fire brigades and political parties were established.'[82] Diggers usually viewed themselves as important catalysts of the changes they described, essentially writing themselves into their community's 'own colonial book of Genesis'.[83] Throughout his autobiography, William Jackson Barry described himself as a friend of the independent digger, an opponent of monopolies and able to beat any villain in a fistfight.[84] James Gascoigne narrates his creation of the first water race at Waitahuna.[85] This act of narrating personal contributions to local development became a form of what Peter Gibbons describes as 'cultural colonisation'.[86] When gold rushes in Otago always occurred on the edge of a colonial frontier, they became an important means through which settlement extended to lands scarcely known by most colonists before the rushes. Autobiographical writing allowed colonists to 'domesticate the incorrigible wilderness' through knowledge, by charting the continued vanishing of the frontier.[87] As elderly prospectors wrote about a landscape that had been transformed by dredging, sluicing and horticulture, they quickly forgot the domination of the rushes by nature and the landscape. Henry Walton, for example, characterised the trek across hills and through snow banks in search of firewood as 'glorious tobogganing' when prospectors slid down hillsides on top of bundles of kindling.[88]

These accounts of personal contributions to local development bear a strong contrast to working-class autobiographies in Britain, which depict the author largely as a member of class rather than an autonomous individual, as demonstrated by Nan Hackett.[89] Working-class autobiographers often presented themselves as 'social atoms' that struggle for autonomy amid the dehumanising forces of the factory and the industrial slum.[90] The dissimilarity between Otago and British working-class autobiographies is especially illuminating given that Otago autobiographers who reflected on their childhood experiences in Britain before overseas migration similarly stress dependence and inequality, juxtaposed against financial successes in the colonies. James Gascoigne recalled his childhood in Norfolk, England:

> Young as I was at that time, I could not but observe the great disparity ... in which the wealth of the country was held. There were the drones, who held more wealth than they could decently use; and there were the workers, who contributed to keep them in their idle grandeur, and who ... were ground down to little better than a crust of bread and a drink of water.[91]

William Smith similarly described his home in Ayrshire in the midst of the potato blight, filled with starvation and destitution.[92] Arthur Scoullar characterised his parents in Glasgow as 'hearty and independent' for their refusal of parish aid amid poverty.[93] For such writers, overseas migration, rather than simply gold seeking, is understood as the axis of their personal life history. Shortly before describing his migration from Scotland to Waikouaiti, Otago, MacLeod Orbell stepped outside of his narrative to tell his readers:

> I have now reached a point in my career, which like a Kaleidoscope, will reveal many changes, varying in character, which I will endeavour to note in such a form that may be of interest to my children.[94]

This follows Erik Erikson's assertion that personal identity becomes most visible during periods of migration when individuals shift from membership in one group to another.[95] However, caution should be made against assuming autobiographies accurately depict personal identity at the time of migration, when there are no known surviving collections of reminiscences and correspondence from the same gold seeker. The masses of letters between prospectors and their relatives in Britain or Ireland, discussed in Chapter One, may indicate that this transformation was likely more gradual than autobiographies document. Alternatively, past hardships could be used to better highlight later accomplishments. Here it should be remembered that autobiographical writings were 'not innocent acts of memory, but attempts to persuade'.[96]

MEMORIES OF THE ANTIPODES: BRITAIN AND THE UNITED STATES

Most accounts published by gold seekers who later returned to Britain or the United States present the Otago rushes as part of a larger string of personal adventures and escapades. For some, the Otago rushes are understood as part of a wider trans-Pacific phenomenon linked together by migration and information exchange. For most, the memory of the Otago rushes was marketed within a genre of adventure literature that saw the empire and the frontier as fields for unbridled adventure and astonishing environments. Charles Ferguson described the Otago rushes as part of a personal odyssey that took him from Illinois to the Californian, Australian and Otago goldfields before he eventually returned home after thirty-four years' absence. Along the way he is ambushed by Indians in Utah, robbed by bushrangers in New South Wales and participates in both the Eureka stockade and the Burke and Wills expedition across the Australian continent.[97] J. Inches Thomson's aptly named *Voyages and Wanderings in Far Off Seas and Lands* catalogues his experiences as a whaler and gold digger around the Pacific and throughout North America. Among other events, he slew a whale, was shipwrecked on a deserted island and was a guest of Te Whiti during the 1881 government invasion of Parihaka.[98] T. E. Crowhurst was first attracted to emigration when he heard that his uncle in South Africa shot lions from his window at night. When he arrived in New Zealand from Sussex he was well-armed, having brought a rifle and a Colt revolver.[99] Robert Booth developed 'boyish and quixotic notions' to emigrate when he read stories of 'wild life in America and elsewhere'.[100] These accounts were part of a larger genre in Britain and the United States that described the frontiers as vivid landscapes for adventure and excitement, in direct contrast to the assumed sedentary situation of their readers. Otago only operates in these accounts as a canvas on which to place a story and was little differentiated from other environments.

In most of these accounts the Otago colonists only hover on the margins. Robert Booth only mentions Dunedin in a brief paragraph as he is passing through from Canterbury on the way to the diggings.[101] When they do emerge, colonists are often described in disparaging terms. Matthew McKeown, for example, characterised them as a backwards group of settlers who were rightly put in their place by gold seekers and never much mattered in the province since.[102]

In his reminiscences, entitled *The Wonders of Providence and Grace*, published in London, Andrew Bools described his experiences of gold seeking in terms of moral depravity and corruption. His little book of under two hundred pages was a sort of confessional, in which he catalogued his spiritual awakening to God's 'providence and grace' operating in his life. It aligned with a genre of autobiographies in Britain and the United States, written in the tradition of St Augustine's *Confessions*, that depicted life as a pilgrimage from darkness to light.[103] Sprinkled throughout the book are expositions on the mercy of God and the depravity of man. Bools told his readers that he was often overcome by 'the wonderful unction of the Spirit' while writing the book.[104] He hoped that *The Wonders of Providence and Grace* would reveal to his readers 'the glory of God and the good of his chosen ones'.[105]

Bools was born in Devonshire to the son of a shipbuilder. At the age of sixteen he found employment on a trading vessel. His journeys took him through Europe, into South America, across the Pacific and on to the Victorian and Otago goldfields. Interspersed within the book are scenes of shipwreck and shanties, brawls and bullfights, and at least thirteen near-death experiences, including with illness (smallpox and yellow fever), shark attacks, knife stabbings and one occasion in which he was bitten by a dog. These scenes are not intended merely as a log of adventure, but as evidence of God's hand in protecting and sustaining him.

Bools identified his experiences digging in Otago as the hinge of his conversion. One night in 1862 at Weatherston's, he returned to his camp after a drinking and gambling spree through which he forged a 'covenant with death [that] leads to destruction'. When he entered his tent, Bolls found a poem about a mother praying for her son who abandoned God in his pursuit of riches and pleasure on the Otago goldfields. At this point, he wrote, 'an unutterable anguish came over me. My sins stood out in dread array ... I dropped on my knees in the tent and began to cry for mercy ... "Oh, God, be merciful to me, a sinner ... who feels as if hell were about to open before him."' As he saw diggers around him becoming sick and dying during the especially difficult winter of 1862, he worried that if he died with a soul corrupted by licentiousness, gambling and greed, he would not be spared 'the wrath of a sin-avenging God'.[106] He left the goldfields, returned to Dunedin and eventually sailed home to Britain.

Settling in Cardiff, Bools tried his hand in shipbuilding before he began his career of preaching and polemicising as an itinerant Baptist minister, establishing a circuit through Wales, Yorkshire and Lancashire. He then went on to write four more books on religious topics[107] and his reminiscences went to a second edition ten years later. There is no solid evidence that this book was read by more than a handful of individuals, but his wide circuit and frequent preaching engagements probably meant he was relatively successful. To Bools, the depravity on the Otago diggings was the result of human corruption, rather than frontier conditions – an impression that for many of his Nonconformist readers and hearers was easily transferable to the music-hall culture developing in their local communities in late-nineteenth-century Britain.[108] Bools' recollection of drunkenness and greed on the goldfields, therefore, was in some ways as much the result of contemporary social circumstances in Britain as Chisholm's forgetting them in Otago twenty years later.

TRANS-TASMAN MEMORIES

While the Otago gold rushes did not create the Tasman World, it more deeply entangled the societies, economies and cultures in Otago and Victoria. When prospectors rushed from Victoria and Otago to the West Coast in the second half of the 1860s, Melbourne and Dunedin competed for control of the West Coast trade. Still retaining a strong commercial connection to each other, the two cities established a triangular trade between Melbourne, Dunedin and Hokitika.[109] Dunedin was always a junior partner in this relationship when Melbourne was both closer and had more resources than Dunedin. By the 1870s, Otago still retained a strong connection to Victoria. As during the early 1860s, prospectors were acutely aware of conditions in both locations through correspondence that flowed across the Tasman Sea in both directions.[110]

There were therefore many in Otago and Victoria during the late 1860s who still understood the gold rushes as trans-Tasman events. It was in this context that Charles Thatcher again set out to make a profit in the late 1860s by commoditising the memories of the gold rushes for its participants on both sides of the Tasman Sea. In 1867 Thatcher launched his last Australasian tour. By the late 1860s, Thatcher and his wife, the vocalist Madame Vitelli, intended to return to England with their two infant daughters.[111] To help finance their travel, and undoubtedly go out with a bang, Thatcher developed a one-man performance, entitled 'Life on the Goldfields: An Entertainment', that re-presented the Victorian gold rushes to his audiences in public houses in Australia and New Zealand. He employed the German immigrant painter John Hennings to paint a diorama through the guise of an itinerant drunk gold seeker.[112] While the panoramas have not survived, Thatcher's script, which was transcribed by Robert Hoskins, provides insight into the retelling of the rushes a short five years after they ended.[113] The performance was part lecture, part musical, and mostly comedy. As Anita Callaway observes, painted landscape panoramas were a popular entertainment medium in the nineteenth century because they 'registered the images not as vertical paintings but as vistas laid out before [their audiences]'.[114] Such images, writes Callaway, implicitly stressed for their audiences a 'natural progression [from] a "desolate wilderness"' to a developed society.[115] Thatcher attempted to satirise this medium at the same time he emphasised its usefulness as a lens into the gold rushes which had already begun to slip into nostalgia by the late 1860s.[116] During his performance, Thatcher recited a series of memorised monologues, each assisted by a corresponding painting and interspersed with his own songs.

The play presented a satiric look at the 'new chum's' transformation into a hardened colonist. It began with the disembarking of the naive hero, 'Thomas Noddy' (Tomnoddy for short) in Melbourne, having left sisters, a sweetheart, a weeping mother and an indulgent father in England. Upon arrival, he was met by the scenes of Melbourne ablaze with a gold rush, and he promptly travelled to the diggings, carrying only a broom and a briefcase. After passing through the Black Forest, where decaying bodies of bullocks lined the road and returning diggers are murdered or robbed by bushrangers, he comes to the goldfield. Thatcher then describes the scene as represented in the panorama:

> Everywhere he sees little mounds of earth cast up & who can tell the feelings that crowd upon his excited imagination as he goes & looks down the first hole he comes to . . . Shouting laughing & swearing such a confusion & noise hundreds of men walking about covered with dirt red shirts & long beards. Tailors with mustachios doctors bank managers clerks & shopmen all on an equality working together.

At this point Thatcher points to two diggers in the background taking a drink, commenting that 'the artist painted this in the best style because he is "quate at home in drinking subjects"'.[117] Next, Thatcher took his audience through a series of events common to goldfield lore, including a mining party jumping a nearby claim, a procession of Chinese diggers and a magistrates' court session. Finally, at the end of the presentation, Thatcher's hero settles down as a squatter and devotes himself to livestock.

After Thatcher completed a successful Australian tour, earning wide applause and favourable reviews in over sixty Australian newspapers, he took 'Life on the Goldfields' to New Zealand, travelling south from Auckland, again earning wide acclaim in performances and in the press. Thatcher seemed to embody a gold rush culture that was as evident in New Zealand as it was in Australia. As his audiences again watched his familiar gestures and heard his familiar songs, memories of their experiences in Otago flooded back. The *West Coast Times* wrote, reflecting on a recent performance in Hokitika, where the audience undoubtedly included many former Otago diggers:

> His appearance on stage was the signal of a boisterous shower of applause which was prolonged for some time and only subsided after frequent acknowledgements from the recipient. Doubtless many of those present last night who were so demonstrative . . . at the sight of that 'old familiar face,' were influenced by recollections of the rosy days of yore, and the glorious incidents that are associated with the name and fame of the celebrated Thatcher.[118]

'Life on the Goldfields' operated at the junction of memory and everyday culture, bringing life on the diggings back to memory just as it receded into the past. Moreover, its generic content made it easily transferable to different communities. The lecture presented an endless stream of caricatures and anecdotes that flowed easily together, and were set alongside each other in stark contrast that defied easy categorisation. The eerie quiet of the Black Forest was followed in the next painting by scenes of chaos in the first weeks of a goldfield. A drunkard prospector was seen digging for gold alongside a doctor. The glamour of riches was set alongside the thrall of poverty, sickness and death.[119]

The performance, however, was as much about the transformation of the new chum into the seasoned colonial as it was about the excitements and anxieties. The period of the gold rushes was still raw. Caricatures still had a certain resonance when many were still prospecting in Otago and on the West Coast. Yet there were even more who, like the hero, had settled down on land or were in waged work. This majority saw that the rushes had indeed passed. Thatcher drew his audience back to the first days of the rushes and pulled them forward to the present. In doing so, he helped individuals to form a narrative that revealed as much about contemporary society as it did about the gold rushes. The play depicted a world in which the gold digger was gradually transformed into the small farmer or the waged worker. This account of Thatcher's diorama aligns with Anita Callaway's reading of Australian moving dioramas, which, she argues, often presented a narrative of constant progress and historical development, placing the individual in sharp contrast to the landscapes he observed.[120] 'Life on the Goldfields', therefore, moved in the spaces between a contemporary event that seemed crude, vulgar and random and a newly formed memory that sought to understand the rushes' significance and how exactly the digger became the settler.

It was also in this context, in which the ongoing connections between Victoria and Otago after the rushes subsided, that Charles Money published his widely circulated and critically acclaimed reminiscences of his experiences during the Otago rushes, entitled *Knocking About in New Zealand*. The book was published in Melbourne in 1871 and sold well enough that it went through two printings within a year. The editors of the *Launceston Examiner* wrote a two-column review in which they described the volume as a 'thoroughly readable' account which 'exhibited Mr Money's craft with words'.[121] The Melbourne *Argus* agreed, applauding the author's avoidance of being 'too slovenly in [his] literary dress' and the 'fine writing' practised by other gentleman travellers. *Knocking About in New Zealand*, the *Argus* asserted, joined the canon of the 'better class of Australian literature'.[122]

Money's vivid account is filled with mateship and egalitarianism: brandy glasses clanked over the din of a packed grog shanty, yarns were exchanged by the glow of the campfire after a long day's tramp, and bonds between diggers congealed through the drudgery of shovelling and swirling wash dirt on a claim.[123] In the book, Otago, and implicitly New Zealand, exist only as a backdrop where these social dramas take place. Dunedin, for example, only surfaces in the narrative when the author is standing at the bar of the Provincial Hotel, surrounded by diggers, and looks at the town drenched in mud, diggers and disease.

While many of the reminiscences about the rushes in New Zealand and Australia tended to be self-complimenting 'pioneering' accounts that swelled 'the pioneer bladder ... to the size of a paragraphic pumpkin', in the words of the Melbourne novelist, Marcus Clarke, the settler and the pioneer are entirely absent in Money's account.[124] It is not a self-patronising account of one's own personal contributions to the creation of the present, like most of the New Zealand reminiscences. Furthermore, the positive reviews *Knocking About in New Zealand* received in the Australian press, and the fact it was reviewed at all, may also indicate that in 1871 many in Australia still thought Australia and New Zealand shared a single history.

Both Thatcher's 'Life on the Goldfields' and Money's *Knocking About in New Zealand* appeared in the midst of the West Coast rushes that continued to link Victoria and Otago in the Tasman World. Both accounts lacked the strong current of nostalgia that dominated New Zealand reminiscences towards the end of the century because the rush to New Zealand goldfields was still occurring in the late 1860s and early 1870s. It is undoubtedly significant that *Knocking About in New Zealand* was the last collection of reminiscences from the Otago diggings published in Australia and reviewed in the Australian press, especially when the high point of New Zealand memoirs was still thirty years away.

TRANS-TASMAN AMNESIA

As the Australasian rushes waned after the 1870s, Victorian memories of the Otago gold rushes began to slip from view at the same time that New Zealand colonists began to remember them as local, rather than transnational, events. By the time of the 1911 Gabriel's Gully Jubilee, the personal and collective memories of the Otago gold rushes, as with all memories, '[depended] upon forgetting'. They necessitated, as Jacquelyn Dowd Hall writes, 'the suppression and repression of contrary, disruptive memories – other people's memories of the same events, as well as the unacceptable ghosts of our own past'.[125] The act of forgetting, whereby some memories fade into oblivion, is as instructive as the encapsulation of memories in autobiographical writings and public recollections.

Within all these debates about what the gold rushes meant for New Zealand society was lost the fact that they were not simply New Zealand events. Absent from nearly the entire jubilee celebration are the gold seekers who did not remain in New Zealand. Upon watching the procession of gold seekers in the parade, the reporter for the *Otago Daily Times* remarked that it represented 'almost all that is left of the once great army'.[126] However, out of the 280 gold seekers attending the celebration there was only one gold seeker who came from Australia (he only returned to Victoria in 1867), and none who came from elsewhere.[127] Moreover, most of those who attended had lived in New Zealand before they joined the Otago rushes. Among the seventy-two reminiscences published by the *Otago Daily Times*, more than half were written by colonists who were already residing in New Zealand. Only a quarter were written by individuals who migrated from Victoria, despite the colony accounting for approximately 90 per cent of Otago miners rushing from Victoria.[128] Moreover, among those who recorded Victorian origins, none make mention of Victorian experiences before arriving in Otago. Victorian experiences fade into oblivion when they are seen by authors and audiences to be unimportant to community building and genealogies of place. Most often, the writer included his place of birth and arrival in Australia as a preface, while the majority of the narrative concerns his New Zealand experience and his 'settling down' in Otago. Most of the autobiographical accounts of the Otago rushes were written by colonists who lived in New Zealand before and after the gold rushes.[129] Moreover, when Victorian experiences are discussed, they are incorporated into a narrative of eventual settlement in New Zealand.[130] Historians of the New Zealand rushes too often have slipped into this narrative that only depicts Victoria as a place from which gold seekers arrived, neglecting the ongoing movement of knowledge, people, capital, commodities and correspondence that linked Victoria and Otago into a single trans-Tasman community.[131] Moreover, while those who remained in New Zealand forgot the rushes' Victorian connections, those who returned often forgot their New Zealand experiences.[132] This may emphasise the social construction of personal memory when late-nineteenth-century recollections often present genealogies of communities in which individuals spent their lives.

CONCLUSION

This chapter has analysed the ways in which the Otago gold rushes were remembered and forgotten by their participants after the rushes subsided. It began with a discussion of the 1911 Gabriel's Gully Semi-Centennial Jubilee, which commemorated the Otago gold rushes as New Zealand events. While debates swirled around the celebration over what type of colony the prospector helped to create, colonists understood the digger as a pioneer and stressed his contributions to local community building, thus forgetting connections to Victoria and the volatile environmental and climatic factors of Otago that helped to push gold seekers off Otago's shores. Private autobiographies written in New Zealand were framed by these broader contemporary social concerns, as individuals presented themselves as active participants in the genesis of local communities, charging recollections with contemporary social contexts. Gold seekers who later returned to Britain or the United States presented the Otago goldfields as generic antipodean landscapes for audiences interested in narratives of excitement or religious conversion. In the late 1860s and early 1870s, prospectors in Victoria and Otago remembered the Otago rushes as part of a series of trans-Tasman rushes, as shown through a discussion of the works of Charles Thatcher and Charles Money. This was due to the ongoing migration of prospectors between Victoria and the West Coast. However, as the Australasian rushes began to wane, memories of the trans-Tasman rushes also began to fade. New Zealand colonists began to compose narratives of national and local development, independent of connections to Victoria. Meanwhile, Victorian colonists forgot the Otago rushes entirely because they seemed, by the early twentieth century, to have little bearing to Australian development.

NOTES

1. *Otago Daily Times*, 22 May 1911, 5.
2. *The Cyclopedia of New Zealand: Otago and Southland Provincial Districts* (Christchurch: Horace J. Weeks, 1903), 168.
3. Chisholm's sermon is published in 'Gabriel's Gully jubilee', *Evening Star*, 29 May 1911, 6 and 30 May 1911, 2. Also see *Otago Daily Times*, 22 May 1911, 5.
4. The published New Zealand autobiographies discussed in this chapter are William Jackson Barry, *Past and Present, and Men of the Times* (Wellington: McKee and Gamble, 1897); Alexander Bathgate, *Colonial Experiences; or Sketches of People and Places in the Province of Otago, New Zealand* (Glasgow: James MacLehose, 1874); Alexander Don, *Early Central Otago; a Bathurst Miner's Reminiscences* (Dunedin: Otago Daily Times, 1932); G. M. Hassing, *Pages from the Memory Log of G. M. Hassing: Sailor, Pioneer, Schoolmaster* (Invercargill: Southland Times Company, 1930); George Ogilvy Preshaw, *Banking Under Difficulties or Life on the Goldfields of Victoria, New South Wales and New Zealand. By a Bank Official* (Christchurch: Kiwi Publishers, 1997); John Wilson, *Reminiscences of the Early Settlement of Dunedin and South Otago* (Dunedin: J. Wilkie and Co. Limited, 1912). The chapter also draws upon

seventy-four reminiscences that were published in newspapers. Of these, seventy-two were from letters submitted to the *Otago Daily Times* in 1911 and were later published in *Gabriel's Gully Jubilee: Reminiscences of the Early Gold Mining Days* (Dunedin: Otago Daily Times, 1911). Two more were composed of series of letters submitted to goldfield newspapers and compiled into manuscript form: J. C. Bremner, 'Memoirs of the Early Diggings', OSM, DC-0986; and David A. Jolly, 'Early Goldfields History: Reminiscences of the Early Goldfields of Central Otago, and Jottings of Early Cromwell History', private collection [David George]. The unpublished autobiographies and reminiscences include William Ayson, *Pioneering in Otago* (Christchurch: Kiwi Publishers, 1995); William F. Heinz, *Bright Fine Gold: Stories of the New Zealand Goldfields* (Wellington: Reed, 1974); W. G. Fail, 'Mr W. G. Fail's First Year's Experience in New Zealand. Delivered at Old Identities Meeting, March 23 1916', OSM, DC-2153; W. G. Fail, 'Address Delivered at Old Identities Meeting, Port Chalmers, on March 10th, 1914', OSM, DC-2153; Sir William Fraser, 'The Early Sixties in Otago: Personal Reminiscences of a Pioneer', HC, DU 484.4 FU283; James Randall Gascoigne, 'The Adventures of a Norfolk Boy for a Half Century from 1847 Onwards. His Early Life as a Sailor, Life on a Copper Mine in 1850, His Goldfields Experience in New South Wales in 1851, in California from 1852 to 1858, in British Columbia from 1858 to 1860, in Victoria in 1861, on the Otago Goldfields from 1861 to 1881', OSM, DC-0483; Frank Harbottle, autobiography, HC, Misc-MS-1654; Richard Hay, 'Old Times in New Zealand', OSM, no call number; Alexander Kerr, 'Reminiscences of the Gold Rush Days in Australia and New Zealand', ATL, MS-1115; William Martin, 'Experiences of William Martin as a Goldminer at Gabriel's Gully in 1861', HC, MS-0203; John McLay, 'Waikouaiti and Dunedin in 1850', OSM, DC-0112; George O'Halloran, autobiography; Orbell, reminiscences, OSM, C084; Arthur Scoullar, reminiscences, OSM, DC-3028; William Smith, 'Reminiscences of a Long and Active Life by an Old Colonist', OSM, C101; James Strachan, 'My First Twelve Years on My Own – commencing from 20th April 1856 –nearly 61 Years Ago', HC, MS-563; J. S. Suisted, reminiscences, OSM, DC-2439; Richard Norman, 'Early Cardrona History', OSM, C-083. Twenty oral histories of participants in the Otago rushes are located in Shaw Taieri Correspondence, OSM, no call number. An additional eight interviews of Otago prospectors are contained in Edith Mary Story, 'Stories of the Gold Diggings', ATL, fMS-Papers-7868.
5. Cf. David Goodman, 'Making an Edgier History of Gold', in Iain McCalman, Alexander Cook, and Andrew Reeves (eds), *Gold: Forgotten Histories and Lost Objects of Australia* (Cambridge: Cambridge University Press, 2001), 38.
6. Much of this literature draws on the work of writing in the cultural

colonisation of New Zealand. See Peter Gibbons, 'Non-fiction', in Terry Sturm (ed.), *The Oxford History of New Zealand Literature in English* (Auckland: Oxford University Press, 1991), 25–104.
7. Chris Hilliard, 'Island Stories: The Writing of New Zealand History, 1920–1940' (MA thesis, University of Auckland, 1997).
8. Peter Gibbons, 'Cultural Colonization and National Identity', *New Zealand Journal of History* 36, no. 1 (2002): 9–12, quotation taken from p. 10.
9. Fiona Hamilton, 'Pioneering History: Negotiating Pakeha Collective Memory in the Late Nineteenth and Early Twentieth Centuries', *New Zealand Journal of History* 36, no. 1 (2002): 77; Seán G. Brosnahan, *To Fame Undying: The Otago Settlers Association, 1898–2008* (Dunedin: Otago Settlers Association, 2008).
10. Miles Fairburn, *The Ideal Society and Its Enemies: The Foundation of Modern New Zealand Society, 1850–1900* (Auckland: Auckland University Press, 1989), 145–52, 203–4, 245.
11. For a discussion of biases inherent in each source, see the introduction of this thesis.
12. Jock Phillips, *A Man's Country?: The Image of the Pakeha Male, a History*, 2nd edn (Auckland: Penguin Books, 1996), viii.
13. John Burnett, *Destiny Obscure: Autobiographies of Childhood, Education and Family From the 1820s to the 1920s* (New York: Routledge, 2013), x–xii.
14. The thesis, however, shies away from drawing evidence from autobiographies about motivations for gold seeking, as they may be more prone to reinterpretation later in life.
15. Sidone Smith, 'Construing Truths in Lying Mouths: Truthtelling in Women's Autobiography', *Studies in the Literary Imagination* 23, no. 2 (1990): 145.
16. Nan Hackett, 'A Different Form of "Self": Narrative Style in British Nineteenth-Century Working-class Autobiography', *Biography* 12, no. 3 (1989): 211.
17. Orbell, autobiography; Gascoigne, 'Adventures of a Norfolk Boy'; William Smith, 'Reminiscences'.
18. William C. Spengemann and L. R. Lundquist, 'Autobiography and the American Myth', *American Quarterly* 17, no. 3 (1965): 502.
19. Susan A. Crane, 'Writing the Individual Back into Collective Memory', *The American Historical Review* 102, no. 5 (1 December 1997): 1377.
20. Ibid., 1381.
21. Liam Harte, *The Literature of the Irish in Britain: Autobiography and Memoir, 1725–2001* (London: Palgrave Macmillan, 2009), xx.
22. Phillips, *A Man's Country*, 27–38.
23. *Otago Daily Times*, 23 May 1911.
24. Ibid., 23 May 1911.

25. *Evening Star*, 22 May 1911.
26. *Otago Daily Times*, 23 May 1911.
27. David Glassberg, *Sense of History: The Place of the Past in American Life* (Amherst: University of Massachusetts Press, 2001), Chapter 7; Malcolm J. Rohrbough, *Days of Gold: The California Gold Rush and the American Nation* (Berkeley: University of California Press, 1998), 289–93.
28. Graeme Davison, 'The Parochial Past: Changing Uses of Australian Local History', in Paul Ashton (ed.), *The Future of the Past? Australian History after the Bicentenary: Proceedings of the Royal Australian Historical Society* (Sydney: Royal Australian Historical Society, 1990), 5–19.
29. Hamilton, 'Pioneering History', especially 66–9.
30. Brosnahan, *To Fame Undying*, 6.
31. Ibid., Chapter 1.
32. Erik Olssen, *A History of Otago* (Dunedin: John McIndoe, 1984), 136–8. The museum is now called the Toitū Otago Settlers Museum.
33. James W. Carey, *Communication as Culture: Essays on Media and Society* (Boston: Unwin Hyman, 1989), 30–5.
34. *The Evening Star*, 22 May 1911.
35. Ibid., 23 May 1911.
36. *Gabriel's Gully Jubilee*, 1.
37. Ibid.
38. *Otago Daily Times*, 22 May 1911.
39. *Gabriel's Gully Jubilee*, 25.
40. Ibid., 13–14.
41. Spengemann and Lundquist, 'Autobiography', 501–2.
42. Keith Sinclair, *A History of New Zealand*, 4th edn (Auckland: Penguin Books, 1988), 178.
43. J. H. M. Salmon, *A History of Goldmining in New Zealand* (Wellington: Government Printer, 1963), 108–10, 120–1, 210.
44. From a conversation with Tom Brooking.
45. *Otago Daily Times*, 23 May 1911.
46. Ibid.
47. *Mount Ida Chronicle*, 31 August 1923.
48. Ibid.
49. Ibid.
50. *Otago Daily Times*, 25 May 1911.
51. Ibid.
52. James Belich, *Reforging Paradise: A History of the New Zealanders from the 1880s to the Year 2000* (Auckland: Penguin Press, 2001), 170–7.
53. Ibid., 177.
54. *The Evening Star*, 22 May 1911.
55. Ibid., 25 May 1911.
56. Ibid., 26 May 1911.

57. Ibid.
58. See, for example, *Otago Daily Times*, 18 March 1911, 24 April 1911; *Gabriel's Gully Jubilee*, 39.
59. Crane, 'Writing the Individual', 1381.
60. Frederick Jackson Turner, 'The Significance of the Frontier in American History', in Frederick Jackson Turner (ed.), *The Frontier in American History* (New York: Henry Holt, 1921), 1–20.
61. Rohrbough, *Days of Gold*, 289.
62. Tom Griffiths, *Hunters and Collectors: The Antiquarian Imagination in Australia* (Cambridge University Press, 1996), 199. Also see Davison, 'The Parochial Past', 7–9.
63. Hamilton, 'Pioneering History', 67.
64. Ibid., 69.
65. See, for example, Ayson, *Pioneering*; Barry, *Past and Present*; Bremner, 'Memoirs'; Don, *Early Central Otago*; Fail, 'First Year's Experience'; Gascoigne, 'Adventures of a Norfolk Boy'; Fraser, 'The Early Sixties'; Hassing, *Memory Log*; Hay, 'Old Times in New Zealand'; Martin, autobiography; Orbell, autobiography; O'Halloran, autobiography; Scoullar, reminiscences; Smith, autobiography; Suisted, reminiscences.
66. Gascoigne, 'Adventures of a Norfolk Boy'.
67. Smith, autobiography.
68. *Christchurch Press*, 27 May 1911.
69. Michael Kowalewski, 'Romancing the Gold Rush: The Literature of the California Frontier', in Kevin Starr and Richard J. Orsi (ed.), *Rooted in Barbarous Soil: People, Culture and Community in Gold Rush California* (Berkeley: University of California Press, 2000), 204–25; Kevin Starr, *Americans and the California Dream, 1850–1915* (New York: Oxford University Press, 1973), 63–8; Susan Lee Johnson, *Roaring Camp: The Social World of the California Gold Rush* (New York: W. W. Norton and Company, 2000), 322–43; Barbara Berglund, 'The Days of Old, the Days of Gold, the Days of '49'; 'Identity, History, and Memory at the California Midwinter International Exposition, 1894', *The Public Historian* 25, no. 4 (2003): 25–49.
70. These reminiscences were republished in *Gabriel's Gully Jubilee*.
71. *Mount Ida Chronicle*, 1 September 1911, 15 September 1911, 29 September 1911, 6 October 1911, 20 October 1911.
72. Ayson, *Pioneering in Otago*, 8.
73. Fail, 'First Year's Experience'. Also see W. G. Fail, 'Address'.
74. Brosnahan, *To Fame Undying*, 14–15. Also see 'Shaw Taieri Correspondence'. For a listing of reminiscences archived in the Toitū Otago Settlers Museum, see the bibliography.
75. Sylviane Agacinski, *Time Passing: Modernity and Nostalgia* (New York: Columbia University Press, 2003), 6–10.
76. Christopher Shaw and Malcolm Chase, 'The Dimension of Nostalgia',

in Christopher Shaw and Malcolm Chase (eds), *The Imagined Past: History and Nostalgia* (Manchester: Manchester University Press, 1989), 8.
77. Harbottle, autobiography; Bremner, 'Memoirs'; Fail, 'Address'.
78. Hay, reminiscences.
79. Orbell, autobiography, 72.
80. Pierre Nora, 'Between Memory and History: Les Lieux de Mémoire', trans. Marc Roudebush, *Representations* 26 (1988): 19.
81. Hamilton, 'Pioneering History', 75. Hamilton references Chris Healy, *From the Ruins of Colonialism: History as Social Memory* (Cambridge: Cambridge University Press, 1997) for this point.
82. Bremner, 'Memoirs'.
83. Davison, 'The Parochial Past', 9.
84. Barry, *Past and Present*, 149–70.
85. Gascoigne, 'Adventures of a Norfolk Boy'. Also see Smith, autobiography; Suisted, reminiscences.
86. Gibbons, 'Cultural Colonization'.
87. Ibid., 10. Also see Gibbons, 'Non-fiction'.
88. *Gabriel's Gully Jubilee*, 14.
89. Hackett, 'A Different Form of "Self"', 208–9.
90. Regina Gagnier, 'Social Atoms: Working-Class, Autobiography, Subjectivity, and Gender', *Victorian Studies* 30, no. 3 (1987): 340–1.
91. Gascoigne, 'Adventures of a Norfolk Boy'.
92. Smith, autobiography, 1–11.
93. Scoullar, reminiscences.
94. Orbell, autobiography, 9.
95. For a discussion of Erik Erikson's understanding of migration and identity, see Philip Gleason, 'Identifying Identity: A Semantic History', *The Journal of American History* 69, no. 4 (1983): 929.
96. Hamilton, 'Pioneering History', 68.
97. Charles D. Ferguson, *The Experiences of a Forty-Niner During Thirty-Four Years' Residence in California and Australia* (Cleveland: Williams Publishing Company, 1888).
98. J. Inches Thomson, *Voyages and Wanderings in Far Off Seas and Lands* (London: Headley Brothers, 1910).
99. T. E. Crowhurst, *Life and Adventures in New Zealand, Including 'The Invisible Hand', 'The Power Within' and 'Why I Became a Spiritualist'* (Auckland: Whitcombe and Tombs, 1920), 2.
100. Robert B. Booth, *Five Years in New Zealand* (London: J. G. Hammond and Co., 1912), 1.
101. Ibid., 57.
102. Matthew C. McKeown, *Some Memories of a Miner's Life, or, Five Years in the Gold Fields of New Zealand* (Barnesville: Matthew C. McKeown, 1893), 30.

103. Spengemann and Lundquist, 'Autobiography'.
104. Andrew Bools, *The Wonders of Providence and Grace, as Illustrated in the Life of the Author, While Doing Business in Deep Waters, in Travels on Sea and Land, and over the Gold Fields of Australia and New Zealand* (London: Frederick Kirby, 1890), 95.
105. Ibid., 1.
106. Ibid., 80–5.
107. *Scripture and the Sevenfold View of the Church of God; Christ Crucified; The Church of the Living God*, and *Meditation of Hab. 3:2*.
108. Peter Bailey, 'Conspiracies of Meaning: Music-Hall and the Knowingness of Popular Culture', *Past and Present* 144 (1994): 138–70; John Burnett, *Liquid Pleasures: A Social History of Drinks in Modern Britain* (London and New York: Routledge, 1999).
109. Philip Ross May, *The West Coast Gold Rushes*, 2nd edn (Christchurch: Pegasus Press, 1967), 464–6.
110. For example, see the correspondence between the Victorian prospector, George Davies, and his acquaintance in Otago. The letters are concerned largely with news of mutual acquaintances in Victoria and Otago. George Davies Letters, HC, MS-0721.
111. Robert H. B. Hoskins, 'Introduction', in Charles Thatcher, *'Life on the Goldfields': An Entertainment*, ed. Robert H. B. Hoskins (Christchurch: University of Canterbury Press, 1996), 1–2.
112. For a biography of Hennings, see Mimi Colligan, 'Hennings, John (1835–1898)', *Australian Dictionary of Biography*, National Centre of Biography, Australian National University, http://adb.anu.edu.au/biography/hennings-john-12976/text23451, accessed 7 October 2013.
113. Thatcher, *Life on the Goldfields*.
114. Anita Callaway, 'A Broad Brush Dipped in Gold: The Expansion of Australian Vision', in Iain McCalman, Alexander Cook, and Andrew Reeves (eds), *Gold: Forgotten Histories and Lost Objects of Australia* (Cambridge: Cambridge University Press, 2001), 327.
115. Anita Callaway, *Visual Ephemera: Theatrical Art in Nineteenth-century Australia* (Sydney: University of New South Wales Press, 2000), 142.
116. Mimi Colligan, *Canvas Documentaries: Panoramic Entertainments in Nineteenth-century Australia and New Zealand* (Melbourne: Melbourne University Press, 2002), 73–4.
117. Thatcher, *Life on the Goldfields*, 43.
118. *West Coast Times*, 18 December 1869.
119. Hoskins, 'Introduction', 10.
120. Callaway, *Visual Ephemera*, 141–2.
121. *Launceston Examiner*, 16 January 1872.
122. *The Argus*, 15 July 1871. The book was also reviewed in the *Australasian* on Saturday after 15 August 1871.

123. See, for example, C. L. Money, *Knocking About in New Zealand* (Melbourne: Samuel Mullen, 1871), 12–20.
124. Marcus Clarke, 'Preface', ibid., vi.
125. Jacquelyn Dowd Hall, '"You Must Remember This": Autobiography as Social Critique', *The Journal of American History* 85, no. 2 (September 1998): 440.
126. *Otago Daily Times*, 23 May 1911; *Gabriel's Gully Jubilee*, 39.
127. *Otago Daily Times*, 23 May 1911; ibid., 32.
128. Twenty-seven reminiscences were written by Otago residents. Eleven were written by colonists who lived in other New Zealand provinces. Twenty-four writers migrated from Victoria, one from New South Wales and another nine authors did not record their place of residence before the Otago rushes. See ibid., 11–48.
129. Ayson, *Pioneering in Otago*; Fraser, 'The Early Sixties'; Richard Norman, 'Early Cardrona History'; Orbell, autobiography; Smith, autobiography; Suisted, reminiscences; John Blair, 'My First Trip to Gabriel's Gully, and How I Got There', *Otago Daily Times*, 24 March 1911.
130. See, for example, Barry, *Past and Present*; Gascoigne, 'Adventures of a Norfolk Boy'; O'Halloran, autobiography.
131. Salmon, *A History of Goldmining*; William Parker Morrell, *The Gold Rushes* (London: Macmillan Company, 1941); Stevan Eldred-Grigg, *Diggers, Hatters and Whores: The Story of the New Zealand Gold Rushes* (Auckland: Random House, 2008).
132. No autobiographies published in Australia that were located for this book discuss experiences of prospecting in Otago. Despite several collections of letters located in the State Library of Victoria, no autobiographical texts were located in the repository. Enquiries at the Mitchell Library in Sydney and the National Library in Canberra also did not reveal autobiographical material.

Conclusion

This book argues that the cultures and societies of the Otago gold rushes were shaped by local social networks and natural environments in colonial Otago and by transnational cultures and networks that both connected individuals back to communities they left behind in Victoria, China and the United Kingdom and influenced the ways in which individuals responded to new environments and work practices in Otago. In doing so, this investigation has implemented a geographic perspective to understand the goldfields as meeting places of the transnational and the local. This analysis has also been comparative, highlighting similarities and differences with goldfield societies in Australia and North America.

While stressing these local and transnational contexts, it is also important to emphasise that they were not two separate aspects of gold rush societies. Rather, work and leisure practices on the diggings constantly entangled localities and transnational networks and cultures. Some individuals gathered gold and spent it on entertainment alongside relatives from Britain, Ireland, China or Victoria. Others depended on gold deposits to send money to loved ones or hoped to finance their return home in wealth. However, time and again individuals found both their work and leisure practices and their expectations of remittances or a return journey inhibited by non-human dimensions of the rushes like precipitation rates, climate and topography. Finally, discussing transnational and local scales within the same analysis has allowed this book to emphasise the limitations of each term. Local points of friction impeded the easy extension of transnational cultures into Otago. Meanwhile, local social bonding on the goldfields and methods by which individuals gathered gold were inseparable from networks and experiences brought from Victoria, China and the United Kingdom.

These local, transnational and comparative approaches differ significantly from other studies of the Otago rushes, which bind the events within New Zealand history. Miles Fairburn incorporates the Otago rushes into a broader history of atomisation in colonial New Zealand.[1] Jock Phillips also draws heavily from gold seekers to depict nineteenth-century New Zealand as a socially bonded, egalitarian male society.[2] More recently, Stevan Eldred-Grigg presents a narrative of lawlessness and licence on the diggings in an effort to strip New Zealand of its past of puritanism and stuffiness.[3] While reaching very different conclusions, these scholars consider the nation as the primary unit of analysis. In contrast to these preoccupations with national history, this book decentres New Zealand, instead analysing the British, Irish, Chinese and trans-Tasman dimensions that were entangled with each other and with natural environments in Otago during the gold rushes.

While Fairburn and Phillips both draw largely from published guidebooks and autobiographies to form their narratives of the Otago rushes, this book relies heavily on contemporary newspapers and unpublished diaries and letters written by gold seekers. Newspapers are used not as objective accounts of the past, but as public conversations that provided the 'cultural ambience' of local communities.[4] As diggers relaxed after a day prospecting or migrating in search of riches, they read reports of gold yields, committee meetings, magistrates' and police court proceedings and weekly entertainments, which collectively presented a particular image of the local community they were helping to form. In this way, the 'work' of community formation on the goldfields never ended when diggers walked off their claims.

Diaries and letters form the other major type of sources used in this book. The analysis of diaries is influenced by Andrew Hassam's argument that the texts were in a constant process of composition by their authors.[5] They, therefore, record the ongoing work of identity formation arising from interactions with other individuals and the natural environment at particular localities. Drawing on David Fitzpatrick's and Angela McCarthy's respective studies of Irish correspondence, this investigation shows that letters illuminate a range of social networks and emotional connections to friends and relatives in Victoria, Britain and Ireland that animated individuals' pursuit of gold in colonial Otago.[6] The use of letters also highlights the difficulties of generalising about the strength of these transnational personal networks or the experiences of and motivations for gold seeking. Left unrecorded are individuals who chose not to write or those whose letters were lost or not located for this book. Moreover, caution should be taken against generalising about those who did write. Some conflicts erupted over home correspondents' expectations of remittances and timetables for gold seekers' return home, like those involving the McDonald brothers and between Oliver McSparron and his father Archibald. Others, like Archibald Henderson and William Ruskin, drifted out of contact with relatives when their letters did not receive responses. Still others, like John Lees, continued regular correspondence before eventually migrating home; however, as Lees' letters show, hopes of a speedy return were repeatedly deferred when the realities of gold seeking continued to fall short of prospectors' expectations. Perhaps, then, the only unifying theme in gold seeker correspondence is the difficulty of maintaining relationships in the age of mass migration and particularly in gold rush societies that intensified itinerancy and made regular communication more difficult. The motivations for prospecting, the resilience of connections to loved ones and the decision to return home or create a new home abroad, while influenced by external factors, were fundamentally psychological choices that, as Frank Thistlethwaite ponders, may be beyond the means of historical investigation.[7]

Autobiographical accounts of the gold rushes are treated in this book as artefacts of their period of composition rather than accurate accounts of the personal historical events they describe. They, therefore, chart the ways in which memories of the gold rushes were taken up into class and national identities in the late nineteenth and early twentieth centuries. New Zealand autobiographies are read alongside New Zealand commemorations, reflecting the interdependence of public and private memory as argued by Susan Crane.[8] British autobiographies present the goldfields as part of generalised landscapes that are embedded in late-nineteenth-century metropolitan representations of Empire. Victorian memories of the Otago rushes written in the late 1860s and early 1870s reveal the relevance of the Tasman World.

In utilising transnational, comparative and local approaches, this book has particularly emphasised the pervasiveness of trans-Tasman connections between Victoria and Otago. Within a few months of Gabriel Read's discovery of gold on the Tuapeka in 1861, the province of Otago was overwhelmed with Victorian ships, Victorian diggers, Victorian merchants and Victorian prostitutes. Prospectors worked alongside mates from Victoria, purchased items previously sold on the Victorian diggings, and attempted to deploy methods of gold extraction used on the other side of the Tasman Sea. To maintain some semblance of order, the Provincial Government created a Goldfields Department run by Vincent Pyke, the former head of the Victorian Goldfields Department, and staffed by former Victorian wardens. The Otago police force was enlarged by recruiting constables from the Victorian diggings. *The Otago Daily Times* was established by Julius Vogel, the former editor of the Victorian goldfield newspapers, the *Maryborough and Dunolly Advertiser* and the *Inglewood and Sandy Creek Advertiser*. As surface deposits evaporated, the Victorian tide turned to New Zealand's West Coast, which became a satellite of Victoria, as has been ably demonstrated by Phillip Ross May.[9] In these varieties of ways, the Otago gold rushes were more a series of events in the history of Victoria than New Zealand.

Several historians of the Otago rushes note the events' Victorian origins, but few studies analyse these origins' relevance to the Otago gold rushes.[10] In the literature about colonial Victoria, the Otago rushes only emerge briefly as individuals leave the colony.[11] Implicit in these narratives is the assumption that individuals were New Zealanders while in Otago and Australians while in Victoria. Absent in the historiography is the two-way traffic of people, commerce and knowledge that fused gold rush migrants into a single trans-Tasman population.

This book, influenced by Erik Olssen's plea, now twenty-six years old, analyses the Victorian foundations to the Otago rushes.[12] It represents the first attempt to discuss the Tasman World not simply as a supplementary motif to a largely national narrative but as a central feature of gold seeking. In doing so, this exploration fills a significant gap in the existing literature on the Tasman World that largely ignores the nineteenth century and emphasises instead the pervasiveness of the twentieth-century Tasman World. This approach is intended to counter James Belich's argument that New Zealand abandoned membership in the Australasian community for a national identity as a 'Better Britain'.[13]

This study of the Otago rushes is also the first study of the nineteenth-century Australasian gold rushes to systematically use newspapers and manuscripts on both sides of the Tasman Sea. Such an approach to the Otago rushes shows that there were two sides to what were essentially trans-Tasman events. For prospectors boarding ships bound for Otago, the rushes represented a moment of excitement and anticipation. For the wives left behind in Victoria who petitioned colonial authorities for aid, the same rushes were events of abandonment and starvation. For parents who scribbled notes about absent sons and missing letters, gold seeking resulted in loneliness and grief. Moreover, the trans-Tasman approach reveals that the Otago gold rushes sometimes resulted in anxiety and dread in Victoria, where colonists feared Melbourne would soon become a satellite of Dunedin with its golden hinterland. The fact that these fears were never realised does not lessen their forcefulness in the early 1860s. Finally, combining a comparative and transnational approach into a single methodology allows this investigation to stress both the enduring connections between Victoria and Otago and the local contexts that allowed Otago in the early 1860s to diverge from its Victorian antecedent ten years earlier. This analytical structure emphasises the importance of transnational networks and cultures while also highlighting the points of local friction that impeded their easy transplantation in new environments.

While certain inferences can be made about the European gold seekers during the early 1860s, conclusions about Chinese prospectors during the last few decades of the nineteenth century are far less certain. The analysis of Chinese prospectors in this book relies heavily on Alexander Don's published diaries of his annual tours among the Chinese in Otago. While his reports were among the most detailed English-language descriptions of a Chinese population on the Pacific Rim, they were manifestly a response against the proto-nationalist language in New Zealand that sought to exclude the Chinese from colonial society in the late nineteenth and early twentieth centuries. Despite this limitation, certain inferences can be made of Chinese prospectors. Like their British and Irish counterparts, most Chinese diggers travelled to Otago within migrant networks and often sought to remain connected to loved ones through remittances, correspondence and eventually return migration. Moreover, again like European prospectors, dreams of returning home in wealth rarely materialised. According to Don's account, connections to home were often stronger than among British and Irish diggers and most Chinese prospectors returned to their native villages, sometimes re-migrating multiple times. Perhaps because of ostracisation from colonial society and the strength of Chinese cultures, few Chinese gold seekers who remained in Otago seem to have assimilated into colonial society.

This book has not attempted to narrate a comprehensive history of the Otago gold rushes. What it has done is retell the story of the events through transnational, local and comparative perspectives. In deploying these new methodologies to an understanding of the history of the Otago rushes, it has also highlighted alternative approaches and topics that could be applied in future research. A study of religious practices and institutions on the goldfields could further elucidate the entangling of leisure practices, social networks and transplanted cultures. Another area of further research is the role of ethnic identity on the goldfields. More research needs to be done which investigates how Otago colonists understood their province's gold rushes. Another line of enquiry could be an examination of the provincial and colonial governments' oversight of the gold rushes. A regional history of the nineteenth-century Tasman World is a long overdue topic for future research. Another area of fruitful research could be a study of the impact of the gold rushes on the Māori and aboriginal Australians. More work is also needed which discusses the impacts of the gold rushes on Britain and Ireland. The comparative and transnational perspectives employed in this book could also be used to analyse the trans-Pacific exchanges between Victoria and California during the 1850s. David Goodman offers a valuable comparative study of cultural perceptions of the gold rushes in California and Victoria, but there has been very little work done plotting the transfer of people, commodities and knowledge.[14] A final field of research could be a comparative study of migrant letters from the Pacific Rim goldfields. David Fitzpatrick and Angela McCarthy have drawn on gold seeker correspondence as part of a broader history of letter writing within a national migrant group, but so far no historian has compared gold seeking correspondence between national groups and goldfield populations.[15]

REMEMBERING AND FORGETTING IN THE PRESENT DAY

This book has argued against the totalising glare of national history that either stresses or minimises the rushes for their role in making New Zealand. The Otago gold rushes, and more broadly the colonial past of the South Island, have receded from view in an academic historiography centred on interactions between Māori and Pakeha in the North Island, in which race relations retain their national importance into the twenty-first century. By contrast, the South Island, 'the land of sheep and gold' to use Erik Olssen's phrase, seems to matter less in contemporary New Zealand when the prospector has vanished and Auckland has supplanted Dunedin as the commercial capital of the country.[16]

In contrast to academic histories, the rushes re-emerge periodically in popular history through re-enactments and celebrations in Otago. The annual Otago Goldfields Cavalcade allows participants to follow 'the steps and trails of the gold miners who sought their fortune in inland Otago'.[17] This popular interest is inseparable from the attention the rushes have garnered from local and family historians, as best illustrated by the events surrounding the 2011 sesquicentennial jubilee of the Otago gold rushes in Dunedin and Gabriel's Gully. In conjunction with this celebration, eighty-six events were organised over four days around the theme of gold and gold seekers in Dunedin alone. The centre of the Dunedin festivities was the recreation of the mock arrival of gold seekers aboard the *Steadfast* at the Dunedin wharf, where they were greeted by five hundred spectators. The group then travelled to the Octagon, the town's central commercial district, which a hundred actors had transformed into a 'Shantytown'. Describing Shantytown, the city's tourism website stated:

> A makeshift camp of miners' tents will be jostling with characters of the day; the Minister, the Salvationist, the Doctor, the destitute, the pick-pocket and the ladies of the night. Boxing, betting and debauchery will greet the new arrivals from the Steadfast and the constabulary will be there maintaining law and order. Merchants will be peddling their wares and at the Assaying Office the scales will be sagging with the weight of gold.[18]

At Gabriel's Gully, the celebrations also entangled spectacle with the work of memory making. A play entitled *The Drama of Tuapeka* was performed in the Gully and featured a cast of ninety in depicting the gold rushes as part of an ongoing history of the locality. As the jubilee pamphlet stated:

> *The Drama of the Tuapeka* will take its audience on a journey that will traverse: the formation of the land and the precious metal within it told through Maori legend; the discovery of gold and the onset of the gold rush; the drama of the lawless Garrett Gang; the hard road the Chinese miners trod; the merchants and their boom time trade; farming and its place down through the years; and the vision of the future. This ambitious spectacle has a cast of almost ninety and features the haunting sounds of Maori wind instruments, the skirl of bagpipes and the stirring sounds of the Roxburgh Silver Band.[19]

The following day, the Gabriel's Gully celebrations formally opened with the arrival of twenty-six horseback riders who had traced the gold rush trail from Dunedin to Gabriel's Gully. The goldfield's weekend activities included gold panning, an antique bicycle show, 'pioneer stories' and a 'Swaggers Dance'. The Lawrence celebration presented the Otago gold rushes as part of an ongoing story of community formation grounded in a particular place, although this local genealogy was sometimes blurred, as when gold seekers arrived on bicycles or in classic cars, and antique tractors processed alongside a twenty-first-century Bobcat.

Above all, what these events demonstrate is an enduring interest among residents in the histories of their local communities. *The Drama of the Tuapeka* was performed by ninety volunteers, most of whom were residents on the former Tuapeka goldfield, presenting a place-based history created by individuals whose daily social interactions were grounded in that particular locality. In Dunedin, anniversary events took a similar tone. The transformation of the Octagon into a 'shantytown' allowed local visitors to reimagine this social and commercial space through the lens of the city's gold rush past. Moreover, in the sesquicentennial brochures, the rushes were overwhelmingly presented as local, rather than national events. New Zealand only emerged in the Gabriel's Gully brochure when the Gully was (incorrectly) described as the first gold rush in New Zealand and the local Sunday church service was anticipated to have a 'New Zealand flavour'.[20] While the Dunedin pamphlet assessed the role of the Otago rushes in national development, the emphasis was on a civic pride in local contributions, as in Dunedin mayor Dave Cull's introduction:

> Gabriel Read . . . truly put Dunedin on the world map . . . The Otago gold rushes became the catalyst that laid the foundations of Dunedin's rich heritage. 'Layers of Gold' [the Dunedin commemoration] celebrates not just the discovery of gold in 1861, but the rich layers of the city's past that have been woven into the fabric that is our vibrant city today . . . The influx of people . . . saw Dunedin transformed from a small and struggling settlement to New Zealand's most prosperous and influential city of the day . . . [These migrants] built a city of 'firsts' with Dunedin leading the way in education, commerce, communications and the arts.[21]

Reflecting on this local interest in the rushes, Jim Read, a grandson of Gabriel Read who attended the anniversary celebrations as an honoured guest, stated in an interview that he 'had no idea how important the discovery of gold was to Lawrence and Otago'.[22]

Finally, while these celebrations were firmly cemented in a local chronology, they were also inseparable from family history. The most visited part of the Gabriel's Gully celebration was a large tent which contained upwards of fifty booths of family historians, interested in sharing stories, letters and artefacts of ancestors who participated in the gold rushes. Three months later, the New Zealand Society of Genealogists also held their annual conference in Dunedin. The conference, entitled 'A Golden Opportunity', dealt exclusively with the gold rushes and how family historians can locate records about their gold-seeking ancestors.[23] This interest in local and family history remained the central feature of the 2011 commemorative celebrations, which drew over a thousand attendees to gold rush events in Dunedin and Gabriel's Gully over the weekend.

While the totalising glare of academic history has often neglected the Otago gold rushes, the events have, in the words of Pierre Nora, emerged periodically as 'sites of memory' which reveal an ongoing personal and local engagement with the past. The memories of the rushes, seen through the lens of popular commemorations, become 'affective and magical' because they take 'root in the concrete, in spaces, gestures, images and objects' rather than a national identity detached from the lived, everyday experiences grounded in a locality.[24] However, as Nora observes, such a memory also 'only accommodates those facts that suit it', leaving the trans-Tasman and Imperial connections, the lost tailings of the Otago gold rushes, largely overlooked.[25]

NOTES

1. Miles Fairburn, *The Ideal Society and Its Enemies: The Foundation of Modern New Zealand Society, 1850–1900* (Auckland: Auckland University Press, 1989), 9–13.
2. Jock Phillips, *A Man's Country?: The Image of the Pakeha Male, a History*, 2nd edn (Auckland: Penguin Books, 1996), 14–40.
3. Stevan Eldred-Grigg, *Diggers, Hatters and Whores: The Story of the New Zealand Gold Rushes* (Auckland: Random House, 2008), 325–37.
4. James W. Carey, *Communication as Culture: Essays on Media and Society* (Boston: Unwin Hyman, 1989), 25.
5. Andrew Hassam, *Sailing to Australia: Shipboard Diaries by Nineteenth-Century British Emigrants* (Manchester and New York: Manchester University Press, 1994), 4.
6. David Fitzpatrick, *Oceans of Consolation: Personal Accounts of the Irish Migration to Australia* (Ithaca and London: Cornell University Press, 1995); Angela McCarthy, *Irish Migrants in New Zealand, 1840–1937: 'The Desired Haven'* (Woodbridge: Boydell Press, 2005).
7. Frank Thistlethwaite, 'Migration from Europe Overseas in the 19th and 20th Centuries', in Rudolph J. Vecoli and Suzanne M. Sinke (eds), *A Century of European Migration, 1830–1930* (Urbana: University of Illinois Press, 1991), 43.
8. Susan A. Crane, 'Writing the Individual Back into Collective Memory', *The American Historical Review* 102, no. 5 (1 December 1997): 1372–85.
9. Philip Ross May, *The West Coast Gold Rushes*, 2nd edn (Christchurch: Pegasus Press, 1967), 125. More recently, Lyndon Fraser also observes these connections between the West Coast and Victoria; however, he notes that his is not a study of the gold rushes so much as an analysis of the 'role of *ethnicity* in the adaptation of migrants to new environments': Fraser, *Castles of Gold*, 18. He, therefore, does not analyse these connections to Victoria to the same extent as May.
10. The only notable exceptions are J. H. M. Salmon, *A History of Goldmining in New Zealand* (Wellington: Government Printer, 1963); Erik Olssen, 'Lands of Sheep and Gold: The Australian Dimension to the New Zealand Past', in Keith Sinclair (ed.), *Tasman Relations: New Zealand and*

Australia, 1788–1988 (Auckland: University of Auckland Press, 1987), 34–51.

11. A few examples are Geoffrey Serle, *The Golden Age: A History of the Colony of Victoria, 1851–1861* (Melbourne: Melbourne University Press, 1963), 228; Geoffrey Blainey, *The Rush That Never Ended: A History of Australian Mining*, 4th edn (Melbourne: Melbourne University Press, 1993), 59; Anthony Edward Dingle, *The Victorians: Settling* (McMahons Point: Fairfax, Syme and Weldon Associates, 1984), 99.
12. Olssen, 'Lands of Sheep and Gold'.
13. A few examples are Philippa Mein Smith and Peter Hempenstall, 'Australia and New Zealand: Turning Shared Pasts into a Shared History', *History Compass* 1 (2003): 1–8; Philippa Mein Smith, Peter Hempenstall and Shaun Goldfinch, *Remaking the Tasman World* (Christchurch: Canterbury University Press, 2008); Philippa Mein Smith, 'The Tasman World', in Giselle Byrnes (ed.), *The New Oxford History of New Zealand* (Melbourne: Oxford University Press, 2009), 297–319; Peter Hempenstall, 'Overcoming Separate Histories: Historians as "Idea Traders" in a Trans-Tasman World', *History Australia* 4, no. 1 (2007): 04.01–04.16. Also see James Belich, *Reforging Paradise: A History of the New Zealanders from the 1880s to the Year 2000* (Auckland: Penguin Press, 2001), 30.
14. Ibid. The most important work in this regard is Jay Monaghan, *Australians and the Gold Rush: California and Down Under, 1849–1854* (Berkeley: University of California Press, 1966).
15. McCarthy, *Irish Migrants in New Zealand*; Fitzpatrick, *Oceans of Consolation*. Lyndon Fraser also draws on migrant correspondences, but his analysis concerns migration paths, ethnic identity and local networks rather than the ways in which identities were created transnationally through the writing and receipt of letters.
16. Olssen, 'Lands of Sheep and Gold', 34-51.
17. 'Welcome', *Goldfields Cavalcade*, accessed 21 September 2013, http://cavalcade.co.nz/2010-2/
18. 'Dunedin Events | Heritage Festival', *Dunedin New Zealand*, accessed 7 October 2013, http://www.dunedinnz.com/visit/events/festivals/heritage-festival
19. [Anon], *Layers of Gold, Dunedin: Otago Anniversary Weekend 18–21 March 2011; [and] Gabriel's Gully 150th Anniversary, Lawrence New Zealand* (Dunedin: Dunedin Heritage Festival, 2011).
20. Ibid.
21. [Anon], *Layers of Gold*.
22. *Otago Daily Times*, 21 March 2011.
23. New Zealand Society of Genealogists Conference, *A Golden Opportunity: Proceedings of the New Zealand Society of Genealogists Annual Conference, Held at John McGlashan College, Maori Hill, Dunedin, June*

3–6, 2011 (Dunedin: Conference Committee of the New Zealand Society of Genealogists – Dunedin Branch, 2011).
24. Pierre Nora, 'Between Memory and History: Les Lieux de Mémoire', trans. Marc Roudebush, *Representations* 26 (1988): 8.
25. Ibid.

Bibliography

PRIMARY SOURCES

Unpublished

Andrew, Thomas. Letters. 1863. ATL, MS-Papers-4802.
Armstrong, Thomas. Letter. 1869. SLV, MS-12164.
Blackwood, J. F. Letters. 1857–63. OSM, DC-2482.
Bowler, Edmund. Diary. 1857–63. OSM, C-012.
Bremner, J. C. 'Memoirs of the Early Diggings.' Autobiography. 1911. OSM, DC-0986.
Brown, John. Letters. 1862. ATL, MS-Papers 8869-2.
Calwell, Dan. Letters. Calwell Family Papers. 1862–3. SLV, MS 11492.
Chapman, William Nixon. Letter. 1862. Private Collection [Evelyn Chapman].
Coles, C. J. Diary. 1860–73. SLV, MS-12398.
Crawford, James Coutts. Diary. 1864. ATL, MS-Papers-1001-012.
Crawford, William. Letter. 1862. HC, Misc-MS-0095.
Dewar, John and William Dewar. Letters. 1863–9. HC, MS-2373/001.
Fail, W. G. 'Address Delivered at Old Identities Meeting, Port Chalmers, on March 10th, 1914.' Reminiscences. 1914. OSM, DC-2153.
———. 'Mr W. G. Fail's First Year's Experience in New Zealand. Delivered at Old Identities Meeting, March 23 1916.' 1916. OSM, DC-2153.
Fraser, William. 'The Early Sixties in Otago: Personal Reminiscences of a Pioneer.' 1906. HC, DU 484.4 FU283.
Frykberg, Bengt. Letter. 1864. HC, Misc-MS-1931.
Garrett, John. 1860–1903. OSM, DC-2670.
Gascoigne, James Randall. 'The Adventures of a Norfolk Boy for a Half Century from 1847 Onwards. His Early Life as a Sailor, Life on a Copper Mine in 1850, His Goldfields Experience in New South Wales in 1851, in California from 1852 to 1858, in British Columbia from 1858 to 1860, in Victoria in

1861, on the Otago Goldfields from 1861 to 1881.' Autobiography. 1902. OSM, DC-0483.
Hallenstein, Bendix. 'Day Book of Bendix Hallenstein.' OSM, DC-1430.
Hamilton, Anne Elizabeth. Oral History Transcripts. 1948. LDM, MU 1080-3.
Harbottle, Frank. Autobiography. 1909. HC, Misc-MS-1654.
Hay, Richard. Reminiscences. 1911. OSM, no Call Number.
Henderson, Archibald. Letters. 1860–75. OSM, DC-2399.
Houston, Allan. Diary. OSM, PC-0216.
Jefferis Family Letters. 1858–64. OSM, AG-190.
Jolly, David A. 'Early Goldfields History: Reminiscences of the Early Goldfields of Central Otago, and Jottings of Early Cromwell History.' Reminiscences. 1908. Private Collection [David George].
Jones, David. Letters. Jones Family Letters. 1862–3. ATL, MS-Papers-6249.
Jones, William. Letter.1864. ATL, MS-Papers-10303.
Kerr, Alexander. 'Reminiscences of the Gold Rush Days in Australia and New Zealand.' Reminiscences. 1870. ATL, MS-1115.
Lees, John. Letters. 1847–67. SLV, MS 10083.
Lindsay, Annie. Letters. 1863–6. OSM, DC-0195.
McDonald, Lachlan. Letters. 1858–68. OSM, DC-2810.
MacLeod Orbell. Reminiscences. OSM, C-084.
Mapleson, Francis Joseph. Letters. 1862–3. SLV, MS 10869.
Martin, William. Autobiography. 1861. HC, MS-0203.
McCourt, Thomas. Diary. 1863–4. LDM, N-2377.
McIlrath, James. Letters. 1860–1906. Transcribed and edited by Angela McCarthy. In McCarthy, Angela Hannah, '"Seas May Divide": Irish Migration to New Zealand as Portrayed in Personal Correspondence, 1840–1937', vol. 2. PhD thesis, Trinity College, Dublin, 2000, 201–11.
McKay, Alexander. Letters. 1864. ATL, MS-Papers-4409-1.
McKinlay, Archibald. Letters. 1854–71. Private Collection [Michael Wallace].
McLay, John. 'Waikouaiti and Dunedin in 1850.' Reminiscences. OSM, DC-0112.
McSparron, Oliver. Letters. 1860–82. Transcribed and edited by Angela McCarthy. In McCarthy, Angela Hannah, '"Seas May Divide": Irish Migration to New Zealand as Portrayed in Personal Correspondence, 1840–1937', vol. 2. PhD thesis, Trinity College, Dublin, 2000, 50–7.
McVicar Family. Letter, 1864. OSM, no Call Number.
Moffat, John. Diary. 1863. OSM, C-0204.
Murison, James. Diary. 1858–69. OSM, C191.
Norman, Richard. 'Early Cardrona History.' Reminiscences. 1911. OSM, C-083.
O'Halloran, George. Autobiography. ATL, 1345/1.
Penderick, John. Diary. 1863. LDM, N-1901.
Pierson, Thomas. Diary. 1852–64. SLV, MS-11646.
Ramsden, Frederic. Diary. 1853–62. SLV, MS-12522.

Robjohns, Charles J. D. Diary. 1864. ATL, MS-Papers-4913.
Rodgers, John. Diary. 1862–3. Private Collection [Dee Mantova].
Roy, Andrew. Letters. 1863–6. OSM, DC-0683.
Ruskin, William. Letters. 1861–79. OSM, DC-0676.
Scoullar, Arthur. 'Arthur Scoullar of Scoullar and Chisholm.' Reminiscences. OSM, DC-3028.
Shaw Taieri Correspondence, OSM, no Call Number.
Smith, Edwin. Letters. 1852–61. SLV, MS-14189.
Smith, William Turnbull. Diary. 1862–64. HC, MS-578-B.
Smith, William. 'Reminiscences of a Long and Active Life by an Old Colonist.' Autobiography. [No Date.] OSM, MS-578-B.
Story, Edith Mary. 'Stories of the Gold Diggings.' Oral Histories. 1914. ATL, fMS-Papers-7868.
Strachan, James. 'My First Twelve Years on My Own – commencing from 20th April 1856 – nearly 61 Years Ago.' Reminiscences. 1915. HC, MS-563.
Suisted, J. S. Reminiscences. OSM, DC-2439.
Thompson, John. Letters. 1861. J. H. Beattie Papers. HC, MS-582/F/33.
Wakefield, George. Letters. 1861–3. SLV, MS 6331.
Walker, John George and William Walker. Letters. 1860–3. OSM, C-128.
Warren, Peter. Diary. 1863. OSM, no Call Number.
Watmuff, John Henry. Diary. 1854–82. Private Collection.
Wilson, William and George Wilson. Letters. 1862–72. OSM, DC-0454.
Williamson, Thomas. 'Account of a Prospecting Trip to the West Coast.' Diary, 1863. OSM.

Published

Ayson, William. *Pioneering in Otago*. Christchurch: Kiwi Publishers, 1995.
Bathgate, Alexander. *Colonial Experiences; or Sketches of People and Places in the Province of Otago, New Zealand*. Glasgow: James MacLehose, 1874.
———. *Colonial Experiences; or Sketches of People and Places in the Province of Otago, New Zealand*. Glasgow: James MacLehose, 1874.
Bonwick, James. *Notes of a Gold Digger and Gold Diggers' Guide*. Melbourne: R. Connebee, 1852.
Bools, Andrew. *The Wonders of Providence and Grace, as Illustrated in the Life of the Author, While Doing Business in Deep Waters, in Travels on Sea and Land, and over the Gold Fields of Australia and New Zealand*. London: Frederick Kirby, 1890.
Booth, Robert B. *Five Years in New Zealand*. London: J. G. Hammond and Co., 1912.
Burns, Thomas. *Early Otago and Genesis of Dunedin: Letters of Rev. T. Burns, D. D., 1848–1865*. Dunedin: R. J. Stark and Co., 1916.
Chudleigh, E. R. *Diary of E. R. Chudleigh, 1841–1920: Settler in New Zealand*. Christchurch: Cadsonbury Publications, 2003.

Crowhurst, T. E. *Life and Adventures in New Zealand, Including 'The Invisible Hand', 'The Power Within' and 'Why I Became a Spiritualist'*. Auckland: Whitcombe and Tombs, 1920.

Don, Alexander. *Annual Inland Tour among Otago Chinese, 1900–1901*. Dunedin: Otago Daily Times, 1901.

——. *Annual Inland Tour among Otago Chinese, 1905–1906*. Dunedin: Otago Daily Times, 1906.

——. *Early Central Otago; a Bathurst Miner's Reminiscences*. Dunedin: The Otago Daily Times, 1932.

Earp, G. Butler. *The Gold Colonies of Australia, and Gold Seeker's Manual: with Illustrations of the Implements Required in the Search for the Gold One, as Well as the Progress of the Gold Mining to the Latest Period, and Ample Notices of Australian Gold Geology and Mineralogy; with the Chemical and Metallurgical Treating of Gold Ore*. London: George Routledge and Co., 1852.

Ferguson, Charles D. *The Experiences of a Forty-Niner During Thirty-Four Years' Residence in California and Australia*. Cleveland: Williams Publishing Company, 1888.

Gabriel's Gully Jubilee: Reminiscences of the Early Gold Mining Days. Dunedin: Otago Daily Times, 1911.

Hassing, G. M. *Pages from the Memory Log of G. M. Hassing: Sailor, Pioneer, Schoolmaster*. Invercargill: Southland Times Company, 1930.

Heinz, William F. *Bright Fine Gold: Stories of the New Zealand Goldfields*. Wellington: Reed, 1974.

Heywood, B. A. *A Vacation Tour at the Antipodes, through Victoria, Tasmania, New South Wales, Queensland and New Zealand in 1861–1862*. London: Longman, Green, Longman, Roberts and Green, 1863.

McKeown, Matthew C. *Some Memories of a Miner's Life, or, Five Years in the Gold Fields of New Zealand*. Barnesville: Matthew C. McKeown, 1893.

Money, C. L. *Knocking About in New Zealand*. Melbourne: Samuel Mullen, 1871.

Mundy, Godfrey Charles. *Our Antipodes: Or, Residence and Rambles in the Australasian Colonies with a Glimpse of the Gold Fields*. Vol. 3. 2nd edn. London: Richard Bentley, 1852.

Preshaw, George Ogilvy. *Banking Under Difficulties or Life on the Goldfields of Victoria, New South Wales and New Zealand. By a Bank Official*. Christchurch: Kiwi Publishers, 1997.

Pyke, Vincent. *History of the Early Gold Discoveries in Otago*. Dunedin: Otago Daily Times and Witness Newspapers, 1887.

Thatcher, Charles. *'Life on the Goldfields': An Entertainment*. Edited by Robert H. B. Hoskins. Christchurch: University of Canterbury Press, 1996.

——. *Thatcher's Dunedin Songster, Containing the Popular Local Songs as Written and Sung by Him at the Theatre Royal, Commercial Hotel*. Vol. 1. Dunedin: Daily Times Office, 1862.

———. *Thatcher's Otago Songster, Containing Many of the Popular Local Songs, as Written and Sung by Him at the Corinthian Hall, Dunedin.* Vol. 2. Dunedin: Joseph Mackay, 1865.
Thomson, J. Inches. *Voyages and Wanderings in Far Off Seas and Lands.* London: Headley Brothers, 1910.
Wekey, Sigismund. *Otago as It Is, Its Gold-Mines and Natural Resources: Handbook for Merchants, Capitalists, and the General Public, and a Guide to Intending Emigrants.* Melbourne: F. F. Baillière, 1862.
Wilson, John. *Reminiscences of the Early Settlement of Dunedin and South Otago.* Dunedin: J. Wilkie and Co. Limited, 1912.

Government records

Appendices to the Journals of the House of Representatives, 1861–5
Statistics New Zealand, 1853–6

Newspapers

Arrow Observer (Otago), 1880
Ballarat Star (Victoria), 1861–4
Bendigo Advertiser (Victoria), 1861–4
Christchurch Star (Canterbury, New Zealand), 1931
Christian Outlook, The (Otago), 1894–5
Colonist (Otago), 1856–63
Daily Telegraph (Otago), 1863–4
Dunstan Times (Otago), 1866
Evening Star (Otago), 1911
Inglewood Advertiser (Victoria), 1862–4
Lake Wakatip Mail (Otago), 1863–4
Lancashire Gazette (England), 1864
Melbourne Argus (Victoria), 1861–4
Mount Alexander Mail (Victoria), 1861–4
Mount Ida Chronicle (Otago), 1871–1911, 1923
New Zealand Presbyterian (Otago), 1882–9
Otago Daily Times (Otago), 1861–1911, 2012
Otago Witness (Otago), 1857–1911
Southland Times (Southland), 1862–4, 1871–88
Tuapeka Times (Otago), 1871–88

Reference

Cardrona Cemetery Registry, HC, no Call Number.
Cousins, John W. *Short Biographical Dictionary of English Literature.* London: J. M. Dent and Sons, 1910.

The Cyclopedia of New Zealand: Auckland Provincial District. Christchurch: The Cyclopedia Company, 1902.
The Cyclopedia of New Zealand: Canterbury Provincial District. Christchurch: The Cyclopedia Company, 1903.
The Cyclopedia of New Zealand: Nelson, Marlborough and Westland Provincial Districts. Christchurch: Horace J. Weeks, 1903.
The Cyclopedia of New Zealand: Otago and Southland Provincial Districts. Christchurch: Horace J. Weeks, 1903.
The Cyclopedia of New Zealand: Taranaki, Hawke's Bay and Wellington Provincial Districts. Christchurch: The Cyclopedia Company, 1908.
The Cyclopedia of New Zealand: Wellington Provincial District. Wellington: The Cyclopedia Company, 1897.
The Cyclopedia of Victoria. Vol. 2. Melbourne: F. W. Niven and Co., 1904.
Eaman, Ross. *Historical Dictionary of Journalism.* Lanham: Scarecrow Press, 2009.
Queenstown Cemetery Registry, HC, no Call Number.

Websites

Colligan, Mimi. 'Hennings, John (1835–1898).' In *Australian Dictionary of Biography*. Canberra: National Centre of Biography, Australian National University. Accessed 11 October 2013. http://adb.anu.edu.au/biography/hennings-john-12976.
Dalziel, Raewyn. 'Vogel, Julius – Biography'. *Dictionary of New Zealand Biography, Te Ara – the Encyclopedia of New Zealand.* Accessed 22 March 2012. http://www.TeAra.govt.nz/en/biographies/1v4/1.
'Dunedin Events | Heritage Festival.' *Dunedin New Zealand.* Accessed 7 October 2013. http://www.dunedinnz.com/visit/events/festivals/heritage-festival.
Hoskins, Robert. 'Thatcher, Charles Robert.' Web page. *Te Ara – The Encyclopedia of New Zealand.* Accessed 4 July 2013. http://www.teara.govt.nz/en/biographies/1t91/thatcher-charles-robert.
Lawn, R. G. 'Lawn, John (1840–1905).' *Dictionary of New Zealand Biography.* Accessed 21 March 2011. http://www.dnzb.govt.nz/.
Palmer-Gard, Sue. 'Canoona Gold Fields – Boom or Bust in 66 Days.' *CQ University Library.* Accessed 1 July 2011. http://library-resources.cqu.edu.au/cqcollection/manuscripts/short-manuscripts/canoona.pdf.
Phillips, Jock and Terry Hearn. 'The Provincial and Gold-rush Years, 1853–70.' *New Zealand History Online.* Accessed 4 February 2010. http://www.nzhistory.net.nz/files/documents/peopling3.pdf.
'Welcome.' *Goldfields Cavalcade.* Accessed 21 September 2013. http://cavalcade.co.nz/2010-2/.

SECONDARY SOURCES

Books

Agacinski, Sylviane. *Time Passing: Modernity and Nostalgia*. New York: Columbia University Press, 2003.

Agnew, John A. *Place and Politics in Modern Italy*. Chicago and London: University of Chicago Press, 2002.

Akenson, Donald Harman. *The Irish Diaspora: A Primer*. Toronto: P. D. Meany, 1993.

Arnold, Rollo. *New Zealand's Burning: The Settlers' World in the Mid-1880s*. Wellington: Victoria University of Wellington Press, 1994.

———. *The Farthest Promised Land: English Villagers, New Zealand Immigrants of the Nineteenth Century*. Wellington: Victoria University of Wellington Press, 1981.

Atkinson, Alan. *Europeans in Australia*. 2 vols. Melbourne and New York: Oxford University Press, 1997.

Bailey, Peter. *Popular Culture and Performance in the Victorian City*. Cambridge: Cambridge University Press, 1998.

Baines, Dudley. *Migration in a Mature Economy: Emigration and Internal Migration in England and Wales, 1861–1900*. Cambridge: Cambridge University Press, 1985.

Belich, James. *Making Peoples: A History of the New Zealanders from Polynesian Settlement to the End of the Nineteenth Century*. Auckland: Penguin Books, 1996.

———. *Reforging Paradise: A History of the New Zealanders from the 1880s to the Year 2000*. Auckland: Penguin Press, 2001.

Blaine, Geoffrey. *A History of Victoria*. Cambridge: Cambridge University Press, 2013.

———. *The Rush That Never Ended: A History of Australian Mining*. 4th edn. Melbourne: Melbourne University Press, 1993.

Bodnar, John. *The Transplanted: A History of Immigrants in Urban America*. Bloomington: Indiana University Press, 1985.

Brands, H. W. *The Age of Gold: The California Gold Rush and the New American Dream*. New York: Doubleday, 2002.

Brosnahan, Seán G. *To Fame Undying: The Otago Settlers Association, 1898–2008*. Dunedin: Otago Settlers Association, 2008.

Bueltmann, Tanja. *Scottish Ethnicity and the Making of New Zealand Society, 1850–1930*. Edinburgh: Edinburgh University Press, 2011.

Burchell, R. A. *The San Francisco Irish, 1848–1880*. Manchester: Manchester University Press, 1979.

Burnett, John. *Destiny Obscure: Autobiographies of Childhood, Education and Family From the 1820s to the 1920s*. New York: Routledge, 2013.

---. *Liquid Pleasures: A Social History of Drinks in Modern Britain*. London and New York: Routledge, 1999.
Calloway, Anita. *Visual Ephemera: Theatrical Art in Nineteenth-century Australia*. Sydney: University of New South Wales Press, 2000.
Cannon, Michael. *Melbourne after the Gold Rush*. Main Ridge: Loch Haven Books, 1993.
Cardell, Kerry and Cliff Cumming (eds). *A World Turned Upside Down: Cultural Change on Australia's Goldfields 1851–2001*. Canberra: Australian National University Press, 2001.
Carey, James W. *Communication as Culture: Essays on Media and Society*. Boston: Unwin Hyman, 1989.
Colligan, Mimi. *Canvas Documentaries: Panoramic Entertainments in Nineteenth-century Australia and New Zealand*. Melbourne: Melbourne University Press, 2002.
Collins, E. J. T. *The Agrarian History of England and Wales*. 2 vols. Cambridge: Cambridge University Press, 2000.
Cronon, William. *Changes in the Land: Indians, Colonists, and the Ecology of New England*. New York: Hill and Wang, 2003.
---. *Nature's Metropolis: Chicago and the Great West*. New York: W. W. Norton and Company, 1991.
Daley, Caroline. *Girls and Women, Men and Boys: Gender in Taradale, 1886–1930*. Auckland: Auckland University Press, 1999.
Dalziel, Raewyn. *Julius Vogel: Business Politician*. Auckland: Auckland University Press, 1986.
Daniels, Roger. *Asian America: Chinese and Japanese in the United States since 1850*. Seattle: University of Washington Press, 1988.
Davies, John. *A History of Wales*. London: Allen Lane, 1994.
Day, Patrick. *The Making of the New Zealand Press: A Study of the Organizational and Political Concerns of New Zealand Newspaper Controllers, 1840–1880*. Wellington: Victoria University Press, 1990.
Delaney, Enda. *Demography, State and Society: Irish Migration to Britain, 1921–1971*. Liverpool: Liverpool University Press, 2000.
Denoon, Donald, Philippa Mein Smith and Marivic Wyndham. *A History of Australia, New Zealand and the Pacific: The Formation of Identities*. Oxford and Malden: Blackwell Publishers, 2000.
Devine, T. M. *Clearance and Improvement: Land, Power and People in Scotland, 1700–1900*. Edinburgh: John Donald, 2006.
---. *The Scottish Nation, 1700–2000*. London: Viking, 1999.
Dingle, Anthony Edward. *The Victorians: Settling*. McMahons Point: Fairfax, Syme and Weldon Associates, 1984.
Eldred-Grigg, Stevan. *Diggers, Hatters and Whores: The Story of the New Zealand Gold Rushes*. Auckland: Random House, 2008.
Emmons, David M. *The Butte Irish: Class and Ethnicity in an American Mining Town, 1875–1925*. Champaign: University of Illinois Press, 1989.

———. *The Ideal Society and Its Enemies: The Foundation of Modern New Zealand Society, 1850–1900*. Auckland: Auckland University Press, 1989.
Fairburn, Miles. *The Ideal Society and Its Enemies: The Foundation of Modern New Zealand Society, 1850–1900*. Auckland: Auckland University Press, 1989.
———. *Nearly Out of Heart and Hope: The Puzzle of a Colonial Labourer's Diary*. Auckland: University of Auckland Press, 1995.
Fetherling, Douglas. *The Gold Crusades: A Social History of Gold Rushes, 1849–1929*. Toronto: University of Toronto Press, 1997.
Ficken, Robert. *Unsettled Boundaries: Fraser Gold and the British-American Northwest*. Pullman: Washington State University Press, 2003.
Fitzgerald, Patrick and Brian Lambkin. *Migration in Irish History, 1607–2007*. Houndmills: Palgrave Macmillan, 2008.
Fitzpatrick, David. *Irish Emigration 1801–1921*. Dundalk: Economic and Social History Society of Ireland, 1984.
———. *Oceans of Consolation: Personal Accounts of the Irish Migration to Australia*. Ithaca and London: Cornell University Press, 1995.
Foster, R. F. *Modern Ireland, 1600–1972*. London: Penguin Books, 1989.
Fraser, Lyndon. *Castles of Gold: A History of New Zealand's West Coast Irish*. Dunedin: Otago University Press, 2007.
———. *To Tara via Holyhead: Irish Catholic Immigrants in Nineteenth-Century Christchurch*. Auckland: Auckland University Press, 1997.
Fredrickson, George M. *White Supremacy: A Comparative Study of American and South African History*. Oxford: Oxford University Press, 1982.
Garden, Donald Stuart. *Australia, New Zealand, and the Pacific: An Environmental History*. Santa Barbara: ABC-CLIO, 2005.
Gerber, David A. *Authors of Their Lives: The Personal Correspondence of British Immigrants to North America in the Nineteenth Century*. New York: New York University Press, 2006.
Glassberg, David. *Sense of History: The Place of the Past in American Life*. Amherst: University of Massachusetts Press, 2001.
Goodman, David. *Gold Seeking: Victoria and California in the 1850s*. Stanford: Stanford University Press, 1994.
Griffiths, Tom. *Hunters and Collectors: The Antiquarian Imagination in Australia*. Cambridge: Cambridge University Press, 1996.
Guy, Laurie. *Shaping Godzone: Public Issues and Church Voices in New Zealand*. Wellington: Victoria University Press, 2011.
Haines, Robin. *Emigration and the Labouring Poor: Australian Recruitment in Britain and Ireland: 1831–1860*. New York: St Martin's Press, 1997.
Hampton, Mark. *Visions of the Press in Britain: 1850–1950*. Urbana: University of Illinois Press, 2004.
Handlin, Oscar. *The Uprooted: The Epic Story of the Great Migrations That Made the American People*. Boston: Little, Brown and Company, 1951.

Hansen, Christine and Tom Griffiths. *Living with Fire: People, Nature and History in Steels Creek*. Collingwood: CSIRO Publishing, 2012.

Harris, Cole. *The Resettlement of British Columbia: Essays on Colonialism and Geographical Change*. Vancouver: UBC Press, 2011.

Harrison, Brian. *Drink and the Victorians: The Temperance Question in England, 1815–1872*. 2nd edn. Staffordshire: Keele University Press, 1994.

Harte, Liam. *The Literature of the Irish in Britain: Autobiography and Memoir, 1725–2001*. London: Palgrave Macmillan, 2009.

Hassam, Andrew. *Sailing to Australia: Shipboard Diaries by Nineteenth-Century British Emigrants*. Manchester and New York: Manchester University Press, 1994.

Healy, Chris. *From the Ruins of Colonialism: History as Social Memory*. Cambridge: Cambridge University Press, 1997.

Heinz, William F. *Bright Fine Gold: Stories of the New Zealand Goldfields*. Wellington: Reed, 1974.

Held, Ray E. *Public Libraries in California, 1849–1878*. Berkeley: University of California Press, 1963.

Hempenstall, Peter. 'Overcoming Separate Histories: Historians as "Idea Traders" in a Trans-Tasman World.' *History Australia* 4, no. 1 (2007): 04.01–04.16.

Holliday, J. S. *The World Rushed In: The California Gold Rush Experience: An Eyewitness Account of a Nation Heading West*. New York: Simon and Schuster, 1981.

Hoskins, Robert. *Goldfield Balladeer: The Life and Times of the Celebrated Charles R. Thatcher*. Auckland: HarperCollins, 1997.

Hsu, Madeline Y. *Dreaming of Gold, Dreaming of Home: Transnationalism and Migration Between the United States and South China, 1882–1943*. Stanford: Stanford University Press, 2000.

Hurtado, Albert L. *Indian Survival on the California Frontier*. New Haven: Yale University Press, 1988.

Hutchins, John Milton. *Diggers, Constables and Bushrangers: The New Zealand Gold Rushes as a Frontier Experience, 1852–1878*. Lakewood: Avrooman-Apfelwald Press, 2010.

Isenberg, Andrew C. *Mining California: An Ecological History*. New York: Macmillan, 2010.

Jalland, Patricia. *Death in the Victorian Family*. Oxford: Oxford University Press, 1996.

Johnson, Susan Lee. *Roaring Camp: The Social World of the California Gold Rush*. New York: W. W. Norton and Company, 2000.

Jones, Aled. *Powers of the Press: Newspapers, Power and the Public in Nineteenth-Century England*. Aldershot: Scolar Press, 1996.

Jones, Gareth Stedman. *Language of Class: Studies in English Working Class History, 1832–1982*. Cambridge: Cambridge University Press, 1983.

King, Michael. *The Penguin History of New Zealand*. Rosedale: Penguin Books, 2003.
Knowles, Anne Kelly. *Calvinists Incorporated: Welsh Immigrants on Ohio's Industrial Frontier*. Chicago: University of Chicago Press, 1997.
Kuhn, Philip A. *Chinese Among Others: Emigration in Modern Times*. Lanham: Rowman and Littlefield Publishers, 2008.
Kulp, Daniel. *Country Life in South China: The Sociology of Familism*. Taipei: Ching-Wu Publishing, 1966.
Lake, Marilyn and Henry Reynolds. *Drawing the Global Colour Line: White Men's Countries and the Question of Racial Equality*. Melbourne: Melbourne University Press, 2008.
[Anon]. *Layers of Gold, Dunedin: Otago Anniversary Weekend 18–21 March 2011; [and] Gabriel's Gully 150th Anniversary, Lawrence New Zealand*. Dunedin: Dunedin Heritage Festival, 2011.
Limerick, Patricia. *The Legacy of Conquest: The Unbroken Past of the American West*. New York and London: W. W. Norton and Company, 1987.
Macmillan, David S. *Scotland and Australia: Emigration, Commerce and Investment*. London: Oxford University Press, 1967.
Mann, Ralph. *After the Gold Rush: Society in Grass Valley and Nevada City, California, 1849–1870*. Palo Alto: Stanford University Press, 1982.
Marks, Paula Mitchell. *Precious Dust: The American Gold Rush Era, 1848–1900*. New York: William Morrow and Co., 1994.
Massey, Doreen. *For Space*. London: Sage Publications, 2005.
May, Philip Ross. *The West Coast Gold Rushes*. 2nd edn. Christchurch: Pegasus Press, 1967.
Mayne, Alan and Charles Fahey (eds). *Gold Tailings: The Hidden History of Victoria's Central Goldfield Region*. Canberra: Australian Scholarly Publishing, 2010.
McCalman, Iain, Alexander Cook and Andrew Reeves (eds). *Gold: Forgotten Histories and Lost Objects of Australia*. Cambridge: Cambridge University Press, 2001.
McCarthy, Angela (ed.). *A Global Clan: Scottish Migrant Networks and Identities Since the Eighteenth Century*. London: Tauris Academic Studies, 2006.
———. *Irish Migrants in New Zealand, 1840–1937: 'The Desired Haven'*. Woodbridge: Boydell Press, 2005.
———. *Scottishness and Irishness in New Zealand since 1840*. Manchester: Manchester University Press, 2011.
McKenzie, Kirsten. *Scandal in the Colonies: Sydney and Cape Town, 1820–1850*. Melbourne: Melbourne University Press, 2004.
McKeown, Adam. *Chinese Migrant Networks and Cultural Change: Peru, Chicago, Hawaii, 1900–1936*. Chicago and London: University of Chicago Press, 2001.

McLintock, A. H. *The History of Otago*. Dunedin: Otago Centennial Historical Publications, 1949.
Mein Smith, Philippa. *A Concise History of New Zealand*. Cambridge: Cambridge University Press, 2005.
Mein Smith, Philippa, Peter Hempenstall and Shaun Goldfinch. *Remaking the Tasman World*. Christchurch: Canterbury University Press, 2008.
Monaghan, Jay. *Chile, Peru, and the California Gold Rush of 1849*. Los Angeles: University of California Press, 1973.
Morrell, William Parker. *The Gold Rushes*. London: Macmillan Company, 1941.
Morse, Kathryn. *The Nature of Gold: An Environmental History of the Klondike Gold Rush*. Seattle: University of Washington Press, 2003.
Ng, James. *Windows on a Chinese Past*. Vol. 1. Dunedin: Otago Heritage Books, 1993.
———. *Windows on a Chinese Past*. Vol. 2. Dunedin: Otago Heritage Books, 1993.
O'Farrell, Patrick. *Letters from Irish Australia: 1825–1925*. Sydney: New South Wales University Press, 1984.
———. *The Irish in Australia: 1788 to the Present*. Sydney: University of New South Wales Press, 2000.
Oakes, Tim and Louisa Schein. *Translocal China: Linkages, Identities and the Reimagining of Space*. London and New York: Routledge, 2005.
Olssen, Erik. *A History of Otago*. Dunedin: John McIndoe, 1984.
———. *Building a New World: Work, Politics and Society in Caversham, 1880s–1920s*. Auckland: Auckland University Press, 1995.
Paul, Rodman W. *California Gold: The Beginning of Mining in the Far West*. Cambridge: Harvard University Press, 1947.
Payton, Philip. *The Cornish Overseas*. Fowey: Alexander Associates, 1999.
Payton, P. J. *The Cornish Miner in Australia: Cousin Jack Down Under*. Trewolsta: Dyllansow Turan, 1984.
Perry, Adele. *On the Edge of Empire: Gender, Race, and the Making of British Columbia, 1849–1871*. Toronto: University of Toronto Press, 2001.
Phillips, Jock. *A Man's Country?: The Image of the Pakeha Male, a History*. 2nd edn. Auckland: Penguin Books, 1996.
Phillips, Jock and Terry Hearn. *Settlers: New Zealand Immigrants from England, Ireland and Scotland, 1800–1945*. Auckland: Auckland University Press, 2008.
Pomeroy, Earl. *The Pacific Slope: A History of California, Oregon, Washington, Idaho, Utah, and Nevada*. 3rd edn. Reno: University of Nevada Press, 2003.
Pooley, Colin and Jean Turnbull. *Migration And Mobility In Britain Since The Eighteenth Century*. London: Routledge, 1998.
Porter, Frances and Charlotte McDonald (eds). *My Hand Will Write What My Heart Dictates: The Unsettled Lives of Women in Nineteenth-Century New*

Zealand as Revealed to Sisters, Family and Friends. Auckland: Auckland University Press, 1996.
Prentis, Malcolm. *The Scots in Australia*. Sydney: University of New South Wales Press, 2008.
Proudfoot, Lindsay and Dianne Hall. *Imperial Spaces: Placing the Irish and Scots in Colonial Australia*. Manchester and New York: Manchester University Press, 2011.
Pyke, Vincent. *History of the Early Gold Discoveries in Otago*. Dunedin: Otago Daily Times and Witness Newspapers, 1887.
Ramirez, Bruno. *Crossing the 49th Parallel: Migration from Canada to the United States, 1900–1930*. Ithaca: Cornell University Press, 2001.
Reid, Richard E. *Farewell My Children: Irish Assisted Emigration to Australia, 1848–1870*. Spit Junction: Anchor Books, 2011.
Richards, Eric. *Britannia's Children: Emigration from England, Scotland, Wales and Ireland Since 1600*. Hambledon and London: Continuum International Publishing Group, 2004.
Richards, Eric, Richard Reid and David Fitzpatrick (eds). *Visible Immigrants: Neglected Sources for the History of Australian Immigration*. Vol. 1. Canberra: Australian National University, 1989.
Roberts, Brian. *American Alchemy: The California Gold Rush and Middle-Class Culture*. Chapel Hill: University of North Carolina Press, 2000.
Rohrbough, Malcolm J. *Days of Gold: The California Gold Rush and the American Nation*. Berkeley: University of California Press, 1998.
Rose, Jonathan. *The Intellectual Life of the British Working Classes*. New Haven: Yale University Press, 2002.
Salmon, J. H. M. *A History of Goldmining in New Zealand*. Wellington: Government Printer, 1963.
Serle, Geoffrey. *The Golden Age: A History of the Colony of Victoria, 1851–1861*. Melbourne: Melbourne University Press, 1963.
Shorter, A. H., W. L. D. Ravenhill and K. J. Gregory. *Southwest England*. London: Thomas Nelson, 1969.
Sinclair, Keith. *A History of New Zealand*. 3rd edn. London: Allen Lane, 1980.
———. *A History of New Zealand*. 4th edn. Auckland: Penguin Books, 1988.
Smith, Duane A. *Rocky Mountain Mining Camps: The Urban Frontier*. Bloomington: Indiana University Press, 1967.
Spence, Jonathan D. *God's Chinese Son: The Taiping Heavenly Kingdom of Hong Xiuquan*. New York and London: W. W. Norton, 1996.
Starr, Kevin. *Americans and the California Dream, 1850–1915*. New York: Oxford University Press, 1973.
Starr, Kevin and Richard J. Orsi (eds), *Rooted in Barbarous Soil: People, Culture, and Community in Gold Rush California*. Berkeley: University of California Press, 2000.
Stedman, Richard (ed.). *A Golden Opportunity: Proceedings of the New Zealand Society of Genealogists Annual Conference, Held at John McGlashan College,*

Maori Hill, Dunedin, June 3–6, 2011. Dunedin: Conference Committee of the New Zealand Society of Genealogists – Dunedin Branch, 2011.

Stivers, Richard. *Hair of the Dog: Irish Drinking and Its American Stereotype*. 2nd edn. New York: Continuum, 2000.

Thomas, Brinley. *Migration and Economic Growth: A Study of Great Britain and the Atlantic Economy*. Cambridge: Cambridge University Press, 1973.

Thompson, Edward P. *Customs in Common: Studies in Traditional Popular Culture*. London: Merlin Press, 2009.

Tyrrell, Ian. *Transnational Nation: United States History in Global Perspective Since 1789*. New York: Palgrave Macmillan, 2007.

Vernon, James. *Politics and the People: A Study in English Political Culture c. 1815–1867*. Cambridge: Cambridge University Press, 1993.

Vincent, David. *Bread, Knowledge and Freedom: A Study of Nineteenth-Century Working Class Autobiography*. London: Europa Publications, 1981.

Wakeman, Frederic E. *Strangers at the Gate: Social Disorder in South China, 1839–1861*. Berkeley: University of California Press, 1966.

Ward, Russell. *The Australian Legend*. Melbourne: Oxford University Press, 1958.

West, Elliott. *The Contested Plains: Indians, Goldseekers, and the Rush to Colorado*. Lawrence: University of Kansas Press, 1998.

———. *The Saloon on the Rocky Mountain Mining Frontier*. Lincoln: University of Nebraska Press, 1996.

Wevers, Lydia. *Reading on the Farm: Victorian Fiction and the Colonial World*. Wellington: Victoria University of Wellington Press, 2010.

White, Richard. *The Organic Machine: The Remaking of the Columbia River*. New York: Macmillan, 2011.

Williams, David. *The Georgia Gold Rush: Twenty-Niners, Cherokees, and Gold Fever*. Columbia: University of South Carolina Press, 1993.

Yuen, William Tai. *The Origins of China's Awareness of New Zealand, 1674–1911*. Auckland: University of Auckland Press, 2005.

Zhu, Liping. *A Chinaman's Chance: The Chinese on the Rocky Mountain Mining Frontier*. Niwot: University of Colorado Press, 1997.

Articles and book chapters

Agnew, John A. 'Space and Place.' In *The Sage Handbook of Geographical Knowledge*, edited by John A. Agnew and David N. Livingstone, 316–24. London: SAGE, 2011.

Angus, John. 'Populism, Parochialism and Public Works: Politics on the Otago Goldfields from the 1860s to the 1880s.' In *Rushing for Gold: Life and Commerce on the Goldfields of New Zealand and Australia*, edited by Lloyd Carpenter and Lyndon Fraser, 69–83. Dunedin: Otago University Press, 2016.

Akenson, D. H. 'Reading the Texts of Rural Immigrants: Letters from the Irish

in Australia, New Zealand, and North America.' *Canadian Papers of Rural History* 7 (1990): 387–406.
Arnold, Rollo. 'Some Australasian Aspects of New Zealand Life.' *New Zealand Journal of History* 4, no. 1 (1970): 62–70.
Bailey, Peter. 'Conspiracies of Meaning: Music-Hall and the Knowingness of Popular Culture.' *Past and Present* 144 (1994): 138–70.
———. 'Parasexuality and Glamour: The Victorian Barmaid as Cultural Prototype.' *Gender & History* 2, no. 2 (1990): 148–72.
Ballantyne, Tony. 'On Place, Space and Mobility.' *New Zealand Journal of History* 45, no. 1 (2011): 50–70.
———. 'Placing Literary Culture: Books and Civic Culture in Milton.' *Journal of New Zealand Literature* 28, no. 2 (2010): 82–104.
———. 'Reading the Newspaper in Colonial Otago.' *Journal of New Zealand Studies* 12 (2011): 47–63.
———. 'Thinking Local: Knowledge, Sociability and Community in Gore's Intellectual Life, 1875–1914.' *New Zealand Journal of History* 44, no. 2 (2010): 138–56.
Ballantyne, Tony and Brian Moloughney. 'Asia in Murihiku: Towards a Transnational History of a Colonial Culture.' In *Disputed Histories: Imagining New Zealand's Pasts*, edited by Tony Ballantyne and Brian Moloughney, 65–92. Dunedin: Otago University Press, 2006.
Barkan, Elliott R. 'America in the Hand, Homeland in the Heart: Transnational and Translocal Immigrant Experiences in the American West.' *The Western Historical Quarterly* 35, no. 3 (October 2004): 331–54.
Bayly, C. A., Sven Beckert, Matthew Connelly, Isabel Hofmeyr, Wendy Kozol and Patricia Seed. 'AHR Conversation: On Transnational History.' *The American Historical Review* 111, no. 5 (December 2006): 1441–64.
Bellesiles, Michael A. 'Western Violence.' In *A Companion to the American West*, edited by William Deverell, 162–78. Malden: Blackwell Publishing, 2007.
Berglund, Barbara. 'The Days of Old, the Days of Gold, the Days of '49: Identity, History, and Memory at the California Midwinter International Exposition, 1894.' *The Public Historian* 25, no. 4 (2003): 25–49.
Blaine, Geoffrey. 'A Theory of Mineral Discovery: Australia in the Nineteenth Century.' *Economic History Review* 23 (1970): 298–313.
———. 'The Momentous Gold Rushes.' *Australian Economic History Review* 50, no. 2 (2010): 209–16.
Brooking, Tom. 'Gold in Otago: Digging for a New Perspective.' In *A Golden Opportunity: Proceedings of the New Zealand Society of Genealogists Annual Conference*, edited by Richard Stedman, 17–22. Dunedin: New Zealand Society of Genealogists, 2011.
———. 'Weaving the Tartan and the Flax: Networks, Identities, and Scottish Migration to Nineteenth-Century Otago, New Zealand.' In *A Global Clan: Scottish and Migrant Networks Since the Eighteenth Century*,

edited by Angela McCarthy, 183–202. London: Tauris Academic Studies, 2006.

Brubaker, Rogers. 'Ethnicity without Groups.' *European Journal of Sociology* 43, no. 2 (2002): 163–89.

Burton, Antoinette. 'Introduction: On the Inadequacy and the Indispensability of the Nation.' In *After the Imperial Turn: Thinking with and through the Nation*, edited by Antoinette Burton, 1–23. Durham, NC: Duke University Press, 2003.

———. 'Not Even Remotely Global? Method and Scale in World History.' *History Workshop Journal* 64, no. 1 (2007): 323–8.

Callaway, Anita. 'A Broad Brush Dipped in Gold: The Expansion of Australian Vision.' In *Gold: Forgotten Histories and Lost Objects of Australia*, edited by Iain McCalman, Alexander Cook and Andrew Reeves, 326–38. Cambridge: Cambridge University Press, 2001.

Campbell, Persia Crawford. 'Chinese Emigration to Canada, Australia, and New Zealand.' In *The Chinese Diaspora in the Pacific*, edited by Anthony Reid, 102–231. Aldershot: Ashgate, 2008.

Cardell, Kerry, Cliff Cumming, Peter Griffiths and Bill Jones. 'Welsh Identity on the Victorian Goldfields in the Nineteenth Century.' In *A World Turned Upside Down: Cultural Change on Australia's Goldfields, 1851–2001*, edited by Kerry Cardell and Cliff Cumming, 25–60. Canberra: Australian National University Press, 2001.

Carey, James W. 'Communications and Economics.' In *James Carey: A Critical Reader*, 60–75. Minneapolis and London: University of Minnesota Press, 1997.

———. 'The Chicago School and the History of Mass Communication Research.' In *James Carey: A Critical Reader*, 14–33. Minneapolis and London: University of Minnesota Press, 1997.

Chan, H. D. Min-hsi. 'Qiaoxiang and the Diversity of Chinese Settlement in Australia and New Zealand.' In *Chinese Transnational Networks*, edited by Tan Chee-Beng, 153–71. Abingdon and New York: Routledge, 2007.

Chen, Yong. 'Understanding Chinese American Transnationalism During the Early Twentieth Century: An Economic Perspective.' In *Chinese American Transnationalism: The Flow of People, Resources, and Ideas Between China and America During the Exclusion Era*, edited by Sucheng Chan, 156–73. Philadelphia: Temple University Press, 2006.

Conzen, Kathleen Neils. 'Mainstreams and Side Channels: The Localization of Immigrant Cultures.' *Journal of American Ethnic History* 11, no. 1 (1991): 5–20.

Crane, Susan A. 'Writing the Individual Back into Collective Memory.' *The American Historical Review* 102, no. 5 (1 December 1997): 1372–85.

Curthoys, Ann. 'We've Just Started Making National Histories, and You Want Us to Stop Already?' In *After the Imperial Turn: Thinking with and through the Nation*, edited by Antoinette Burton, 70–89. Durham, NC: Duke University Press, 2003.

Davison, Graeme. 'Gold Rush Melbourne.' In *Gold: Forgotten Histories and Lost Objects of Australia*, edited by Iain McCalman, Alexander Cook and Andrew Reeves, 52–66. Cambridge: Cambridge University Press, 2001.

———. 'The Parochial Past: Changing Uses of Australian Local History.' In *The Future of the Past? Australian History after the Bicentenary: Proceedings of the Royal Australian Historical Society*, edited by Paul Ashton, 5–19. Sydney: Royal Australian Historical Society, 1990.

Dean, Heather. '"The Persuasion of Books": The Significance of Libraries in Colonial British Columbia.' *Libraries and the Cultural Record* 46, no. 1 (2011): 50–72.

Delaney, Enda. 'Our Island Story? Towards a Transnational History of Late Modern Ireland.' *Irish Historical Studies* 37, no. 148 (2011): 599–621.

Denoon, Donald. 'Re-membering Australasia: A Repressed Memory.' *Australian Historical Studies* 34, no. 122 (2003): 290–304.

Devine, T. M. 'Introduction: The Paradox of Scottish Emigration.' In *Scottish Emigration and Scottish Society: Proceedings of the Scottish Historical Studies*, edited by T. M. Devine, 1–15. Edinburgh: John Donald, 1992.

Dykstra, Robert R. 'Quantifying the Wild West: The Problematic Statistics of Frontier Violence.' *The Western Historical Quarterly* 40, no. 3 (2009): 321–47.

Fahey, Charles. 'Labour and Trade Unionism in Victorian Goldmining: Bendigo, 1861–1915.' In *Gold: Forgotten Histories and Lost Objects of Australia*, edited by Iain McCalman, Alexander Cook and Andrew Reeves, 67–84. Cambridge: Cambridge University Press, 2001.

Fairburn, Miles. 'A Discourse on Critical Method.' *New Zealand Journal of History* 25 (1991): 158–77.

Fitzpatrick, David. 'Irish Emigration and the Art of Letter-Writing.' In *Letters Across Borders: The Epistolary Practices of International Migrants*, edited by Bruce S. Elliott, David A. Gerber and Suzanne M. Sinke, 97–106. New York: Palgrave Macmillan, 2006.

Forrest, James. 'Population and Settlement on the Otago Goldfields, 1861–1870.' *New Zealand Geographer* 17, no. 1 (1961): 64–86.

Fotheringham, Richard. 'Theatre from 1788 to the 1960s.' In *The Cambridge Companion to Australian Literature*, edited by Elizabeth Webby, 134–58. Cambridge: Cambridge University Press, 2000.

Fraser, Lyndon. 'The Working Lives of Irish Men on the Antipodean Goldfields.' In *Deeper Leads: New Approaches to Victorian Goldfields History*, edited by Keir Reeves and David Nichols, 21–38. Ballarat: Ballarat Heritage Services, 2007.

Frost, Warwick. 'The Environmental Impacts of the Victorian Gold Rushes: Miners' Accounts During the First Five Years.' *Australian Economic History Review* 53, no. 1 (2013): 72–90.

Gabaccia, Donna R. 'Is Everywhere Nowhere? Nomads, Nations and the Immigrant Paradigm of United States History.' *The Journal of American History* 86, no. 3 (1999): 1115–34.

Gagnier, Regina. 'Social Atoms: Working-Class, Autobiography, Subjectivity, and Gender.' *Victorian Studies* 30, no. 3 (1987): 335–63.

Garden, Don. 'Catalyst or Cataclysm?: Gold Mining and the Environment.' [Article in a Special Issue Celebrating 150 Years of Goldmining in Victoria.] *Victorian Historical Journal (1987)* 72, no. 1–2 (2001): 28–44.

Gerber, David A. 'Epistolary Ethics: Personal Correspondence and the Culture of Emigration in the Nineteenth Century.' *Journal of American Ethnic History* 19, no. 4 (2000): 3–23.

Gerber, James. 'Gold Rushes and the trans-Pacific Wheat Trade: California and Australia, 1848–57.' In *Pacific Centuries: Pacific and Pacific Rim History Since the Sixteenth Century*, edited by Dennis O. Flynn, Lionel Frost and A. J. H. Latham, 125–51. London: Routledge, 1999.

Gibbons, Peter. 'Cultural Colonization and National Identity.' *New Zealand Journal of History* 36, no. 1 (2002): 5–17.

———. 'Non-fiction.' In *The Oxford History of New Zealand Literature in English*, edited by Terry Sturm, 25–104. Auckland: Oxford University Press, 1991.

———. 'The Far Side of the Search for Identity: Reconsidering New Zealand History.' *New Zealand Journal of History* 37, no. 1 (2003): 38–49.

Gleason, Philip. 'Identifying Identity: A Semantic History.' *The Journal of American History* 69, no. 4 (1983): 910–31.

Goodman, David. 'Gold Fields/Golden Fields: The Language of Agrarianism and the Victorian Gold Rush.' *Australian Historical Studies* 23, no. 90 (1988): 19–41.

———. 'Making an Edgier History of Gold.' In *Gold: Forgotten Histories and Lost Objects of Australia*, edited by Iain McCalman, Alexander Cook and Andrew Reeves, 23–36. Cambridge: Cambridge University Press, 2001.

Green, Nancy L. 'The Comparative Method and Poststructural Structuralism: New Perspectives for Migration Studies.' *Journal of American Ethnic History* 13, no. 4 (1994): 3–22.

Hackett, Nan. 'A Different Form of "Self": Narrative Style in British Nineteenth-Century Working-class Autobiography.' *Biography* 12, no. 3 (1989): 208–26.

Hall, Jacquelyn Dowd. '"You Must Remember This": Autobiography as Social Critique.' *The Journal of American History* 85, no. 2 (1998): 439–65.

Hamilton, Fiona. 'Pioneering History: Negotiating Pakeha Collective Memory in the Late Nineteenth and Early Twentieth Centuries.' *New Zealand Journal of History* 36, no. 1 (2002): 66–81.

Handelman, Donald. 'The Organization of Ethnicity.' *Ethnic Groups* 1 (1977): 187–200.

Hearn, Terry. 'Irish on the Otago Goldfields, 1861–1871.' In *A Distant Shore:*

Irish Migration and New Zealand Settlement, edited by Lyndon Fraser, 75–85. Dunedin: Otago University Press, 2000.

———. 'Mining the Quarry.' In *Environmental Histories of New Zealand*, edited by Eric Pawson and Tom Brooking, 84–99. New York: Oxford University Press, 2002.

———. 'Review of Diggers, Hatters & Whores: The Story of the New Zealand Gold Rushes.' *New Zealand Journal of History* 43, no. 1 (2009): 77–9.

———. 'Scots Miners in the Goldfields, 1861–1870.' In *The Heather and the Fern: Scottish Migration and New Zealand Settlement*, edited by Tom Brooking and Jennie Coleman, 67–86. Dunedin: Otago Univesity Press, 2003.

Hellier, Donna. '"The Humblies": Scottish Highland Migration into Nineteenth Century Victoria.' In *Families in Colonial Australia*, edited by Patricia Grimshaw, Chris McConville and Ellen McEwen, 9–18. Sydney: Unwin Hyman, 1985.

Hempenstall, Peter. 'Overcoming Separate Histories: Historians as "Idea Traders" in a Trans-Tasman World.' *History Australia* 4, no. 1 (2007): 04.01–04.16 [no page numbers].

Hoerder, Dirk. 'Introduction. From Dreams to Possibilities: The Secularization of Hope and the Quest for Independence.' In *Distant Magnets: Expectations and Realities in the Immigrant Experience, 1840–1930*, edited by Dirk Hoerder and Horst Rössler, 1–32. New York and London: Holmes and Meier, 1993.

Hsu, Madeline. 'Trading with Gold Mountain: Jinshanzhuang and Networks of Kinship and Native Place.' In *Chinese American Transnationalism: The Flow of People, Resources, and Ideas Between China and America During the Exclusion Era*, edited by Sucheng Chan, 22–33. Philadelphia: Temple University Press, 2006.

Jackson, Hugh. 'Churchgoing in Nineteenth-Century New Zealand.' *New Zealand Journal of History* 17 (1983): 43–59.

Johnson, Susan Lee. '"My Own Private Life": Toward a History of Desire in Gold Rush California.' In *Rooted in Barbarous Soil: People, Culture and Community in Gold Rush California*, edited by Kevin Starr and Richard J. Orsi, 316–48. Berkeley: University of California Press, 2000.

Jones, Aled and Bill Jones. 'The Welsh World and the British Empire, c. 1851–1939: An Exploration.' *Journal of Imperial and Commonwealth History* 31, no. 2 (2003): 57–81.

Jones, Bill. 'Welsh Identities in Colonial Ballarat.' *Journal of Australian Studies* 25, no. 68 (2001): 34–43.

Keane, Patrick. 'Useful Knowledge and Morality: The San Francisco Mechanics' Institute, 1854–1906." *Adult Education Quarterly* 35, no. 1 (1984): 26–50.

Kellaway, Roger. 'Immigration from New Zealand: The Tasmanian Select Committee of 1864.' *New Zealand Geographical Society Conference Proceedings, 1999* (2000): 171–4.

———. 'Tasmania and the Otago Gold Rush, 1861–1865.' *Papers and Proceedings. Tasmanian Historical Research Association* 46, no. 4 (1999): 213–29.

Kowalewski, Michael. 'Romancing the Gold Rush: The Literature of the California Frontier.' In *Rooted in Barbarous Soil: People, Culture and Community in Gold Rush California*, edited by Kevin Starr and Richard J. Orsi, 204–25. Berkeley: University of California Press, 2000.

Kraus, Hildie V. 'A Cultural History of the Mechanics' Institute of San Francisco, 1855–1920.' *Library History* 23 (2007): 115–28.

Kuch, Peter. 'The Irish and the Australasian Colonial Stage – Confrontation and Compromise.' *Australasian Journal of Irish Studies* 10 (2010): 105–18.

Lambert, David and Alan Lester. 'Introduction: Imperial Spaces, Imperial Subjects.' In *Colonial Lives Across the British Empire: Imperial Careering in the Long Nineteenth Century*, edited by David Lambert and Alan Lester, 1–31. Cambridge: Cambridge University Press, 2006.

Lawrence, Susan. 'After the Gold Rush: Material Culture and Settlement on Victoria's Central Goldfields.' In *Gold: Forgotten Histories and Lost Objects of Australia*, edited by Iain McCalman, Alexander Cook and Andrew Reeves, 250–66. Cambridge: Cambridge University Press, 2001.

Lawton, Richard. 'Population.' In *Atlas of the Industrializing Britain, 1780–1914*, edited by John Langton and R. J. Morris, 10–29. London: Methuen and Co., 1986.

Lester, Alan. 'British Settler Discourse and the Circuits of Empire.' *History Workshop Journal* 54 (2002): 25–48.

———. 'Imperial Circuits and Networks: Geographies of the British Empire.' *History Compass* 4, no. 1 (2006): 124–41.

Lilley, Keith D. '"One Immense Gold Field!" British Imaginings of the Australian Gold Rushes, 1851–59.' *Landscape Research* 27, no. 1 (2002): 67–80.

Limerick, Patricia Nelson. 'Going West and Ending up Global.' *Western Historical Quarterly* 32, no. 1 (2001): 5–23.

Lovejoy, Valerie. 'Chinese in Late Nineteenth-Century Bendigo: Their Local and Translocal Lives in "This Strangers' Country".' *Australian Historical Studies* 42, no. 1 (2011): 45–61.

McDonald, Charlotte. 'Too Many Men and Too Few Women: Gender's "Fatal Impact" in Nineteenth-century Colonies.' In *The Gendered Kiwi*, edited by Caroline Daley and Deborah Montgomerie, 17–35. Auckland: Auckland University Press, 1999.

MacLennan, Hugh Dan. 'Gu Fearann an Òir: To the Land of Gold.' *Journal of Australian Studies* 25, no. 68 (2001): 44–53.

Macmillan, David S. 'Sir Charles Trevelyan and the Highland and Island Emigration Society.' *Journal of the Royal Australian Historical Society* 44 (1963): 161–88.

Magee, Gary B. and Andrew W. Thompson. 'The Global and the Local:

Explaining Migrant Remittance Flows in the English-speaking World, 1880–1914.' *Journal of Economic History* 66, no. 1 (2006): 177–202.
Matthews, Gethin. 'Gold Fever: The Stampede from South Wales to British Columbia in 1862.' *North American Journal of Welsh Studies* 5, no. 2 (2005): 54–83.
Mayne, Alan. 'Family and Community on the Central Victorian Goldfields.' In *Gold Tailings: Forgotten Histories of Family and Community on the Central Victorian Goldfields*, edited by Charles Fahey and Alan Mayne, 234–43. North Melbourne: Australian Scholarly Publishing, 2010.
McCalman, Iain, Alexander Cook and Andrew Reeves. 'Introduction.' In *Gold: Forgotten Histories and Lost Objects of Australia*, edited by Iain McCalman, Alexander Cook and Andrew Reeves, 1–36. Cambridge: Cambridge University Press, 2001.
McConville, Chris. 'The Victorian Irish: Emigrants and Families, 1851–91.' In *Families in Colonial Australia*, edited by Patricia Grimshaw, Chris McConville and Ellen McEwen, 1–8. Sydney: Allen and Unwin, 1985.
McEvoy, Arthur F. 'Towards an Interactive Theory of Nature and Culture: Ecology, Production and Cognition in the California Fishing Industry.' In *The Ends of the Earth: Perspectives on Modern Environmental History*, edited by Donald Worster, 211–29. New York: Cambridge University Press, 1988.
McGowan, Barry. 'The Working Miners of Southern New South Wales: Adaptability, Class and Identity.' *Australasian Mining History Journal* 1, no. 1 (2003): 95–109.
McKeown, Adam. 'Conceptualising Chinese Diasporas.' *Journal of Asian Studies* 58, no. 2 (1999): 306–37.
Mei, June. 'Socioeconomic Origins of Emigration: Guangdong to California, 1850–1882.' *Modern China* 5 (1979): 463–501.
Mein Smith, Philippa. 'The Tasman World.' In *The New Oxford History of New Zealand*, edited by Giselle Byrnes, 297–319. Melbourne: Oxford University Press, 2009.
Mein Smith, Philippa and Peter Hempenstall. 'Australia and New Zealand: Turning Shared Pasts into a Shared History.' *History Compass* 1 (2003): 1–8.
Moloughney, Brian, Tony Ballantyne and David Hood. 'After Gold: Reconstructing Chinese Communities, 1896–1913.' In *Asia in the Making of New Zealand*, edited by Henry Johnson and Brian Moloughney, 58–75. Auckland: Auckland University Press, 2006.
Moloughney, Brian and John Stenhouse. '"Drug-besotten, Sin-begotten Fiends of Filth": New Zealanders and the Oriental Other, 1850–1920.' *New Zealand Journal of History* 33 (1999): 43–64.
Morris, R. J. 'Samuel Smiles and the Genesis of Self-Help; The Retreat to a Petit Bourgeois Utopia.' *The Historical Journal* 24, no. 1 (1981): 89–109.
Mouat, Jeremy. 'After California: Later Gold Rushes of the Pacific Basin.' In

Riches for All: The California Gold Rush and the World, edited by Kenneth N. Owens, 263–95. Lincoln and London: University of Nebraska Press, 2002.

Nerone, John. 'Newspapers and the Public Sphere.' In *A History of the Book in America Vol. 3: The Industrial Book, 1840–1880*, edited by Scott E. Casper, Jeffrey D. Groves, Stephen W. Nissenbaum and Michael Winship, 230–48. Chapel Hill: University of North Carolina Press, 2007.

Nora, Pierre. 'Between Memory and History: Les Lieux de Mémoire.' Translated by Marc Roudebush. *Representations* 26 (1988): 7–24.

Olssen, Erik. 'Lands of Sheep and Gold: The Australian Dimension to the New Zealand Past.' In *Tasman Relations: New Zealand and Australia, 1788–1988*, edited by Keith Sinclair, 34–51. Auckland: University of Auckland Press, 1987.

———. 'Where to from Here? Reflections on the Twentieth-Century Historiography of Nineteenth-Century New Zealand.' *New Zealand Journal of History* 26, no. 1 (1992): 54–77.

Payton, Philip. 'Cornish Emigration in Response to Changes in the International Copper Market in the 1860s.' *Cornish Studies* 2, no. 3 (1995): 60–82.

———. 'Cousin Jacks and Ancient Britons: Cornish Immigrants and Ethnic Identity.' *Journal of Australian Studies* 25, no. 68 (2001): 54–64.

Phelps, Robert. '"All Hands Have Gone Downtown": Urban Places in Gold Rush California.' In *Rooted in Barbarous Soil: People, Culture and Community in Gold Rush California*, edited by Kevin Starr and Richard J. Orsi, 113–40. Berkeley: University of California Press, 2000.

Phillips, Jock. 'Of Verandahs and Fish and Chips and Footie on Saturday Afternoon: Reflections on 100 Years of New Zealand Historiography.' *New Zealand Journal of History* 24, no. 2 (1990): 118–34.

Prentis, Malcolm. '"It's a Long Way to the Bottom": The Insignificance of "the Scots" in Australia.' *Immigrants and Minorities* 29, no. 2 (2011): 195–219.

Ramirez, Bruno. 'Canada in the United States: Perspectives on Migration and Continental History.' *Journal of American Ethnic History* 20, no. 3 (2001): 50–70.

Reeves, Keir. 'Tracking the Dragon Down Under: Chinese Cultural Connections in Gold Rush Australia and Aotearoa, New Zealand.' *Graduate Journal of Asia-Pacific Studies* 3, no. 1 (2005): 49–66.

Reeves, Keir, Lionel Frost and Charles Fahey. 'Integrating the Historiography of the Nineteenth-Century Gold Rushes.' *Australian Economic History Review* 50, no. 2 (2010): 111–28.

Richards, Eric. 'An Australian Map of British and Irish Literacy in 1841.' *Population Studies* 53, no. 3 (1999): 345–59.

———. 'Highland and Gaelic Immigrants.' *The Australian People: An Encyclopedia of the Nation, Its People and Their Origins*. Cambridge: Cambridge University Press, 2001.

———. 'St Kilda and Australia: Emigrants at Peril, 1852–3.' *Scottish Historical Review* 71 (1992): 129–55.
Rohrbough, Malcolm. 'No Boy's Play: Migration and Settlement in Early Gold Rush California.' In *Rooted in Barbarous Soil: People, Culture and Community in Gold Rush California*, edited by Kevin Starr and Richard J. Orsi, 25–43. Berkeley: University of California Press, 2000.
Rosenwein, Barbara. 'Worrying About Emotions in History.' *American Historical Review* 107, no. 3 (2002): 821–45.
Ryan, Greg. 'Drink and the Historians: Sober Reflections on Alcohol in New Zealand 1840–1914.' *New Zealand Journal of History* 44, no. 1 (2010): 35–53.
Sandos, James A. '"Because He Is a Liar and a Thief": Conquering the Residents of "Old" California, 1850–1880.' In *Rooted in Barbarous Soil: People, Culture and Community in Gold Rush California*, edited by Kevin Starr and Richard J. Orsi, 86–112. Berkeley: University of California Press, 2000.
Sewell, Jr., William H. 'The Concept(s) of Culture.' In *Beyond the Cultural Turn: New Directions in the Study of Society and Culture*, edited by Victoria E. Bonnell and Lynn Hunt, 35–61. Berkeley: University of California Press, 1999.
Shaw, Christopher and Malcolm Chase. 'The Dimension of Nostalgia.' In *The Imagined Past: History and Nostalgia*, edited by Christopher Shaw and Malcolm Chase, 1–17. Manchester: Manchester University Press, 1989.
Smith, Sidone. 'Construing Truths in Lying Mouths: Truthtelling in Women's Autobiography.' *Studies in the Literary Imagination* 23, no. 2 (1990): 145–63.
Spengemann, William C. and L. R. Lundquist. 'Autobiography and the American Myth.' *American Quarterly* 17, no. 3 (1965): 501–19.
Stafford, R. A. 'Preventing the "Curse of California": Advice for English Emigrants to the Australian Goldfields.' *Historical Records of Australian Science* 7, no. 3 (1987): 215–30.
Thelen, David. 'The Nation and Beyond: Transnational Perspectives on United States History.' *The Journal of American History* 86, no. 3 (1999): 965–75.
———. 'Of Audiences, Borderlands, and Comparisons: Toward the Internationalization of American History.' *The Journal of American History* 79, no. 2 (1992): 432–62.
Thistlethwaite, Frank. 'Migration from Europe Overseas in the 19th and 20th Centuries.' In *A Century of European Migration, 1830–1930*, edited by Rudolph J. Vecoli and Suzanne M. Sinke, 17–49. Urbana: University of Illinois Press, 1991.
Thompson, E. P. 'Time, Work-discipline and Industrial Capitalism.' *Past & Present* 38 (1967): 56–97.
Tilly, Charles. 'Transplanted Networks.' In *Immigration Reconsidered: History, Sociology, and Politics*, edited by Virginia Yans-McLaughlin, 79–95. Oxford: Oxford University Press, 1990.

Traue, J. E. 'Fiction, Public Libraries and the Reading Public in Colonial New Zealand.' *Bulletin of the Bibliographical Society of Australia and New Zealand* 28, no. 4 (2004): 84–93.

———. 'Reading as a "Necessity of Life" on the Tuapeka Goldfields in Nineteenth-century New Zealand." *Library History* 23, no. 1 (2007): 41–8.

———. 'The Public Library Explosion in Colonial New Zealand.' *Libraries and the Cultural Record* 42, no. 2 (2007): 151–64.

Turner, Frederick Jackson. 'The Significance of the Frontier in American History.' In *The Frontier in American History*, edited by Frederick Jackson Turner, 1–20. New York: Henry Holt, 1921.

Tyrrell, Ian. 'American Exceptionalism in an Age of International History.' *The American Historical Review* 96, no. 4 (1 October 1991): 1031–55.

———. 'Making Nations/Making States: American Historians in the Context of Empire.' *The Journal of American History* 86, no. 3 (1999): 1015–44.

———. 'Peripheral Visions: Californian-Australian Environmental Contacts, c. 1850s–1910.' *Journal of World History* 8, no. 2 (1997): 275–302.

Vertovec, Stephen. 'Conceiving and Researching Transnationalism.' *Ethnic and Racial Studies* 22, no. 2 (1999): 447–62.

White, Richard. 'Discovering Nature in North America.' *The Journal of American History* 79, no. 3 (1992): 874–91.

———. 'The Nationalization of Nature.' *The Journal of American History* 86, no. 3 (1 December 1999): 976–86.

Willbold, Matthias, Tim Elliott and Stephen Moorbath. 'The Tungsten Isotopic Composition of the Earth's Mantle before the Terminal Bombardment.' *Nature* 477, no. 7363 (September 2011): 195–8.

Williams, Michael. 'Hong Kong and the Pearl River Delta Qiaoxiang.' *Modern Asian Studies* 38 (2004): 257–82.

Withers, Charles W. J. 'Place and the "Spatial Turn" in Geography and in History.' *Journal of the History of Ideas* 70, no. 4 (October 2009): 637–58.

Theses/dissertations

Angus, Wayne R. 'Queenstown 1862–1864: The Genesis of a Goldfields Community.' BA (Hons) thesis, University of Otago, 1987.

Campbell, Scott. 'Community Formation in a Colonial Port Town: Port Chalmers, 1860–1875.' MA thesis, University of Otago, 2012.

Chivers, Susan. 'Religion, Ethnicity and Race: The Mission of the Otago Church to the Chinese 1860–1950.' MA thesis, University of Otago, 1992.

Clarke, Ali. 'Feasts and Fasts: Holidays, Religion and Ethnicity in Nineteenth-century Otago.' PhD thesis, University of Otago, 2003.

Davy, Daniel. 'Selling Australia: New South Wales Emigrant Guidebooks and Scottish Perceptions of Australia, 1818–1850.' MSc thesis, University of Edinburgh, 2007.

Dickinson, Jennifer L. 'Picks, Pans and Petticoats: Women on the Central Otago Goldfields.' BA (Hons) thesis, University of Otago, 1993.
Gillespie-Needham, Dulcie. 'The Colonial and His Books: A Study of Reading in Nineteenth Century New Zealand.' PhD thesis, Victoria University of Wellington, 1971.
Hearn, Terence J. 'Land, Water and Gold in Central Otago, 1861–1921: Some Aspects of Resource Use Policy and Conflict.' PhD thesis, University of Otago, 1981.
Hilliard, Chris. 'Island Stories: The Writing of New Zealand History, 1920–1940.' MA thesis, University of Auckland, 1997.
Marks, Robin. 'The Lawrence Athenaeum and Miners' Institute: a Fragment of Goldfields History.' MA thesis, University of Otago, 1973.
Marshall, Daniel Patrick. 'Claiming the Land: Indians, Goldseekers, and the Rush to British Columbia.' PhD thesis, University of British Columbia, 2000.
McClean, Rosalind. 'Scottish Emigrants to New Zealand, 1840–1880: Motives, Means and Background.' PhD thesis, University of Edinburgh, 1990.
McGowan, Barry. 'Dust and Dreams: A Regional History of Mining and Community in Southeast New South Wales, 1850–1900.' PhD thesis, Australian National University, 2002.
Morton, Grahame. '"Gold, Law, and Freemasonry": A Biographical Analysis of Vincent Pyke as a Goldfields Administrator in Otago, 1862–1867.' BA (Hons) thesis, University of Otago, 1994.
Quick, Sandra. '"The Colonial Helpmeet Takes a Dram": Women Participants in the Central Otago Goldfields Liquor Industry, 1861–1901.' MA thesis, University of Otago, 1997.
Sedgwick, Charles P. 'The Politics of Survival: A Social History of the Chinese in New Zealand.' PhD thesis, University of Canterbury, 1982.
Storey, Kenton Scott. '"What Will They Say in England?" Violence, Anxiety, and the Persistence of Humanitarianism in Vancouver Island and New Zealand, 1853–1862.' PhD thesis, University of Otago, 2011.
Sullivan, Kim. 'Scots by Association: Scottish Diasporic Identities and Ethnic Associationalism in the Nineteenth–Early Twentieth Centuries and the Present Day.' PhD thesis, University of Otago, 2011.
Van der Voorn, Marianne. 'The Police Department on the Otago Goldfields: Dunstan, 1861–1864.' BA (Hons) thesis, University of Otago, 1979.
Williams, Michael. 'Destination Qiaoxiang: Pearl River Delta Villages and Pacific Ports, 1849–1949.' PhD thesis, University of Hong Kong, 2002.

Index

agriculture, 5, 28–30, 33, 45, 89n69, 193, 217, 222
   agricultural labourer *see* labour
alcohol, 150–2, 211, 217–19
   alcoholism, 208
   ale, 151
   beer, 151, 219
   gin, 2, 149, 151
   in palace, 75, 148
   liquor, 121, 150–2, 154, 159–60, 169n68, 217, 219
   poisoning, 150–1
   whisky, 141, 151, 161, 219
   wine, 151
   see also drink
ale *see* alcohol
ancestors, 44, 183–5, 247
Argus (newspaper), 66–7, 70, 80, 82–3, 145, 156, 229
association *see* company
atomisation, 5, 17n19, 126, 150–1, 198, 210, 241
Auckland, 190, 228, 245
Australasia, 7, 12–13, 19n34, 23, 25–6, 29, 31, 33–4, 43, 45, 47, 50, 65, 71, 73–5, 77, 96, 101–2, 117, 124, 136n169, 145, 159, 169n66, 176, 180–1, 191, 227, 230, 232, 243
Australia, 2–3, 6–8, 12–14, 15n3, 17n22, 27–8, 32–4, 37–8, 43, 47, 49, 64–5, 67–70, 76, 79, 81, 96, 176, 179, 190–2, 209, 213, 219–20, 224, 227–32, 240, 243, 245; *see also* New South Wales; South Australia; Victoria; Tasmania
autobiographer, 209–11, 220, 222–3
   autobiography, 53n25, 67, 149, 209–11, 219–25, 231–2, 232n4, 234n14, 241–2
   see also reminiscences
Autumnal Equinox, 186

ballad, 152, 154–5
   sentimental, 142, 155, 158–9
barmaid, 11, 141, 152–4
Barry, William Jackson, 223, 232n4
Bathgate, Alexander, 155–6
beer *see* alcohol
blizzard, 1–2, 71, 114, 121, 159, 220
Bools, Andrew, 106, 225–6
Brazil, 28
Bremner, John, 221–2
Britain, 2–3, 5, 7–8, 13, 24–33, 36–7, 40, 42–4, 46–50, 61n152, 62n153, 66, 72–5, 77, 85, 89n66, 91n87, 97, 99–102, 112, 124, 141–2, 144–5, 148–9, 151–3, 155, 164, 169n66, 177–8, 186, 190, 209, 211, 216–17, 222–6, 232, 240–1, 243, 245; *see also* England; Scotland; Wales
British Columbia, 30, 99, 118, 191, 201n34
brothel, 158, 162, 184, 211
bushfire *see* fire

Caledonian Games, 21n65, 153
Caledonian Societies, 222
Calwell, Daniel, 40, 100–11
campfire *see* fire
Canterbury, 35, 38, 88n31, 100–1, 225
Cape Town (South Africa), 161
Cargill, E. B., 156, 195
Carroll, James, 211, 213, 216
Chapman, William Nixon, 38–9, 41, 43, 48, 101
Chartism, 12, 124–6, 129n252, 144
China, 2, 7, 13, 26, 175–6, 178–83, 185–8, 190–1, 197–8, 201n34, 240
   Guangdong, 177–9, 181, 183–4, 186–8, 197, 201n34
   Guangzhou, 177–80, 200n28
   Panyu, 177, 181, 188
   Pearl River Delta, 177–9, 181

Siyi, 178
Taishan, 180
Zengcheng, 177
Chinese Immigrants Bill, 192
Chinese New Year, 186
Chisholm, Revd James, 208, 215
church, 211, 222, 247
  Free Church, 156
  leaders, 196
  Presbyterian Church, 196, 207–8
claim, 1, 6, 10, 38, 42, 45, 68–70, 72–4, 80, 85, 98, 100, 109, 111, 114–21, 123–4, 126, 142, 148, 150, 154, 158, 161, 164, 184, 221, 229, 241
  claim jumping, 123, 215, 228
  see also diggings
climate, 40, 71, 74, 98, 106–7, 113, 116, 220, 240; see also blizzard; cold; drought; snow; weather; winter
coal, 29, 54n37; see also mining
cold, 1, 71, 104, 107, 112, 115–16, 197
Collingwood, 78, 159
colonial, 4, 6–9, 32, 34–5, 42, 44–5, 48–50, 66, 72–3, 77, 80, 102, 145–6, 151, 161, 164, 171n113, 174–5, 177, 182, 186, 191, 194, 196–7, 209, 214, 220, 222–3, 229, 240–1, 243, 245
  government, 33–4, 104, 125, 161, 191, 244
  society, 3–4, 15, 61n152, 185, 187, 195–6, 209–10, 244
  see also network, colonial
colonisation, 3, 31, 37, 73, 209–10, 217, 223
Colonist (newspaper), 145–6, 167n41, 195
colonist, 4–5, 14, 49, 69, 75, 79, 83–4, 88n31, 91n87, 103, 107, 150–1, 153, 156–7, 175, 189–98, 208, 213–14, 223, 225, 227, 230–2, 239n128, 243–4
colony, 5, 14, 23, 26, 33, 35, 40, 66–70, 72–3, 75–6, 79–80, 82, 84, 97, 102, 150, 154, 174, 182, 190, 192, 194–5, 208, 231–2, 243
comedy, 155, 209, 215, 227
commercial, 74–5, 82, 146–7, 191, 222, 226, 245–7
  commercialised, 14, 148, 152–3
  see also network, commercial
commodities, 13, 31, 66, 75, 152, 179, 231, 245
communication, 11, 35, 38, 43, 47–8, 79, 141–2, 145, 147, 153, 161, 242, 247
community, 5, 7, 11–13, 25, 27, 29, 34, 37, 40–1, 45, 47–51, 81–2, 84, 98, 101, 119, 121, 123–7, 142, 145–8, 150, 152–3, 155–7, 159–61, 163–4, 172n122, 175, 179–82, 185, 188, 197, 208–10, 213, 217, 220–2, 226, 228, 231–2, 240–1, 243, 246
company, 72, 119, 124, 152
  Arrow Miners' Association, 196
  Ballarat Sluicing Company, 124
  Grand Junction Company, 124
  Manuherikia Company, 124
  mining, 38, 72, 118, 124, 193
  Nelson Reef Company, 86n3
  New Zealand Company, 55n53
  Nil Desperandum Gold Mining Company, 124
  Waitahuna Mining Association, 124
  Waitahuna Sluicing Company, 119
concert, 146, 152, 154
Convention of Peking, 191, 204n106
cooperation, 97, 117–19, 127, 197
copper, 28
correspondence, 13, 24–5, 30, 35, 37, 39–40, 44–5, 47–50, 61–2n153, 71, 76–7, 80, 85n3, 93n124, 93n131, 99, 138n230, 143–4, 147, 156, 176, 179–81, 183, 198, 224, 227, 231, 238n110, 241–2, 244–5, 249n15
correspondent, 2, 37, 40–3, 45, 47, 49, 70, 81–4, 109, 114, 126, 146, 161, 181, 192, 207, 219, 241
  see also letter
cotton, 23, 27, 44, 61n153, 178
court, 78, 147, 160–4, 185, 228, 241
  courthouse, 126, 142, 160–3
  courtroom, 126, 161, 163
  Lakes District, 140n254
  records, 149, 151
  Warden's, 126, 140n254
cradle, xiv, 37, 115, 118–19, 147
crime, 4, 122–3, 138n230
Croker, Major, 212
cultural, 2–4, 6–8, 10–12, 14, 16n10, 37, 50–1, 77–80, 96–9, 117, 123–7, 141–2, 144, 148, 150–4, 160–4, 175–6, 180–2, 186, 190, 197–8, 209–10, 219, 223, 226, 228, 234n6, 240–1, 244–5
  flow, 21nn52–3
  formation, 11, 65, 97–8, 142, 160, 164, 209

Daily Telegraph (newspaper), 83, 145, 167n41
dam, 118, 126
dance hall, 158
death, 2, 40–1, 48, 84, 103, 110, 120–1, 184, 188
  alcohol-induced, 150
  and autobiography, 220
  and mourning, 39, 44
  from disease, 103, 110, 116
  see also murder; suicide

destitute, 69–70, 72, 78, 104, 150, 184, 246
　destitution, 31, 40, 44–5, 61n153, 73, 81, 100, 102, 115, 184, 223
diary, 14, 35–6, 64, 76, 78, 99–100, 106, 116, 120–1, 124, 137n196, 138n230, 143–4, 146, 149, 154, 156, 158, 210, 241, 244
disease *see* sickness
Don, Revd Alexander, 14, 77, 177, 181–8, 197
Dragon Boat Festival, 186
drink, 149, 151–2, 154, 188, 228
　drinking, 4, 148, 150–2, 154–5, 162, 219, 226, 228
　drunk, 83, 122, 149, 151, 162, 194, 218–19, 227
　drunkard, 150, 163, 228
　drunkenness, 150, 162, 169n66, 194, 217–18, 226
　see also alcohol
drought, 2, 72, 81, 112
　dry spell, 113, 115
Dunedin Temperance Council, 218
Dunstan News (newspaper), 145
Dunstan Times (newspaper), 146

ecology, 96–7, 119, 127; *see also* environment; nature
economy, 29, 31, 43, 65, 71–2, 81, 125, 148, 152, 177, 180, 195, 213
　economic, 11–13, 15, 25–7, 29, 32, 34, 46, 48, 50–1, 72–4, 97–100, 125, 127, 141, 144, 146, 154, 167n41, 176–9, 191, 196, 221
egalitarian, 4, 11, 16n15, 17n22, 77, 216, 229, 241
England, 23, 25–9, 38, 41, 43, 46, 53n29, 54n37, 64, 71, 101, 104, 153, 155, 223, 227
　Birmingham, 23
　Cheshire, 30
　Cornwall, 28
　Devonshire, 27–8, 225
　Dorset, 27
　Exeter, 27
　Hull, 23
　Lancashire, 23–5, 27, 30, 42–4, 61–2n153, 73, 101, 145, 226
　Liverpool, 29
　London, 10, 23, 28, 30, 33–6, 38, 40, 46, 48, 75, 99, 148–9, 153–5, 179, 193, 225
　Manchester, 10
　Midlands, 32
　Norfolk, 220, 223
　Plymouth, 27
　Somerset, 27
　Sussex, 225
　York, 23
　Yorkshire, 27, 32, 226
entertainment, 14, 142, 147–8, 152–5, 159–61, 163–4, 184, 227, 240–1
environment, 2, 8–9, 16n10, 19n33, 25, 45, 97, 99, 104, 107, 113, 117, 127, 141–2, 148, 150, 152, 211, 215, 221, 225, 241, 244, 248n9
　in Australia, 49
　in California, 118
　in Dunedin, 96, 102
　in Dunstan, 118
　in New Zealand, 4–5, 9, 49, 96, 150
　in North America, 112
　in Otago, 10, 12–14, 71, 80, 85, 96, 98–9, 107, 112–13, 117, 119, 125, 127, 175, 215, 224, 232, 240–1
　in Tuapeka, 112
　in Upper Taieri, 118
　in Victoria, 112, 118
　in Wakatipu, 118
　see also ecology; nature
ethnic, 11–12, 21n65, 30, 34, 56n75, 123–4
ethnicity, 11–13, 19n33, 124, 205n139, 248n9
　see also identity; network, ethnic
Evening Star (newspaper), 214–15, 218

family, 6–7, 10, 14, 23–8, 30, 32, 34–7, 39–46, 48, 50, 62n153, 62n164, 64, 77–8, 92n112, 97–8, 101, 111, 124, 152, 175–6, 179–84, 187–9, 195, 197–8, 201n34, 211, 221, 245, 247; *see also* kin; network, family
famine, 33, 61n153, 79, 197
fan-tan, 184, 186
farce, 149, 153, 155, 172n120, 212
farm, 25, 28, 31, 41, 46, 100–1, 180
　farmer, 27, 29, 31, 47, 100, 217, 229
　farming, 36, 40, 73, 100, 178, 181, 193, 246
fire, 71, 115–16, 161, 212, 220
　bushfire, 115
　campfire, 40, 76, 107, 141–3, 229
　firewood, 116, 119, 223
　wildfire, 69
flax, 104, 178
flood, 1–2, 10, 27–8, 68, 70, 73, 75, 80, 84, 102, 111, 113–15, 120–1, 126, 145, 158, 178, 184, 190, 213, 228
food, 81, 104, 106, 176, 179, 185, 187, 220
frostbite, 70

gambling, 64, 122, 149, 176, 184, 202n61, 226
　house, 176, 183–6

Garrett, Henry, 122
Gascoigne, James, 74, 76, 100, 104, 118, 220, 223
geology, 9, 71, 111, 118
gin *see* alcohol
gold pan, xiv, 2, 37, 117–18, 119, 161, 246
gold rush, 2–10, 12–15, 15n3, 19n33, 21n52, 26–7, 30–1, 34, 36–8, 40, 42–3, 45, 49–50, 65–7, 69–77, 79–82, 84–5, 91n87, 93n124, 96–9, 101–2, 107, 109, 111–13, 115, 117, 120–6, 128n230, 142–54, 156–9, 162, 169n66, 174–5, 179, 191, 193, 195–6, 199, 204n105, 208–15, 217–23, 227–31, 240, 242–7, 248n9
  American, 3, 21n53, 75, 220
  Arrow River, 124
  Australasian, 7, 19n34, 73, 232
  Australian, 3, 15n3, 17n22, 43, 65, 230
  Bendigo, 64
  British Columbian, 99
  Dunstan, 28, 69, 81–2, 84, 100, 106, 145, 195
  California, 43, 98, 138n230, 149, 179, 220, 245
  European, 14, 25, 174, 196, 198
  Gabriel's Gully, 28, 107
  Lakes District, 81–2
  New Zealand, 3, 99, 174, 209–10, 230–1
  North American, 112, 128n230
  Otago, 2–3, 6, 8, 10, 12–15, 17n23, 25, 27, 32, 39, 44, 46, 48, 50, 64–5, 73, 75–7, 79–80, 82, 84–5, 96, 104, 111–12, 118, 125, 127, 138n230, 144, 155–6, 164, 167n41, 174, 207–9, 221, 223–4, 226, 229–32, 233n4, 239n128, 240–8
  Picton, 36
  Port Curtis, 67, 83
  Victoria, 7, 26–7, 42, 67, 72, 89n69, 96–8, 104, 106, 112, 118, 138n230, 143, 150, 154, 169n68, 227, 245
  Tasman World's, 2
  Thames, 48
  Tuapeka, 26, 31, 74, 80, 82, 106, 109, 121, 161, 211
  Waipori, 60n128
  Wakamarina, 28
  Wakatipu, 73, 69
  West Coast, 7, 11, 28, 48, 65, 230
goldfield, 1–5, 7, 9–11, 12–14, 19n34, 23, 26–30, 31–2, 34–38, 40–3, 45–8, 49–51, 56n61, 60n128, 64, 66–85, 87n15, 88n31, 90n69, 91n86, 92n112, 96–110, 112–13, 115–18, 120–7, 133n100, 138n227, 138n230, 141–55, 157–63, 167–8n44, 172n122, 174, 176, 179–80, 182, 184–7, 189–91, 193, 195, 197, 202n60, 204n105, 210–11, 215–16, 221, 224–30, 232, 233n4, 240–6; *see also* Dunstan; Hamiltons; Mount Ida; Round Hill; Taieri; Tuapeka; Wakatipu
gossip, 24–5, 37, 82, 101, 161–2
government, 25–6, 31–4, 70, 73, 103, 138n230, 161, 167n44, 178, 180, 186, 188, 192, 194, 196, 215–17, 224
  aid, 78
  assistance, 32–3
  British, 176, 191
  Chinese, 191, 204n106
  New Zealand, 192
  Otago, 76
  Otago Provincial, 12, 70, 76, 78, 89n69, 104, 123, 125, 242, 244
  Tasmanian, 70
  Victorian, 70, 78
  see also colonial, government
Graham, Jock, 212
Greenland, 26
gum san (gold letter), 181

Hakka, 178
Hallenstein, Bendix, 75
Halliday, Florence, 162–3
Hartley, Horatio, 100, 112–13
Henderson, Archibald, 31, 36, 41–2, 47–8, 100, 242
Highland and Islands Emigration Society (HIES), 32, 62n153
home, 3, 7, 13–14, 16n10, 23–6, 30–2, 34–8, 40–50, 62n164, 64, 71, 73, 75–7, 80, 84, 99–101, 103–4, 116, 143, 152, 154, 161, 175–6, 179–89, 195, 198, 216, 223–4, 226, 228, 240–2, 244
  homeland, 40, 45, 185
  homeward bounders, 42
  see also network, home
Hong Kong, 38, 101, 178–81, 186, 191–2
horticulture, 223
hospital, 39, 109, 121, 185
  City Cholera, 103
  Committee, 110
  Dunedin, 104, 120
hotel, 81, 99, 111, 141, 146, 153, 157
  Golden Age, 163
  Provincial, 153, 155, 229
  Royal, 153
  Shamrock, 155
hung san (empty letter), 181

identity, 11, 49, 98–9, 129n13, 155–6, 183, 194, 209, 217, 237n95, 241
  class, 177
  ethnic, 11–12, 244, 249n15

identity *(cont.)*
   national, 3–4, 10, 159, 186, 198, 220, 243, 248
   New Zealand, 216, 221
   Old, 12, 156–8, 215
   personal, 11, 45, 49, 224
   social, 47, 211
   trans-Tasman, 10
   working-class, 193–4
illness *see* sickness
immigrant, 3, 12, 177, 222
   Chinese, 177, 192
   European, 194; German, 227
   see also Chinese Immigrants Bill; migrant; emigrant
immigration, 3, 5, 69, 73, 88n33, 194
   Chinese, 175–7, 191–6, 198, 201n28
   New Zealand, 89n6
   see also migration; emigration
imperial, 27, 96, 176, 180, 186, 190–1, 248
   Imperial policy, 187
   see also Chinese imperialism; government, imperial
India, 10, 27, 75
Indonesia, 179, 181
Industrial Revolution, 25, 27, 30–1, 46, 141
industry, 3, 9, 23, 27–32, 44, 53n29, 61n153, 100, 107, 112, 154, 161, 193–4, 208, 213, 216
Ireland, 2, 5, 7, 13, 24–7, 29–30, 32–3, 37, 40–1, 43–4, 46–50, 61n153, 66, 72–5, 77, 85, 91n87, 97, 100–2, 142, 144–5, 151–3, 155, 224, 240–1, 245
   Antrim, 33
   Cavan, 33
   Clare, 33
   Down, 33, 36, 41
   Kerry, 33
   Killinchy, 36
   Limerick, 33
   Londonderry, 33
   Munster, 33
   Tipperary, 33
   Ulster, 33
iron, 147, 160
   manufacturing, 29
   tray, xiv
   see also mining, iron

Jackson, Thomas, 160
jinshanzhuang, 179
Jones, David, 30, 41–3, 71, 111, 116
Jones, Shadrach, 153, 155
Jones, William, 39, 46, 116
jubilee, 208, 210–11, 213–17, 221, 230, 246
   Gabriel's Gully Semi-Centennial, 207, 211–14, 221–2, 230–2

semi-centennial, 14, 199, 208, 211, 213
sesquicentennial, 245, 247

kin, 14, 30, 33–4, 37, 41, 45, 47, 49, 78, 159, 181, 184, 188
kinship, 7, 11, 13, 345, 56n75, 57n80, 77, 124, 185, 198
   see also family; network, kinship
Klondike Gold Rush, 97, 117
knowledge, 7–9, 25, 65–6, 76, 79–80, 82, 84–5, 117, 125, 144–6, 187, 223, 231, 243, 245

labour, 12, 14, 26, 29, 40, 82, 111, 120, 125, 141, 144, 160, 175, 180, 193–4, 221; agricultural labourer, 33; labourer, 29, 31–3, 63n169, 89n69, 103, 180, 193–5, 215
Lake Wakatip Mail (newspaper), 140n254, 145–6, 154, 156, 159, 162
Lees, John, 23–5, 37, 42, 46–7, 72, 101, 242
leisure, 4, 11, 13–14, 41, 85, 98, 120, 127, 141–5, 148, 152–3, 176, 184, 240, 244
letter, 1, 25, 37–40, 44–5, 49–50, 53n25, 61n153, 64, 74–6, 78–9, 83, 86n3, 115, 124, 143, 145, 148, 153, 161, 189, 210, 216, 219, 224, 238n110, 239n132, 241–2, 245, 247, 249n15
   acquaintances from home, 35–6, 49
   asking for more frequent correspondence, 40, 43–4, 78
   cost of sending, 40
   difficulty composing, 39–40, 46, 49
   fraying relationships, 47, 184
   from family, 2, 30, 38, 40–2, 44–6, 50, 76–7, 92n112, 101, 142, 159, 181, 184, 187
   lost or delayed, 38, 41, 44, 243
   migration, 30, 45, 76
   money, 24, 30, 43–5, 77, 100, 183–4
   published in newspapers, 56n63, 82–4, 94n153, 147, 156, 193, 214, 217, 219, 233n4
   remittances, 181, 183, 198
   returning home, 23–4, 42, 46, 101, 187, 242
   to family, 10, 23–4, 30, 34–6, 38–43, 45–6, 48, 101, 116, 143, 180–1
   see also correspondence; correspondents; *hung san* (empty letter); *gum san* (gold letter)
library, 144
Lindsay, Anne, 36
liquor *see* alcohol
literature, 144, 149, 209, 211, 224, 229; *see also* novel
livestock, 31, 33, 81, 228

loneliness, 5, 24, 79, 150, 184, 243
Long Depression, 193
long tom, 118
Love, John, 1–2, 101, 121, 159

McCourt, Thomas, 70–1, 116, 154
McDonald, Lachlan, 32, 38–9, 41, 43–5, 69, 116, 242
McIlrath, Hamilton, 36, 41–2, 109
McIlrath, James, 41–2, 60n128
McIlrath, John, 41–2, 60n128
magistrate, 78, 104, 147, 149, 151, 162–3, 228, 241
Manila (Philippines), 198
Maniototo Early Settlers' Association, 221
Māori, 3, 121, 209, 245–6
  iwi, 3
  Māori–Pakeha conflicts, 3
  Māori–Pakeha relations, 3, 174
  see also war, Māori Wars
Martin, William, 31, 121, 151
melodrama, 149, 152, 154–5
memory, 11, 15, 67, 154, 156–7, 159, 198, 208–11, 217–19, 221, 224, 226–30, 232, 242, 246–8
  collective, 210, 219, 230
  colonial, 209
  historical, 65
  local, 220–2
  personal, 210, 221, 231
  private, 209, 219, 242
  public, 208, 242
  social, 211, 214
merchant, 26, 47, 66, 75, 81, 91n86, 109, 147, 149, 154, 160–1, 175, 178–80, 186, 193, 196, 242, 246
migrant, 7, 11–14, 16n10, 19nn33–4, 24–6, 29–34, 37, 42–3, 49, 55n50, 59n116, 66, 68, 72, 74, 76–7, 80, 84, 87n29, 89n69, 100, 102, 106, 124, 153, 175–7, 179–82, 185–8, 190–2, 196–7, 211, 243–5, 247, 248n9, 249n15; see also emigrant; immigrant; migration
migration, 7–8, 11, 13, 24–6, 30–1, 34–5, 37, 45, 49–50, 57n82, 72, 74, 76–7, 81, 84–5, 91n83, 93n131, 102, 107, 109, 115, 117, 180, 224, 237n95, 242, 249n15
  across North America, 117
  across the Pacific Ocean, 117
  across the Tasman Sea, 7, 31, 65
  Chinese, 14, 175–6, 178–9, 191, 197, 204n106, 244
  European, 84, 197
  from Ireland, 26–7, 32–3, 74, 77, 61n153
  from Dunedin, 65
  from England, 153
  from London, 23
  from Britain, 26–7, 74, 77
  from Melbourne, 65
  from New South Wales, 239n128
  from North Wales, 29
  from Otago, 6, 65–6, 78, 84–5, 244
  from Scotland, 223–4
  from the Isle of Tiree, 43
  from the Highlands and Islands, 32
  from Victoria, 6–7, 19n34, 30, 51, 65–6, 72, 74, 84–5, 117, 231–2, 239n128
  from Wales, 29–30
  from the West Coast, 232
  in China, 181
  internal, 180
  overseas, 33, 180, 197, 204n106, 223
  to America, 44
  to Australasia, 26, 33, 74
  to Australia, 13, 28, 31–2
  to Britain, 26, 33, 74
  to New Zealand, 7, 19n34, 35, 59n116
  to Dunedin, 65, 153, 200n14
  to Dunstan, 112, 118
  to England, 29, 43
  to Lancashire, 43, 61n153
  to Melbourne, 65
  to Otago, 6, 13–14, 25, 28, 30–1, 34, 36, 44–5, 51, 65–6, 70–2, 74, 79–80, 84, 91n86, 112, 178, 183, 197, 223–4, 239n128
  to Tyree, 61n153
  to Upper Taieri, 118
  to Victoria, 6, 19n34, 23, 28, 29, 30, 33–4, 65–6, 84, 100, 232
  to Wakatipu, 118
  to Wellington, 200n14
  trans-oceanic, 80
  trans-Tasman, 74, 76, 85
  see also emigrate; migrate
miner, 1–2, 11–12, 14, 28, 32, 80–1, 103–4, 121, 123–5, 141, 148, 152, 154, 156, 158, 161–3, 174–5, 181, 184, 186–90, 193–7, 201n34, 202n70, 205n139, 208, 212, 214, 216, 231, 245–6; see also digger; prospector
Miner's Pension Act, 218
Miners' Relief Fund, 216
mines, 28, 125, 210
  coal, 30
  coal and iron, 29, 54n37
  gold, 76
ming (fate), 184
mining, 1, 28, 38, 44, 53n29, 68, 72, 75, 77, 81, 106, 118, 121, 124, 143, 148, 193, 228
  coal, 29, 124, 193
  copper, 28
  gold, 11, 28, 87n15, 108, 114, 125, 193, 201n34

mining (cont.)
    quartz, xiv, 72, 104
    rock, 29
    see also claim; company; prospecting
missionary, 14, 177, 182, 187
Moffat, John, 115–16, 120, 137n196
money, 7, 23, 43–4, 62n164, 74, 78, 81, 97, 100, 104, 106, 121–2, 149, 157, 176, 180–1, 183–5, 187–9, 195, 198, 229–30, 232, 240; see also remittance
Money, Charles, 104, 149, 229–30, 232
mud, 9–10, 101–4, 106–9, 111, 114, 150, 156, 158, 230
Munro, George, 212
murder, 122–3, 140n254, 147, 197, 227; see also death

nationalism, 174, 187, 197–8
    Chinese, 186
    New Zealand, 14–15, 208
nature, 4, 9–10, 15, 34, 37, 45, 72, 76, 97–8, 101, 107, 111–12, 121, 123–6, 223; see also ecology; environment
network, 2, 6–8, 10–11, 13, 26, 35, 48, 50, 66, 74–5, 77, 85, 96–9, 107, 112, 127, 142, 144, 147, 164, 176, 178–82, 198, 240, 244
    colonial, 34, 48
    commercial, 74, 76, 85, 179
    communication, 38
    community, 13, 34, 175, 197
    ethnic, 5, 19n31, 198
    family, 24, 26, 34, 36–7, 49, 175, 197
    financial, 76
    friendship, 34, 37, 40, 49
    home, 35, 49, 57n82
    kinship, 7, 11, 13, 25, 31, 34–6, 50, 77, 198
    local, 14, 176, 197, 249n15
    migration, 24, 197
    neighbourhood, 26, 35
    personal, 25, 66, 74, 76, 79, 241
    press, 79, 82, 176, 191
    social, 13, 34, 65, 74, 97–8, 123, 210, 240–1, 244
    transnational, 14, 45, 142, 175–6, 183, 240–1, 244
New Iniquity, 12, 170n106, 195, 209, 211, 215
New South Wales, 1, 32–3, 67, 75, 189–92, 224, 239n128
New Zealand, 1–9, 13–15, 16n10, 18n26, 19n34, 20n47, 27, 35–8, 41, 44, 47–50, 55n53, 59n116, 65, 67, 76, 78, 85, 87n31, 89n69, 96, 99, 101, 140n254, 148, 150, 153, 155, 164, 167n44, 171n113, 171n115, 174, 176–7, 188–95, 198, 200n14, 201n34, 208–11, 213, 215–17, 219–22, 225, 227–32, 232n4, 239n128, 241–5, 247; see also Auckland; Canterbury; North Island; Otago; South Island; Southland; West Coast
New Zealand House of Representatives, 167n44
New Zealand Society of Genealogists, 247
newspaper, 9, 13, 26, 30, 42–3, 47, 56n63, 66–7, 71–3, 75–6, 80–5, 94n153, 102, 107, 115, 121, 123–4, 126, 141–8, 150–1, 156, 159, 162–4, 166n30, 181–2, 186–7, 189, 191, 193, 198, 209–10, 214, 217, 219, 222, 228, 233, 241, 243; see also press
North America, 6–7, 12, 18n30, 43, 75, 112, 117, 124, 138n230, 179–81, 191, 224, 240
North Island, 3, 5, 100, 147, 222, 245
novel, 115, 144–5; see also literature

Old Age Pension Act, 216, 218
opium, 176, 183–4, 186; house, 183; see also war, Opium Wars
Orbell, MacLeod, 108, 121, 222, 224
Otago, 1–2, 5–15, 17n23, 21n65, 23–51, 52n25, 55n53, 56n63, 64–85, 86n3, 87n15, 88n31, 89n69, 91nn86–87, 92n112, 96, 98–107, 111–13, 115–20, 122–5, 127, 138n230, 142–51, 153–61, 164, 174–9, 181–4, 186–98, 204n105, 207–11, 213–17, 219–32, 238n110, 239n128, 240–8
    Alexandra, 184
    Anderson Bay, 103
    Arrow River, 77, 118, 120, 124, 126, 145, 162–3
    Arrowtown, 38, 120–1, 126, 137n196, 159, 189, 197
    Arthur's Point, 107, 121
    Bell Hill, 104–5
    Bluff, 32, 38, 66
    Campbell's Gully, 1, 114, 116
    Cardrona, 197
    Clyde, 31, 150
    Dunedin, 5, 10, 14, 31, 36, 38, 64–70, 72, 75–6, 80, 82–4, 91n86, 96, 98, 102–6, 109–10, 113, 125, 140n254, 146, 150–1, 153, 155–8, 162, 176, 179–80, 189, 191, 193–4, 196–7, 200n14, 213, 216–18, 222, 225–6, 229, 243, 245–7
    Dunstan, 1, 10, 26, 28, 41, 60n128, 69–70, 75, 78, 81, 84, 99–100, 106, 108, 110, 112–16, 118, 122, 124, 145–6, 153, 163, 167n44, 195, 217
    Fiordland, 119
    Fox's Flat, 38
    Frankton, 121

INDEX

Fraser's River, 124
Gabriel's Gully, 28, 64, 67–9, 74, 80, 84, 87n15, 104, 107–9, 124, 150, 161, 207–8, 211–14, 221–2, 230–1, 245–7
Hamiltons, 67, 75, 143, 189
Hogburn, 115, 122, 150
Invercargill, 38, 46, 67, 70, 119, 121, 155, 160, 180, 188, 192
Kawarau River, 1, 40, 100, 106, 112–13, 115, 120
Lake Waihola, 10, 106
Lake Wakatipu, 150, 157–8
Lakes District, 38, 70, 75, 81–2, 114, 123, 125, 140n254, 154
Lawrence, 144–5, 161, 181, 207–8, 211, 219, 246–7
Maniototo Plains, 106
Manuherikia River, 112
Maori Point, 38, 41, 120
Milford Sound, 120
Moke Creek, 113, 140n255, 162
Molyneux River, 100, 110, 112–13, 115, 122, 126, 184
Molyneux, 36, 84
Mount Highlay, 69
Mount Ida goldfield, 221
Mount Ida, 70, 195, 222
Naseby, 186
Nevis, 181
Northeast Valley, 103
Oamaru, 31
Old Man Range, 1, 101, 110, 121, 159
Pigburn, 184
Pomahaka Creek, 114
Port Chalmers, 26, 32, 67, 72, 80, 102–3, 156–7
Puketoi, 106
Queenstown, 75, 110, 114, 143, 145, 155, 157–9, 162–3, 197
Rock and Pillar range, 67
Round Hill, 181, 184–5
St Bathans, 216
Shotover River, 70, 108, 113–14, 118, 120–1
Skipper's Canyon, 70, 114–15
Taieri, 108, 122, 209, 221
Tokomairiro, 44
Tuapeka, 10, 26, 31, 60n128, 67–70, 74, 76–7, 80, 82, 88n31, 100–1, 105–6, 109, 112–14, 116–19, 121, 126, 144, 146, 161, 167n44, 183, 208, 211–12, 214, 220, 242, 246
Upper Nevis, 189
Waikaia, 216
Waikouaiti, 224
Waipori, 32, 43, 60n128, 69, 106, 116, 124, 144
Waitahuna, 38, 67, 69, 121, 161, 223

Wakatipu (goldfield), 66, 69–70, 73, 75, 81, 107, 109, 113–15, 118, 120–3
Weatherston's, 64, 67, 69, 109–10, 118, 144, 149, 226
Wendon, 216
Otago Bible Society, 196
Otago Daily Times (newspaper), 2, 42, 66, 68, 75, 80, 82–4, 114, 140n254, 145, 156, 161–2, 191–4, 207, 214–15, 217–18, 221, 231, 243
Otago Early Settlers Association, 213–14, 221
Otago Goldfields Cavalcade, 245
Otago Provincial Council, 156, 160, 196
Otago Witness (newspaper), 47, 66–7, 80, 83–4, 145, 150, 189

Pacific Ocean, 117, 164, 179, 181, 191, 193, 224–5, 245
  Pacific Rim, 177, 192, 202n60, 244–5
pakapu, 184, 186, 202n60
Penderick, John, 70, 110, 114, 116, 154
Peru, 175, 180
  Lima, 198
petition, 70, 100, 104, 125–6, 153, 167n44, 175, 178, 188, 192, 194, 197, 243
pickpocket, 122, 163; *see also* theft
pioneer, 76, 97, 198, 208–9, 211–13, 215–17, 219–20, 230, 232, 246
  myth, 215, 219
political, 8, 11–12, 79, 124–6, 146, 177–8, 186, 197, 217, 222
pooled resources, 68, 118, 123, 126
Poonti, 178, 185
population, 13, 24–5, 27, 29–32, 42, 53n29, 56n61, 67, 69–70, 73, 78, 81, 83, 88n31, 89n69, 98, 116, 144, 147–8, 174, 179–80, 184, 190–1, 195, 211, 213, 245
  Chinese, 176–7, 186, 190–2, 196, 198, 200, 204n105, 244
  Cornish, 28
  English, 54n39
  European, 176, 204n105
  flow, 21n52, 66, 85
  Irish, 123
  New Zealand, 200n14
  Otago's, 151
  Scotland's, 32, 54n39, 56n61, 59n116
  trans-Tasman, 9, 65–6, 243
  Victorian, 67
  Welsh, 29–30
post office, 35, 37–8, 49, 148, 161
postage, 40
potato blight, 31, 223
poverty, 24, 43, 74, 77–8, 187, 223, 229
Presbyterian, 14, 177, 182, 187, 196; *see also* church, Presbyterian

press, 9, 13, 30, 43, 69, 76, 79–80, 82–5, 100, 145, 186, 214, 228, 230; see also network, press; newspaper
prohibition, 194, 219
prospect, 1, 12, 24, 28, 30–2, 34, 43–4, 46, 48–50, 64, 69, 72, 77, 86n3, 98, 100–3, 105–7, 109, 111–12, 115–24, 126, 142–4, 146, 180, 184, 187, 190, 195, 198, 212, 229, 231, 241–2
prospector, 2, 7–12, 14, 24–5, 29, 31, 33–4, 36, 39–43, 45, 47, 49–50, 65, 69–74, 76, 78, 82, 84–5, 92n112, 97–101, 103–4, 106, 108–12, 114–21, 123–6, 141, 143–6, 158, 160, 164, 174–7, 179, 181, 183, 186, 188–9, 195, 197–8, 199n2, 208–9, 211–12, 214, 216217, 220–1, 223–4, 226–8, 232, 233n4, 238n110, 242–5; see also miner; digger
prostitute, 158, 162–3, 184, 242
  prostitution, 184
public house, 80, 104, 119, 122, 141–2, 144, 147–54, 157–60, 164, 172n122, 218, 227; tavern, 152; see also alcohol
public meeting, 100, 124–6, 192
publican, 11, 67, 75, 81, 103, 121, 141, 148–9, 152–4, 160, 162–3
Pyke, Vincent, 242

qiaoxiang (native place), 180–1, 185, 187
quartz, 72, 112, 146, 222
  reefs, 68, 71
  see also mining, quartz

racism, 175, 190–3
railway, 26–9, 73, 75–6, 106
rain, 41, 108, 112–13, 161
  rainfall, 71, 73, 107–9, 111–12, 114
rat, 10, 110–11, 114
  ratcatcher, 110
Read, Gabriel, 67, 207–8, 212, 242, 247
reading, 39, 41, 64, 76, 80, 84, 142, 144–7, 164, 229
Red Turban Revolt, 178
Reilly, Christopher, 112–13
religion, 13, 83, 176, 186, 196, 226, 232, 244
  Chinese, 182–4
reminiscences, 5, 48, 100, 124, 198, 209–12, 214–15, 219–22, 224–6, 229–31, 233n4, 236n70, 239n128; see also autobiography; autobiographer
remittance, 43, 45, 50, 176, 179–81, 183–5, 188, 198, 240, 242, 244; see also money
ritual, 148, 150, 175–6, 185–7, 198
river, 2, 50, 71, 85, 98, 107, 110–13, 116, 118, 120–1, 123–4, 126, 147, 193

road, 3, 10, 26, 68, 78, 82, 103, 105–7, 121–2, 124–5, 146, 197, 227, 246
  Main South Road, 103
  Taieri Road, 122
  Waipori Road, 122
robbery, 5, 140n254, 123; see also theft
Rocky Mountains (United States), 75, 124, 197
routine, 13, 102, 141–2, 150, 176, 210
  daily, 11, 37, 98, 101, 120, 143, 161
Roy, Andrew, 36, 38–41, 43, 46, 159
rush see gold rush
Ruskin, William, 38, 42, 48, 242

saloon, 149, 184
satire, 155–6
school, 211; see also Lawrence High School, Lawrence School Cadets
Scotland, 25, 27, 29–32, 47–8, 56n61, 59n116, 73, 224
  Aberdeen, 75, 148
  Ayrshire, 48, 73, 223
  Caithness, 32
  Edinburgh, 103–4
  Fife, 26, 36–7
  Glasgow, 2, 26, 31, 34, 101, 159, 223
  Glendevon, 25, 40, 46
  Inverness, 32
  Islands, 31–2, 59n116, 104
  Lanarkshire, 31
  Midlothian, 38
  Orkney, 32
  Perth, 41, 62n164
  Scottish Borders, 30
  Scottish Highlands, 30–2, 59n116, 62n153, 104
  Scottish Lowlands, 30–1, 40, 55n53, 59n116
  Shetland, 32
  Skye, 32
  Sutherland, 32
  Tiree, 32, 38–9, 43–4, 61n153, 116, 136n169
  Wigtown, 31
Scoullar, Arthur, 26, 73, 223
settler, 12, 15n3, 49, 55n53, 97, 150, 156, 174, 177, 179, 190, 192, 195–7, 208–9, 213–15, 217–18, 220–2, 225, 229–30
sewage, 103, 109
sheep, 106, 189, 245
  shearing, 38
  station, 70, 106, 132n90, 216
ship, 26, 32, 34–5, 38, 66–7, 70, 102–3, 156, 192, 242–3
  shipbuilder 225
  shipbuilding, 31, 226
  shipping, 75, 85, 147, 179, 190–1, 193

shopkeeper, 67, 75, 81, 85, 121, 141, 143, 197, 222
sickness, 44, 46, 78, 103, 109–11, 120, 150, 185, 188, 226, 229
　disease, 103–4, 110, 230
　llness, 120, 161, 216, 225
silk, 178–9, 197
singer, 152, 155, 158–9
sluice, 115, 119–20, 193, 221, 223
　box, 111, 119, 141
Smith, Fred, 111
Smith, William, 27, 48, 107, 113, 116, 123, 220, 223
Smith, William Turnbull, 106, 144
snow, 1, 9, 111–14, 116, 143, 223
　snowdrift, 1, 9, 101, 112, 116
　snowstorm, 114
　see also environment, nature
society, 3–5, 9, 11–12, 14, 16nn15–16, 20n47, 25, 32, 49, 61n152, 62n153, 65, 75, 78, 81–2, 97, 107, 112, 120, 123–4, 127, 149–51, 155–6, 160–4, 177, 182, 184, 187, 192–8, 208–9, 211, 213, 215, 217, 227, 229–30, 241
　social, 2, 8, 11–13, 15, 25, 35, 37, 40, 44, 47, 51, 80, 97–8, 117–19, 125–7, 141–2, 144–6, 151, 154, 160–2, 164, 167n41, 176–8, 182, 190–1, 193, 198, 209–11, 215, 217, 219–21, 223, 226, 229, 231–2, 246–7
　bonding, 4–5, 20n47, 98, 121, 148, 151, 211, 240
　structures, 11, 24, 26, 117, 127, 175
　see also identity, social; memory, social; network, social
song, 143, 154–60, 212, 227–8
South America, 225
South Island, 3, 119, 213, 245
Southland, 39, 69, 88n31, 160, 176, 188, 192
　Riverton, 184–5, 192
speculation, 32, 44–5, 72, 161
squatter, 101, 193, 216, 228
spree, 121, 148–51, 162, 218, 226
starvation, 44, 70, 82, 84, 223, 243
steamer, 68, 76, 157; steamship, 26, 79, 106
Strachan, James, 26, 121
Stuart, Revd D. M., 196
sugar, 75, 178, 186
suicide, 189; *see also* death
surface deposits, 71, 100, 118, 123, 243

Taiping Rebellion, 178
Tasman Sea, 2, 7, 9, 34, 51, 65–6, 71–4, 80, 104, 110, 164, 209, 227, 242–3; *see also* Trans-Tasman
　Tasman World, 2, 7–8, 10, 13, 65, 76, 217, 226, 230, 242–3, 245

tavern *see* public house
tea, 10, 75, 116, 179
technology, 17n22, 79, 98, 106, 221
telegraph, 76
　telegraphic cable, 176
Thatcher, Charles, 142, 155–61, 227–30, 232
theatre, 146, 152–5, 160
　Princess', 153
　Royal, 157
　Royal Victoria, 155
theft, 122; *see also* pickpocket
tobacco, 104, 149, 153–4, 159, 178
topography, 9–10, 106, 112–13, 115, 118, 240
trade, 141, 178, 191, 194, 222, 226, 246
　Chinese, 27, 178
　global, 27, 179
　iron-manufacturing, 29
　West Coast, 226
translocal, 26, 47, 50, 52n13, 101, 185–7
transnational, 6–7, 10, 12, 14, 36–7, 45, 49, 51, 65, 85, 96, 98, 142, 164, 174–6, 183, 192, 198, 219, 230, 240–2, 244–5, 249n15
trans-Pacific, 224, 245
transport, 29, 85, 102, 151, 190
transportation, 15n3, 28–9, 33, 71, 106, 180
trans-Tasman, 7–10, 13, 51, 65–6, 74–7, 79, 84–5, 96, 164, 191, 209, 226–7, 230–2, 241–3, 248; *see also* Tasman Sea; Tasman World; translocal; transnational
Tuapeka Mounted Rifles, 212
Tuapeka Recorder (newspaper), 145
tussock, 119

United Kingdom, 8, 13, 25–6, 30, 34, 37, 40, 43, 47, 49–51, 56n61, 127, 142, 145, 155, 159, 161, 240; *see also* Britain; England; Ireland; Scotland; Wales
United States of America, 3, 8, 28, 30, 37, 44, 74, 79, 97, 99, 141, 148, 155, 180, 182, 192, 201n34, 209, 219–20, 224–5, 232
　California, 14, 17n23, 26, 43, 97–100, 118, 123–4, 138n230, 143, 148–50, 176, 179, 181, 190–3, 213, 220, 224, 245
　Georgia, 117
　Hawaii, 175, 180, 198
　Illinois, 26, 224
　San Francisco, 75, 181, 191–2
urban, 29, 31, 102, 104, 148, 151, 194–5
urbanisation, 5, 15n3, 148

vaudeville, 152, 154
Victoria, 4, 6–7, 10–13, 19nn33–4, 23–30, 32–6, 38, 42–3, 50–1, 55n50, 62n153, 64–85, 87n15, 88n33, 89n69, 96–8, 100–4, 106–7, 111–12, 115–19, 123–4, 127, 142–5, 150–6, 158–9, 161, 171n108, 175, 179, 190–3, 209, 216, 226–7, 229–32, 238n110, 239n128, 239n132, 240–5, 248n9
    Ararat, 73
    Ballarat, 30, 67–8, 70–1, 73, 76–8, 81, 87n15, 153
    Bendigo, 28, 31, 64–5, 67–8, 70, 72, 75, 77, 81, 86n3, 104, 153, 155, 201n34
    Braybrook, 101
    Buckland Valley, 76
    Castlemaine, 28, 67, 76
    Chewton, 77
    Creswick, 73
    Dunolly, 67
    Forrest Creek, 33
    Geelong, 44, 67, 106
    Gippsland, 31
    Inglewood, 69–70
    Maldon, 68
    Melbourne, 8, 10, 31, 33, 38, 64–9, 71–3, 75–7, 79–81, 85, 91n86, 104, 106, 145, 147, 153, 159, 179, 191, 193, 201n34, 226–7, 229–30, 243
    Moonambel, 68
    Ovens, 68
Victorian Goldfields Department, 242
violence, 5, 122, 138n230
Vitelli, Annie, 155, 159, 227
Vogel, Julius, 80, 84, 146, 243

Wales, 25, 29–30, 39, 41, 46, 54n37, 111, 116, 226
    Bangor, 25, 39, 46, 116
    Caernarfon, 30
    Cardiff, 226
Walker, John George, 35–6, 41, 43, 45, 70–1, 99, 106, 110, 113, 143, 145

Walker, William, 35–6, 45, 70–1, 110
war, 27, 31, 147, 178, 186
    American Civil War, 78, 145
    French Wars, 31
    Māori Wars, 147
    New Zealand Wars, 3
    Opium Wars, 178
    Second Opium War, 191
    Sino-Japanese War, 186–7
    South African wars, 216
Warren, Peter, 70, 143
water, xiv, 9, 11, 101, 103–4, 109–15, 117–19, 151, 223
    conveyance, 124
    race, xiv 11, 38, 109, 115, 119, 126, 146, 223
    waterline, 111
    waterway, xiv, 11, 72, 126
Watmuff, John Henry, 36, 64–5, 71, 74, 76–7, 85–6n3, 116, 121, 123, 143–4, 146, 149, 151, 158
weather, 40
    patterns, 2, 9, 71, 98, 112–13, 144
West Coast, 11, 28, 65, 76, 243
    Hokitika, 7, 39, 156, 226, 228
whisky *see* alcohol
whiteness, 12, 192; *see also* racism
wildfire *see* fire
wine *see* alcohol
winter, 70–1, 101, 110, 112–16, 121–2, 226
wool, 27–9
work, 4–5, 8–9, 11–14, 28–9, 31–2, 34–6, 38, 40–1, 64, 70, 72, 76–7, 85, 97–102, 104, 108, 110–12, 115–17, 120–4, 126–7, 138n230, 141–7, 150, 154, 158, 161, 163–4, 175–6, 178, 180, 184, 189, 192–8, 209–10, 215–16, 220, 222–3, 228–9, 234n6, 240–2, 245–6, 249n14
worker, 175, 193–1, 217, 223, 229; *see also* labourer

'yellow peril', 191, 197, 216
yun (luck), 184

EU representative:
Easy Access System Europe
Mustamäe tee 50, 10621 Tallinn, Estonia
Gpsr.requests@easproject.com